Religion in the Age of Shakespeare

RELIGION IN THE AGE OF SHAKESPEARE

Christopher Baker

THE AGE OF SHAKESPEARE

GREENWOOD PRESS
WESTPORT, CONNECTICUT • LONDON

Library of Congress Cataloging-in-Publication Data

Baker, Christopher Paul, 1946–
    Religion in the age of Shakespeare / Christopher Baker.
        p. cm. — (The age of Shakespeare, ISSN 1936–6388)
    Includes bibliographical references and index.
    ISBN-13: 978–0–313–33636–2 (alk. paper)
    ISBN-10: 0–313–33636–9 (alk. paper)
    1. Shakespeare, William, 1564–1616—Religion.   2. Christianity and
literature—England—History—16th century.   3. Christianity and literature—England—History—17th century.   4. England—Church history—16th
century.   5. England—Church history—17th century.   6. Religion in
literature.   I. Title.
    PR3011.B35   2007
    822.3'3—dc22   2007017752

British Library Cataloguing in Publication Data is available.

Library of Congress Catalog Card Number: 2007017752
ISBN-13: 978–0–313–33636–2
ISBN-10: 0–313–33636–9
ISSN: 1936–6388

First published in 2007

Greenwood Press, 88 Post Road West, Westport, CT 06881
An imprint of Greenwood Publishing Group, Inc.
www.greenwood.com

Printed in the United States of America

The paper used in this book complies with the
Permanent Paper Standard issued by the National
Information Standards Organization (Z39.48–1984).

10 9 8 7 6 5 4 3 2 1

In memory of my parents and brother

CONTENTS

PREFACE

Then Ariel, Hamlet, & all—all done in sport with the free daring pencil of a Master of the World. He leaves his children with God.

Ralph Waldo Emerson, *Journals* (1832)

After God, Shakespeare has created most.

Alexandre Dumas *père*
"How I Became a Playwright" (1863)

This book offers the student and general reader an overview of the major religious contexts and themes within Shakespeare's works and his era, as well as of significant scholarly approaches to these themes. It can be read both as a survey of the religious factors that enter his works and as a reference guide to other more specialized studies from researchers who have probed these issues from various critical perspectives. Within the past decade, increasing attention has been paid by historians and literary critics to the role of religion within Elizabethan culture and especially to Shakespeare's own religious background. We can only surmise about the faith of the mature Shakespeare, and the dramatist's individual religious convictions, like so much else about him that we are curious to know, remain hidden. However, this is not to say that Christianity or even religion in general, broadly defined as the ways in which belief in the divine is held to be influential in human affairs, is a minor theme in his works.

In Shakespeare's era, much more than in twenty-first century Europe or North America, religious belief had broad social, political, and personal implications. Religion was deeply ingrained in the daily lives of English people at every level of culture and was a part of all major rites of passages for each individual, from birth to marriage to death. In his Meditation XVII, seventeenth-century English poet and priest John Donne, for example, could ask his readers to contemplate "for whom the bell tolls," knowing that they would often have heard the tolling of church bells for the dead, especially during times of plague. As the dominant faith of the English monarchs swung away from Roman Catholicism under Henry VIII, back to Rome under Mary Tudor, and toward an Anglicanism somewhere between these poles under Shakespeare's Elizabeth I, dying for one's faith was also a real possibility. Martyrs were not simply figures of history but could possibly be members of one's own family, like Henry Donne, John's brother, who died in prison for having hidden a priest from the authorities. In Europe, the massacre in Paris of Hugeunots (French Protestants) by King Charles IX on the feast of St. Bartholomew (August 24, 1572), reminded the English of the cost of discipleship, prompting Christopher Marlowe to write his play *The Massacre at Paris*.

The highly charged religious atmosphere in which Shakespeare flourished invites the expectation that religious issues will clearly figure in his plays and poems. But, because he is not essentially a didactic writer, it is characteristic of Shakespeare that these concerns will sometimes be raised in indirect, inventive, and even skeptical ways. Unlike his fellow dramatist Ben Jonson, his goal is not to impose a clearly defined point of view on the topics he raises. Rather, Shakespeare characteristically "disappears" into his own works, leaving us with theatrical experiences first and "dramatic messages" second. Writers of the English Romantic era, who often viewed Shakespeare as the highest English example of creative genius, prized the fact that he was both allusive and elusive. As William Hazlitt wrote in his essay "On Genius and Common Sense" (1821), "Shakespear [*sic*] (almost alone) seems to have been a man of genius raised above the definition of genius. . . . His genius consisted in the faculty of transforming himself at will into whatever he chose: his originality was the power of seeing every object from the exact point of view in which others would see it. He was the Proteus of human intellect." Poet John Keats famously remarked in an 1817 letter to his brothers, George and Thomas, that "Shakespeare possessed so enormously" the most essential of poetic talents that Keats called negative capability: "that is when a man is capable of being in uncertainties, Mysteries, doubts, without any irritable reaching after fact & reason." Shakespeare brilliantly portrays the complex interplay of personal faith with doubt, with the institutional church, and with politics, but he is more concerned with depicting the drama of individuals who experience these dynamic situations than with offering neat labels or tidy explanations for their behavior.

Whatever conclusions we reach about Shakespeare's own religious inclinations or the major religious themes of his works will therefore have to be grounded in an understanding of the religious currents of his own day. Although Ben Jonson, in his dedicatory poem to the 1623 First Folio (the first collected edition of the plays), said that Shakespeare was "not of an age, but for all time," the dramatist clearly is of an era in which religious issues were fundamental to the ways in which men and women dealt with one another, made decisions, and governed their nation. A knowledge of the major changes in English religious belief during the sixteenth century is essential for a fuller understanding of his works.

The emergence of Christianity as the dominant faith of Western Europe is the subject of the first chapter. After the crucifixion of Jesus in around 33 A.D., the faith spread throughout the Mediterranean, and its expansion was accelerated after the Roman Emperor Constantine became a convert and encouraged its growth within the empire. The faith that had been "catholic," in the sense of being universal or widespread, became the Roman Catholic faith after the

Bishop of Rome was established as its primary administrator or Pope. The "early Church" of such theologians as St. Augustine and St. Jerome, among other so-called Fathers of the Church, endured a series of conferences and councils (some lasting years) that hammered out the foundational doctrines of the faith. By 800, the Carolingian monarchs (members of the dynastic family of Charlemagne) ruled in a thoroughly Christianized Europe, one in which the authority of the Roman Catholic church was undisputed. The spread of monasticism, the rise of major universities, the efforts of Crusaders to convert Islamic nations, and the deep influence of the philosophy of Aristotle upon theology all profoundly marked the eleventh and twelfth centuries, also the age of the great Gothic cathedrals, known as the High Middle Ages.

But the church's influence did not remain uncontested after the close of the Middle Ages. The second chapter will examine how the tremendous wealth and burgeoning influence of the church, together with the moral and spiritual laxity of many of the clergy and even some popes, led to open protests, which grew to become the Protestant Reformation, a complex historical event in which theology, nationalism, an emerging intellectual skepticism, and even technology combined to fracture the centuries-old influence of Roman Catholicism. This intellectual revolution moved Europe from an "age of faith" into the early modern world in which Catholicism was made to share its influence with rapidly multiplying and more individualistic Protestant denominations. With the rise of competing nation-states and contending religious sects, the earlier concept of "Christendom" as a homogeneous group of like-minded believers was profoundly challenged and finally dismantled by the protests of men such as Martin Luther and Ulrich Zwingli and the theologically-based vision of society advanced by John Calvin and the later English Puritans. However, unlike the often bloody confrontations that marked this process on the continent, England benefited from a monarch in the mid-sixteenth century, Queen Elizabeth I, who managed to balance these competing factions without open conflict. Bloody struggle would come later in the seventeenth century, as Oliver Cromwell attempted to institutionalize the precepts of a political Calvinism by first executing Charles I in 1649 and then establishing a commonwealth. But Elizabeth was as interested in political stability as religious piety, and, rather than advancing such an openly monolithic plan for government, she maintained a balanced rule by fostering a *via media* or "middle way." The Anglican Church (the Church of England) sought to tolerate beliefs drawn from both Catholicism and the new reformers within the nationally mandated rituals of its *Book of Common Prayer,* government-approved homilies or sermons, and the English Geneva Bible.

The mingled strains of Catholic, Protestant and (in the case of *The Merchant of Venice*) Jewish belief in Shakespeare's works is the focus of Chapter 3. The comedies and late romances all portray a dramatic movement toward unification and harmony that suggests the permanence of such spiritual values as love, forgiveness, and redemption, although the "problem comedies" temper these themes with greater ambiguity and more serious moral issues. Comedies by design of course end happily, but the final romances especially (*Pericles, The Winter's*

Tale, Cymbeline, and *The Tempest*) possess overtones of divine grace or heavenly intervention, which suggest more emphatically a beneficial providence than such romantic comedies as *Much Ado About Nothing* or *As You Like It* or the earlier comedies based on classical models, such as *The Comedy of Errors.* In keeping with Shakespeare's famed openness to experience, however, the tragedies as a genre challenge this "spiritual" optimism with a much darker vision. The tormented protagonists of the great tragedies (e.g., Hamlet, Othello, Macbeth, King Lear) seem to inhabit worlds in which God is either utterly absent or else disturbingly silent. Here the great and painful paradoxes of faith are raised, and Shakespeare presents figures who grapple with such ancient biblical questions as the existence of evil and the meaning of suffering. The history plays engage religion less in a philosophical or psychological sense than, predictably, in the course of political change. Shakespeare scrutinizes how concepts such as divine providence and divine right were adapted and even subverted by monarchs and nobility in their quest for power, specifically in the rise of the Tudor dynasty. He challenges a complacent optimism about England's divine favor, which was a keystone of the "Tudor Myth."

Chapter 4 examines the ways in which productions of Shakespeare's plays have approached the topic of religion and portrayed the issues and themes outlined in the previous chapters. Shakespeare's theatrical depiction of Christian concepts is fundamentally influenced by the English religious drama of the Middle Ages. Richard III, for example, self-consciously refers to himself as "the formal vice, iniquity," an allusion to a character from the medieval morality plays who reinforces for the audience not only his purposeful evil, but his fiendish delight in committing sin, while he invites the audience to admire his devilish ingenuity. Shakespeare's own spectators would have caught this medieval reference; modern audiences, however, are more likely to respond to the moral quality of the vice itself without considering its medieval religious ancestry, but Shakespeare's histories invite our constant examination of the religious and moral assumptions made by their characters, who may or may not believe all that they espouse. Among modern stage productions, John Caird's staging of *Hamlet* in 2000 is notable for its intentional portrayal of the Danish prince as a theologically aware character, attuned to the divine implications of his actions. Because most modern audiences will experience Shakespeare on film rather than on stage, close attention will be given to the religious aspects of four films: Orson Welles's expressionistic *Macbeth,* Grigori Kozintsev's socialist *King Lear,* Peter Brook's existentialist *King Lear,* and Baz Luhrmann's contemporary *Romeo + Juliet.* In varying ways, these films raise religious issues that can be muted in other modern Shakespeare films, such as Richard Loncraine's 1995 film of a totalitarian *Richard III.*

The response of critics and scholars to Shakespeare's use of religious materials is truly vast. Chapter 5 summarizes some of the main currents in this history of scholarship. As with the evolution of the plays' stage production, critical approaches to the plays have been shaped by cultural influences since the dramatist's death. While scholars continue to explore the theological dimensions of his works, it has become increasingly common in recent decades for these religious dimensions to be seen within the context of social or cultural factors. When Portia announces in *The Merchant of Venice* that the "quality of mercy is not strained," she is certainly drawing upon the central Judaeo-Christian belief in a loving God, one whose benevolence is freely given. Yet some critics argue that she is merely using such religious language as a means to an end, a strategy with which to justify Shylock's defeat in court and ensure Venetian Christians' dominance over him. Others have noted that, although Shakespeare's audience may have viewed Shylock's enforced conversion as a good thing spiritually (he is led to acknowledge Christ as the fulfillment of the Old Testament covenant with the Hebrews), modern audiences who have come of age in the shadow of the Holocaust find it almost impossible not to see it as a state-approved erasure of Shylock's Jewish identity. For modern critics, religion is increasingly seen as one among many intertwined issues of ethnicity, gender, politics, and economics. For modern audiences of Shakespeare, it has become difficult to separate religion from ideology.

Chapter 6 offers a collection of written texts documenting the influence of religious issues in printed works of Shakespeare's era. This selection of poems, sermons, and other documents helps to portray the kinds of texts that readers and audiences would have found important in shaping their own religious understanding. The historical conjunction of the Reformation with the invention of the printing press guaranteed that this religious revolution would spread rapidly. As literacy rates began to rise and the Bible became translated into vernacular languages, the authority of institutional churches to assert theological conclusions about the sacred texts was necessarily shared with individual believers. Some evidence of this changing religious environment can be seen from the references to both the Bible and the Anglican *Book of Common Prayer* in Shakespeare's plays.

The Bibliography lists general studies to supplement the individual References at the ends of the chapters, directing readers to printed and electronic sources. A Glossary is also provided to briefly define selected major terms and concepts.

Readers will note variations in the spelling of Shakespeare's name, especially among writers of the nineteenth century and earlier. English spelling in the Renaissance had not yet become regularized; David and Ben Crystal point out in *The Shakespeare Miscellany* (2006) that during the playwright's lifetime his name was spelled 25 different ways (108). The modern spelling is "Shakespeare," but quotations in this book from earlier eras which used "Shakspere" or "Shakespere" have not been changed.

Quotations from and dates of Shakespeare's works are taken from the second edition of *The Riverside Shakespeare*, edited by G. Blakemore Evans (Boston: Houghton Mifflin, 1997). Unless otherwise noted, all biblical quotations are from the Authorized or King James Version.

I wish to thank the Office of the Vice President and Dean of Faculty at Armstrong Atlantic State University for funding an academic research leave that significantly aided the completion of this book. The staff of the Lane Library at Armstrong, especially Melissa Jackson and Barbara Brown, has been unfailingly helpful in helping me locate books and materials. I also benefited from the helpful comments and suggestions of David Bevington, the Rev. Robert Carter, John Ford, Richard Harp, Maurice Hunt, Carol Jamison, Darryl Tippens, Mary Villeponteaux, and David Wheeler. John Caird graciously agreed to be interviewed about his Royal National Theatre production of *Hamlet*. Computer assistance was provided by Christy Mroczek and Annette Ramos. William O. Deaver, Jr. and Ana Torres offered valuable advice on the Hispanic background of Baz Luhrmann's *Romeo + Juliet*. Ronald Fritze has given continued assistance and encouragement on this project. Thanks go also to George Butler, my editor at Greenwood Press, for his prompt and helpful guidance. As always, the love, patience, and good humor of Barbara and Matt were invaluable.

1

BACKGROUND

Shakespeare is certainly the greatest author of the English Renaissance and, arguably, of English literature. But by linking him to the historical term "Renaissance," which names the "rebirth" of a scholarly interest in classical Greek and Roman culture by Europeans beginning in the fourteenth century, we may be led to an incomplete assumption about his importance for us. Seeing him as a Renaissance author could lead us to value him only for the glimpse he offers of the values that the ancient world has left us and the ways in which his own era adapted them to its own needs. The cultures of Rome and Athens offered guidance to the Renaissance in government, education, the arts, philosophy, and literature. Shakespeare's Roman plays and *Venus and Adonis*, his poem in the manner of the Roman poet Ovid, bear witness to this heritage, the gateway to which lay through a knowledge of Latin, which Elizabethan schoolboys studied thoroughly. Crudely put, Shakespeare might thus appear to be a "rear-view mirror," a writer who primarily reflects the importance of classical ideas for his post-medieval society. But he also is a writer of perennial relevance, and historians and critics in recent decades have tended to describe him and his era as "Early Modern," a label that stresses how he reveals attitudes that we have come to view as more similar to our own. From this perspective, we might say that Shakespeare is more a "spotlight" than a "mirror"; he illuminates what is to come as much as he reflects what has been. The most accurate label for him (if it is even possible to choose only one) must of course combine both views: he was a writer of such comprehensive outlook that no single, simplistic metaphor can do him justice or capture his complexity.

This duality in Shakespeare's work, his capacity for touching both past and future, ancient culture and modern society, is also at work if we consider him in a religious context. The medieval period that preceded the Renaissance is sometimes termed an "age of faith," while Shakespeare's own era, despite the intense conflicts of Catholics against emerging Protestant denominations, was marked by an individualism and an increasingly skeptical intellectual outlook largely foreign to the middle ages. The main character in *Othello*, for example, demands "ocular proof" (3.3.360) before he will believe Desdemona's dishonesty, and Horatio declares he would not have believed the appearance of Hamlet's ghost "without the sensible and true avouch / of mine own eyes" (*Hamlet*, 1.1.57). A new emphasis upon factual evidence laid the foundation for the later secularism of the eighteenth-century Enlightenment and the high value placed on rationalism in the modern world. (More recent postmodern suspicions about the validity of this rational Enlightenment "project" are beyond the scope of this discussion.) It is helpful to recall that the Renaissance itself was built upon a synthesis of pagan and Christian values, a blending known as Christian Humanism (not to be confused with the later so-called secular humanism), which sought to fuse the best insights of both worldviews. Classical assertions about the value of humanity and its high potential—summed up in the words of the Greek philosopher Protagoras (c. 480–c. 410), "Man is the measure of all things"—are thought by Christians to have been fulfilled in the life of Jesus, believed by them to be both God and man. A Renaissance writer such as Pico della Mirandola (1463–1494) could thus base his "Oration on the Dignity of Man" (c. 1487) upon both the humanistic confidence of the ancients as well as the faith of the New Testament: "O Supreme generosity of God the Father, O highest and most marvelous felicity of man! To him it is granted to have whatever he chooses, to be whatever he wills."

Like his most famous dramatic character, Shakespeare blends skeptical and spiritual outlooks: Hamlet is both the inveterate asker of questions and yet the sage who can see that there is "more in heaven and earth" than is "dreamt of" in his friend Horatio's philosophy (1.5.166–67). In *Antony and Cleopatra*, Cleopatra describes the vigor of Antony's life by saying that "His delights / Were dolphin-like, they showed his back above / The element they liv'd in" (5.2.88–90). Shakespeare similarly tested, probed, and inquired above and beyond his own age, yet he never lets us forget the cultural climate of his own day. In discussing Shakespeare's religious background, this chapter and the next do not attempt to define his own religious outlook but, rather, offer a succinct picture of the "element" he "liv'd in." The historian Mark Noll has commented that all attempts to explain the history of Christianity in any one narrative are to some extent "failures" because its story is too complex to be captured in a single book (Shelley, xiii). The following discussion can only sketch some of the primary factors in the spread of this faith, which was later to influence Shakespeare's works so decisively. Historian Diarmaid MacCulloch has commented that "Social or political history cannot do without theology in understanding the sixteenth century" (107). Shakespeare's religious context likewise cannot be ignored if we are to gain the fullest appreciation of his work.

THE MINISTRY OF JESUS

As a force in the development of Western European culture from the reign of the Roman Emperor Constantine the Great (c. 288–337) until the mid-seventeenth century, Christianity has no equal. It spanned nations, cultures, languages, and political systems. It influenced literature, government, morality, and philosophy. It inspired great works of art, music, sculpture, and architecture. It also fostered devastating wars, self-righteous cruelty, and unthinking bigotry. Its early history is the record of survival against a variety of problems and obstacles. Its founder never married, amassed no wealth, obtained no official rank, left no personal writings or descendents, and was regarded by both Jewish leaders and Roman officials as at least a social nuisance and at most a dangerous political and religious threat. In about the year 35, he suffered a grisly crucifixion at the hands of the Romans. After his death, his small band of followers scattered, and 35 years later the Romans destroyed the Jewish temple in Jerusalem, the focal point of the faith in which he had been raised. Thirty years after that, Peter and Paul, two of his most ardent followers, were martyred in Rome. What did Jesus teach and why did he provoke so much immediate hostility, followed by 2,000 years of devotion?

Apart from some minor differences, the gospels (written accounts of Jesus's life and teachings) of Matthew, Mark, and Luke center on several consistent essential details of his life and ministry; for this reason they are referred to as the *synoptic* gospels (the gospel of John is more theological and departs from the synoptics' historical pattern). E. P. Sanders has summarized those features of Jesus's life that are known with greatest certainty. He was born about 4 B.C. (though some suggest a somewhat earlier date) in Bethlehem, a town in southern Palestine, a region known to the Romans as Judaea, but he spent his youth in the Galilean village of Nazareth. He was baptized by John the Baptist, chose twelve apostles, taught mostly in the rural areas around Galilee, and entered Jerusalem around the year 30 for the Jewish feast of Passover, where he disrupted the activities of the Temple. After a meal with the twelve disciples, he was arrested and questioned by the Jews, then executed by order of the Roman procurator Pontius Pilate.

The core of Jesus's teachings was already contained within the "old covenant," the spiritual commitment between God and the tribes of Israel as recorded in the Torah, the first five books of the Old Testament. Recent scholars have re-emphasized the "Jewishness" of Jesus, John P. Meier terming him "a marginal Jew," John Dominic Crossan labeling him "a Mediterranean peasant," and Bruce Chilton calling him "rabbi Jesus." In his three-year ministry to the Jews living in and around the sea of Galilee, traveling no more than a distance of some 200 miles, he rejected the overemphasis upon legalistic ritual and empty ceremony that he found among the Israelites. Instead, preaching the "kingdom of God," he called for a new focus upon personal moral and spiritual conversion (in Greek, *metanoia*, or "change of mind"). Instead of emphasizing obedience to the more than 600 obligatory laws of the Old Testament, he stressed only two as necessary to "inherit eternal life": "Thou shalt love the Lord thy God with all thy heart, and with all thy soul, and with all thy strength, and with all thy mind; and thy neighbor as thyself" (Luke 10: 27). It was this outlook of the heart, the inner orientation of the believer, that Jesus counted as most important in a right relationship with God, and he could be harshly uncompromising about those who merely appeared to be holy but lacked true devotion. On numerous occasions he spurned the Pharisees and Saduccees, the ruling Jewish priests and authorities who would later interrogate him, for maintaining the letter, but not the spirit, of a genuine faith: "Woe unto you, scribes and Pharisees, hypocrites! For ye are like unto whited sepulchres, which indeed appear beautiful outward, but are within full of dead men's bones and of all uncleanness" (Matthew 23: 27).

However, to the large crowds of people at the bottom of the social ladder who followed him, to the sick, the poor, and the outcast, Jesus showed remarkable forgiveness and affection. In his famous Sermon on the Mount (Matthew 5), he claimed that the "poor in spirit," the peacemakers, the humble, the persecuted, the merciful, and those who mourn, were all "blessed." Everyone, regardless of rank or wealth, was the object of God's loving concern: "Are not five sparrows sold for two farthings, and not one of them is forgotten before God? But even the very hairs of your head are all numbered. Fear not therefore: ye are of more value than many sparrows" (Luke 12: 6–7; Matthew 10: 29. Hamlet alludes to this statement when he says "There is special providence in the fall of a sparrow" [5.2.219–20]). He favored parables, or brief instructional stories, to illustrate his beliefs, as in the account of a traveler who is attacked by robbers and left for dead (Luke 10: 25–37). A Jewish priest and a Levite (a member of the Jewish tribe of Levi) ignored the traveller's plight, but a Samaritan (a group despised by the priests) stopped to aid him. In the words of Donald Guthrie, Jesus thereby "shows how even a Samaritan may be nearer to the kingdom than a pious, but merciless, Jew" (905). On another occasion Jesus is brought a woman who was accused of adultery by the Pharisees, who, hoping to entrap him in a legal question, remind him that according to the Law of Moses she must be stoned to death. But Jesus instead says to them, "Let he who is without sin cast the first stone" (John 8: 4–11). After they leave, he refuses to condemn the woman and simply tells her to sin no more, offering her an acceptance like that of the loving father in the parable of the Prodigal Son (Luke 15). The fact that Jesus would even speak with an accused woman, much less refuse to condemn her, raised serious suspicions about him in the minds of the Jewish authorities but reveals his characteristic unconditional love. Additionally, crowds were drawn to Jesus because of the miracles he performed, events which were seen and heard by the disciples: "The blind receive their sight, and the lame walk, the lepers are cleansed, and the deaf hear, the dead are raised up, and the poor have the gospel preached to them" (Matthew 11:5).

What these stories and many others like them illustrate is the remarkable combination of intelligence, compassion, perception, and persistence we find in the character of Jesus; his steadfast unwillingness to be dissuaded from his ministry of reform; and his refusal to be judged according to standards and expectations that he found misguided or self-serving. Jesus was clearly a person of dynamic character and deep integrity; the gospels reveal that it was the personal impact of his presence as well as the concepts he taught that won him both acclaim and censure. Nor was his gospel a simple one, as sentimental accounts of his life may suggest. As Ralph Sockman has pointed out, his message was often deeply paradoxical as he spoke of easy burdens, losing one's life to save it, and turning the other cheek to evil. More recently, Jaroslav Pelikan has argued that the place of Jesus in western culture hinges on his many-sided roles such as the "divine and human model," "the universal man," and "the teacher of common sense."

Such a compelling yet provocative person, like most shapers of history, was bound to unsettle established customs and familiar assumptions. In the popular phrase, Jesus "comforted the afflicted and afflicted the comfortable." Official Jewish opposition to him was based upon the drastic reinterpretation he placed upon traditional Hebrew teachings. Like all revolutionaries, Jesus posed a threat to the establishment, in this case the religious hierarchy of Jerusalem. By claiming that God demanded personal amendment of life more than obedience to the institutional ritual of the Temple, he effectively redefined what it meant to be a believing Jew. In fact, when he entered Jerusalem shortly before his death, he shocked the authorities by going straight to the Temple and driving out the money-lenders and others for whom it was no longer a religious sanctuary but a place of business: "Jesus went into the temple, and began to cast out them that sold and bought in the temple, and overthrew the tables of the moneychangers, and the seats of them that sold doves . . . And he taught, saying unto them, Is it not written, My house shall be called of all nations the house of prayer? But ye have made it a den of thieves" (Mark 11: 15, 17). This flagrant act of defiance guaranteed that the high priests would no longer tolerate his presence; they "sought how they might destroy him: for they feared him, because all the people was astonished at his doctrine" (Mark 11: 18).

Jesus also proved to be a disturbing problem to the Jewish rulers politically as well as religiously. Their Mosaic tradition and ancient prophets had predicted that God, working through the events of history, would send a messiah (Hebrew for "anointed one"; the equivalent Greek word is *christos*), who would lead the nation into an era of godly peace and freedom from oppression like that imposed on the Jews by the Romans during Jesus' lifetime. Jesus was at first assumed to be this messiah by the twelve apostles he himself had chosen to become the teachers of his message; the crowds who greeted him on his arrival into Jerusalem assumed as much. But he rejected the role of governmental leader and political figurehead who sought influence through force. As he said to Pilate before his final sentencing, "My kingdom is not of this world: if my kingdom were of this world, then would my servants fight, that I should not be delivered to the Jews: but now is my kingdom not from hence" (John 18: 36). The "kingdom of God" about which Jesus preached was, rather, both personal and public, both immediate and to come. The reformation of the individual that came with obedience to God's love established a "kingdom" within the believer—what John Milton in *Paradise Lost* would later call a "paradise within" (XII, 587)—while the spread of such believers would hopefully result in a social kingdom whose values were rooted in love and justice. While Jesus accepted the Jewish expectation for a messiah, once again—as with his understanding of the law—he redefined that concept, rejecting a political or social reformation in favor of a necessary prior spiritual or moral awakening. These concepts come together in the Sermon on the Mount as he declared, "Think not that I am come to destroy the law or the prophets: I am not come to destroy, but to fulfill. . . . For I say unto you, that except your righteousness shall exceed the righteousness of the scribes and Pharisees, ye shall in no case enter into the kingdom of heaven" (Matthew 5: 17, 20).

The Jews at this time were but one of the countless peoples who were held in the huge geographical embrace of the Roman empire, but they were an especially troublesome group, for they steadfastly refused to acknowledge the multitude of Roman gods, among whom was the emperor himself, Caesar Augustus. In place of this polytheism, they worshipped only Jahweh: "Hear, O Israel, the Lord our God is one Lord" (Deuteronomy 6: 4). The Roman government, more concerned about obedience within its empire than allegiance to its state religion, had nevertheless reached a workable compromise with the Jewish leaders that preserved a measure of stability. The presence of Jesus threatened to destroy the relative peace that Rome had achieved in this troublesome region. For the Roman occupiers of Jerusalem, Jesus was a dangerous agitator whose increasing popularity with the masses could provoke revolution. Certainly some of his comments hinted at social reform, as in his parable of the workers in the vineyard who all receive the same pay regardless of their work: "the last shall be first, and the first last" (Matthew 20: 16).

The betrayal of Jesus into the hands of the Roman legal system was the inevitable outcome of his ministry. To have avoided death would have required him to abandon all that he stood for. During the Jewish feast of Passover, he ate a last supper with his followers, "and as they were eating, Jesus took bread and blessed it and broke it and gave it to the disciples and said, 'Take, eat for this is my body.' And he took the cup and gave thanks and gave it to them saying, 'Drink ye all of it. For this is my blood of the new testament, which is shed for many for the remission of sins'" (Matthew 26: 26–28). This communion meal or *eucharist* (Greek for "thanksgiving") became the central rite of the church, whether viewed as a powerful memorial symbol (among many Protestants) or as a sacramental event in which Jesus was spiritually truly present (among Roman Catholics, Anglicans, and Orthodox). It also became the source of gossip among his enemies, leading some groups to believe that Christians practiced cannibalism.

Jesus had foretold his own death and resurrection (Luke 18: 32–33). But, in an important sense, the death of Jesus was in fact the birth of what would become known as the Christian faith. The gospels record that three days after his death, his friends found his tomb empty, though he was later seen by many before he was taken up into heaven. Whether his resurrection is understood literally as a miracle by which his body was physically reanimated or, as some modern theologians such as John Spong claim, it was instead the profound awareness of his message that transformed the lives of his followers, there is no doubt that his triumph over death (celebrated annually in the feast of Easter) was the keystone of this new religious movement. As the apostle Paul put it, "If Christ be not raised, your faith is in vain" (1 Corinthians 15: 17). According to E. P. Sanders, his followers "believed that he would return to found the kingdom; they formed a community to await his return and sought to win others to faith in him as God's Messiah" (11).

THE EARLY CHURCH: FROM PAUL TO CONSTANTINE

The first five centuries of the church's history are among its most tumultuous, for in these years it expanded its influence throughout the empire and struggled to define and codify its core beliefs (orthodoxy) and reject erroneous theological ideas (heresies). In the decades shortly after the death of Jesus, this process of expansion and unification was aided most notably by the tireless work of the apostle Paul (who died c. 64–67), an educated Roman Jew who had himself persecuted Christians before being converted during a momentous revelation as he was traveling to Damascus (Acts 9: 3–9). Journeying throughout Asia Minor and North Africa to the budding churches in such cities as Ephesus, Corinth, and Thessalonica, he instructed, encouraged, and cajoled the young centers of faith. His job was aided by the fact that he enjoyed the privilege of Roman citizenship and spoke both Aramaic and Greek. He was able to take advantage of the excellent Roman road system, the political peace that prevailed throughout the empire (the *pax Romana*), and the fact that many Jewish synagogues and temples were potential sites for the growth of Christianity, which had not yet completely grown beyond its identity as a branch of Judaism. Paul and his fellow proselytizers were to change this.

It was in the large city of Antioch in Asia Minor, for example, where the followers of Jesus were first called "Christians." Paul's missionary travels, told in the book of Acts, form an adventurous story of conflicts and successes, often at great risk to himself "in much patience, in afflictions, in necessities, in distresses, in stripes, in imprisonments, in tumults, in labors, in watchings, in fastings" (2 Corinthians 6: 5). Paul's ability to straddle the Roman and Jewish worlds, together with his knowledge of Greek and Roman philosophy, expanded Christian thinking beyond the limits of Jewish culture and history. "He established the right to think in the full Hellenistic sense," says Paul Johnson, "and thus showed that the Christian faith has nothing to fear from the power of thought" (40). A dominating force in the history of Christianity, Paul is a protean figure, at once a Jew, a Roman, a Hellenist, a mystic, an activist, and a theologian (Meeks).

These scattered groups of early believers were bound by a common faith in Christ, but in practice that faith often took different forms or found expression in varying beliefs. Because these early Christians had first been Jews, a crucial question arose as to the admission of Gentiles (non-Jews) to the church. Should new adherents be made to follow Mosaic laws and Jewish rituals, specifically circumcision—the requirement for all Jewish males? The book of Acts (written sometime after 70 A.D.) records that a council in Jerusalem concluded that circumcision was unnecessary. This confirmed the position that Paul had taken in his letter to the church in Galatia (c. 55 A.D.) that there were no preconditions for becoming a Christian: "There is neither Jew nor Greek, there is neither bond nor free, there is neither male nor female: for ye are all one in Christ Jesus" (Galatians 3: 28). The freedom to be Christian without first being Jewish was rooted in both a practical reality as well as a theological truth, for the emperor Vespasian (and later his son Titus) had begun to enforce an even stricter control over Israel. In 70 A.D. they destroyed the temple at Jerusalem. For Christians there was now no returning to the city of their origin even had they wanted to, and it was not possible any longer to consider Christianity as merely some unique branch of Judaism. The church's new home was the world; it was now catholic (universal), rather than local or national.

At first flourishing in those cities Paul visited and wrote to in his letters, Christianity would later move west, into France, Spain, and Britain, and as far east (according to tradition) as India during the first century. The need for a system to administer and maintain these churches was met by the growth of an episcopal structure, or governance by bishops (from the Greek, *episcopos* or bishop). In Mark Noll's words, these "designated successors of the apostles [were] charged with carrying on the apostolic work of testifying to Christ and organizing lives of service to him" (41). They became especially important after the martyrdoms of Paul and Peter in Rome, sometime between 64–67 under the emperor Nero. The early centers of Christian faith had as yet no common definition of their central tenets of belief, and the spread of theological differences posed a threat to the developing church just as the debate over the admission of Gentiles had. It was up to influential bishops and theologians of the first six centuries (referred to as the Church Fathers) to hammer out in often lengthy and contentious councils the foundational concepts of Christian belief by beating back a series of heretical ideas that threatened to crack the young religion's fragile unity.

Heresy came to mean any belief that contradicted the convictions of the major-ity of believers; it was the opposite of *orthodoxy* (Greek for "right thinking"). While there were many heresies the church had to combat, church historian Martin Marty has identified three as most influential. The first was Gnosticism. Gnostics varied in their specific doctrines, but all believed that they possessed a special knowledge (from the Greek *gnosis*), which would lead to salvation. They were dualists who felt that the universe was governed by spirits of good and evil, and that the evil spirit expressed itself in material nature; what was truly good was spirit, not matter. Gnostic knowledge was a mixture of Christian, pagan, and Jewish ideas, but it was grounded in the desire to seek salvation by repudiating the physical, fleshly world. Jesus Christ therefore could not have actually been truly a man, because this would have compromised his spiritual nature; he only seemed to be a man (this aspect of Gnosticism resembled the related heresy of *docetism*). From this it followed that it was not the divine Christ who was crucified, but only the physical body of Jesus. A vigorous critic of the Gnostics was the church father Irenaeus, bishop of Lyon (c. 125–c. 202), who composed the treatise *Adversus Haereses* (*Against the Heretics*). He defended the apostolic succession of bishops, asserted the centrality of the four gospels, and confuted the Gnostics' claim of special knowledge about spiritual duality by reaffirming the unity of God.

A second major heresy was Marcionism, after its proponent Marcion who flourished in Rome around 140. Influenced by Gnostic thinking, Marcion found the Old Testament God of the Jews to be a stern lawgiver interested only in harsh justice. However, the New Testament God was a fatherly spirit lovingly concerned for the well-being of his people. Marcion therefore rejected the Old Testament totally and in fact regarded only parts of the gospel of Luke and ten of Paul's letters as the truly "genuine" New Testament. In so doing, he elevated Paul's importance almost to the level of Jesus and stripped the church of its Jewish heritage and the spiritual importance of the Old Testament covenant. "Marcion posed an even greater threat to the church than did the Gnostics," explains Justo González, "[because] he organized a church with its own bishops and its own scripture" (I, 62). The prolific and influential theologian Origen (c. 185–c. 254) included Marcion among the various heresies he combated. According to Henri Crouzel, "Against the Marcionites he affirmed the goodness of the creator, his identity with the Father of Jesus, the agreement of the two Testaments and the value of the Old" (12).

The third major heresy appeared between 156 and 170, spread by Montanus and his two female prophets, Priscilla and Maximilla. By the second century, widespread belief had faded in the New Testament conviction that Jesus had inaugurated the last age of history, the endtime. Montanus attempted to correct this apparent failure of belief by declaring that he himself was the divinely sent spirit of the last age. He and his prophetesses were convinced that the action of the Holy Spirit took precedence over the authority of scripture and that the New Testament was subordinate to an individual's own private revelation.

Not only did these and other heresies contradict one another at many points, all of them ran afoul of doctrines that were emerging as common beliefs among a large number of Christians. If the church as a whole was to keep itself from splintering, an effort had to be made to set down the defining articles of Christian faith. A crisis emerged in the challenge posed when a theologian named Arius asserted that the three-fold nature of God—the trinity of God the Father, God the Son (Jesus), and God the Holy Spirit—was in fact hierarchical instead of equivalent. That is, rather than each being equal to and somehow part of the others, Arius contended that the Father was distinctly superior to the Son, a concept that would have diminished the authority of Jesus as living Messiah. In 325 the emperor Constantine (who was himself later to convert in 337, shortly before his death) summoned a council of bishops at Nicaea. The result was the Nicene Creed (from its first word in Latin, *credo*, "I believe"), a revision of a statement formerly used as a summary of the faith by those to be baptized. It was a declaration of the central faith-statements of the church, one of which was that Jesus was "the Son of God, begotten of the Father, Light of Light, very God of very God, begotten, not made, being of one substance with the Father." Luke Timothy Johnson points out that "The orthodox saw the Arian position as a reduction of the mystery of Jesus to what seemed 'reasonable,' as one-sidedly emphasizing some scriptures and suppressing others, and above all, as denying the full Christian experience of Jesus. This section of the creed is therefore fundamentally a piling up of epithets to characterize Jesus Christ's relationship to God, precisely in order to safeguard the belief that Jesus Christ is our savior" (111–12). The creed also rejected Gnosticism by asserting the unity, not duality, of God, and it rejected Marcionism by declaring that Jesus Christ was fully human ("born of the Virgin Mary"). Arian's ideas were the lifelong target of Athanasius (c. 297–373), bishop of Alexandria, author of *Orations against the Arians* (c. 340). His first two orations, in the view of Charles Kannengieser, "provide a strong articulation of baptismal faith in the divine Trinity with central attention given to the substantial relation between Father and Son in line with the Creed of Nicaea" (19). Later councils, extending even into the twentieth century, methodically continued to build the theological foundation of the faith: in 381 the divinity of the Holy Spirit was asserted at Constantinople; in 431 at Ephesus Mary was designated *theotokos*, the "bearer of God"; and at Chalcedon in 451 the fathers affirmed the nature of Christ as both fully human and fully divine.

The early councils also benefited from the growth of the scriptural canon, the set of holy writings judged to be authoritative for the faith. The word "bible" is taken from the Latin *biblia* or "books," and Jews and Christians alike were known in antiquity as "the people of the book." The church fathers accepted the Old Testament as the old, or original, covenant between God and his people. Some Old Testament books, present in the Greek Old Testament (the Septuagint) but not accepted in the Hebrew scriptures, were called the *Apocrypha* (Greek, "hidden"). Eastern Christians tended not to accept them as authentic (a position later adopted by European Protestants), while the church in the west agreed with the view of Augustine that they should be canonical; this became the Roman Catholic stance. The record of the life and ministry of Christ formed the new covenant, which fulfilled the old, written accounts of the life of Jesus that were in existence prior to the four gospels, which began to be composed around 60 or 70 A.D. A method of allegorical interpretation known as "typology" arose in which events in the Old Testament became foreshadowings of events in the New Testament, which they were thought to parallel, and the links forged between the Hebrews and the followers of Jesus were seen to be not just historical but theological as well. (Marcion's rejected effort to discount the entire Old Testament would have severed the Christian canon from these Hebrew spiritual roots.) The story of the willingness of Isaac to be sacrificed by his father in Genesis 22 was read, for example, as a precursor to the willing crucifixion of Jesus, and Jesus himself was seen as the "second Adam." The Hebrew Old Testament had been translated into Greek about 250 B.C. Called the Septuagint because it was supposedly the work of seventy scholars, it provides evidence for other manuscripts now lost. A list of New Testament canonical works in use at Rome around 200 A.D. indicates some agreement about the content of the Christian texts. Origen, around 250, and Eusebius, a half-century later, advocated their own canons, containing some disputed texts such as the Shepherd of Hermes and the Letter of Barnabus. These and other debated works were finally dropped from the text adopted by the Council of Carthage in 397, which adopted a list of books put forward by Athanasius. The New Testament canon had been set, and the church could now advance with an authorized group of guiding documents.

In addition to resolving internal problems of self-government, doctrine, and canon, the faithful also had to cope with a persistent external problem—Roman persecution. Christians had been intermittently persecuted from their faith's inception. Although the Roman empire practiced a fair degree of toleration for other religions besides its own state religion, Roman paganism posed a problem for the monotheistic Christians just as it had for the Jews. Jesus had told his followers to "render to Caesar the things that are Caesar's and to God the things that are God's" (Mark 12: 17). Caesar deserved the taxes and political recognition that were his due. He did not deserve worship as a god. But rejection of the emperor-god was viewed by the Romans as a rejection of the empire, and Christians were branded "atheists." Christians also aroused suspicion for their generosity, mutual love, and peaceful behavior, traits quite different from many of their more libertine pagan contemporaries. The earliest persecutions, which employed a wide variety of excruciating public deaths, began under the mentally unstable emperor Nero (54–68) and continued principally under Domitian (81–96), Aurelius (161–180), Decius (249–251), and Diocletian (284–305), the last two being most severe. An edict of toleration in 311 by Galerius finally ended the Roman persecutions, but not before the Christians had impressed many by the strength of their faith—just the opposite of what the oppressing emperors had hoped for. Those who died for their faith in the early church became models of piety for those who lived. The famous comment of the early theologian Tertullian (c. 160–c. 230) probably best sums up the importance of the persecutions in the church's history: "The blood of the martyrs is the seed of faith."

The church's vitality within this early period was also strengthened by those who chose not death but the desert. In the later third century, individuals seeking a deeper religious experience grounded in solitude and meditation gravitated toward the Egyptian desert to live as hermits. Thus began monasticism, a form of religious life emphasizing silence, austerity, prayer, and study. In the mid-fourth century, a communal form of monasticism arose, with monks living together in groups under a commonly accepted rule of life. The founder of monasticism was Anthony of Egypt (251–356), a close friend of Athanasius, whose biography of Anthony became, according to Charles Kannengieser, "the first Christian bestseller after the bible" (21). Monks flourished as well in Palestine, Syria, and North Africa, later spreading to northern Italy, Gaul, Spain, and Ireland. The teachings of these early monastics, often expressed as pithy, aphoristic statements, were later collected as "Sayings of the Desert Fathers." Roughly two centuries later monasticism would find its most effective administrator in Benedict (c. 480–c. 547), a monk born in Nursia, Italy. He established a famous monastery at Monte Cassino in Italy on the site of a temple to Apollo. Benedict's *Rule* offered practical guidelines for the efficient management of monasteries and the daily lives of their monks, which would lay the basis for the great flourishing of medieval monasticism six centuries later. His guiding principle was *Orare est laborare, laborare est orare* ("To pray is to work, to work is to pray").

THE CHURCH IN LATE ANTIQUITY: FROM CONSTANTINE TO CHARLEMAGNE

On October 28, 312, the emperor Constantine confronted Maxentius, a challenger to his title, at the Milvian bridge over the Tiber river near Rome. Constantine was emboldened when, according to a legend recounted in the history written by Eusebius, patriarch of Constantinople, he glimpsed a flaming cross in the sky together with the words *In hoc signo vinces* ("In this sign, conquer"). He went on to defeat his enemy and become unchallenged emperor. Although Constantine did not convert to Christianity until shortly before his death in 337, he had long been interested in and sympathetic to the religion. Was he was drawn to the faith because of a genuine belief or because he sensed in it a unifying force that could draw his empire together, only about one-fifth of whom were Christian? There is probably truth in both points, but his decision to summon the Council at Nicaea was a pivotal step in the growth of the church, as well as a crucial link in the developing relationship between it and the state: what had been the catholic church had begun its gradual progression toward becoming the Roman Catholic church. While Constantine did not enforce the acceptance of Christianity in the empire, he did favor its advance and made it more difficult for pagans to practice their beliefs. He demolished their shrines and replaced them with churches, such as the temple to Aphrodite on the site of Christ's tomb, which was replaced with the Church of the Holy Sepulchre. He legalized the giving of wills and legacies to the church, which benefited greatly from the generosity of widows. He named the first day of the week a day of rest, and the first recording of the date of Christmas as December 25 occurs during his reign. His mother Helena designated Bethlehem and the Mount of Olives as Christian sacred sites, and it was said that she had discovered the true cross on which Jesus had died.

In a decision of historic consequence, Constantine also decided to move the capital of his empire far to the east, to a city along the Bosporus named Byzantium, which he renamed Constantinople. It would later become Istanbul in the twentieth century. This was an anchor for the empire in the east, the Byzantine empire, and it took advantage of the rich trade and commerce of the region, which stretched from the Serbian and Croat lands along the Adriatic Sea eastward through Turkey to the western fringes of Russia. But, just as one circle cannot have two centers, the church now experienced a tension between Rome and Constantinople that would ultimately lead to a rupture. Though the Council of Chalcedon in 451 declared these cities of equal administrative importance, Pope Leo I wielded sufficient influence to maintain the primacy of Rome. Orthodox Christianity, as the faith of the Byzantine empire came to be called, remained the second most influential branch of the church until the Protestant Reformation of the sixteenth century. Constantine's decision had in effect created a theocracy in the east, an empire in which civil authority and religious authority were united, unlike the western empire where bishops and secular princes would vie for power, land, and wealth for centuries to come. This unity was physically expressed in Constantinople in the completion of the colossal church of St. Sophia, an architectural masterpiece of the emperer Justinian (527–565).

For Orthodox Christians, painted images or icons of Jesus, Mary, and the saints were vital elements of worship, offering visual aids for meditation and prayer. They were pictures to be contemplatively looked through, so to speak, rather than merely looked at. Western Catholics, however, viewed these icons as forms of idolatry and opponents of these images, called iconoclasts or "image-breakers," argued that they must be stripped from the churches. After a lengthy period of contention, the struggle was decided by the Council of Nicea in 787, which held for the Orthodox practice and condemned the iconoclasts. But other theological differences flared over the nature of the eucharist and the language of the creed. Finally, in 1054, Pope Leo IX officially excommunicated the Orthodox church, and the split between Rome and Constantinople was sealed. In 2007, more than a dozen national Orthodox churches exist, primarily in eastern Europe, such as the Greek, Russian, and Serbian.

As the political might of the Roman empire declined, the vigor of the Roman church increased. Theodosius I succeeded the empire's first Christian emperor, and Theodosius did not hesitate to legally enforce Christianity as the state religion, a step Constantine had never taken. Those who refused, he said, "We adjudge demented and insane, [and] they shall sustain the infamy of heretical dogmas, their meeting places shall not receive the name of churches, and they shall be smitten first by divine vengeance and secondly by the retribution of our own initiative" (Shelley, 97). When a crowd of Greeks rioted and killed their governor because a favorite charioteer was not released from prison to enter a race, Theodosius ordered 7,000 Thessalonians executed in one day for the governor's death. Ambrose, bishop of Rome, refused to administer the sacraments to the Byzantine emperor until he had confessed to his horrendous sin. This incident highlighted the growing strain between Rome and Byzantium, between the power of the pope (as the Bishop of Rome had come to be known) and the authority of secular government, an issue that would become a recurring theme in later European church history. Despite the relocation of the empire's capitol to Constantinople, Rome had steadily increased its influence as the center of Church administration and doctrinal authority. Bishops of Rome were regarded as the direct apostolic descendents of its first bishop, St. Peter, while the fact that Peter and Paul had both been martyred there further enhanced its spiritual status. Eventually, Augustine of Hippo could simply condemn a heresy with his famous, attributed remark: *Roma locuta est, causa finita est* ("Rome has spoken; the case is closed").

The multi-talented Augustine (354–430) was probably the greatest single opponent of heresy in the church's first 500 years. He ultimately rose to become Bishop of Hippo (in what is today northeastern Algeria). More than 300 of his letters and 500 of his sermons survive. Augustine was raised by a devout Christian mother but found himself drawn to pagan Manichean ideas as a youth. He enjoyed what he regarded (in his autobiographical *Confessions*) as a pleasure-loving life of young adulthood, and he did not accept baptism until the sermons of the anti-Arian Bishop Ambrose of Milan (c. 340–397) had convinced him to reject the dualistic concepts of Manicheism, especially its denial of human responsibility for sin. "In his later thought," comments Robert Markus, "the unity of the person and his responsibility for his actions often appear as the nub of Augustine's confrontation with Manicheism and the decisive point over which he rejected its teaching" (503). A second heresy Augustine rejected was Donatism. The Donatists were a populous sect of Christians in North Africa who believed that the effectiveness of the church's sacraments (the ritual symbols through which divine grace was imparted to the believer) depended upon the moral virtue of the priest who administered them, as well as the doctrinal integrity of those who had ordained the priest. Augustine countered that the true agent of sacramental grace was Christ, not the priest, who was nevertheless an essential administrator of the sacraments. The sacraments were thus valid regardless of the moral state of the clergy, a fundamental element of church doctrine known as *ex opere operato* (literally, "from the work performed"). Augustine's third theological target was the heresy of Pelagianism. The monk Pelagius (c. 355–c. 425) rejected the concept of original sin by asserting that Adam's sin of disobedience was not passed down to all mankind; there was thus no need for the "washing away" of sin through baptism. Everyone possessed the divine grace to achieve sanctity, and even unbaptized pagans were able to reach heaven. Augustine, however, stressed the fallen nature of man, his inability to achieve heaven without divine grace, and, furthermore, that God had chosen an "elect" whom he intended to save. God's divine favor was thus more significant than human effort in achieving salvation. The argument over Pelagianism would begin a debate over the nature of free will and divine predestination that would persist throughout the church's history and become especially important in the Protestant Reformation.

The later reign of Theodosius was marked by the great translation of the Bible into Latin (called the Vulgate or "common" edition) by the theologian St. Jerome (c. 347–c. 420). However, although the church grew under Constantine and Theodosius, the empire had begun its infamous downfall. The decline and fall of the Roman empire was a vast historical process straddling the fifth and sixth centuries, with causes too numerous and complex to be addressed in this short overview. A loss of social unity; a weakened army; a conflict between the powers of church and state; the gradual influx of diverse, invading cultures—each of these and more made for internal fractures. Outside its borders lurked first the barbarian nomads and later the aggressive armies of the newly emerging Arab religion, Islam. Germanic peoples had begun to infiltrate the Roman empire at the start of the fifth century. In Richard McBrien's summary, the primary groups were "the Visigoths in southern France (Gaul) and Spain, the Vandals in North Africa, and the Ostrogoths and Lombards in Italy . . . Those migrations were to last for six hundred years and were to come in three waves: the continental Germans in the fifth and sixth centuries, the Saracens in the seventh and eighth centuries, and the Scandinavians and Vikings in the ninth and tenth centuries" (618). The Angles, Saxons, and Jutes of lower Scandinavia intermingled once they reached the British Isles, resulting in the culture named Anglo-Saxon. These infiltrations were probably less violent than outright invasions, but they were steady and largely unstoppable by the weakened Roman army. While they whittled away at the structure of the old Roman empire, which officially fell in 476, these groups swelled the ranks of the church because many of them were, or were about to become, Christians (though mostly adherents of the Arian heresy). The christianization of the invaders was pursued by the vigorous Pope Gregory the Great, who reigned from 590–604. He dispatched St. Augustine of Canterbury (not to be confused with Augustine of Hippo, author of the *Confessions*) to minister to the peoples of Britain. This process of conversion was so thorough that by the time Charlemagne was crowned in 800, a broad foundation had been laid for the culture of medieval Catholicism.

THE CHURCH OF THE MIDDLE AGES

Like Constantine before him, King of the Franks and Emperor Charlemagne (c. 742–814) was both religiously pious and politically astute. His Carolingian dynasty eventually extended through what are now France and Germany and included portions of Italy. After Charlemagne's death, the German Otto I attempted to retain a political unity by establishing the Holy Roman Empire (962–1806). A rudimentary nationalism among the various peoples of this so-called empire began to make for a growing political cohesiveness after the fall of the Roman Empire on which it was modeled. Two centuries later, from 1220–1270, France would benefit from the careful administration of Louis IX, which contributed to the intellectual vigor of the thirteenth century. The administrative structure of the church likewise began a period of sustained growth and consolidation, as bishops grew in wealth and influence, and church policies and doctrines or "canons" were more effectively promulgated. (Shakespeare's Hamlet refrains from committing suicide because he knows that "the everlasting" has "fix'd his canon 'gainst self-slaughter" [1.2.132].) The papal system of authority was to become so effective that 500 years later Thomas Hobbes, the seventeenth-century philosopher, would say in his *Leviathan* (1651) that "The Papacy is no other than the ghost of the deceased Roman empire, sitting crowned upon the grave thereof." Social unity was further strengthened by the system of interlocking allegiances among landholders and their dependents known as feudalism. Although the rich and rising middle-class shopkeepers were a class apart, the predominately agricultural economy of medieval Europe was governed by the authority of many local dukes and nobles (or *suzerains*), who pledged to provide protection and legal adjudication for those (their *vassals*) who worked their lands (or *fiefdoms*) and who promised to fight for them in time of war. Prior to the emergence of modern national states, the social structure of this period of European history was thus a trinity composed of those who worked (the peasants), those who fought (the aristocratic knighthood and landholders), and those who prayed (the church clergy). With its countless bishops, priests, monks, and friars spread across boundaries from England to the Baltic; with its vast and influential holdings of wealth and land; and with its centralized rule under the Roman pope, the church had thus become the single most unifying factor in medieval society.

One result of this growing social stability was the development of monastic learning and, towards the end of the twelfth century, of the universities. Monks preserved and copied manuscripts for the sake of prayer and meditation, and this practice expanded with the spread of the Benedictine order centered at Cluny in France, which eventually numbered close to one thousand locations throughout Europe. But the devotional study of the cloisters differed from the more inquisitive learning springing up at the universities. At first little more than guilds, or groups of students associated with one or more teachers, the rise of the universities was a key factor in what has been termed "the Renaissance of the twelfth century" or the "medieval Renaissance." The earliest university was in Bologna

(1088), with later schools at Oxford (1167), Cambridge (1209), Padua (1222), and elsewhere. At Paris in 1231, Robert Sorbon established a school of theology, which later became the Sorbonne. The curriculum of medieval education, which persisted into the Renaissance largely unchanged until the seventeenth century (when it was vigorously criticized by John Milton), consisted of the seven ancient liberal arts: the trivium (grammar, rhetoric, and logic) and the quadrivium (astronomy, music, geometry, and arithmetic). Central to this curriculum was the great respect accorded the philosopher Aristotle. As C. H. Lawrence observes, "The books of Aristotle's logic provided a system of rational analysis that could apparently be applied in every field of learning. In the course of the twelfth century the application of dialectic or analytic logic to the materials of study created new sciences of theology and canon law, as well as new secular sciences of logic, jurisprudence, and medicine" (139). When applied to theology, this Aristotelian method of thinking resulted in the intellectual movement that most typified medieval thought: scholasticism.

Scholasticism sought to explain and defend the tenets of Christianity (apart from certain mysteries of the faith such as the trinity, incarnation, and resurrection) by means of classical logic, based upon the assumption that there could finally be no conflict between religious truth and philosophical truth. Its motto was *fides quaerens intellectum* or "faith seeking understanding." A key founder of scholasticism was Anselm (c. 1033–1109), a British monk who sought to fuse the insights of reason and revelation, most notably in his *Monologium* and *Proslogium* (c. 1070), which offered an ontological proof for the existence of God. The most important scholastic thinker of the Middle Ages was Thomas Aquinas (1225–1274), a Dominican friar educated at Monte Cassino who made his reputation as a professor of theology in Paris. The "Dumb Ox," as he was nicknamed for his corpulence and slow manner of working, is best known for his *Summa Theologica* (1267–1273), which set forth the principles of theology according to Aristotle's logic. Aquinas's particular method of scholasticism came to be known as Thomism, and after his death its principles became the foundation for traditional Roman Catholic theology.

The growth, power, and influence of the Roman Catholic church throughout Europe from the tenth through the fourteenth centuries can be visually summed up in the great architectural movement of the medieval era: the Gothic style. Termed "Gothic" by later Renaissance historians because it emerged north of the Alps (though it had nothing to do with the Gothic tribes that invaded those regions), it first appeared in the French abbey of St. Denis, rebuilt during 1140–1144. Gothic architecture was the physical expression of the medieval spirit of faith, a human longing for God translated into pointed arches, stained glass windows that portrayed biblical scenes for the illiterate, and cross-shaped churches with long, central naves whose height was over twice their width. This proportion gave Gothic cathedrals a tremendous sense of height and a feeling of transcendent airiness that belied their vast structure. This feeling of transcendence was enhanced by music and incense at the celebration of the Mass, which became a sensory experience for the worshippers.

The twelfth century was the great age of cathedral building; Bruce Shelley notes that "between 1170 and 1270 more than 500 great churches were built in Gothic style in France alone" (183). Cathedrals embodied the authority of the bishops whose "seats" (*cathedra* in Latin) they were, as well as the competitive spirit of the rich middle-class merchants who financed them and who competed with each other to see whose town could build the highest and most impressive structure. The cathedrals were marvels of engineering, built only of wood and stone and with huge external supports called flying buttresses to hold up the walls, which held beautiful but fragile windows. In some cases construction skills could not keep up with civic ambitions, as in the collapse of the 500-foot high Beauvais cathedral in 1284. In addition to their religious and civic importance, because cathedrals drew large crowds on religious feast days, they swelled the population of their towns and aided the growth of commerce and business. Cathedrals often fostered schools for the training of clergy. Later, as the schools filled with more students who did not wish to become priests, the schools became secular centers of education for their communities as well.

The medieval church's growing successes both intellectually and materially did not come without strains, however. The influence that Charlemagne and later rulers were able to wield became a point of contention against the authority of the church, especially where the appointment, or investiture, of new bishops was concerned. This "investiture controversy" appeared in eleventh-century Germany and was essentially a struggle between the church, which asserted the primacy of spiritual authority in such matters, against the Holy Roman Emperors, who held that their temporal authority should prevail. A compromise of sorts was reached at the Concordat of Worms in 1122, but it marked only one aspect of a continuing struggle between church and state, which was to rear its head again in England a generation before Shakespeare's birth when Henry VIII sought a papal divorce from his wife, Catherine of Aragon.

A second source of friction became clear as the lives of medieval bishops grew increasingly lax, and their wealth increased through donations of money and property, arousing calls for a return to a life of simplicity and holy poverty among the clergy. Around 1176, Peter Waldo, a French merchant, gave away his possessions in a gesture of voluntary poverty as the path to holiness. He and his followers, known as the Waldenses, believed in the efficacy of lay preaching, rejecting papal authority and the significance of the Mass. Not surprisingly, they were vigorously condemned as heretical by the church hierarchy. Eighty members were burned at the stake in Strasbourg in 1211, but their movement lived on into the nineteenth century. Also prompted by the attraction of a severely disciplined life, the Albigensians were a group of heretics in Albi, France, who not only denied clerical authority, but held to a dualistic theology of good and evil similar to the Manicheans whom the early church had condemned. Part of an even larger movement called Catharism, the Albigensians were so resistant to correction that in 1208 Pope Innocent III began the Albigensian Crusade to root them out of southern France. The crusade ended in 1229, but the heretics were only eradicated in the mid-fourteenth century after Pope Gregory IX established an inquisition to interrogate and eliminate them. The most memorable and least divisive effort in this era to rededicate the church to a mission of humble service was the life and work of Giovanni Bernardone, known to history as Francis of Assisi (1182–c. 1226). The son of a wealthy Italian merchant, Francis underwent a conversion experience in his early twenties, gave away his possessions, and made a pilgrimage to Rome in 1206. However, unlike the Waldenses and Albigensians, Francis was devoted to the church and managed to receive permission from Pope Innocent III to travel freely and preach even though he was not ordained a priest. Thus were born the Franciscan friars, mendicants who lived on the generosity of those they ministered to and who performed simple labor for daily wages. Eventually, the church sanctioned four orders of friars: Franciscans, Augustinians, Dominicans, and Carmelites. Francis's life of poverty, service, and humility has made him one of the best-loved saints of the church. (There are six different friars in Shakespeare's plays, the most famous probably being Friar Laurence, who performs the tragic marriage of Romeo and Juliet.)

Innocent III's crusade against the Albigensians recreated in France one of the most historic military and religious events of the Middle Ages: the Crusades against the Muslims. Over three centuries later Shakespeare composed *Richard II*, in which Henry Bolingbroke usurps King Richard, and then, in *Henry IV, Part 1*, announces his intent to expiate this sin by mounting a crusade of his own against Islam:

> Therefore, friends,
> As far as to the sepulcher of Christ—
> Whose soldier now, under whose blessed cross
> We are impressed and engag'd to fight—
> Forthwith a power of English shall we levy,
> Whose arms were moulded in their mother's womb,
> To chase these pagans in those holy fields,
> Over whose acres walk'd those blessed feet
> Which fourteen hundred years ago were nail'd
> For our advantage on the bitter cross. (1.1.22–27)

Although Henry never fulfilled his wish, it is significant that he chose such a public and expensive way in which to demonstrate the depth of his faith. By imitating the medieval crusaders (and recalling the Knight in Chaucer's *Canterbury Tales*, who had fought "As wel in cristendom as hethenesse"), he called attention to that series of protracted but ultimately ineffective medieval campaigns whose effects still reverberate in the Middle East of the twenty-first century, whose Islamic extremists condemn American soldiers as "crusaders."

Sometime between 570 and 580 A.D., the prophet Mohammed was born in Mecca, a city near the Red Sea coast in Arabia. After a long period of prayer and meditation, he received a divine revelation in 611 instructing him to present the message of God to the various disunited Arab tribes. The full record of his revelation is found in the *Koran*, the holy book of Islam (the name Islam means "submission to God"). According to Islam, Mohammed is the final prophet of

God, preceded by Adam, Noah, Abraham, Moses, and Jesus. Christians, Jews, and Muslims thus find some agreement in these revelations of a single God, though Muslims regard the Hebrew and Christian Bibles as misinterpretations of the genuine scripture. Muslims, whose name means "the submitted," believe in a heaven of reward and a hell of punishment, and they must satisfy five demands during their lives. They must commit to the belief that "There is no god but God and Mohammed is his prophet," pray five times daily, give alms, keep the holy feast of Ramadan, and make a pilgrimage to Mecca. Finding it difficult to establish Islam in his home city, Mohammed traveled northeast to Medina, establishing there a religiously governed center of believers. From there he then mounted a campaign to conquer Mecca, which he achieved in 624.

The spread of Islam had begun. By Mohammed's death eight years later, all of Arabia had become Muslim. By the ninth century, the vast Muslim Abbasid empire stretched from present-day Afghanistan in the east, through the entire Arabian subcontinent, westward across North Africa, and into the southern half of Spain, which had been assaulted in 711. The center of Orthodox Christianity, Constantinople, had weathered two attacks in the late seventh and early eighth centuries; Sicily was conquered in 827; Rome was struck in 846. It seemed clear to medieval Christians that their faith and culture were in peril. And despite whatever links existed between Koranic and Christian beliefs, it was obvious to them that the Muslims held to a heretical rejection of the incarnation and resurrection of Jesus. As Richard Fletcher points out, attitudes between Christians and Muslims were marked by "misunderstanding, resentment, [and] hostility" (28). In 1071, Byzantine forces made a stand against the Muslim Turks at Manzikert, Turkey. The Turks were the decisive victors, and the terrified Byzantines then called upon the nations of western Christianity for assistance. The result was a series of no less than nine Crusades, lasting from 1095 until 1272, which fruitlessly attempted to drive the Muslims from their footholds. The last stronghold to fall to Islam was the northern Palestinian city of Acre in 1291, an event possibly hinted at in Henry IV's reference to the "acres" over which Jesus walked. Despite the loss of sacred cities such as Constantinople and Jerusalem, Europeans did benefit in lasting ways from the Crusades because of improved trade routes, importation of new and exotic foods and spices, and a greater knowledge of world geography and ancient manuscripts. Intellectually, the protracted interactions, often surprisingly cooperative, between the two cultures led to a vital transmission of classical knowledge by way of Latin translations of Arabic copies of Greek and Arabic works on such topics as philosophy, medicine, astronomy, and mathematics.

The failure of the Crusades of the thirteenth century signaled the end of the great era of church intellectual culture during the High Middle Ages of the eleventh and twelfth centuries. Though the popes had been able to summon forces to fill the crusading armies, their power and influence waned dramatically in the fourteenth and fifteenth centuries. The increasing power of national rulers such as Edward I in England and Philip the Fair in France posed threats to the secular power of the popes. Pope Boniface VIII attempted to reassert this power in the papal bull or pronouncement of 1302, *Unam Sanctam*. But Philip's agents captured Boniface at his summer residence in Italy and held him temporarily in a show of force. Boniface died shortly thereafter, and Philip's influence led to the coronation of a Frenchman, Clement V, as the next Pope. He and the succeeding popes for the next 72 years reigned not from Rome, but in the French town of Avignon, a period called the "Babylonian Captivity" of the papacy. In 1377, Urban VI was elected pope and chose to remain in Rome, but the French cardinals acted independently and picked their own pope, Clement VI, who like his French predecessors, chose to stay in Avignon. This so-called Great Schism, in which there was not one but two popes (and even three in the early fifteenth century) divided European Christendom. Finally, the Council of Constance in 1417 decided that the influence of the council itself could settle the issue. This "conciliar movement" resulted in the unseating of the popes with the election of Martin V, who promptly declared the council invalid and heretical. The existence of multiple popes had ceased but so had the attempt to govern the church through a representative council rather than a single authority. The centralized power that remained, plus the immorality and wealth of the succeeding popes such as Alexander VI, was to fan the flames of a growing call for sweeping change within the church. The seeds of the Protestant Reformation had been sown.

REFERENCES

Chilton, Bruce. *Rabbi Jesus: An Intimate Biography*. New York: Doubleday, 2000. Rpt. 2002.

Crossan, John Dominic. *The Historical Jesus: The Life of a Mediterranean Jewish Peasant*. San Francisco, CA: HarperSanFrancisco, 1991.

Crouzel, Henri. "Origen." In *Key Thinkers in Christianity*. Ed. A. Hastings, A. Mason, and H. Pyper. Oxford, UK: Oxford University Press, 2003. 8–16.

Fletcher, Richard. *The Cross and the Crescent: Christianity and Islam from Muhammed to the Reformation*. New York: Viking, 2003.

González, Justo L. *The Story of Christianity*. 2 volumes. New York: HarperCollins, 1984.

Guthrie, Donald and J. A. Motyer. *The New Bible Commentary Revised*. New York: Eerdmans, 1970.

Johnson, Luke Timothy. *The Creed*. New York: Doubleday, 2003.

Johnson, Paul. *A History of Christianity*. New York: Atheneum, 1980.

Kannengieser, Charles. "Athanasius." In *Key Thinkers in Christianity*. Ed. A. Hastings, A. Mason, and H. Pyper. Oxford, UK: Oxford University Press, 2003. 17–23.

Lawrence, C. H. *Medieval Monasticism*. 3rd ed. Harlow, England: Longman, 2001.

MacCulloch, Diarmaid. *The Reformation*. New York: Viking, 2003.

Markus, Robert A. "Life of Augustine." In *Augustine through the Ages: An Encyclopedia*. Ed. Allan D. Fitzgerald, O.S.A. Grand Rapids, MI: Eerdmans, 1999. 498–504.

Marty, Martin. *A Short History of Christianity*. Philadelphia, PA: Fortress Press, 1987.

McBrien, Richard P. *Catholicism*. New edition. New York: HarperCollins, 1994.

Meeks, Wayne. "The Christian Proteus." In *The Writings of St. Paul*. Ed. Wayne Meeks. New York: Norton, 1972. 435–444.

Meier, John P. *A Marginal Jew: Rethinking the Historical Jesus*. 3 volumes. New York: Anchor Bible, 1991–2001.

Noll, Mark. *Turning Points: Decisive Moments in the History of Christianity*. 2nd ed. Grand Rapids, MI: Baker Academic, 2000.

Pelikan, Jaroslav. *Jesus Through the Centuries: His Place in the History of Culture*. New Haven, CT: Yale University Press, 1985.

Sanders, E. P. *The Historical Figure of Jesus*. London: Penguin Press, 1993.

Shelley, Bruce L. *Church History in Plain Language*. Updated 2nd ed. Dallas, TX: Word Publishing, 1995.

Sockman, Ralph W. *The Paradoxes of Jesus*. New York: Abingdon Press, 1936.

Spong, John Shelby. *Resurrection: Myth or Reality?* San Francisco: HarperSanFrancisco, 1995.

2

RELIGION IN SHAKESPEARE'S WORLD

After the Great Schism, the church hierarchy drifted even further away from a vital spiritual direction and into a variety of worldly temptations. The most notorious pope of this period—or any other—was Alexander VI, Rodrigo Borgia, who climbed his way to the papacy through the nepotism of his uncle, Pope Calixtus III, and had four children and numerous mistresses. When the outspoken Florentine Dominican friar Girolamo Savonarola (1452–1498) protested Alexander's immorality, he was hanged. Other church officials freely granted indulgences, or remission of punishment for sins, to any with money or gifts to pay for them, oftentimes the gullible poor. Church positions were also sold to wealthy patrons, a practice called *simony* after Simon Magus who sought to buy the gifts of the Holy Spirit from Peter (Acts 8). A graphic picture of this corruption at the grassroots level can be seen in Chaucer's *Canterbury Tales,* which portrays the morally dubious behavior of a variety of clerics in the last decades of fourteenth-century England. Chaucer's portraits are ironically satirical, but the abuses he depicts were all too real. A prioress, the administrator of a women's cloister, is rather too fond of her pets, fine food, and courtly manners, and she wears a bracelet engraved with a line from the pagan Roman poet Ovid—*Amor vincit omnia.* "Love conquers all," but is this meant in a spiritual or a romantic sense? The monk, who should be pale from an indoor life of prayer and meditation, is "full fat" and fond of hunting, while the friar, who should be well-tanned from a wandering life serving villagers, has a neck as white as a lily from spending his days in "tavernes." The summoner, a church official who called defendants into ecclesiastical courts, is as "lecherous as a sparwe [sparrow]," and the pardoner, licensed to pardon sins upon receipt of charitable contributions, is expert at duping the poor with fake relics such as "pigges bones." Only the "poore Person [Parson]" escapes Chaucer's barbs, receiving undiluted praise: "riche he was of holy thought and work." Lest we miss the contrast between the one good cleric among so many corrupt colleagues, Chaucer hammers home his point with blunt medieval emphasis: "And shame it is, if a preest take keep [notice], / A shiten shepherde and a clene sheep." That these abuses existed was not news to anyone, but Chaucer ensured that they would be vividly remembered.

While the Protestant Reformation may seem, from the vantage of five centuries of history, to be a single, monolithic movement in religious history, it is on closer examination a series of distinct yet interrelated corrections launched against these and other problems by various thinkers in different countries. Beginning with the earliest protestors and including both the Protestant and Catholic Reformations, these interlocking phases spanned three centuries, from the birth of John Wyclif in about 1324 to the death of the Jesuit missionary Matteo Ricci in 1610, or possibly even to the end of the Thirty Years' War in 1648. Even allowing for the many differences among them, the reformers tended to be bound by several broad attitudes, which not only linked them together, but also formed a complex bridge between the historical movements we know as the Reformation and the Renaissance.

First, they adapted the Renaissance humanist emphasis on the importance of the individual (a concept with its roots in ancient classical thinkers such as Protagoras, noted earlier) and made it, rather than the organizational church, the starting point for one's relationship with God. Each person had the potential to develop an understanding of and commitment to God, with "potential" here meaning "responsibility" as much as "capability." However, following St. Augustine, the reformers also recognized man's sinful state and the essential need of divine grace for a person to accomplish this commitment; God met the effort of each person with his own offer of love. In this way, the "church" became not so much the bricks and mortar of a building or the accumulated wisdom of the early fathers, but the group of those persons, whatever their denomination, who were united in a deliberate choice to follow Christ. This naturally meant a redefinition of the nature of ministry itself and, even for Protestants like Luther who retained the ordained clergy, it was this "priesthood of believers" that was paramount. As Article XIX of the Anglican Book of Common Prayer would state, "The visible church of Christ is a congregation of faithful men."

Secondly, influenced by the humanists' love for the discovery and analysis of ancient writings, the reformers were text-centered. They took seriously the fact that, according to the opening verse of the Gospel of John, "In the beginning was the word" and that God had revealed himself in written as well as human form. This meant that each believer should strive to apprehend for himself the holy text. As Calvin stated in a sermon, "we must follow the rule which is given us in the Word of God. . . . let us not entangle ourselves with the superstitions of men but be content with what is contained in the pure simplicity of the gospel" (149). A famous prayer composed by Thomas Cranmer for the 1549 Book of Common Prayer also expresses this goal: "Blessed Lord, who hast caused all holy Scriptures to be written for our learning; Grant that we may in such wise hear them, read, mark, learn, and inwardly digest them, that by patience, and comfort of thy holy Word, we may embrace, and ever hold fast the blessed hope of everlasting life." To rely only upon versions of the Bible sanctioned by the Pope, such as Jerome's Vulgate, was counter to the divine command to *personally* seek the word of God. The great Dutch humanist Desiderius Erasmus (1466?–1536) had published his own Latin edition of the New Testament in 1516 based upon his personal study of Greek manuscripts, and Luther would bring out his own German translation of the whole Bible in 1534.

Hence the Reformation was a great era of biblical translation, as we shall notice later; the reformers believed there was no reason why every commoner should not have a Bible in his own language. Though some thinkers advocated views based only upon what the Bible had directly permitted, while others took a more liberal stance and advanced ideas that the Bible did not expressly forbid, scripture itself was the deciding authority. Whether by historical coincidence or divine purpose, Gutenberg's invention of moveable type around 1436 provided exactly the technological means for enabling this Protestant love of the word to rapidly spread by making tracts, Bibles, sermons, and essays available to an ever-increasing readership. As Roland Bainton notes, "More pamphlets were issued in Germany from the beginning of 1521 to the end of 1524 than in any other four years of her history, and the bulk of them dealt with the Reformation" (251).

Finally, as the careers of Wyclif, Huss, and others demonstrate, the Reformation was a religious movement with distinctly national overtones for each of its major denominations. Theologians were usually quite sensitive to their own political environments (sometimes because their lives were at stake!), while monarchs were aware that politics and religion could make unexpected bedfellows, as both they and the reformers in their countries were often opposed to papal interference, though for varying reasons. After Luther, it became clear that the old medieval idea of a single, homogenous, European "Christendom" was dead. In its place a new religious pluralism was taking shape in which various Christian denominations each claimed a measure of theological validity. Full acceptance of this variety did not happen until after the Thirty Year's War (1618–1648), but it was apparent long before then. Italian and Spanish Catholics, English Anglicans, Scottish Calvinists, German and Scandinavian Lutherans—believers in each country emerged with a sense of their own theological identity mingled with a distinctly cultural stamp as well. Though some nations were less unified than others (e.g., there were French Protestant Hugenots and south German Catholics), the individualism that the reformers prized had become, at the level of the nation-state, part of a cultural character. Stressing the "complexity of the English reformation," A. G. Dickens points out that "Above all, in England as in the Netherlands, Protestantism became at last inextricably involved with the national self-assertion of a people fighting for its place in a new European and extra-European order" (*English Reformation*, 325). Although Shakespeare's *Henry V* retells events of a still-Catholic England in the early fifteenth century, Henry knows that his subjects would respond enthusiastically to his union of God, king, country, and patron saint as he urges his men forward against the French: "The game's afoot! / Follow your spirit; and upon this charge / Cry, 'God for Harry, England, and St. George!'" (3.1.32–34).

REFORMATION FORERUNNERS: WYCLIF AND HUSS

The most outspoken reformer in late medieval England was the Oxford professor John Wyclif (c. 1324–1384). A zealous reformer well aware of the abuses Chaucer had so memorably mocked, Wyclif became convinced that the true and only authority in the church was God and that only those who served him in a state of grace were his true vicars on earth (see Primary Document 1). Clearly, this excluded the immoral clergy of his day, including the Pope, whom he labeled the Antichrist. God, he felt, expressed himself most fully through the Bible itself, not through the magisterium or ancient hierarchy of the church. In these two stances he foreshadowed Calvin's later emphasis on the sovereignty of God and the Lutheran emphasis upon the unalterable authority of the "scripture alone" (*sola scriptura*). So great was Wyclif's belief in the importance of the Bible that he began and saw through to completion the first English translation of it, though how much of it was his own work and how much that of his colleagues, such as Nicholas Hereford, is unclear. Additionally, Wyclif held that, though Christ was truly present in the Eucharist, the Roman Catholic concept of transubstantiation was wrong; that the church has only spiritual, not political, authority, hence clergy are not exempt from taxation; and that a life of Franciscan-style poverty was appropriate for all clerics. He obviously aroused the enmity of church authorities, but, though condemned for heresy twice, he ended his days in relative peace as the rector of his parish church at Lutterworth.

Wyclif's followers, a group of knights who were devoted to preaching and spreading his ideas, became known as Lollards (meaning "mumblers" of prayers). In Chaucer's prologue to the *Shipman's Tale*, the host Harry Bailey calls the parson "a Lollere," though Chaucer himself was probably not a Lollard, and in Christopher Marlowe's *Tragical History of Dr. Faustus*, Faustus speaks of "lollards and bold schismatics / And proud disturbers of the Church's peace" (3.2.178–179). Their influence persisted into Henry VIII's reign and their name long after. Shakespeare's famous comic knight Sir John Falstaff was based in part on an actual Lollard knight, Sir John Oldcastle (c. 1377–1417), who is mentioned in a history play Shakespeare probably used as a source. Oldcastle had been a valuable military leader for Henry IV, but his involvement in the Lollards brought him a charge of heresy in 1413. Later imprisoned, he escaped from the Tower of London but was captured and burned to death. The dramatist's portrayal of Falstaff offended Oldcastle's family, causing Shakespeare at the end of *Henry IV, Part 2* to disavow any link between his character and the Lollard: "Oldcastle died an martyr, and this [Falstaff] is not the man" (Epilogue, 32). As A. G. Dickens notes, the Lollard movement "argued with force that the materialism, the pride, the elaborate ritual and coercive jurisdiction of the Church found no justification in the lives of Christ and his disciples as recorded in the New Testament" (*English Reformation*, 25).

The wife of England's Richard II was the king of Bohemia's sister, and an intellectual exchange existed between the two countries whereby Czech churchmen became aware of Wyclif's writings. Thus Jan Huss (c. 1372–1415), a preacher in

Prague, became closely influenced by Wyclif in his own criticism of the Bohemian church. Denouncing many of the same abuses that Wyclif had, in 1412 he attacked Pope John XXII's decision to sell indulgences to pay for a war against the king of Naples, a supporter of his rival Pope Gregory XII. The king of Bohemia banished Huss for two years, during which time he composed his treatise on the church, De ecclesia. Though less strident than Wyclif (he did not share the Englishman's rejection of transubstantiation), Huss received support from the Lollards. He was summoned to the Council of Constance in 1414 to recant his heretical ideas. Demanding to be shown which portions of scripture he had violated, Huss denied the accusations made against him, but in July 1415 he was sentenced to death and burned. Throughout his trials, he never lost broad popular support, and his followers, the Hussites, later became known as the Bohemian Brethren during the Reformation. Luther was later to say of German Protestants that "We are all Hussites without realizing it" (qtd. Ozment, 222). While it is true that Wyclif, Huss, and Savonarola sounded the alarm over widespread flaws in the late medieval church, they never worked in concert to advance their views, and their movements were suppressed in the fifteenth century, so it is more accurate to term them forerunners rather than originators of the Reformation. Even had they not lodged their protests, Luther would still have penned his Ninety-five Theses. Nevertheless, they foreshadowed many of the same theological conflicts that he and Calvin were to experience and revealed the depth of discontent felt throughout European Christendom.

LUTHER AND CALVIN

The work of Martin Luther (1483–1546) and John Calvin (1509–1564) is the bedrock upon which the Protestant Reformation stands. Each is an example of the way in which the flow of events at a particular historical moment can combine with the talents of unique individuals to produce decisively far-reaching cultural change. "It has often been said," declares Jaroslav Pelikan, "difficult though it may be to substantiate, that more is published about Luther each year than about any other figure in the history of the church except Jesus Christ" (154). Luther was born in Eisleben, Germany in 1483, a descendant of peasants. His father was a fairly prosperous miner who had hopes that his son would become a lawyer. Luther earned a bachelor's degree from the University of Erfurt in 1501 and his master's four years later. But Luther, after fearing for his life during a violent thunderstorm and promising St. Anne that he would become a monk if he survived, kept his word and entered an Augustinian monastery in 1505. He was an exemplary monk and student of scholastic theology, earning a doctorate from the University of Wittenberg (later to be Hamlet's alma mater) in 1515. But these were difficult years for him spiritually, for he struggled with deep feelings of unworthiness and an inability to satisfy the demands of a God whom, he later said, he had come to hate instead of love. According to Martin Brecht, Luther in fact wrestled with periods of spiritual discontent, which he termed

Anfechtungen, for a decade (130). He lectured on the Psalms and on the book of Romans, and it was through his meditation on Romans 1: 17 that his momentous breakthrough came, probably early in 1518. Instead of the strenuous works of piety to which he had dedicated himself, personal efforts to gain grace from God through intense devotions, he found spiritual enlightenment in these words: "The just shall live by faith." It became clear to him that grace was a divine favor not earned by men but freely given by God. This insight, which years later he described as his *Turmerlebnis* or "tower experience," was the basis for his conviction of salvation by faith alone. This was one leg of the Reformation triangle of foundational beliefs: *sola fides, sola gratia, sola scriptura* (faith alone, grace alone, scripture alone). Only through faith and not works, granted only by God's grace and not merit, grounded only in the Bible and not a magisterial church authority, could one achieve justification. As Heiko Oberman points out, the implications of Luther's inspiration were broad and deep. "Luther's discovery was not only new, it was unheard-of; it rent the very fabric of Christian ethics. Reward and merit, so long undisputed as the basic motivation for all human action, were robbed of their efficacy. Good works, which Church doctrine maintained as indispensable, were deprived of their basis in Scripture" (154). This theological discovery, says Martin Brecht, "became the nucleus of Luther's reformation as a theological and religious achievement of an individual and as a paradigmatic shift almost without parallel in the history of Christendom" (132).

Luther had been emotionally tested by this experience; he would struggle with doubts and insecurities throughout his life, especially after the death years later of his young daughter Magdalena in 1542. He was tested as well by the historical influences around him. Johann Tetzel (c. 1465–1519), a Dominican monk who was highly successful at selling indulgences, had been working near Wittenberg while Luther pondered Paul's epistle to the Romans. Luther was incensed at the selling of indulgences, reductions in the spiritual punishment for sins, a practice summed up in Tetzel's poetic slogan: "As soon as the coin in the coffer rings / The soul from purgatory springs." This was the historical occasion for Luther to write his Ninety-five Theses, criticisms not only of the sale of indulgences, but of the papal system that sanctioned them; he expected his challenges would serve as the basis for a debate on them and other church flaws. Number 28 answered Tetzel's jingle directly: "It is certain that when money clinks in the money chest, greed and avarice can be increased; but when the church intercedes, the result is in the hands of God alone." And, because Tetzel functioned with the pope's approval, Luther's statements also constituted an attack on the church hierarchy, as in number 50: "Christians are to be taught that if the pope knew the exactions of the indulgence preachers, he would rather that the basilica of St. Peter were burned to ashes than built up with the skin, flesh and bones of his sheep" (Luther, *Basic Writings*, 24, 26).

Whether Luther, as tradition holds, really nailed the theses to the door of the Wittenberg Castle Church in 1517 as an act of public defiance, or actually mailed them to the Archbishop of Mainz, or did both, they soon drew the anger of the church authorities. He was summoned to Augsburg in 1518 to debate the theses

Martin Luther.

with papal representative Cardinal Cajetan, a three-day confrontation in which Luther refused to recant. The next year, Luther was ordered to answer to the skillful debater Johannes Eck in the Leipzig Disputation. Despite Eck's intricate questioning and accusations that Luther was a follower of heretical Hussite views (it was Eck who first used the term "Lutherans"), Luther displayed a superior knowledge of scripture and once again refused to alter his stand. The following year, on June 15, 1520, he was threatened with excommunication in a papal bull that labeled him a "wild boar"; he defiantly burned this bull on December 10, and his formal excommunication was pronounced on January 3, 1521. With his life now in jeopardy, Frederick the Wise, the Elector of Saxony who admired Luther's character though not all of his theology, arranged for one last hearing by the Diet, or general assembly meeting, at Worms. Luther was pointedly asked if he would withdraw his criticisms and submit to the church authorities. His traditional reply is one of the great statements of the Reformation: "Unless I am convicted by scripture and plain reason—I do not accept the authority of Popes and Councils for they contradict each other—my conscience is captive to the Word of God. I cannot and will not recant anything, for to go against conscience is neither right nor safe. God help me. Amen." Early printed accounts of the hearings added the famous, and possibly apocryphal, statement: "Here I stand, I cannot do otherwise." Luther's refusal for a third time to acquiesce to Rome was the pivotal moment of the Reformation; after this point, it would prove impossible to reverse the current of religious change. His stand was scripturally grounded, anchored in a hard-won personal faith, and expressed through his complex yet tenacious personality. He brought to full growth the seeds sown by Wyclif and Hus and went beyond the more moderate and scholarly objections raised by Erasmus, who chose never to break with the Roman Catholic church. The Diet declared Luther a heretic, and he left Worms in April 1521. Frederick the Wise, now fearing for Luther's safety, hustled him off to Wartburg Castle in a benevolent exile, which lasted until December of that year.

During these months in seclusion, he completed his own translation of the New Testament and would eventually translate the entire Bible into a German that was both accessible to common readers and possessed of distinct literary style; it was influential in the growth of the German language itself and, in Jaroslav Pelikan's words, "may well be his most important accomplishment" (204). Luther was a prodigious author; it has been estimated that he published some form of written work on an average of every two weeks for his entire lifetime, enough to supply the three printing presses in Wittenburg; the American edition of his collected works fills 55 volumes. Three works of 1520 deserve special notice. His *Address to the German Nobility* reinforced his concept of the priesthood of all believers by calling upon German princes to exercise administrative authority in the church and summon a council that would condemn the abuses of the pope. Luther's point was not that the princes were superior to the clergy but that they possessed an equal spiritual authority that empowered them to aid in reforming the church. *The Babylonian Captivity of the Church* criticized the church's help-lessness within the grip of medieval theology; the papacy that had maintained this grip he now bluntly labeled the Antichrist. The only genuine sacraments were baptism, penance, and communion, the latter to be taken in both bread and wine, as at the Last Supper, although Luther disputed the church's doctrine of transubstantiation. (Luther later designated only baptism and communion as valid sacraments.) He also put forward a German language mass. The most influential of these three works was *The Freedom of a Christian*, which outlined what Luther saw as the central concept—and paradox—of the Christian's life: "A Christian is a perfectly free lord of all, subject to none. A Christian is a perfectly dutiful servant of all, subject to all" (Luther, *Basic Writings*, 596). Luther relied on the biblical metaphor of the bridegroom and the bride to stress the joy that the Christian feels upon being united with Christ. Spiritually the believer owes obedience to none but Christ, yet this obedience obligates him to be the servant of others for Christ's sake.

By 1525 Luther's tracts had provoked church authorities to the point that he had become a man living under a Roman Catholic death sentence. Neverthe-less, in that year he married Katherine von Bora, a former nun, and she bore him six children, of whom only four survived. He had his staunch supporters, such as the moderate Philip Melanchthon (1497–1560), but more radical reformers such as Thomas Müntzer adapted his ideas in ways that seemed to him politically inflammatory. Müntzer supported the efforts of German peasants, who had suffered genuine grievances, to launch an armed revolt against the nobility. Luther bridled at having his doctrines turned to revolutionary purposes, and he vigorously condemned the peasants in a pamphlet of that year entitled *Against the Murderous and Thieving Peasants*, whom he said, in his characteristically outspoken way, deserved to be ruthlessly eliminated.

The final two decades of Luther's life saw completion of his German translation of the Bible, his small and large Catechisms, various disputations, and the gradual spread of his reforms throughout most of Germany and into Scandinavia. He was also a prolific composer of hymns, of which the most famous is "A Mighty Fortress is Our God." In 1529 he debated the Swiss reformer Ulrich Zwingli (1484–1531) at the Colloquy of Marburg, in which each spelled out his understanding of the nature of communion. Luther asserted that Christ's words at the Last Supper "This is my body" (Matt. 26: 26–8; Mark 14: 22–4; Luke 22: 19) were to be taken literally, hence his body must be actually present in the elements of bread and wine. Luther took issue with the Roman Catholic explanation of how this actually took place. Zwingli countered by saying that "is" meant "signifies" or "represents," especially since Christ's body had ascended to God after his resurrection. For Zwingli, the sacrament of communion was a memorial or symbolic act.

Lutheranism as a movement acquired greater cohesiveness that same year when a group of Lutheran princes protested the decision of the Diet of Speyer to forbid them from worshipping in predominantly Catholic districts; it was here that the term "Protestant" was born. The following year saw the drafting of the Augsburg Confession, largely the work of Melanchthon, the defining statement of the Lutheran church. The first part presented its agreement with the historic creeds, a rejection of the heresies of Pelagianism and Donatism, assertion of justification by faith, and a statement on confession and the sacraments. The second portion rejected the following Roman Catholic practices: the withholding of communion wine from the laity, clerical celibacy, the Mass as a "sacrifice," required confession, celebration of certain festivals, validity of monastic vows, and the civil authority of bishops.

Luther was the pioneer Protestant. As Martin Brecht says, "almost all the other reformations grew out of Luther's and shared essential contents with it or at least owed significant impulses to it" (129). Luther died on February 14, 1546 without ever having met John Calvin, the other great sixteenth-century pillar of Protestantism. But they did correspond and developed a respect for each other, despite their theological and personal differences; Calvin certainly felt Luther's influence in his own work and thought. Though history has somewhat exaggerated the images we have of them, they were men of clearly different temperaments. In contrast to Luther's extroverted personality, Diarmaid MacCulloch observes that Calvin was "the buttoned-up French exile who wanted to stop the citizens of Geneva dancing" (*Reformation*, 234). Whereas Luther could be outspoken, paradoxical, and combative, Calvin, no less devoted to reform, tended more towards an austerely private, scholarly, and legalistic cast of mind. His great *Institutes of the Christian Religion,* unlike the many spontaneous writings that Luther had composed in response to issues of the moment, was a systematically planned and carefully reasoned statement of theological principles on which the Reformed Church (as churches that followed Calvinism came to be called) were based.

John Calvin (Jean Cauvin) was born in Noyon, Picardy, France and at an early age seemed headed for a career in the ministry. He attended the Collège de Montaigu in Paris in the early 1520s, but in 1528 began to study law, first at Orleans and then Bourges; he was influenced by the humanists and in 1532 published his commentary on Seneca's *De Clementia.* His sympathies for reformed theology were growing, and at some point in the mid-1530s he experienced what he later termed a "sudden conversion." He befriended the like-minded Nicholas Cop, rector of the University of Paris. Cop delivered a strongly Protestant speech to the university in 1533, which provoked such criticism that he fled the city, with Calvin leaving two years later and arriving in Basle, Switzerland. Here in 1536 Calvin published in Latin the first edition of his *Institutes.* That same year, while traveling through Geneva, he was persuaded by the Swiss reformer Guillaume Farel (1489–1565) to help unify the Protestants there, whose numbers were swelling with French refugees in need of a leader. But in 1538 the city government told Calvin to leave, having found his ideas a threat to their more Zwinglian convictions. For several years he served as the pastor of a French church in Strasbourg, where he strengthened his ties to another reformer, Martin Bucer (1491–1551), who influenced his thoughts on the need for social discipline. Here he refined his *Institutes,* publishing an expanded version in 1539, as well as marrying an Anabaptist widow. The Anabaptists, led by Müntzer and others, were a more radical Protestant branch who advocated strict personal morality, direct inspiration by the Holy Spirit, and an avoidance of religious artwork and images in churches (which Luther had allowed).

In 1541 Calvin published a French edition of the *Institutes,* written in a style that contributed to the growth of that language as much as Luther's Bible translation had for German. Because of its systematic organization, clear style, and widespread dissemination across Europe, Calvin's *Institutes* was the single most influential work of theology of the Reformation. Its first edition, modeled on Luther's catechism, contained but six chapters: the Ten Commandments; the Apostle's Creed; the Lord's Prayer; the two genuine sacraments (like Luther, Calvin recognized only baptism and communion); the five "false sacraments"; and church government. By its final French edition in 1560, it had grown to 80 chapters. As Calvin's followers modified and adapted his ideas into the religious ideology that came to be known as "Calvinism," several principles emerged that distinguished it from "Lutheranism" and "Zwinglianism." Calvin's emphasis upon the absolute majesty and sovereignty of God over all of life underlay his emphasis on predestination. Luther, Augustine, and Aquinas had also acknowledged that God had chosen an elect to be saved, but Calvin stressed that God's predestination was his sole prerogative, that it affected every individual, and that it determined both those to be saved and those to be damned (a doctrine known

John Calvin. Courtesy of The H. Henry Meeter Center for
Calvin Studies, Calvin College.

as "double predestination"). Man's salvation was solely in God's hands, the Fall
of Adam having irreparably depraved the human soul and will. Secondly, Calvin
asserted that the authority of the Bible was paramount, hence preaching of the
word and close study of sacred scripture were essential. Calvin's humanist respect
for the written word here supported his theology; reformed thinkers generally
valued formal education as preparation for study of the holy text, and they would
later establish numerous schools and colleges throughout Europe and in North
America (such as Harvard College) to this end. Third, Calvin differed from both
Luther and Zwingli in his conception of communion. All three rejected the
Roman Catholic concept of transubstantiation, which held that the elements of
bread and wine were themselves transformed into the body and blood of Christ.
Luther favored consubstantiation; namely, that Christ's body was distinct from
but actually present with and in the elements. Zwingli, as noted earlier, believed
the Lord's Supper to be a memorial, the bread and wine commemorative symbols
of Christ's presence. Calvin's position was that Christ was a "real presence" in
the elements of communion; the exact nature of this presence was hard to clarify,
but the sacrament was held to contain a spiritual reality and was not merely a
symbolic event.

In September, 1541, the Genevan city fathers, realizing again their need of his organizational ability, invited Calvin to return. Over the next 14 years there, he crafted policies that created a city known for its grounding in the principles spelled out in his *Ecclesiastical Ordinances*. This was, according to Patrick Collinson, "a document of seminal importance and a model to be followed throughout Calvinist Europe. It defined the normative ministry of pastors, doctors [teachers of theology], elders, and deacons, and their functions; provided for weekly meetings of a company of pastors; called for what would become the Geneva Academy; and set up the consistory, a meeting of ministers and elders to oversee church attendance and morals" (*Reformation*, 92). But these changes were accomplished only with difficulty; Calvin was vigorously resisted by many who resented having to relinquish such pleasures as dancing and gambling. He persisted, even in the face of a death threat, gradually converting the city to his views primarily through a barrage of almost 200 sermons a year. The result of his efforts was a theocratic republic founded on Biblical principles, which became a model throughout Reformed Europe. The Scots reformer John Knox proclaimed Geneva and its academy "the most perfect school of Christ that ever was in the earth since the days of the apostles" (qtd. McNeill, 178).

It is perhaps too easy to overemphasize Calvin's penchant for organization and structure and to label him, as Patrick Collinson does, a "quintessential control freak" (*Reformation*, 90). A more balanced view is that of William Bouwsma, who suggests that Calvin was a complex personality who held together two contrasting tendencies that characterized the whole sixteenth century: Calvin the rationalist philosopher strove for a harmonious and conservative orthodoxy, while Calvin the rhetorician and humanist was "flexible to the point of opportunism and a revolutionary in spite of himself" (230–231). No matter how we view him, it is difficult to underestimate the impact that he had in his own and later generations. He had an immediate effect upon his native France; Collinson notes that "In 1560 there may have been two million Protestants, 10 percent of the population, more than there would ever be again in French history" (*Reformation*, 97). And just as Luther had invigorated the printing industry in Germany, so did Calvin for Geneva. His thinking influenced not only the course of Christian theology, but also such fields as political theory, morality, sociology, and economics. In the twentieth century his ideas were linked to the rise of capitalism in two famous works: Max Weber's *The Protestant Ethic and the Spirit of Capitalism* (1904) and R. H. Tawney's *Religion and the Rise of Capitalism* (1926). Calvin's frail health and tireless efforts finally wore him down, and comforted by the presence of his younger disciple Theodore Beza (1519–1605), he died on May 27, 1564, one month after Shakespeare was born.

THE HENRICIAN REFORM IN ENGLAND

King Henry VIII, eight years younger than Martin Luther and the second of the Tudor monarchs, was born on June 28, 1491 and ascended the throne in 1509, the year of Calvin's birth. Red-haired, over six feet tall, and a man of tremendous ego, Henry read several languages, was excited by military exploits, was adept in music and dancing, loved jousting and the trappings of chivalry, and fancied himself something of a theologian. His expansive personality, like Luther's, lends itself to stereotype. As J. J. Scarisbrick writes, "he was to grow into a rumbustious, noisy, unbuttoned, prodigal man—the 'bluff king Hal' of legend—exulting in his magnificent physique, boisterous animal exercise, orgies of gambling and eating, lavish clothes" (16). Two months after his coronation, he married Catherine of Aragon (1485–1536), his deceased brother Arthur's widow and daughter of King Ferdinand and Queen Isabella of Spain, the monarchs who, when Henry was one year old, had dispatched Christopher Columbus on his first voyage of discovery. After close to 20 years of marriage, Catherine had borne Henry a daughter, Princess Mary, but had not given him a son. His fears grew that there would be no smooth succession of the monarchy without a male heir. By 1527 he had fallen in love with a young woman of the court, Anne Boleyn (1507–1536), and he had begun to contemplate divorcing Catherine to seek a queen who might give birth to a prince. But what began as a divorce became a religious reform.

Catherine was a devout Catholic, and Henry himself had been named *defensor fidei* ("defender of the faith") by the pope for having composed a treatise supporting the validity of the seven sacraments against Luther's opinions. But he had become convinced of—or was appropriating for his own purposes—the injunction in Leviticus 20: 21 against marriage with the wife of one's brother. Relying on the political skills of Thomas Wolsey, his cardinal, papal legate, and Lord Chancellor, Henry hoped to persuade Pope Clement VII to grant him an annulment. Catherine, however, maintained that her marriage to Arthur had never been consummated, so Henry was not in fact contradicting the Old Testament law. An even greater obstacle to a divorce was the fact that Catherine's nephew Charles V, the Holy Roman Emperor, had in 1527 invaded Rome and held the pope hostage; the pope was unlikely to make any decision which would again place the papacy in jeopardy. If Henry were to be free to marry Anne Boleyn, he would have to justify a unilateral decision, and to this end his supporters began to assemble historical documents, which they felt demonstrated that England had always been a free and sovereign nation, under the sway of no foreign prince or pope.

Wolsey failed to obtain the annulment, and he fell from power in 1529. In his place the king elevated Sir Thomas More to the post of Lord Chancellor, but More's deep devotion to the church (he was later raised to sainthood) was greater than his support for the king's "great matter" (see Primary Document 2). Although More could not in good conscience support Henry's bid for a divorce, the so-called "Reformation Parliament," influenced by the shrewd policies of Henry's powerful principal secretary Thomas Cromwell, nevertheless passed between 1529 and 1534 a variety of bills that were inexorably moving England away from papal jurisdiction and influence. These culminated in the Act of Supremacy of 1534, by which the king was declared the administrative head of the church in England (see Primary Document 3).

Thomas More, who retained his Catholic integrity to the end, was executed on July 6, 1535, and his head was placed on a pike as a public example to others who might challenge the king's will. More, whose story was popularly told in Robert Bolt's play *A Man for All Seasons* (1960), was both a humanist and a model of traditional Catholic piety (he wore a penitential hair shirt his entire life). Yet he was a shrewd lawyer and a challenging defendant for his prosecutors to deal with. He had been as forthright in his prosecution of early reformers as Henry was of him: the earliest Protestant martyrs in England were burned while he was Lord Chancellor. For Catholics, his death was a tragedy. For Martin Luther it was justice, as we read in Luther's *Table Talk:* "He was a cruel tyrant. He was the king's counselor; a very learned and wise man, doubtless, but he shed the blood of many innocent Christians that confessed the Gospel" (442). The conflict between More and Henry offers in microcosm a glimpse of the clashing concepts of the English Reformation.

It may seem from this very compressed summary of an extremely complex process that the church of Shakespeare's baptism thus sprang from a purely legal response to the king's personal and political preferences. As Maurice Powicke long ago put it, "The one definite thing which can be said about the Reformation in England is that it was an act of state" (1). Equally as important, however, was the king's unstoppable will; Luther, who had refused an amazing request from Henry to approve his second marriage, had said, "Junker Heinz [Knight Henry] will be God and does whatever he lusts [desires]" (qtd. Scarisbrick, 526). G. W. Bernard has recently argued that Henry, rather than being the mere subject of his powerful advisors, capably influenced the parliamentary and religious forces at work on him. But other factors beyond the royal court were also shaping the context of Parliament's decisions.

First, the unsettled political environment fueled the lingering sparks of Lollardism and, invigorated by the steady flow into England of Lutheran pamphlets and tracts, an emerging evangelical presence was gathering strength. Henry was not the only individual eager for a break with Rome, but others had less personal motives for doing so. Luther's works were circulating in England just two years after he had posted the Ninety-five Theses in Wittenberg, and, despite a burning of Lutheran books at Cambridge in 1520, a group of reform-minded men had begun meeting at the White Horse Inn there to discuss his theology. They included Matthew Parker (1504–1575, later to be Queen Elizabeth's first Archbishop of Canterbury), Nicholas Ridley (c. 1500–1555, Edward VI's Bishop of London), Hugh Latimer (c. 1490–1555, Bishop of Worcester), and William Tyndale (c. 1494–1536, translator of the first Bible printed in English). The most influential among them was Thomas Cranmer (1489–1556). As Archbishop of Canterbury, he dissolved the king's marriage to Catherine, officiated at the second royal wedding, and as we shall see, was instrumental in the reign of Edward VI. Cromwell and the new queen herself likewise favored the new theology.

Second, a number of English intellectuals were becoming increasingly influenced by the work of continental humanists such as Lorenzo Valla (1407–1457), who had used linguistic and historical criticism to debunk the Donation of Constantine, a document purporting to grant lands to the papacy. Erasmus also visited England, staying for a while with Thomas More and spending time at

Oxford University. Professors such as John Colet (1467–1519), Thomas Linacre (c. 1460–1524), and William Grocyn (1446–1519) advocated a close study of ancient languages and their inclusion into university curricula along with a renewed interest in the study of biblical texts. King Henry's own teachers had had humanist training. More's *Utopia* (1515) was a fictional vision of an ideal society based on humanist ideals, and Erasmus' *Praise of Folly* (1509) mocked the shortcomings of the church, though not for the doctrines of Luther but, rather, for the sake of a stronger Catholicism.

This new and inquisitive intellectual vitality was aided by a third factor, a spreading anticlericalism and antipapalism. In addition to the neglectful short-comings of the English clergy that Chaucer had noted, Thomas Wolsey's 14-year tenure as the king's minister had angered many by his flagrant love of wealth and his pompous displays of power and influence. It seemed that continued obedience to the pope would mean condoning such conspicuous elitism. Wolsey's failure to obtain the king's divorce was matched by his success at earning the people's disgust. This antipathy, aggravated by an economic crisis, contributed to a popular uprising in the north of England in 1536–1537, the Pilgrimage of Grace.

In short, Henry's break with Rome occurred within a context of social, intel-lectual, and religious ferment that extended far beyond the Privy Chamber. And the situation was further complicated by the fact that the old religion still enjoyed widespread support in many parts of England. Even the king's theology, as revealed in the Six Articles Act of 1539, appeared surprisingly conservative, though to evangelicals this act was a "bloody whip with six strings." Intended to eradicate "diversity in opinions," it asserted the doctrine of transubstantiation, eliminated communion in both bread and wine, ordered celibacy for priests, reas-serted the validity of monastic vocations, and legitimized private masses and per-sonal confessions. The influence of late medieval Catholicism in England was still strong, with the most ardent Protestants located primarily in the southern region. Chaucer's view of church abuses had, after all, been that of a Londoner. But an attitude of reform, especially among members of the merchant middle class who had influential seats in Parliament, was growing. From the Catholic perspective, Henry's dissolution of the monasteries, the appropriation of their goods and the scattering of their clergy, made his ruling practice of "caesaropapism" seem worse than the alleged papal despotism he was defying. The monies he gained from confiscated church properties were actually many times greater than what had previously gone to the pope. To the reformers, however, legislation such as the Six Acts seemed to be little more than a return to Catholicism minus the pope. What eventually emerged from this collision of reformist and traditional outlooks was a church that managed to combine elements of both in a set of doctrines and beliefs that came to be known as the Anglican *via media*, the "middle way," though it would take a long and bloody road to put this concept into practical effect.

Ironically, Shakespeare's rendition of Henry's tumultuous influence on English religious history is contained in one of his least satisfying history plays, *Henry VIII*. It may have been the last play he wrote, and he seems to have written it in collaboration with John Fletcher, with whom he co-authored *Two Noble*

Kinsmen. It was during a performance of this play on June 29, 1613 that a cannon fired during the first act set fire to the roof of the Globe Theatre, burning it to the ground in an hour (it was later reconstructed). The play has been faulted for being more a series of set speeches and theatrical displays of colorful panoply than a cohesively constructed analysis of Henry's administration. A traditional view of the play contends that Shakespeare "had no philosophical conception of the reign" (Berdan and Brooke, 149), while more recent critics find its ambiguities of characterization interesting. Its parallels to the style of the late romances, such as *The Winter's Tale*, defy easy comparison with the eight earlier history plays of the two tetralogies, yet, according to F. David Hoeniger, "a Christian note sounds more strongly through *Henry VIII* than in any other of Shakespeare's plays—at least it receives more overt expression" (783).

Though its language tends to be pedestrian and its plot condenses over 40 years of history, the portrayals of Wolsey and Catherine are especially effective on stage. Wolsey, despite being a "bold bad man" (2.2.43), meets his downfall with a penitent recognition of his shortcomings in a way reminiscent of the medieval morality plays:

> Mark but my fall, and that that ruin'd me.
> Cromwell, I charge thee, fling away ambition.
> By that sin fell the angels: how can man then,
> The image of his Maker, hope to win by it?
> . . .
> O Cromwell, Cromwell,
> Had I but served my God with half the zeal
> I served my king, he would not in mine age
> Have left me naked to mine enemies. (3.2.339–442, 454–457)

Though Wolsey's sudden compunction—like Leontes' in *The Winter's Tale*—may strain credulity, he experiences the peace that passes understanding (Philippians 4: 7): "I know myself now; and I feel within me / A peace above all earthly dignities, / A still and quiet conscience" (3.2.378–380). His awareness of God's guiding hand in English affairs is echoed by Buckingham, who, though sent to death by Wolsey, believes that "Heaven has an end in all" (2.1.124).

Queen Catherine, declaring that she is "the most unhappy woman living" (3.1.147), remains a model of devout Christian patience despite her humiliating fall from the affections of the king, who still praises her "meekness saintlike" (2.4.139). Henry sees his lack of a son as God's sign that he has in fact violated the rule in Leviticus, for which his new marriage is a "remedy":

> This was a judgment on me; that my kingdom,
> Well worthy the best heir o' the world, should not
> Be gladded in't by me.
> . . .
> Thus hulling in
> The wild sea of my conscience, I did steer
> Toward this remedy . . . (2.4.195–197, 200–202)

Wolsey has no love for Anne Boleyn, whom he terms a "spleeny Lutheran" (3.2.99), but Cranmer, a "heretic, an arch one" (3.2.102), confidently prophesies at the play's end that her daughter shall bring "Upon this land a thousand thousand blessings, / Which time shall bring to ripeness" (5.4.19–20). The threat of Catholicism declines as Catherine leaves the play in act 4, while Cranmer's reforming influence rises to prominence. Elizabeth's birth is itself a kind of revelation: "God shall truly be known; and those about her / From her shall read the perfect ways of honor" (36–37).

Mark Noll has compared Shakespeare's historical perspective in this play to those of modern historians of the Reformation. "Shakespeare with A. G. Dickens locates the Reformation in the reign of the early Tudors, but with Christopher Haigh he emphasizes its political and national rather than its pietistic character. He also raises the fruitful suggestion that the spirituality of the English Reformation may have consisted in a return to general godliness more than to the religion of any contending ecclesiastical party" (100). Henry's marriage to Anne Boleyn produced a daughter, Elizabeth, who would later become more than the equal of any royal son he could have wished for. But Anne was accused of adultery and executed in 1536, four months after Catherine's death. Henry was betrothed to Jane Seymour (1509–1537) the day after Anne's death, but Seymour died the following year after giving birth to Edward VI. Henry went on to marry three more times, but the principle actors in the further development of the Anglican church—Edward, Mary, and Elizabeth—were now on stage.

EDWARD VI AND MARY TUDOR

Henry's only son Edward was a sickly lad who took the throne at the age of nine in 1547, dying of a lung infection just six years later. Though he had received a good humanist education, his youth made the power of his two regents significant. The policies of these men, Edward Seymour, Duke of Somerset, and John Dudley, Duke of Northumberland, both adherents of Luther and Calvin, moved the nation farther from the old religion by guiding Parliament to undo the legislation it had so recently passed under Henry. The provisions of the Six Articles were overturned; the Act Against Revilers And Receiving in Both Kinds reinstated a Protestant understanding of communion; and The New Injunctions For Religious Reform mandated widespread removal of Catholic church trappings. As Eamon Duffy has documented for one typical town, "there were to be no Candlemas ceremonies, no ashes, no palms, no creeping to the cross, no sepulcher, no paschal candle, no blessing at the font" (462). Attacks on the Catholic Eucharist are epitomized by the Protestant mockery of the words of consecration from the Mass: *Hoc est corpus meum* ("This is my body") became "Hocus-Pocus," an abusive term connoting magical superstition. But the old religion did not go quietly: to cite just once incident, in 1548 a mob led by a Catholic priest attacked and murdered an agent sent to supervise the stripping of the altars (Duffy, 458–459). Reforms from within were accompanied by reformers from without. Clergy from the continent arrived in England in larger numbers, taking up influential university posts. Calvin's friend Martin Bucer became a professor at Cambridge,

and the Italian Protestants Peter Martyr Vermigli and Bernardo Ochino migrated
to Oxford and Canterbury Cathedral, respectively. John Knox, later to found the
Reformed church in Scotland, was also in England at this time.

Edward's reign was the highpoint of the career of Thomas Cranmer, the Archbishop of Canterbury who had thus far managed to navigate the fluctuating tides
of religious change. Educated at Cambridge, he rejected clerical celibacy and
married the daughter of Lutheran theologian Andreas Osiander. His patient,
scholarly work in defending the king's divorce from Catherine was rewarded in
1532 with his appointment as archbishop. Cranmer's theology grew more radical
from this point, but as a gesture of unity, he instituted changes in the national
church slowly. Susan Brigden has summed up the challenge faced by him and
other advocates of Anglicanism: "As the leaders of the new Church tried to make
real their vision of a truly evangelical Church, they struggled to carry with them
a whole people, most of whom were still hostile to it, and at the same time to
defend it against their fellow reformers who, by setting their individual and unas-
sailable consciences against the institutional Church, threatened to split English Protestantism" (196). Cranmer's two most significant written responses to
this challenge were the publication of the *Book of Homilies,* a series of sermons
approved for preaching in parishes nationwide, and compilation of *The Book of
Common Prayer,* the guiding document for the church's doctrine and worship (see
Primary Documents 5–11).

The martyrdom of Thomas Cranmer as depicted in Foxe's *Acts and Monuments.* By
permission of the Folger Shakespeare Library.

The first set of twelve homilies appeared in 1547. It went through three more editions in the sixteenth century and by 1687 contained 33 sermons, which together stressed state control of the church (a doctrine known as Erastianism), justification by faith, reliance upon scripture, and a flexibility in dealing with points of theology considered "indifferent"—the *adiaphora*. According to Terence Murphy, "Of all the books published in early modern England—not excluding the Bible, *The Book of Common Prayer*, and John Foxe's *Acts and Monuments*—the *Book of Homilies* had the widest audience over the longest time and thus the greatest influence" (195). One of its most significant sermons was the "Exhortation Concerning Good Order and Obedience to Magistrates," stressing submission to the king's divine authority: "It is intolerable ignorance, and wickedness for subjects to make any murmuring, rebellion or insurrection against their most dear and most dread sovereign Lord and King, ordained and appointed by God's goodness for their commodity, peace and quietness" (qtd. Joseph, 176). Such obedience to what Claudius in *Hamlet* calls the "divinity that doth hedge a king" (4.5.124) emerges in John of Gaunt's refusal to condemn the abuses of the king in *Richard II* when he declares, "God's is the quarrel. . . . I may never lift / An angry arm against his minister" (1.2.37–41). But the repetition of the sermons over time made them tiresomely predictable, a fact Shakespeare puts to comic use in *As You Like It* when Rosalind says to Celia, "O most gentle Jupiter, what tedious homily of love have you wearied your parishioners withal, and never cried 'Have patience, good people!'" (3.2.155–157).

The very title of *The Book of Common Prayer*, whose literary qualities we shall glance at later, signified yet another effort at national unity: this was to be the book by which all of England would worship in common. Cranmer drew upon earlier devotional works, both English and continental, in a volume that contained the psalms, the services for morning and evening prayer, the communion, petitionary prayers known as "collects," and a variety of other services, including baptism, confirmation, and marriage. Its language was carefully ambiguous in places, in an attempt to satisfy both Catholics and reformist worshippers, but the first edition in 1549 pleased neither group. A second edition appeared in 1552, revising the communion service in a decidedly more Protestant direction by giving a Zwinglian understanding of the Lord's Supper: this was a memorial service and not a sacrificial experience of the "real presence" of Christ. The Elizabethan edition published in 1559 would become Shakespeare's prayer book, and in the words of John E. Booty, "It, rather than a set of doctrines or a particular person, provided the basis for uniformity in religion. It was also the basis for doing theology in the Elizabethan church and after" (192).

Cranmer's second prayer book had been in effect for less than a year when Edward VI died and, after an abortive attempt to place on the throne Lady Jane Grey (granddaughter of Henry's sister), his half-sister Mary ascended the throne. Mary married Philip II of Spain, a match that proved both childless and unpopular with reformers because it hinted at a return to papal authority. Catherine's ardently Catholic daughter set about dismantling the work of the English reformers (see Primary Document 12). Aided by Cardinal Reginald Pole, she executed 300 non-Catholics, earning the name "Bloody Mary" and driving over 800 out of the country. Heresy laws, reinstated in 1554, sanctioned the torture and burning of any who resisted her policies; these so-called "Marian martyrs" included such men as Ridley, Latimer, and even Cranmer himself. Before his death Cranmer recanted his Protestant views six times, but in a dramatic turnabout he publicly retracted these recantations as the flames rose around him, thrusting first into the fire his right hand, which had signed those documents (see Primary Document 13). Mary's administration worked hard to reestablish the medieval faith of England, reinstalling much of what had been demolished or removed in the churches during the Henrician and Edwardian periods: altars, linens, artwork, vestments, crucifixes, rood screens, candles (Duffy, 543–554). But Mary's reign, marked at the end by widespread outbreaks of disease across the country, ended after only five years when she died on November 17, 1558. That very day, newly released from prison, Elizabeth I became queen of England at the age of 25 (see Primary Document 16).

THE ELIZABETHAN SETTLEMENT

Four hundred years after her death, the personal faith of Elizabeth I is still something of a mystery; perhaps we should be reassured by the fact that her contemporaries seem to have been just as puzzled. Certainly she was an observant Protestant and had composed a number of devout prayers, but in an age in which precise definitions of belief carried more weight (and danger) than they do now, she was able to display either evangelical or Catholic leanings as situations warranted to obtain her political and religious goals. Her own beliefs appeared to combine Protestant and Catholic elements. William Camden's *Annals or History of Queen Elizabeth* (the first half published in 1615) notes that she had forbidden her bishop to lift up the consecrated bread at Mass (a Roman Catholic gesture) and allowed the litany, epistle, and gospel to be read in English, all of which suggested a reformist outlook. "But concerning the Cross, the Blessed Virgin, and the Saints," wrote Camden, "she had no contemptuous opinion, nor ever spake of them but with reverence, nor suffered others patiently to speak unreverently of them" (17–18), gestures which leaned more towards Catholicism. She could also say, apparently impatient with theological arguments, that "There is only one Jesus Christ, and the rest is a dispute over trifles." At a time when issues of politics or religion were often identical, she could use each as the tool of the other with the result that, in the words of Calvinist John Knox, she appeared to be "neither good Protestant nor yet resolute Papist" (qtd. Spitz, 257). In *The First Blast of the Trumpet Against the Monstrous Regiment of Women* (1558), Knox may have strenuously objected to the authority of female rulers such as Elizabeth and Mary, Queen of Scots, but Elizabeth remained undeterred, maintaining the forces of Catholicism and Protestantism in a kind of dynamic tension rather than allowing them to ignite into open religious conflict or letting herself succumb to the influence of either side. Like Shakespeare, Elizabeth managed to submerge her personal convictions within her work.

This delicate balancing act lay at the heart of what has come to be called the Elizabethan Settlement. Elizabeth ruled for 45 years (1558–1603), just four years less than her three royal predecessors combined. This longevity enabled her to sustain this fragile religious equilibrium long enough for the Anglican church to become an accepted part of the fabric of English culture. Within living memory—some 50 years—the nation's official faith had been first officially Roman Catholic, then that of Henry VIII's church, then Catholic again, and now it would become Anglican. She sensed the need for and the benefits that stability would bring to both church and state, bringing to this process a blunt pragmatism by refusing, as Francis Bacon said of her, to "make windows into men's souls" so long as they obeyed the laws of religious observance (Partington). The road ahead would not be smooth; two generations later the English inheritors of Calvinism would execute their Anglican king Charles I in a bloody civil war. But when peace returned with the restoration of the monarchy in 1660, the church in which Shakespeare was baptized and buried would return with it.

Queen Elizabeth I. Note the sword of justice (*Justitia*) resting on the Bible, the word of God (*Verbum Dei*). By permission of the Folger Shakespeare Library.

Strong anti-papal sentiments persisted when Elizabeth ascended the throne, but many among her own administration favored the old faith, and she made a number of political concessions in their favor. Theologically, however, Cranmer's prayer book, with a few modifications, would become the rock on which Elizabeth would build her church. A key alteration was made to the communion service. The 1559 book, adopting a "middle way," joined both the "real presence" language of the 1549 book and the more Zwinglian language of the 1552 book into one statement: "The body of our Lord Jesus Christ which was given for thee preserve thy body and soul into everlasting life; and take and eat this, in remembrance that Christ died for thee, and feed on him in thy heart by faith, with thanksgiving" (Booty, 264). Those for whom the Lord's Supper was a memorial could find their faith confirmed that this was a "remembrance," while those who believed in a genuine spiritual presence of Christ would find it in the reference to his "body . . . given for thee." In the words of Diarmaid MacCulloch, Cranmer "would not have known what Anglicanism meant, and he would probably not have approved if the meaning had been explained to him, but without his contribution the unending dialogue of Protestantism and Catholicism which informs Anglican identity would not have been possible" (*Thomas Cranmer*, 629).

The settlement was secured through additional parliamentary legislation. The 1559 Act of Uniformity, opposed by many in the House of Lords, narrowly passed into law and mandated that the new book be used in all English churches. The Six Articles passed down by Henry VIII in 1539 had grown to 42 under the reign of Edward VI; under Elizabeth they were reduced by three and the Thirty-Nine Articles, the Anglican statement of doctrine, was legislated by the Subscription Act of 1571. The settlement did not extend into Scotland, where the establishment of Protestantism had been advanced by John Knox. Knox, who in the mid-1550s had assisted Calvin's work in Geneva, returned to Scotland in 1559 to oppose the Catholic efforts of the queen regent, Mary of Lorraine. English and Scottish troops united in January, 1560 to confront her French troops; she died that June. In August, the Scots parliament formally approved the Calvinist confession of faith (drawn up by Knox and five other ministers) for the Church of Scotland, severing ties with Rome. The efforts of Mary, Queen of Scots, to continue her mother's pro-Catholic policies eventually failed, and she relinquished the throne to her son James VI, later to succeed Elizabeth on the English throne.

By the time Shakespeare's first plays appeared in London in the 1590s, the Anglican prayer book and its theology had had over a generation in which to mold the faith, worship, and language of the country. Elizabeth's own personality and public image were a key factor in achieving this settlement. She was very much her father's daughter: confident, intelligent, well-educated, and politically savvy. As she told the troops in her famous 1588 speech at Tilbury, "I know I have the body of a weak and feeble woman, but I have the heart and stomach of a King, and a King of England too." Witty and sharp-tongued, she was jealous of her prerogatives, admonishing even high-ranking clergy; as she wrote to one bishop: "You know what you were before I made you what you are now. If you do not immediately comply with my request, I will unfrock you, by God" (qtd. Marty, 189). She avoided the physical excesses and spendthrift ways of her father, and by not marrying, the threat of permanent alliances and threats to her throne. Among the people, she came to be known as "Good Queen Bess" and the "Virgin Queen," while the poet Edmund Spenser termed her "Gloriana" in his *Faerie Queene*. Whether or not she in fact remained a "vestal" virgin, this polite fiction was the basis for Shakespeare's allusion to her in A *Midsummer Night's Dream*:

> A certain aim [Cupid] took
> At a fair vestal thron'd by [the] west,
> And loos'd his love-shaft smartly from his bow
> As it should pierce a hundred thousand hearts;
> But I might see young Cupid's fiery shaft
> Quenched in the chaste beams of the wat'ry moon
> And the imperial vot'ress passed on,
> In maiden meditation, fancy free. (2.1.157–164)

Shakespeare's few references to her maintain this laudatory tone, as in *Henry VIII* where Cranmer praises her future greatness:

> Truth shall nurse her,
> Holy and heavenly thoughts still counsel her.
> She shall be lov'd and fear'd: her own shall bless her;
> Her foes shake like a field of beaten corn,
> And hang their heads in sorrow. Good grows with her;
> In her days every man shall eat in safety
> Under his own vine what he plants, and sing
> The merry songs of peace to all his neighbors. (5.4.28–35)

THE PURITANS

But, inevitably, not everyone was happy. Elizabeth now had the problem of retaining her church in the face of continued opposition from ardent English Calvinists who despised the settlement for containing too many "Romish" elements. Seeking to purify the Anglican church—and some sought to purify it out of existence—they became known as Puritans. Puritanism was not so much a specific religious denomination as it was a religious outlook or frame of mind, which, opposed to any remnants of Catholic faith or practice, came to be shaped by several key Calvinist concepts: the absolute primacy of the Bible as the answer to questions theological, governmental, moral, and social; opposition to aspects of worship that seemed idolatrous, including Anglican church decorations, music, or rituals that could not be biblically justified; a belief in such doctrines as divine sovereignty, the innate depravity of all men after the Fall, and predestination; and an obligation to root out sin both in themselves and in their society by practicing and imposing stricter moral codes. The Puritan attitude emerged, for example, in the so-called Vestiarian Controversy in the 1560s over whether Anglican priests (a word Puritans disliked) should wear religious vestments during services rather than plain gowns. In March 1566, Archbishop Matthew Parker commanded the London clergy to wear the prescribed surplice, but he received from many only grudging agreement. The queen, however, was adamant and, once again, a religious issue had become a case of obedience to royal authority, which served to coalesce Calvinist opposition to the settlement.

The Puritan attitude itself raised thorny problems that these "precisianists," as they were also called, had to grapple with. How could one be obedient both to the authority of the Bible and to one's sovereign? (This had been Cranmer's problem, too, once Mary Tudor became queen.) How was it possible for sinful men to reform a sinful society? Did personal efforts to lead a godly life contradict the doctrines of *sola gratia* and *sola fides*? Furthermore, not all Puritans sought change in the same ways. Many, perhaps most, remained members of the Anglican church and sought to renew it from within. Others, opposing the episcopal system of bishops' rule, favored with John Knox the creation of synods or groups of ruling elders; these were the Presbyterians, and Knox's form of church government became the basis for the established church in Scotland. Still others, the more radical Separatists, broke with the Church of England completely, many leaving England for Amsterdam in 1593 and 1597, from whence they departed as pilgrims for North America to found the Massachusetts Bay Colony. Except for the Anglicans among them, Puritans and the more extreme Anabaptists and Quakers were also termed Nonconformists for their refusal to adhere completely to the settlement.

Official opposition to Puritanism increased under Elizabeth's third archbishop, John Whitgift, her "little black husband," who strictly enforced policies against nonconformism. In October, 1588 the Puritans fought back when Whitgift's policies were lampooned in the Martin Marprelate tracts, penned most likely by the Presbyterian Job Throckmorton (see Primary Document 23). He wrote a total of seven tracts, the last appearing in September 1589, which satirized such Anglican features as the authority of bishops, wearing of the surplice, and making of the sign of the cross. Whitgift's men indicted Throckmorton and hunted down his printers, effectively eradicating this cell of Puritanism. Protestant hopes rose after James I ascended the throne in 1604, but to their calls for abolition of the episcopacy, he famously replied, "No bishop, no king." Taking a measured stand against the Puritans, he retained his bishops and disciplined the extremists but allowed more moderate Puritan voices, such as the preachers Richard Sibbes and John Preston, to remain. The Puritan tide would rise again after Charles I took the throne in 1625, nine years after Shakespeare's death, and lead on to civil war.

Eager to reform themselves and their society, Puritans became familiar objects of mockery in literature of the day, and the name "Puritan" itself gradually broadened to become a pejorative term for any narrow-minded or self-righteous person regardless of religious persuasion (see Primary Documents 18, 19, and 21). This is the sense in which Maria, in Shakespeare's *Twelfth Night*, refers to Olivia's overly precise steward Malvolio: "Marry, sir, sometimes he is a kind of Puritan . . . an affectioned ass" (2.3.140; 148). Angelo, the governor in *Measure for Measure*, likewise—at least initially—displays the strictly moral attitude, self-disciplined habits, and readiness to punish wrongdoers typical of many Puritans. He is, as Lucio says of him,

> a man whose blood
> Is very snow-broth; one who never feels
> The wanton stings and motions of the sense
> But doth rebate and blunt his natural edge
> With profits of the mind: study, and fast. (1.4.57–61)

A more comic glance at the Puritans occurs in *Henry IV, Part 1*, when Falstaff (the living antithesis of a Puritan) parodies their moralizing conversation and their tendency to refer to themselves as "saints" as he portrays himself the victim of Prince Hal's allegedly bad example: "O, thou hast damnable iteration, and art indeed able to corrupt a saint. Thou hast done much harm upon me, Hal, God forgive thee for it! Before I knew thee Hal, I knew nothing, and now am I, if a man should speak truly, little better than one of the wicked" (1.2.90–95).

"PRAY SPEAK IN ENGLISH"

It should not be surprising, as Elizabeth's popularity grew and a rising sense of nationalism spread across the land (intensified after the defeat of the Spanish Armada in 1588), that an English church should increasingly prefer to read God's word and pray to God in English. During her father's reign, Latin was still the official language of court, church, and university; however, Shakespeare rather surprisingly injects a linguistic nationalism into *Henry VIII* from an unlikely source—the king's Spanish wife. In act 3, shortly before Katherine's departure from court, Wolsey begins a conversation with her in Latin, but she objects:

> O, good my Lord, no Latin;
> I am not such a truant since my coming,
> As not to know the language I have lived in.
> A strange tongue makes my cause more strange, suspicious;
> Pray speak in English. . . .
>   Lord Cardinal,
> The willing'st sin I ever yet committed
> May be absolved in English. (3.1.42–46, 48–51)

Despite her Catholicism, Katherine's eagerness to speak English ironically reflects Cranmer's conviction that religious rites such as absolution be conducted in a language "understood of the people." The intimate link between religion and politics in Tudor England was mirrored by the equally close bond between the growth of the Church of England and the publication of seminal English texts that helped promulgate its reformation. William Tyndale (c. 1490–1536), the single most influential English translator of scripture, vigorously defended English as a language of translation for Greek and Hebrew texts: "For the Greek tongue agreeth more with the English than with the Latin. And the properties of the Hebrew tongue agreeth a thousand times more with the English than with the Latin" (qtd. Hammond, 648). Just as Luther's writings benefited from, and aided the growth of, the printing press, so too did the English bibles of the sixteenth century build upon and contribute to the flowering of English as a language of vigor, accuracy, and emotional power. Among the flood of influential religious English writings during Shakespeare's era, the prayer book, Foxe's *Acts and Monuments,* and the King James translation of the Bible were predominant. These works are worth pausing over, because they helped foster the literary awareness of the English people before Shakespeare reached maturity. When his plays gained the stage, his audiences were better prepared to appreciate not only their religious aspects, but their stylistic achievements as well.

After receiving his bachelor's degree from Oxford, John Foxe (1516–1587) traveled to Strasbourg to complete a Latin history of the Lollards. Later visiting Frankfurt and Basle, he expanded his work up to the death of Cranmer, returning to England in 1560 to be ordained by Edmund Grindal, the second of Elizabeth's three archbishops of Canterbury. Recognizing the mass influence of the printed word, he began work on a history in English of the Protestant martyrs (beginning shortly after the crucifixion!) whose complete title summarized the book: *Acts and Monuments of these latter and perilous days, touching matters of the church, wherein are comprehended and described the great persecution and horrible troubles that have been wrought and practiced by the Romish prelates specially in this realm of England and Scotland from the year of Our Lord a thousand to the time now present.* The first edition of almost 2,000 pages appeared in 1563; the 1570 version was twice as long, and a copy was placed in every cathedral; the final edition exceeded 6,000 pages. Five editions would be published before the century closed, and it soon became readily available in churches throughout the nation. As Patrick Collinson states, "No other book, after the English Bible and *The Book of Common Prayer,* had more influence on the religious self-consciousness of England as a largely Protestant nation" ("Foxe, John," 122).

Foxe's *Book of Martyrs* (as it came to be called) was an instant hit owing to Foxe's straightforward, graphic style; his inclusion of pious biographical details as well as gruesome death scenes; and his seemingly exhaustive (and exhausting) volume of background information. He had combed manuscripts and letters, talked to witnesses, and read trial transcripts. He had also fabricated some details to enhance his polemical purpose, which was no more extreme than that of many other contemporary sectarian works. Foxe's book was at once popular religious history, Protestant propaganda, gripping narrative, and instructive morality tale; while portions of it may have been fictionalized, it was at least—as Hollywood might say today—"based on real events." Foxe provided for Protestants an equivalent to the Roman Catholic hagiography or history of saints. One of its most quoted episodes records the burning of Hugh Latimer and Nicholas Ridley at the same stake during the Marian persecution (see Primary Document 14). Shakespeare drew upon Foxe in his portrayal of the plot against Cranmer in *Henry VIII.*

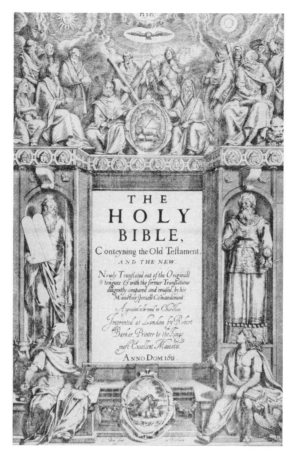

The ornate title page of the first edition of the King James Version of the Bible (1611). By permission of the Folger Shakespeare Library.

The steady stream of biblical translations during sixteenth-century England was a rich religious, social, and literary phenomenon. Driven by the humanist revival of interest in ancient languages as well as the desire to achieve fuller, more accurate, and, as in the case of the Geneva Bible, more doctrinally assertive versions, these translations also were the means by which the monarchy could attempt to enforce uniformity by mandating an "authorized version" that all must read (see Primary Document 15). And as bibles became more readily available, they both enabled and demanded a more literate populace; in the case of the King James Version, the people were given a text of distinctive stylistic achievement (see Primary Document 30). This century of biblical translation would enable the seventeenth-century Anglican scholar William Chillingworth (1602–1644) to confidently proclaim, "The Bible, I say the Bible only, is the religion of Protestants" (qtd. Sykes, 175).

There had been portions of scripture in Anglo-Saxon before the year 1000, and the more than 100 surviving manuscript copies of Wyclif's translation attest to its popularity. But it is to William Tyndale that we owe the first published New Testament in English, based upon his study of Greek and Hebrew original sources, plus the translations of Luther, Erasmus, and others (see Primary Document 4). Unable to gain support in England, he traveled to Germany to print his work, which became available in England in 1526. But the strongly reformist tone of his prefaces and notes earned him the animosity of Henry VIII and Sir Thomas More. For example, he had translated "priest" as "elder," "church" as "congregation," and "penance" as "repentance," and, drawing upon the Greek word *agape* he used "love" in 1 Corinthians 13 instead of "charity" (from the Latin word *caritas*). He was finally hunted down in Belgium, strangled, and burned at the stake; according to Foxe's account, his last words were a prayer: "Lord, open the King of England's eyes." Tyndale's version managed to keep the directness and vigor of spoken English, which still gives it a contemporary ring. According to David Daniell, Tyndale "made for the Bible not only a strong direct short prose line, with Saxon vocabulary in a basic Saxon subject-verb-object syntax, but also showed a range of English styles which, coming out of the 1530s, astonishes the knowledgeable reader. No one else was writing English like this in the 1530s" (136).

Tyndale's work provided momentum for other important translations. The first complete bible printed in English was the work of Miles Coverdale (1488–1568), who drew upon Tyndale's work as well as other sources, though not the original ancient languages. While not royally authorized, when published in 1535, it contained an illustration of preachers receiving copies from the king. The psalms of Coverdale's version were beautifully phrased and were used later in the Book of Common Prayer. From him we get such phrases in Psalm 23 as "thou anointest my head with oil" and "the valley of the shadow of death." Matthew's Bible (1537) was the first to be licensed by the king; Taverner's Bible (1539), the first to be entirely printed in England; and the Great Bible (1539), the first to be authorized by the crown. During the reign of Mary Tudor, reformers left the country for more sympathetic, Protestant lands, resulting in a new English translation later produced by Calvinist scholars in Geneva in 1560 and dedicated to Queen Elizabeth. The first bible to have its chapters divided into verses, this Geneva Bible would be the prevailing English bible—and thus Shakespeare's—until the King James Version some 50 years later. It was supplemented by maps, summaries, and marginal explanations, or glosses, whose Protestant tone upset Catholics. For example, the note for Revelations 9: 11 glossed the "angel of the bottomless pit" as "Antichrist the Pope, king of hypocrites and Satan's ambassador." A Catholic English translation of the New Testament, the Rheims-Douay text, came out in 1582 (see Primary Document 20). It had polemical notes of its own: the "two masters" in Matthew 6: 24 are identified as "God and Baal, Christ and Calvin, Masse and Communion, the Catholike Church and Heretical Conventicles" (qtd. Wikgren, 91–93).

A newly authorized version in 1568, the Bishops' Bible, though it became the version read in churches, never succeeded in displacing the popular Geneva version, but at the Hampton Court Conference of 1604, James I approved yet another new translation. (In fact, James gave no formal "authorization" for it, and it only acquired the label of "Authorized Version" much later.) Starting in 1604, 54 scholars at Oxford, Cambridge, and Westminster Abbey finished their work in 1608. This was not a translation, as David Daniell reminds us, but a revision, drawing from previous versions but taking roughly 80 percent of its language from Tyndale (440–448). It adopted a more Latinate style than Tyndale's and gradually became the English bible preferred above all others, inserting into the language a number of familiar phrases ("salt of the earth," "the skin of my teeth"), and exerting a tremendous impact upon the style of written English generally. Its phrasing, as in John 3: 16 seen here in comparison with two other early versions (all in their original spelling), reveals the subtle changes in style that have made this revision so memorable:

Tyndale (1534): For God so loveth the worlde yt [that] he hath geven his only sonne that none that beleve in him shuld perisshe: but shuld have everlastinge lyfe.

Geneva (1560): For God so loueth the world, that he hath geuen his only begotten Sonne: that none that beleue in him, should peryshe, but haue euerlasting lyfe.

King James (1611): For God so loued the world, that he gaue his only begotten Sonne: that whosoeuer beleeueth in him, should not perish but haue euerlasting life.

Together with the King James Version, the Book of Common Prayer is one of the written glories of Renaissance Anglicanism. Thomas Cranmer was as gifted a writer as Tyndale, and his book likewise helped to define religious language for generations of English people, prescribing the order of service for the major rites of their worship. When Shakespeare in sonnet 116 writes, "Let me not to the marriage of true minds / Admit impediments" he is recalling the marriage service's demand that the couple reveal any "impediment why ye may not be lawfully joined together. . . . " Also familiar with the prayer book was Mistress Page in *The Merry Wives of Windsor,* of whom Mistress Quickly remarks that she is one "that will not miss you morning nor evening prayer" (2.2.98–99). One of Cranmer's most noted compositions is the General Confession from Morning Prayer (see Primary Document 9). This is not a completely original prayer of Cranmer's composing. Rather, his genius appears in his skilfull synthesis of no less than 16 different biblical passages, as Massey Shepherd has pointed out. Notable also is his rhetorical use of a similar repeated phrase ("We have") at the start of clauses (a device called *anaphora*), alliteration ("devices and desires," "thou . . . them"), rhyme ("undone . . . done"), assonance ("own . . . offended . . . holy"), varying sentence lengths, and the presence of a marked prose rhythm, aided by the use of numerous monosyllabic words. In Diarmaid MacCulloch's words, Cranmer was an "adventurous connoisseur of words" (*Thomas Cranmer,* 421).

THE CATHOLIC REFORMATION

The abuses in the Roman church that Luther and Calvin, both raised as devout Catholics, had sought to correct had not gone unnoticed by Catholics who chose not to break from the great medieval institution but to renew it from within. Yet it was clear that the rising tide of reformers posed a threat to the Catholic faith that demanded a response. Were the changes made by sixteenth-century Roman Catholic leaders essentially an initiative of, by, and for the church itself, or were they basically a reaction to Protestantism? A. G. Dickens answers with a rhetorical question: "Was it not quite obviously both?" The labels "Catholic Reformation" as well as "Counter-Reformation" are both valid for this phase of Catholic church history. "Undoubtedly," says Dickens, "this crisis stimulated self-reforming Catholicism to greater effort, while the tasks of self-defense and counter-attack demanded no small share of its growing resources" (*Counter-Reformation*, 7).

In 1517, the same year in which Luther proclaimed his Ninety-five Theses, a new and influential Catholic religious order was established throughout Italy. Members of The Oratory of Divine love, such as Bishop Giovanni Caraffa, Jacopo Sadoleto (who would later contend with Calvin), Reginald Pole (who became Mary Tudor's archbishop), and the Venetian layman Gasparo Contarini, emphasized works of charity and devotion to the Mass. This order was followed by establishment of the Camaldolese and the Capuchins in the late 1520s, the Theatines in 1524, the Somaschi in 1532, the Barnabites in 1533, and an order for women, the Ursulines, in 1535. All were devoted to lives of increased prayer and work among the poor and destitute. Better known is the Spanish mystic St. Teresa of Avila (1515–1582), who founded the Discalced ("barefoot") Carmelites in 1562. With her protégé St. John of the Cross (1542–1591), she became one of the great spiritual guides of the church, prompting the poet and critic Matthew Arnold three centuries later to comment acidly that "there was more of Jesus in St. Teresa's little finger than in John Knox's whole body" (352).

However, it was the creation of the Society of Jesus, the Jesuits, that was to have the greatest intellectual and missionary impact beyond Italy and Spain. Founded by the Basque knight Ignatius Loyola (1491–1556) and officially established in 1540, this order was the vanguard of the Catholic response to the reformers. Highly motivated, deeply spiritual, and rigorously trained in a twelve-year course of study, the Jesuits countered the Protestant movement in written works such as Loyola's influential *Spiritual Exercises* (1548), in the creation of seminaries and colleges, and in a willingness to infiltrate Protestant nations (such as Elizabeth's England) to serve oppressed Catholics and convert heretics. They also were unquestioningly obedient to the authority of the church, as one of Loyola's rules made clear: "If we wish to proceed securely in all things, we must hold fast to the following principle: What seems to me white, I will believe black if the hierarchical church so defines" (qtd Heinze, 265). The spiritual intensity of the Jesuits

A commemorative medal in honor of Ignatius Loyola.

grew out of the Catholic Reformation, while its evangelical purpose was a sign of its Counter-Reformation roots.

Harsher ways to crush heresy also gained favor. In 1477 the medieval inquisition had been revived in Spain to root out Moslems, Jews, and Protestants; interrogation by torture followed by execution was the fate of more than 2,000 under the administration of the infamous Tomás de Torquemada (1420–1498). Its intensity later grew so strong that even St. Teresa and Ignatius Loyola were scrutinized. In 1542 the inquisition was brought to Rome by Pope Paul III, and it soon was in place in France as well. To control heresy in print, Giovanni Caraffa, now Pope Paul IV, created in 1559 the first official Index of Prohibited Books, which included works by Erasmus, Boccaccio's *Decameron,* and non-Vulgate Bibles. This Index had papal approval, though the destruction of heretical works was not new: Torquemada had burned some 6,000 volumes at Salamanca in 1490 (Estep, 285). The inquisition and the list of banned books demonstrate that, despite the spiritual vitality that St. Teresa, Ignatius Loyola, and the new religious orders may have brought to the church, the Counter-Reformation meant for its hierarchy a defensive posture of unequivocal theological pronouncements and sterner measures for coping with unapproved doctrines.

The church's position was gradually spelled out in the protracted Council of Trent, which met in three sessions over 18 years, from 1545–1563. Its tone was decidedly opposed to any cooperation with Protestantism, earlier efforts at conciliation in the colloquies at Worms (1540) and Regensburg (1541) having failed. Its declarations would determine the course of Catholic theology and policy until at least the nineteenth century. It affirmed the equal authority of both scripture and tradition, claiming for the church the sole right of biblical interpretation; established the Vulgate as the normative biblical text; pronounced the validity of all seven sacraments; condemned the Lutheran doctrine of justification by faith; asserted the dogma of transubstantiation; declared the Mass (to be said only in Latin) a sacrificial offering, with communion to be given in one kind only; and made the pope the final arbiter for questions of church dogma and governance.

The Council of Trent empowered the Roman Catholic church by defining its foundational doctrines unambiguously and establishing the centrality of the papal office with new emphasis. While it did not succeed in eradicating all of the flaws that its critics had condemned (though it did eliminate the sale of indulgences), the church was able to flex its organizational muscle and prepare for a protracted contest with the forces of Protestantism, that would last well into the seventeenth century. The ripples of this contest naturally affected Shakespeare's England. Elizabeth herself was excommunicated by the pope in 1570, Catholics in England openly practiced their faith at their peril, and Shakespeare's rival Christopher Marlowe penned his play *The Massacre at Paris* to condemn the 1572 slaughter of French Huguenots on St. Bartholomew's Day. Though Elizabeth may have succeeded in keeping her settlement from dissolving, and so preserved a level of social and political unity in her kingdom, Shakespeare's religious world was forged on the anvil of reformation. While his works do not take sides with a particular theology or denomination, they do reflect a knowledge of the dominant religious texts of his day and were informed by the volatile religious environment in which he wrote.

REFERENCES

Arnold, Matthew. "Literature and Dogma." In *The Complete Prose Works*. Ed. R. H. Super. 11 vols. Ann Arbor: University of Michigan Press, 1960–1977. 6, 139–411.

Bainton, Roland. *Christianity*. Boston, MA: Houghton Mifflin, 1987.

Berdan, John M., and Tucker Brooke, eds. *The Life of King Henry the Eighth*. New Haven, CT: Yale University Press, 1925.

Bernard, G. W. *The King's Reformation: Henry VIII and the Remaking of the English Church*. New Haven, CT: Yale University Press, 2005.

Booty, John E., ed. *The Book of Common Prayer 1559: The Elizabethan Prayer Book*. Charlottesville: University of Virginia Press, 1976.

Bouwsma, William. *John Calvin: A Sixteenth-Century Portrait*. New York: Oxford University Press, 1988.

Brecht, Martin. "Luther's Reformation." In *Handbook of European History, 1400–1600*. Ed. Thomas A. Brady, Jr., et al. 2 vols. Grand Rapids, MI: Eerdmans, 1995. II, 129–159.

Brigden, Susan. *New Worlds, Lost Worlds: The Rule of the Tudors 1485–1603*. New York: Penguin, 2002.

Calvin, John. "The Word Our Only Rule." In *A Treasury of Great Preaching*. Ed. Clyde E. Fant, Jr. and William M. Pinson, Jr. 13 vols. Dallas, TX: Word Publishing, 1995. 2, 146–153.

Camden, William. *The History of the Most Renowned and Victorious Princess Elizabeth Late Queen of England*. Ed. Wallace T. MacCaffrey. Chicago, IL: University of Chicago Press, 1970.

Collinson, Patrick. "Foxe, John." In *The Oxford Encyclopedia of the Reformation*. Ed. Hans J. Hillerbrand. 4 vols. New York: Oxford University Press, 1996. 2, 122–122.

———. *The Reformation*. New York: The Modern Library, 2004.

Daniell, David. *The Bible in English*. New Haven, CT: Yale University Press, 2003.

Dickens, A. G. *The Counter-Reformation*. New York: Harcourt 1969.

———. *The English Reformation*. New York: Shocken Books, 1964.

Duffy, Eamon. *The Stripping of the Altars: Traditional Religion in England 1400–1580*. New Haven, CT: Yale University Press, 1992.

Estep, William R. *Renaissance & Reformation*. Grand Rapids, MI: Eerdmans, 1986.

Foxe, John. *Foxe's Book of Martyrs*. Nashville, TX: Thomas Nelson, 2000.

Hammond, Gerald. "English Translations of the Bible." In *The Literary Guide to the Bible*. Ed. Robert Alter and Frank Kermode. Cambridge, MA: Harvard University Press, 1987. 647–666.

Heinze, Rudolph W. *Reform and Conflict: From the Medieval World to the Wars of Religion, A.D. 1350–1648*. Grand Rapids, MI: Baker, 2005.

Hoeniger, F. David, ed. *Henry VIII: The Complete Pelican Shakespeare*. Ed. Alfred Harbage. Baltimore, MD: Penguin, 1969.

Joseph, B. L. *Shakesepare's Eden: The Commonwealth of England: 1558–1629*. New York: Barnes and Noble, 1971.

Luther, Martin. *Martin Luther's Basic Theological Writings*. Ed. Timothy F. Lull. Minneapolis, MN: Fortress Press, 1989.

———. *Table Talk*. Gainesville, FL: Bridge-Logos, 2004.

MacCulloch, Diarmaid. *Thomas Cranmer*. New Haven, CT: Yale University Press, 1996.

———. *The Reformation*. New York: Viking, 2003.

Marty, Martin. *A Short History of Christianity*. Philadelphia, PA: Fortress Press, 1987.

McNeill, John T. *The History and Character of Calvinism*. New York: Oxford University Press, 1954.

Murphy, Terence R. "Book of Homilies." In *The Oxford Encyclopedia of the Reformation*. Ed. Hans J. Hillerbrand. 4 vols. New York: Oxford University Press, 1996. 1, 194.

Noll, Mark A. "The Reformation and Shakespeare: Focus on *Henry VIII*." In *Shakespeare and the Christian Tradition*. Ed. E. Beatrice Batson. Lewiston, NY: The Edwin Mellen Press, 1994. 83–101.

Oberman, Heiko. *Luther: Man between God and the Devil*. Trans. Eileen Walliser-Schwarzbart. New Haven, CT: Yale University Press, 1989.

Ozment, Stephen. *The Age of Reform 1250–1550: An Intellectual and Religious History of Late Medieval and Reformation Europe*. New Haven, CT: Yale University Press, 1980.

Partington, Angela, ed. *The Oxford Dictionary of Quotations*. 4th ed. rev. Oxford: Oxford University Press, 1996. 274.

Pelikan, Jaroslav. *The Melody of Theology: A Philosophical Dictionary*. Cambridge, MA: Harvard University Press, 1988.

Powicke, F. M. *The Reformation in England*. London: Oxford University Press, 1941.

Scarisbrick, J. J. *Henry VIII*. Berkeley: University of California Press, 1968.

Shepherd, Jr., Massey. *The Oxford American Prayer Book Commentary*. New York: Oxford University Press, 1950.

Spitz, Lewis W. *The Protestant Reformation*. 1985. Rpt. Saint Louis, MO: Concordia Publishing, 2001.

Sykes, Norman. "The Religion of Protestants." In *The Cambridge History of the Bible*. 3 vols. Cambridge, MA: Cambridge University Press, 1963. 3, 175–198.

Wikgren, Allen. "The English Bible." In *The Interpreter's Bible*. Ed. G. A. Buttrick, et al. 12 vols. Nashville, TN: Abingdon, 1952. 1, 84–105.

3

RELIGION IN SHAKESPEARE'S WORKS

In Henry Fielding's novel *Tom Jones* (1749), Mr. Thwackum remarks, "When I mention religion I mean the Christian religion; and not only the Christian religion, but the Protestant religion, and not only the Protestant religion, but the Church of England" (127). If we expect Shakespeare's expressions of religion in his works to be as simple and straightforward as Mr. Thwackum's, we shall certainly be disappointed. Many scholars have warned against an overemphasis upon a presumed Christian or religious dimension in his works, and the American philosopher George Santayana (c. 1880–1946) even argued in an essay for "The Absence of Religion in Shakespeare." Forty years ago, W. R. Elton contended that *King Lear* is not grounded in any Christian vision but, rather, upon an exploration of "heathen religious attitudes" (338) influenced by early seventeenth-century skepticism. Harold Bloom similarly asserts that *King Lear, Hamlet, Macbeth* and *Measure for Measure* "do not yield to Christianization" (51), and Jonathan Dollimore reads the tragedies as portraits of a deeply divisive Renaissance culture, as profound questionings of the supposedly stable intellectual and religious underpinnings mapped out by more traditional commentators.

Yet the cultural importance of religion in Shakespeare's England and in his literary output should not be underestimated. Jeffrey Knapp has challenged the "view of Shakespeare as a writer so miraculously disinterested that religious beliefs—indeed, beliefs of any kind—could have no hold on him" (2). More specifically, David Evett argues that the hierarchical system of master and servant, which was so central to Elizabethan culture and so prominent in the plays, was not simply a secular relationship of social power and rank, but was linked to the Christian paradox of the perfect freedom found in service, as mentioned in the Collect for Peace in the *Book of Common Prayer;* the greatest social and individual freedom stemmed from all members of society observing their appointed places within it. While recognizing that Shakespeare's plays are not theological allegories, these and other commentators acknowledge the potent influence of religion upon his works. In the words of Donna B. Hamilton, "No contribution to the issue of Shakespeare and religion has been more important than the validation of the relevance of religion to the study of Tudor and Stuart drama" (187). It is as unwise to assume that Shakespeare's works are consistently skeptical of religion as it is to presume that a religious perspective alone is the only useful vantage from which to judge them. What we do find in his plays is a religious awareness, largely Christian but not uncritically so, and without any exclusive allegiance to a specific denomination or sect. While Shakesepeare's audiences may have found these dramas religiously instructive, it is more likely that his immediate purpose was to gain a profitable popularity rather than to be a public proselytizer. Nevertheless, they reveal a perceptive religious sensibility, responsive to the impact of organized religion in society and to the presence of a spiritual reality that Hamlet termed the "divinity that shapes our ends" (5.2.10).

As the previous chapters on the history and growth of Christianity suggest, the word "religious" in this volume refers to the ways in which Shakespeare employs the theology, rituals, and terminology of organized Christianity, whether Roman Catholic or Protestant. Critics reading the plays and poems from this perspective typically will link the works in some fashion with printed texts, doctrines, or seminal figures in Christian history, especially from Shakespeare's own era. An obviously religious dramatic moment, for example, occurs at the end of act 4 in *Henry V* when the king orders the victorious English to sing the *Non nobis* (Psalm 115) and the *Te Deum* (a hymn of praise and thanksgiving). Other commentators, however, including some postmodern critics such as Ewan Fernie, prefer to speak of the *spirituality* of Shakespeare's work rather than its "religion," emphasizing the paradoxical, mysterious, or unpredictable way in which a nonmaterial truth may infiltrate the lives of his characters. The presence of the spiritual may be marked by some inexplicable yet deeply significant event, such as the moment when Hermione's statue comes to life in *The Winter's Tale* to complete the reunion of her family. These *religious* and *spiritual* dimensions of the plays are also enhanced by a third aspect, the *supernatural*. Plays such as *A Midsummer Night's Dream*, *Macbeth*, or *The Tempest* contain ghosts, witches, fairies, sprites or deities from classical mythology or native folklore (including the Roman plays and their references to pagan religion), which are not Christian but which do lend a divine perspective to their stories. As we might expect from Shakesepare, these three dimensions are not kept separate and distinct but mingle and combine in dramatically fruitful ways and always point toward his interest in the meeting of the human with the sacred or the supernatural.

Shakespeare's portrayal of the religious aspect of experience springs in part from the mosaic of Christian outlooks he encountered in his youth. As seen earlier, the Elizabethan Settlement was not the triumph of one denomination over another but, rather, the delicate balancing of Catholicism and Protestantism within the newly established Anglican church whose influence had only just begun to take root at the time of Shakespeare's birth. But, as James Shapiro notes, "those labels failed to capture the layered nature of what Elizabethans, from the queen on down, actually believed" (148). Extreme Catholics and Puritans, who ardently held to their own faiths and opposed all others, mingled with Anglicans who were pleased with the new settlement or with those who were Anglican in name but secretly held to old Catholic beliefs (the so-called "church papists" whom

Arthur Marotti terms "a great muddled middle in English Christianity" [219]) or else adhered to newer reformist ideas. And there were likely others for whom these distinctions meant little, whose beliefs were totally idiosyncratic.

Shakespeare himself was baptized in the Church of England on April 26, 1564 in the market town of Stratford-upon-Avon. Because baptisms typically took place several days after birth, his birthday is traditionally recognized as April 23, which, appropriately, is also the feast day of St. George, the patron saint of England; he died on this date in 1616. His parents, John Shakespeare and Mary Arden, came from old Catholic families, but after the Elizabethan Settlement they, like all English, were expected to conform to Anglicanism. However, John Shakespeare was cited in 1592 for failing to attend church, and in 1757 his will, worded according to a Roman Catholic devotional book, was found in the roof of his house and led to speculation that he may have secretly practiced the old faith. Had it been hidden there purposely to avoid prosecution by Elizabethan authorities? It has been argued that Shakespeare's father was a recusant, one who refused to attend Anglican services out of allegiance to Catholicism (see Primary Document 24). Did Shakespeare's Catholic heritage and the strong Catholic presence in his region (the Jesuit missionary Edmund Campion had been active nearby) incline him more toward Rome than Canterbury?

This is possible, although weekly church attendance in Stratford would also have given him ample background in the basic texts of the Anglican faith. There he would have heard the language of the Book of Common Prayer and the Bishop's Bible, as well as sermons from the book of homilies enjoining obedience to the state church. One result of this immersion is that we find references in the plays to no fewer than 42 different Biblical books (Noble, 20). Based upon the scanty facts, scholars offer varying answers to the question of Shakespeare's personal faith, asserting that he was born and died a Catholic (Sams, 12), that he had been raised a Catholic but probably ceased to be one by the time he wrote *Hamlet* around 1600 (Wood, 78), or that he was a conforming Anglican (Rowse, 240). Citing the famous seventeenth-century remark of Anglican priest Richard Davies that Shakespeare "died a Papist," the Jesuit scholar Peter Milward has argued at length that, although the playwright was baptized and buried in an Anglican church, his works strongly imply his personal allegiance to Rome. Some have also suggested that the marked absence of any explicitly personal religious references in the plays indicates that Shakespeare intentionally sought to hide his beliefs, but that they can nevertheless be inferred from "codes" in the works (Asquith). According to this argument, such reticence would have been necessary only if he were a Catholic, not an Anglican. However, based on his study of biblical allusions in the works, Naseeb Shaheen notes that it is "most unlikely that Shakespeare possessed a copy or was familiar with" the Catholic Rheims-Douai translation of the Bible (*Tragedies*, 30). Recently, Stephen Greenblatt has argued that the plays are the work of someone who chose to leave a Catholic heritage, replacing it with a devotion to his art (*Will in the World*, 321). The most prudent view is to acknowledge that our meager evidence is inconclusive (Schoenbaum, 50). As John D. Cox observes, "recent arguments for Shakespeare as a traditional believer or a lapsed believer (i.e., a man of no faith) are less credible in principle than arguments that he was a man whose precise faith commitment is impossible to determine, though it is likely to be somewhere in the English Church" (556). Given that he seems so conversant with both the theology of the "old religion" and the language and liturgy of the Book of Common Prayer, Shakespeare's own faith could well have been solidly in the Anglican "middle way." The presence of Roman Catholic details in his works does not necessarily indicate Shakespeare's personal faith because the cultural remnants of Catholicism were widespread throughout the England of his day. "Shakespeare's evocation of England's abandoned cultural heritage—church furniture, paintings, liturgy, and the mystery plays—was available to the playwright and his audience whether they, or he, were convinced Catholics, lapsed church papists, or simple Protestants with retentive memories and developed aesthetic sensibilities" (Groves, 33).

By the time he began to write for the stage, Shakespeare had absorbed the varieties of religious experience in his native land deeply enough to allow him to create portrayals of almost every outlook. Whether or not he personally believed in the inclusive Anglican *via media* that his queen advocated, he was able to create a literary version of something like it in his own works by dramatizing all sorts and conditions of faith, even—at moments in *King Lear* and *Macbeth*—its absence. Echoing Coleridge's comment that Shakespeare had "no religion," Harold Bloom has asserted that Shakespeare in his works had "no theology" (56). It is perhaps more accurate to say that he had "no *single* theology" but instead a range of theologies through which to portray a variety of human responses to the divine. Maurice Hunt has termed this Shakespeare's "syncretistic method" of blending the differing religious outlooks that impinged upon his literary output. "The frequent simultaneity of Shakespeare's introduction of often studied, complex Protestant and Catholic motifs and systems of thought into his plays suggests a preoccupation with resolving, or harmonizing, conflicting points of view that had cost, and were costing, men and women their lives in England and throughout northern Europe" (ix, xii). The aim of this chapter is to suggest some of the ways in which this religious sensibility emerges throughout Shakespeare's works.

THE HISTORIES

Modern audiences of Shakespeare need not be reminded of the intimate relationships that can develop between political convictions and religious beliefs. Twenty-first century global events continue to demonstrate the vigorous debates and even conflicts caused when nations contend with each other over issues of "God and country." As seen in the previous chapter, the line between religion and politics was often erased completely or just as often thought not to exist in the close embrace of church and state typical of Shakespeare's Europe. Audiences of his history plays would therefore have heard the religious references in these plays filtered through not only the events portrayed on stage, but also through the often unpredictable social changes of their own times. Shakespeare's history plays are theatrical investigations of the complex interactions of faith and politics rather than reenactments of historic conflicts safely resolved by a divine providence for whom England is the Renaissance equivalent of God's chosen people. Religious belief, religious leadership, and even religious language emerge in these plays as potent devices by which those in or out of power seek to gain or keep influence. Shakespeare is careful to show that genuine piety and deep political need can exist in the same individual, such as Richard II, while the trappings and rituals of faith can be exploited as steps to power by those, such as Richard III, to whom they mean nothing or for those, such as Henry V, whose eagerness for military victory strikes many audiences as more convincing than the religious language with which they justify them.

History plays, or "chronicle plays" as they were also called, were popular in the 1590s, and audiences enjoyed such works as Robert Greene's *James IV*, Christopher Marlowe's *Edward II*, and George Peele's *Edward I*. They offered playgoers fresh portrayals of famous notables, dramatic lessons in statecraft and political leadership, interesting studies of personal morality, and opportunities to express feelings of nationalism. Shakespeare wrote ten plays about English history, eight of them grouped into two sets of four, called "tetralogies," and all written during the first half of his dramatic career. The earlier tetralogy consists of the three parts of *Henry VI* (1589–1591) and *Richard III* (1592–1593). The second tetralogy includes *Richard II* (1595), the two parts of *Henry IV* (1596–1596, 1598) and *Henry V* (1599). *Henry VIII* (1612–1613), noticed earlier, and *King John* (1594–1596) are not part of either of these chronological sequences. *King John*, however, poses issues about the legitimacy of kingship that link it to other histories with similar themes, such as *Richard II*. Taking perhaps greater liberty with historical accuracy than in his other history plays, Shakespeare depicts John as both ambitious yet ineffective, first defying the papal legate Pandulph in terms that would have appealed to Elizabethan Protestant audiences, but later relinquishing his authority to the pope in exchange for aid against the French. John, having usurped the throne from his nephew Arthur, rules with a suspect legitimacy. Both John and Pandulph are, in Roy Battenhouse's view, devoid of true religion, Pandulph especially being "implicitly a spokesman more concerned to maintain face for 'mother church' (whose policies are adulterous) than to fulfil the duty of Christ's faithful servant" ("Religion in *King John*," 144). The play's interwoven themes of politics, religion, and ambition are explored in the eight-play group as well.

Shakespeare employed two primary sources for his tetralogies, Edward Hall's *Union of the Two Noble and Illustrious Families of Lancaster and York* (1548) and Raphael Holinshed's *Chronicles of England, Scotland and Ireland* (1577, expanded in 1587). These books recounted the history of two protracted conflicts in English history: the Hundred Years War between the English ruling Plantagenet family and the French House of Valois (1337–1453), and the Wars of the Roses (1455–1485) between two powerful families, the Yorks (symbolized by the white rose) and the Lancasters (the red rose). Shakespeare's dramatic portrayal of these events is his own; he does not always follow precise details of history exactly, nor does he always feel bound by the historical biases of these authors. Instead, he invites an audience to question their narrative by calling attention to the para-doxes and ambiguities of kings and would-be kings whose religious convictions are tempered by their political ambitions.

The first tetralogy spans the period from shortly after the start of Henry VI's reign (1421) to the death of Richard III (1485). The piety of Henry VI is insuf-ficient to make him an effective monarch; as his frustrated queen remarks, "all his mind is bent to holiness, / To number Ave Marias on his beads" (*Henry VI, Part 2*, 1.3.55–56). More than faith is necessary if he is to rule successfully, and he is contrasted in Part 1 with the dynamic Lord Talbot, English leader in the Wars of the Roses, who seeks to regain territory in France won by Henry V. Shakespeare does not hesitate to employ the nationalistic and pejorative tone of his sources concerning Joan of Arc ("Joan La Pucelle"), who is regarded as a French trollop who summons fiends to aid her (5.3). But in Part 2 it is the simplistic faith of the king himself that is held up as a defect of leadership when the supposedly blind Simpcox suddenly regains his vision. The king is overwhelmed, saying, "God's goodness hath been great to thee" (2.1.82), but his uncle, Humphrey, Duke of Gloucester, through skeptical questioning, soon reveals Simpcox's trick-ery. Shakespeare borrowed the story of this false "miracle" at St. Albans from Foxe's Book of Martyrs, thus injecting a Protestant distrust of miracles into an otherwise pre-Reformation play. The Bishop of Winchester later confesses his part in Humphrey's death, taking his dream of the dead Gloucester to be "God's secret judgment" (3.2.31) on his guilt; the English church hierarchy, not merely Joan of Arc, is cast in a critical light.

Compounding the naivety of the religious king and the chicanery of politi-cal prelates is the political rebellion of Jack Cade. Cade, a hotheaded anarchist who distrusts anyone who can read (4.2.95–110), announces, "my mouth shall be the parliament of England" (4.7.14–15). Cade exemplifies the threat of social disorder that so disturbed Tudor political theorists. Shakespeare's staging of inci-dents of political unrest and the questions they posed signals that his plays are not mere vehicles for the dominant ideas of his day but a means of probing those ideas and examining received beliefs. The frequency with which the legal and religious powers exhorted the English to live their lives in peaceful obedience to divinely established authority suggests the constant maintenance required to keep that peace. The threat of political instability conflicted with a social ideal based upon the harmonious Christian universe, as expressed most notably in Richard Hooker's treatise on Anglican polity (church government), *Of the Laws of Ecclesiastical Polity* (1593) (see Primary Documents 25–26). All human law was thought to be rooted in the law of nature revealed in the predictable structure and motions of the physical universe, the loss of which would plunge the world back into chaos. As Hooker asserts, "See we not plainly that obedi-ence of creatures unto the law of Nature is the stay of the whole world?" (I, 517). Shakespeare makes Hooker's discussion of the structured plan of the universe the basis of Ulysses' famous speech on order or "degree" in the dark comedy *Troilus and Cressida* (1.3.103ff), and Queen Elizabeth, through the appointed homilies preached in her churches, could make it clear that defiance of her authority was not merely a political offense, but a violation of divine law, as in the 1571 homily *Against Disobedience and Wilful Rebellion* (see Primary Document 17). It asserted that rebellion "nameth the whole puddle and sink of all sins against God and man, against his prince, his country, his countrymen, his parents, his children, his kinsfolks, his friends and against all men universally; all sins, I say, against God and all men heaped together, nameth he that nameth rebellion" (qtd. Joseph, 177). But Ulysses' grandiloquent speech is spoken by a political manipulator who, to get Achilles to return to battle, later appeals to Achilles' pride rather than to any nobler theological ideas, and his effort eventually fails. Similarly, Hooker's treatise had careful theological underpinnings, but these made it even more attractive as a key intellectual weapon in Elizabeth's political arsenal. In Ulysses' case, the ideal natural law is finally ignored, while in Elizabeth's case, religious principle could be pressed into service for political ends—such as the torture of Catholics—which were far less virtuous than the beliefs on which they were based. Shakespeare's history plays dramatize how religious belief and political principle qualify each other in ways often more complex than that suggested by his sources.

The first three plays of the first tetralogy also dramatize the steady rise to power of Richard, Duke of York. He relies on the concept of divine right—that kings ruled by a divine authority and were answerable to God for that right— but he exploits that right for his own power-hungry ends. With an echo of the sin of simony in his words, Richard declares, "Ah, *sancta majestas* [holy majesty], who would not buy thee dear?" (*Henry VI, Part 2*, 5.1.5). Far more sinister than Jack Cade, Richard takes his breech birth and limping, hunchbacked body as signs that he has been fated to live a uniquely evil life, declaring, "since the heavens have shap'd my body so, / Let hell make crook'd my mind to answer it" (*Henry VI, Part 3*, 5.6.78–79). His perverse misrepresentation of heaven's purpose for his life is but one of the sinister aspects of his character in the fourth play of the tetralogy, *Richard III*. Schemer, murderer, ruthless politician, and skilled rhetorician, he willfully and delightedly defies any ethical or religious code that stands between himself and the throne. Having declared that he could "set the murtherous Machiavel to school" (*Henry VI, Part 3*, 3.2.193), he allies himself with a political theorist who was notorious for his pragmatic approach to politics. In 1532 Niccolo Machiavelli (1469–1527) published *The Prince*, a treatise on government, which argued that princes (like those he had personally observed in Italy) should not hesitate to rule by fear if that were necessary to keep them in power. The "machiavel" thus became a character on the English stage who sought raw power with little concern for morality or religious law; speaking the prologue to Christopher Marlowe's *The Jew of Malta* (1592), Machiavel announces, "I count religion but a childish Toy" (265). For Richard to declare himself not the student but the teacher of such an atheist is to defy the authority of religion altogether. (Shakespeare was certainly aware that Marlowe himself had been accused of atheism.)

In true Machiavellian fashion, Richard will not hesitate to use the appearance of religious faith to manipulate his victims:

> But then I sigh, and with a piece of scripture,
> Tell them that God bids us do good for evil:
> And thus I clothe my naked villainy
> With odd old ends stol'n forth from holy writ,
> And seem a saint, when most I play the devil. (*Richard III*, 1.3.333–337)

He openly announces his own hypocrisy by comparing himself to a character from the medieval morality plays: "Thus, like the formal Vice, Iniquity, I moralize two meanings in one word" (3.1.82–83). The medieval Vice was a malicious and often humorous figure who depicted the human tendency toward sin, which he incited in those around him while mocking their suffering. Richard's allusion prompts Shakespeare's audience to understand his character by recalling these traditional religious and moral plays that many of them may have seen firsthand. Richard again mocks piety when his advocate Buckingham designs a charade to convince the Londoners of Richard's Christian virtue. With obvious symbolic intent, the stage directions call for Richard to appear "aloft, between two Bishops." Buckingham's fulsome comments are intended to sway the onlookers' reactions, but the word *ornaments* suggests that Richard's bishops and prayer book are little more than trappings:

> Two props of virtue for a Christian prince,
> To stay him from the fall of vanity;
> And see, a book of prayer in his hand—
> True ornaments to know a holy man. (3.7.96–99)

Old Queen Margaret, Henry VI's widow, condemns him repeatedly and wishes for his death: "Earth gapes, hell burns, fiends roar, saints pray, / To have him suddenly conveyed from hence" (4.4.75–76). Richard's eventual "fall of vanity" is an object lesson stressing the civic and religious values he had flouted, but once again Shakespeare provides an example implying that the concept of divine right can be exploited and undermined and that invoking it offers no guarantee of wise governance. With obvious irony, Richard reminds Margaret and his mother not to demean his presumed right, though Henry VI's authentic right had not kept Richard from killing him: "Let not the heavens hear these tell-tale women / Rail on the Lord's anointed" (4.4.150–151). Richard dies in the Battle of Bosworth Field (1485) at the hands of Henry Tudor, the Earl of Richmond, later King Henry VII and Elizabeth I's grandfather. Richmond is the founder of the Tudor dynasty who viewed Richard, in Stephen Greenblatt's words, as "a horrible instrument of God's wrath, a virtual devil incarnate" (*Richard III*, 507). However, historians have pointed out that Richard, while guilty of numerous faults, was likely far less malicious than his stereotype, and there seems little factual basis for his having been hunchbacked.

With his second tetralogy, Shakespeare moves backward in time to recount the rise of Henry V. *Richard II* is constructed upon the tragedy of the fall of Richard II and the rise of his usurper, Henry Bolingbroke, Duke of Hereford, later to be Henry IV.

Unlike Richard III, Richard II gained the throne legally but wrongly expects that the honor due the "Lord's anointed" will excuse the shortcomings of his twenty-two year administration (1377–1399). Though poetically creative, Richard emphasizes the power and trappings of his office instead of effective policies; his attraction to medieval ceremony is no match for the efficient designs of Bolingbroke, who overthrows Richard after the king fails to manage the power struggles among his nobles and seizes their property, including Bolingbroke's. Just as Bolingbroke's return from banishment to seek his rightful lands and title barely disguises his desire for the throne, Richard's pervasive use of religious language expresses a genuine faith yet is a manipulative ploy for sympathy after he has mismanaged the crown. Intertwining religion, politics, and personalities, Shakespeare raises the question of just how the nation should respond to a divinely sanctioned yet ineffective monarch and whether usurpation can ever be justified as more than a Machiavellian grab for power.

John of Gaunt (Richard's advisor and Bolingbroke's father), convinced that no action should be taken against "God's substitute, / His deputy anointed in his sight" (1.2.37–38), refuses to oppose the king, who clings desperately to the spiritual authority of his throne and declares, "Not all the water in the rough rude sea / Can wash the balm off from an anointed king" (3.2.54–57). The desertion of his agents Bushy, Bagot, and Green prompts the king to call them "Three Judases, each one thrice worse than Judas" (3.2.132), thus casting himself in the role of the tormented Christ or worse, when he later recalls his former supporters:

> Were they not mine?
> Did they not [sometimes] cry "All hail" to me
> So Judas did to Christ; but He, in twelve,
> Found truth in all but one; I in twelve thousand, none. (4.1.168–171)

Richard prophesies an Old Testament vengeance on his enemies ("God omnipotent / Is mustering in his clouds on our behalf / Armies of pestilence" [3.3.85–87]), but he is deposed in act 3. We are reminded that kings themselves are subject to temptation and fall through the comments of a gardener who muses that the king should have tended the "garden" of England more carefully. He is rebuked by the Queen, who also employs the image of the fall of man:

> Thou old Adam's likeness, set to dress this garden,
> How dares thy harsh rude tongue sound this unpleasing news?
> What Eve, what serpent, hath suggested thee
> To make a second fall of cursed man? (3.4.73–76)

Though Richard II may have gained the throne by rightful succession, his sin lay in assuming that he was infallible, that the power of his crown mattered more than his kingly character. Shakespeare presents us with multiple "falls." Besides his individual fall from personal authority, Richard's fall from the royal position of monarch of England—which Gaunt calls "This other Eden, Demi-paradise"

(2.1.42)—reiterates Adam's fall from the Garden of Eden, taking humanity with him. England itself, like all of mankind, is also a "fallen" nation, thus inviting audiences to consider how Elizabethan goals of stability and order can be achieved in the face of such radical human imperfection. Both Adam and Richard fall as a result of the cardinal sin of pride, later reflected in Richard's smashing of a mirror, a medieval metaphor for vanity (4.1.289).

The Duke of York, reiterating Gaunt's reliance upon God, is convinced that "heaven hath a hand in these events, / To whose high will we bound our calm contents" (5.2.37–38). But this possibly providential transition of power is undercut with Richard's murder by an agent supposedly acting for Bolingbroke—now Henry IV. This is an act for which the new king, who admits having wished for Richard's death, feels the need to atone: "I'll make a voyage to the Holy Land, / To wash this blood off from my guilty hand" (5.6.49–50). Rebellions at home will later keep him from this chance to be absolved of his sacrilege, and he enters his reign bearing a moral burden. Shakespeare again challenges theatergoers with the knotty relationship of religion and governance. Can the removal of a rightful yet weak king be spiritually justified? How does divine will operate through the actions of men, especially through violent acts? What is the new king's authority to rule if he has gained the throne by sanctioning the breaking of the sixth commandment?

Henry IV's sense of guilt extends into the next play, the first part of *Henry IV*. The "unthrifty" behavior of his son Prince Hal (*Richard III* 5.3.1) he takes to be the "hot vengeance and the rod of heaven, / To punish my mistreadings" (3.2.10–11). The two parts of Henry IV trace Hal's growth into a politically adept monarch who has gained his skills by spending time among the lowest rungs of the social ladder. Outwardly a wastrel, Hal shrewdly acquires social and political skills that will equip him for leadership, as he predicts in his "reformation" speech, which draws upon Ephesians 5:15–16: "See then that ye walk circumspectly, not as fools, but as wise, redeeming the time, because the days are evil."

> My reformation, glitt'ring o'er my fault,
> Shall show more goodly and attract more eyes
> Than that which hath no foil to set it off.
> I'll so offend, to make offense a skill,
> Redeeming time when men think least I will. (1.2.213–17)

Hal's reference to this Pauline epistle may reveal that he is actually more religious than he seems, or it may be a carefully rhetorical statement designed to convince us that he is more devout than he really is. As Marjorie Garber comments, "Whereas Richard III was a devil pretending to be an angel, Hal is a virtuous man pretending to be a madcap thief—or is he?" (330). In either case, Shakespeare seems eager to hold up the multi-layered nature of Hal's "reformation" for our scrutiny because it is underscored by the repeated use of the word "redeem" later on (1.3.86, 1.3.180, 1.3.206, 3.2.132).

Hal also shares a complex friendship with Sir John Falstaff. He enjoys the old knight's rowdy nightlife, yet carefully refuses to commit himself to the fat man's indulgent values. A wonderfully comic and pragmatic character—selfish, witty, insightful, lazy, and satirical—Falstaff represents a moral and religious laxity that the prince must see, know, and yet abstain from. Hal terms him "that reverent Vice, that grey Iniquity, that father ruffian, that vanity in years," an "old white-bearded Sathan" (2.4.453–454, 463). The frequent biblical allusions in their dialogues suggest the extent to which the nation's language and people at every level had been influenced by the Book of Common Book and by English translations of scripture that they had heard and read (Baker, "Christian Context"). For example, Falstaff, who can recall what "the inside of a church is made of" (3.3.7–8), defends himself with an allusion to Matthew 7:17 when he says, "If then the tree may be known by the fruit, as the fruit by the tree, then peremptorily I speak it, there is virtue in that Falstaff" (2.4.428–430). Shakespeare may also be parodying the sanctified speech of Puritans through these allusions (Poole). These biblical references extend even to popular slang, as Hal refers to himself as a "Corinthian" (2.4.12), and Falstaff's cronies are "Ephesians . . . of the old church" (*Henry IV, Part 2*, 2.2.150), a reference which J. A. Bryant contends offers a Pauline background for both *Henry IV* plays (52–67). At the end of *Henry IV, Part 1* Hal kills the ambitious rebel Hotspur, whose rash behavior was driven by an egotistic desire for military glory; his death dramatically illustrates Proverbs 16:18: "Pride goeth before destruction, and an haughty spirit before a fall." Upon becoming king and rejecting his wayward youth, Hal turns his back on Falstaff: "Presume not that I am the thing I was" (5.5.56). This "Corinthian," taking Paul's advice from 1 Corinthians 13: 11, has "put away childish things." His words of dismissal to Falstaff are cruelly blunt—"I know thee not old man, fall to thy prayers" (5.5.47)—but in them we hear an appropriate echo of "Get thee hence, Satan" (Matthew 4: 10).

The ethical extremes of Falstaff or Hotspur alone do not create the amendment of life that Hal seeks, but from both men he learns to craft an emotional *via media* to emerge as the balanced, capable monarch in *Henry V*. His stunning rejection of Falstaff's profligate life seems to suggest that he will be "the mirror of all Christian kings" (act 2, Chorus 6), but modern judgments of this play, pointing out the uncertainties Shakespeare raises about Henry's reign, have modified an older view that it offers a largely flattering portrait of this king. Is the assurance of his bishops a valid justification for Henry to wage war on France, or is he merely seeking a pretext for invasion? To what degree does divine right (clouded by his father's removal of Richard II) keep him morally innocent of the deaths of his own men in battle? Is the chorus's praise of him merely promotional publicity little different from Buckingham's flattery of Richard III's pretended piety? Stephen Marx has discussed the ways in which Henry's career parallels those of Old Testament heroes (40–58), yet this biblical background only deepens these and other questions the play raises about the relationships between organized religion and historical events. In the very first scene the Archbishop of Canterbury and the Bishop of Ely realize that their favorable decision on Henry's wish to invade France might result in his persuading the House of Commons to stop a bill that would strip the church of valuable land. As Graham Holderness writes, "They view the church not as the community of Christ's faithful, or as a means of bringing men closer to God, but as an administrative and political apparatus . . . not an unfolding of God's providence." (145–146). This is a view with which the Romantic critic William Hazlitt (1778–1830) would have agreed; in his view Henry "seemed to have no idea of any rule of right or wrong, but brute force, glossed over with a little religious hypocrisy and archepiscopal advice" (qtd. White, 156). Shakespeare's history plays present us with an England in which religion was a vital force in national affairs, yet it was a force that was always intimately joined to the pressures of political events and contending personalities.

THE COMEDIES

Falstaff, a comic figure in the history plays, is evidence of Shakespeare's ability to mingle dramatic genres and moods, and Falstaff is in fact the central figure of fun in a comedy of his own, *The Merry Wives of Windsor*. The roots of his theatrical character reach back, as Bernard Spivack has shown, to the medieval Vice figure and to the Lord of Misrule, an anarchic overseer of carnival mayhem, a kind of Jack Cade with a rubber sword. His sardonic, biblically-laced quips suggest that he is also, as Battenhouse argues, a "holy fool," a jester who leads others to wisdom through laughter instead of lectures. W. H. Auden observes that Falstaff's "untiring devotion to making others laugh becomes a comic image for a love which is absolutely self-giving" (206), linking him to ritual celebration, the comic attitude, and the Christian spirit. Falstaff illustrates that the comic outlook affirms physical pleasure and a zest for life; when moderated by a sense of responsibility (which he fails to fulfill), the comic spirit is also a path to love and social harmony. Shakespearean comedies end with a joyously ordered society created not by the external rules of homilies or laws but by the inner renovation of personalities.

Religious approaches to Shakespeare's comedies have not only noted these plays' use of Christian doctrine and ritual, but have often emphasized their reiteration of mythic patterns found in the earliest pagan comedies. The origins of dramatic comedy lie in the cycle of religious fertility ceremonies of ancient Greece, based upon the mythic stories that explained natural processes (Cornford). As Wylie Sypher notes, "the entire ceremonial cycle is birth: struggle: death: resurrection," and he asks if "the drama of the struggle, death, and rising—Gethsemane, Calvary, and Easter—actually belongs in the comic rather than the tragic domain." "Comedy," he says, "is essentially a Carrying Away of Death, a triumph over mortality by some absurd faith in rebirth, restoration, and salvation" (220). Comedy in this sense is not a momentary amusement arousing laughter, but the more profound gaining of wholeness and happiness after trial and struggle. From a mythic perspective, Shakespearean comedy celebrates birth and renewal, echoing the pagan seasonal celebrations (Northrop Frye). From a Christian vantage, his comedies uphold the loving virtues of forgiveness, redemption, and reconciliation; hence they typically end with marriages, feasts, and reunions, the human enactments of resurrection from misguided outlooks or destructive behaviors. Comedy by its nature is not necessarily Christian, but, as Dante reminds us, Christianity is divinely comic. Comic laughter is restorative because, in provoking our laughter *at* foolish characters, it enables theatergoers to identify shortcomings and pass moral judgment upon them, verifying an awareness of good and evil. By provoking laughter *with* these characters, it helpfully guards audiences against a false moral superiority or a self-righteous pride that would conveniently hide their own ludicrous foibles.

Probably Shakespeare's first staged drama, *The Comedy of Errors* (1592–1594) employs mistaken identity, physical humor, and verbal ingenuity, drawing upon the classical Roman plays of Plautus and Terence. Two brothers (both named Antipholus) are forced apart in a shipwreck shortly after birth; their father, Aegeon, reared one, while their mother, Aemilia, and the other son were rescued separately. The family members converge in Ephesus and eventually identify one another, with the action complicated by a set of identical servants. Aemilia, now the abbess of a priory, reveals herself to Aegeon after numerous confusions. Despite its classical structure and Greek setting, Catholic details appear: the characters "know what 'tis to fast and pray" (1.2.51), use rosaries (2.2.188), and speak of "limbo" (4.2.32) and "Pentecost" (4.1.1). The concerns of this family suggest a theme of Paul's letter to the Ephesians, which stressed the early church's spiritual unity despite its geographical dispersion: "Now therefore ye are no more strangers and foreigners, but fellowcitizens with the saints, and of the household of God" (2: 19). Aegeon's family is similarly drawn together, their separation as strangers ended in act 5 when the abbess appears with an almost queenly command of the situation, balancing the play's Catholic allusions with a possible hint at Elizabeth I's oversight of church and country. Having longed for her family's reunion for 33 years (Christ's traditional lifespan), she invites everyone to a feast celebrating the miraculous, Christmas-like birth of their new life together: "After so long grief, such nativity!" (5.1.407).

Written at about the same time, *The Taming of the Shrew* (1593–1594) continues an emphasis upon physical comedy and verbal fireworks, as Petruchio comes to Padua seeking a wife. He chooses the challenge of wooing "Kate the cursed" (2.1.186), whom no man will have because of her terrible temper. Petruchio proceeds to treat Kate as roughly as she does him, and he finally "tames" her into marriage, leading to her final, much-debated speech on the virtues of wifely submission to husbands. Although her change in temperament has been read as either her total submission to masculine will, or as only an ironic appearance of this to preserve her own autonomy, the spirit of her last speech also recalls Rosalind's advice to Phoebe in *As You Like It* to "thank heaven, fasting, for a good man's love" (3.5.58). Kate's statement on male superiority in marriage, rather than being a license for husbands' domination (though this may often have been the case in actual Renaissance marriages), is contingent upon the husband's wholehearted devotion to his wife's welfare: "Thy husband is thy lord, thy life, thy keeper, / Thy head, thy sovereign; *one that cares for thee, / And for thy maintenance*" (5.2.146–148; emphasis added). This mutuality lies at the heart of Paul's comment on marriage in Ephesians: "Nevertheless, every one of you in particular so love his wife even as himself; and the wife see that she reverence her husband" (5: 33). Kate, however, is not simply a personification of Paul's ideas, and her unexpected change of outlook adds depth to her unique personality.

Several types of New Testament love, as discussed by C. S. Lewis in *The Four Loves*, disclose a religious dimension of *The Two Gentlemen of Verona* (1594). The deep friendship (*philia*) of two men, Valentine and Proteus, is tested by *eros* (romantic love) when Proteus falls in love with Sylvia, Valentine's beloved, and betrays his friend's plan to escape with her against the wishes of her father, the Duke of Milan. The Duke's opposition to their marriage also raises the issue of *storge*, or the love between members of a family; his is the role of the father who obstructs young love, not unlike Egeus in *A Midsummer Night's Dream*, thereby posing a test of its validity. Religious language in this play overlaps the descriptions of the ideal mistress common to Petrarchan love poetry popular among Elizabethans; Sylvia is "holy, fair, and wise" (4.2.42). She recognizes that Proteus has sacrificed genuine *eros* and *philia* for selfishness and diagnoses his emotional and spiritual problem: "Thou hast no faith left now" (5.4.50). When Valentine also confronts Proteus as one "without faith or love" (5.4.62), Proteus declares, "My shame and guilt confounds me. / Forgive me, Valentine" (5.4.73–74), whereupon Valentine quickly pardons him and surrenders Sylvia to him, saying, "Who by repentance is not satisfied / Is nor of heaven nor earth" (5.4.79–80). The Duke, now impressed by the suitor he had despised, decides that Sylvia should instead marry Valentine. Proteus is united with his first love, Julia, and all celebrate "one feast, one house, one mutual happiness" (5.4.173). The Duke forgives the outlaws with whom Valentine has been hiding; by welcoming them back into his kingdom, he demonstrates *agape*, the compassionate love of God for all men. The play's rapid resolution may seem contrived (and Sylvia is given no say in her romantic fate), but it dramatizes the powerful effect of Proteus's contrition, as well as Valentine's forgiveness and selfless acceptance of him.

Love's Labor's Lost (1594–1595) lacks a theological theme as prominent as this, but it warns that interfering with spontaneous love is contrary to the natural order. The King of Navarre and three noblemen swear to abstain from romance for a year and devote themselves to philosophy, but their plans go awry when they are smitten by the Princess of France and her three ladies-in-waiting. Eventually Berowne declares, "To fast, to study, and to see no woman—/ [Is] Flat treason 'gainst the kingly state of youth" (4.3.288–289). They deny their previous oath, accepting that love "Lives not alone immured in the brain" (325) but requires fulfillment in flesh and action. It is worth breaking an oath for, Berowne concludes, alluding to Romans 13: 8: "It is religion to be thus forsworn / For charity itself fulfills the law" (360–361). The play's numerous references to oaths echo the homily "Against Swearing and Perjury" (Shaheen, *Plays*, 119ff.)

With *A Midsummer Night's Dream* (1595–1596), a play possibly commissioned for an actual wedding, Shakespeare forms a synthesis of Christian love with the world of fairies, sprites, and a pagan celebration of nature's fertility; Theseus, for example, mentions both "the rite of May" and Saint Valentine's Day (4.1.133, 139). The play is a festival of comic reconciliation as Theseus (Duke of Athens) and Hippolyta (Queen of the Amazons) are married, and the quarreling king and queen of fairies, Oberon and Titania, make up, and two sets of young lovers unite. The confusions of the young lovers Lysander and Hermia and Demetrius and Helena, as well as the metamorphosis of Bottom the weaver into an ass with whom Titania falls in love, are metaphors for the profound and mystifying changes wrought by love, whether understood in pagan or Christian terms. Shakespeare combines the pagan classical belief that gods and their relationships directly affect natural seasons and human affairs with the Christian belief that love transforms the lovers, lifting them to a vision of the divine. Bottom's description of his dream of love sounds foolish—"The eye of man hath not heard, the ear of man hath not seen, man's hand is not able to taste, his tongue to conceive, nor his heart to report, what my dream was" (4.1.211–214)—until we recognize its parallel with Isaiah 64: 4 and 1 Corinthians 2: 9: "Eye hath not seen, nor ear heard, neither have entered into the heart of man, the things which God hath prepared for them that love him." Bottom changed into an animal recalls Falstaff's animal appetites, but each is a "holy fool" uttering wisdom. The playlet of Pyramus and Thisbe amusingly parodies the loves of the noble youths, but it, like the entire play, is also a testament to the power of art to express the inexpressible. When Theseus states that the poet's "imagination bodies forth / The forms of things unknown" (5.1.14–15), his definition of the artist's vision approaches Paul's understanding of religious faith as "the substance of things hoped for, the evidence of things not seen" (Hebrews 11: 1).

The preceding early comedies of Shakespeare were followed by *The Merchant of Venice* (1596–1597), a play that some have termed a tragicomedy because the title character's imminent death is surprisingly averted. The play is built upon a series of contrasts: Portia's idyllic, romantic life in Belmont and the risky world of Venetian commerce; the mutual distrust between Jews and Christians; the moral demands of justice and mercy; Old Testament legalism and New Testament forgiveness; the conflict of prejudice with equality. When Antonio, the merchant of Venice, borrows a large sum from Shylock the Jewish moneylender to enable his friend Bassanio to woo the beautiful Portia, the theme of friendship in *The Two Gentlemen of Verona* is put to a much greater test. When Antonio proves unable to repay Shylock, Antonio, according to the bond, must pay with a pound of his flesh. But when Shylock demands payment, Portia, disguised as a lawyer, counsels him to reject his legalistic demand and show mercy: "The quality of mercy is not strained, / It droppeth as the gentle rain from heaven . . . It is an attribute of God himself" (4.1.184–185,195). Shylock refuses, and she reminds him that the bond calls only for flesh, not blood; he can take one but not the other. In a theatrically effective turnabout, he is defeated by his own insistence on the letter of the law, made to pay a fine, and ordered to become a Christian. The legal stipulations of the Old Testament are thus superseded by the New Testament emphasis upon mercy. Shylock leaves the play in act 4; the brief final act is devoted to the marriages of Portia and Bassanio and Jessica and Lorenzo, but the morally troubling fate of the moneylender overshadows the romantic plot.

Historically, Jews had been ordered out of England in 1290, leaving only a few in London, who were perhaps *conversos* or converts to Christianity. We can only surmise whether Shakespeare knew any Jews himself, but an incident in 1594 placed them in the public eye. Dr. Roderigo Lopez, a Jewish Portuguese physician who had served the Queen, was executed on charges of having tried to poison her. Shakespeare's play took advantage of this well-known event. To Shakespeare's Christian audience, Shylock's enforced conversion may have seemed a benefit that enables him to gain salvation, especially after his open contempt for Antonio ("I hate him for he is a Christian" [1.3.42]), his comically sinister delight in wealth, and his overbearing attitude towards his daughter (who flees his house to marry a Christian and become one herself). But, though Shylock's hatred of Christians threatens to transform him into a stereotypical villain, Shakespeare complicates our perception of him by giving him a moving speech on the evils of prejudice (3.1.53–73), which reveals the plight of Jews as victimized aliens in European Christendom. Shylock is nevertheless morally at fault for having tried to exploit the law for a verdict that served his wish for revenge, while the Christians—who rely on his moneylending to serve their business dealings but deny him economic and social equality—distort the sacrament of baptism by using it to reinforce their own social superiority. Especially for modern audiences with a knowledge of the Holocaust—when Jews were murdered in the fatherland of the Reformation—this comedy remains profoundly relevant, and the question of its possible anti-Semitism is continually debated.

From these religious conundrums, Shakespeare turned to a jovial farce. *The Merry Wives of Windsor* (1597–1601), supposedly written in just two weeks to satisfy the queen's desire to see "Falstaff in love," presents the old knight in pursuit of Mistress Page and Mistress Ford. This is not quite the quick-witted Falstaff of the histories, because the women dupe him into being dumped into a stream with dirty laundry, beaten (while wearing a dress) by Mr. Ford, and singed with candles by tricksters in the forest. The play resembles the city comedies of Ben Jonson whose characters with exaggerated flaws are mocked out of their "humours," but Falstaff, whose room is "painted about with the story of the Prodigal" (4.5.7–8), also parallels the sinful characters punished in the morality plays (Tippens). Shakespeare blends Christian elements with native English folklore in act 5 suggestive of the world of A *Midsummer Night's Dream*. Falstaff, wearing staghorns in imitation of the mythical Hearne the Hunter, is lured into the park near Windsor where he is accosted by the would-be forest spirits who pinch him and taunt him with lighted candles as punishment for his greed and lechery. Falstaff's horns are also Satanic, as Mr. Page observes: "Heaven prosper our sport! No man means evil but the devil, and we shall know him by his horns" (5.2.12–14). The candle flames suggest hellish or purgatorial fires verifying his sin: "if he start [flinch]," says Anne Page, "It is the flesh of a corrupted heart" (5.5.87). As a stag, Falstaff compares himself to such ancient legends as Europa's union with a bull and Leda's with the swan, observing that love "in some respects makes a beast a man; in some other a man a beast" (5.5.4–6). Lest we miss the echo here of Bottom's transformation, he reminds us: "I do begin to perceive that I am made an ass" (5.5.119). From a Christian perspective, Falstaff undergoes a baptism of shame in the laundry ditch and the burning away of his sins in a comic penance leading to conversion; from a mythic perspective, the forest pranksters (including the Welsh parson disguised as a fairy) ritually subdue the uninhibited natural force of procreation, channeling it into the socially approved marriages of the last act.

In Shakespeare's three most accomplished romantic comedies, characters undergo the expulsion of misguided attitudes and selfish outlooks to recover their true selves and enjoy healthy relationships. This transformation suggests a conversion, and their behavior carries religious overtones as they undergo the process of learning to love. *Much Ado About Nothing* (1598–1599) puns in its title on "nothings"—inconsequential details mistaken for important truths—and "noting" or observing the behaviors of others and then (mis)interpreting them. The tendency of the lovers to mistake appearance for reality is the basis of a trick by which Don Pedro convinces Beatrice and Benedick to accept their love for each other, while Claudio must discount false rumors of Hero's immorality, which he has too quickly believed. After he wrongly condemns Hero at their marriage altar as an "approved wanton" (4.1.44), Friar Francis falsely announces her death. This unjust "death" of the innocent convinces Claudio of his transgression. He admits his mistake to Don Pedro in religious terms: "Impose me to what penance your invention / Can lay upon my sin; yet sinn'd I not / But in mistaking" (5.1.273–275). Hero later unmasks herself at a ball in a romantic resurrection ("One Hero died defiled, but I do live" [5.4.63]), and Claudio sees his sinful error. Robert G. Hunter has argued that Claudio represents *humanum genus* or "the human race" undergoing a process of sin, confession, penance, and then forgiveness (*Forgiveness*, 85–105). Beatrice comments that "man is a giddy thing" (5.4.108) who must learn to deflect illusions with a balance of mind and heart. She and Benedick declare that they love each other "no more than reason" (74), suggesting that they have achieved, as sonnet 116 puts it, a "marriage of true minds" (1). Spiritually, this union of love and reason creates "A miracle!" (5.4.91).

Most of *As You Like It* (1599) occurs in the Forest of Arden, a locale critics term a "green" or "secondary" world in which conflicts originating in the realistic urban world may be resolved through human or spiritual means. Kept from his inheritance by his vindictive older brother Oliver, Orlando defeats the murderous Charles the wrestler (incited by Oliver) in a seemingly unequal match reminiscent of David's defeat of Goliath (1 Samuel 17). He flees to the forest, an Edenic place beyond time ("there's no clock in the forest" [3.2.300–301]) and inhabited by the usurped Duke Senior who praises its pastoral simplicity—"Here feel we not the penalty of Adam"—and its enriching benefits of "tongues in trees, books in the running brooks, / Sermons in stones, and good in everything" (2.1.5,16–17). But, as in the true Eden, temptations must be conquered. Oliver, having fallen asleep under an oak and menaced by a snake and a lioness, is rescued by Orlando who overcomes two temptations to leave his evil brother to die. In an act which recalls John 15: 13, Orlando's "kindness" and "nature" enable him to defeat the lioness (which wounds him) and save his brother, who relates that this unselfish act converted him from his former malicious self: "I do not shame / To tell you what I was, since my conversion / So sweetly tastes, being the thing I am" (4.3.135–137). Alice-Lyle Scoufos observes that "By spilling his blood for his brother, [Orlando] resembles the Second Adam [Christ] whose blood is the premier symbol of sacrifice and love in Christianity" (223). Duke Frederick the usurper enters the forest hunting Duke Senior but "meeting with an old religious man,/ After some question with him, was converted / Both from his enterprise and from the world" (5.4.160–162). These two conversions are complemented by four marriages, which conclude the romantic plotline. William Watterson sees these "eight that must take hand" (5.4.128) as "symbolic of the eight who were saved entering Noah's ark" (121). Thus "earthly things . . . Atone together" (5.4.109–10), and all prepare to return to court reconciled.

The title of Shakespeare's third romantic comedy, *Twelfth Night* (1601–1602) recalls the feast of Epiphany, which in the early church "commemorated not only the coming of the Magi with gifts to Bethlehem, but two later events in the life of Christ: his baptism, and the miracle at Cana" at which Jesus changed water into wine (Barton, 438). As gift-bringers themselves, Viola and her brother Sebastian, swept ashore in Illyria after a shipwreck, will bring the present of self-knowledge and true love to Duke Orsino, who is in love with being in love, and to Olivia, a countess neurotically devoted to seven years of mourning for her dead brother. Within Olivia's household, her steward Malvolio ("ill will") is mocked for his self-importance by fun-loving Maria, who calls him "a kind of puritan," not for his religious views but for being "a time pleaser, an affection'd ass," "so cramm'd (as he thinks) with excellencies, that it is his grounds of faith that all that look on him love him" (2.3.140,148–152). Sir Toby Belch recognizes Malvolio's Puritanism as an excessive self-righteousness: "Dost thou think because thou art virtuous there shall be no more cakes and ale?" (2.3.114–116). Toby and Maria (who eventually marry) appreciate the blending of the material and the spiritual as displayed at the wedding feast of Cana (John 2: 1–12). Malvolio's pride blinds him to this truth, and he leaves the play unrepentant, vowing revenge on them all. Typically, it is the clown Feste who utters a telling diagnosis of him, borrowing from Exodus 10: 22: "I say there is no darkness but ignorance, in which thou art more puzzled than the Egyptians in their fog" (4.2.42–44). Sebastian's marriage to Olivia is a gift freeing her from her unhealthy grief. Viola, who has been disguised as Orsino's servant-boy Cesario, is threatened with death by the Duke as an act of revenge against Olivia's refusal of his affection; "I'll sacrifice the lamb that I do love," he says. Viola, out of her love for him, "a thousand deaths would die" (5.1.130,133). Her willingness to die for love like a sacrifical lamb lends a Judaeo-Christian aspect to her selflessness.

Shakespeare's next three plays are generally termed "dark comedies" or "problem comedies." Though they do not end tragically, they explore moral or ethical issues with a seriousness absent from the romantic comedies. Their endings may seem contrived, their moods more inconsistent or cynically satirical than jovial, and their central characters and themes more ambiguous than the previous comedies. *Troilus and Cressida,* composed at about the same time as *Twelfth Night* (1601–1602) but variously termed a history, tragedy, and comedy in early printings, challenges that play's optimistic rejection of hypocrisy and introversion. The title characters are attracted to each other more by physical desire, fanned by Cressida's prurient uncle Pandarus, than by romantic love. Balancing this seamy affair among the Trojans is the egotism of the headstrong Greek heroes, which has destroyed their military discipline. The acidly satirical comments of Thersites condemn the armies' laxity and the foolishness of a war over Helen of Troy: all is "Lechery, lechery, still wars and lechery" (5.2.194–195). Ulysses' grandiloquent speech on order points ironically to its absence in this play: "The speciality of rule hath been neglected" (1.3.78). He alone seems convinced that "There is a mystery . . . in the soul of state, / Which hath an operation more divine / Than breath or pen can give expressure to" (3.3.201–204), but, as Cassandra reminds Hector, "The gods are deaf to hot and peevish vows" (5.3.16). "Despite the play's epic machinery," comments David Bevington, "the gods are nowhere to be found" (456). These warring heroes ignore any religious or fixed standards beyond self-interest. The play raises the question of whether ideal values exist or if morality is instead only a matter of individual judgment. When Troilus asks, "What's aught, but as 'tis valu'd?" (2.2.52), he echoes Hamlet's comment that "There is nothing either good or bad, but thinking makes it so" (2.2.249–250). The characters' unwillingness or inability to enact morally redemptive ideals has led some critics to view this play from a Christian vantage as an ironic portrayal of a fallen world.

It is perhaps not a coincidence that Helena, the saintly heroine of *All's Well That Ends Well* (1602–1603) shares the same name with St. Helena, mother of Constantine, the first Christian emperor of Rome. With her father's medical knowledge, she promises to cure the King's ailment; when he is skeptical, she assures him that her cure is providential: "it is presumption in us when / The help of heaven we count the act of men." He replies, "Methinks in thee some blessed spirit doth speak" (2.1.151–152,175). She also displays a heavenly patience in coping with the cruel rejection of the selfish and undeserving Bertram, whom she loves and, to some critics, deviously schemes to entrap. After she leaves the court on a pilgrimage to seek him, the Countess remarks that Bertram can only avoid a downfall if "her prayers, whom heaven delights to hear / And loves to grant, reprieve him from the wrath / Of greatest justice" (3.4.27–29). This in fact happens after Helena persuades his new beloved, Diana, to change places with her for a night of love, and Diana exchanges rings with Bertram in this bed-trick, a common folktale device. Confident that Helena is dead, Bertram expects to keep his new bride. But when Diana announces "one that's dead is quick [alive]" (5.3.303), this last-act resurrection of the saintly lover ensures that Helena will gain happiness and that Bertram, a morally "fallen" character, will be saved by her unconditional forgiveness and love—an act of grace. Though it makes sense theologically, this ending strikes many as too quick to be theatrically satisfying; this, plus the cynical Parolles' salacious patter throughout the play, lends a problematic tone to this comedy.

Measure for Measure (1604) takes its title from Christ's Sermon on the Mount: "Judge not, that ye be not judged. For with what judgment ye judge, ye shall be judged: and with what measure ye mete, it shall be measured to you again" (Matthew 7: 1–2; cf. 5.1.411). The Duke of Vienna ends his own lax government by installing as ruler the strict Angelo, a "precise" individual who "scarce confesses / That his blood flows" (1.3.50–52) and thus a puritanical figure of repressive self-control. When Claudio is arrested for the unmarried Julietta's pregnancy and sentenced to death, his sister Isabella, a devout novice in a religious order, pleads for Angelo to be merciful and imitate Christ's love for sinners: "How would you be / If He, which is the top of judgment, should / But judge you as you are?" (2.2.75–77). But Angelo, who is not the "angel" his name implies, suddenly finds himself lusting for her as much as a sinner in a morality play: "O cunning enemy [Satan], that to catch a saint, / With saints doth bait thy hook!" (2.2.179–180). Shakespeare's focus here is on the dangers of religious self-righteousness and the lack of self-knowledge, whether among Protestants or Catholics (Puritans often referred to each other as "saints," and Vienna was a Catholic city). If Isabella surrenders to Angelo with "sweet uncleanness," she may "redeem" Claudio (2.4.53–55), but she refuses, instead preserving her religious chastity and presenting us with a more complex religious personality than Helena's in *All's Well That Ends Well*. The play questions whether Isabella's willingness to sacrifice a life to preserve her vow to God is more truly religious than the sacrifice of her holy chastity to save her brother's life. Unlike Orlando's willingness to lay down his life for his unworthy brother in *As You Like It*, Isabella fails to extend to Claudio the mercy she asks from Angelo, while he fails to apply to himself the strict morality he expects from others. The play is also darkened by the lewd commentary of Lucio, a Parolles-like character. The Duke eventually resolves the play's dilemmas like an absolutist king governing by divine right (perhaps a glance at James I), when he arranges for the marriages of himself and Isabella, Claudio and Julietta, and Angelo and Mariana (in their case through another a bed-trick). This happy ending seems to contradict the sense of the play's title because both Isabella and Angelo receive a forgiveness they themselves have not shown, but the Duke's actions towards them nevertheless implies the forgiving mercy of God's judgment. By marrying, both forgo their solitary self-righteousness and are poised for a comic redemption to learn the love they should have shown earlier. Although the dark comedies raise problematic questions largely absent from the more optimistic romantic comedies, all of these plays explore variations on the processes by which misguided or "sinful" characters experience an eventual "redemption."

THE TRAGEDIES

The world of comedy presents human experience as more of a problem than a mystery. This is not to diminish the depth of insight comedy offers, but only to say that it is an art form whose conflicts will be resolved in laughter rather than death. The world of tragedy, however, is a world of enigma. Tragedies may offer answers, but they do not provide solutions. Characters' understanding and resolution of problems evolves through their suffering, and, though they may come to a deeper understanding of the world, they do not neatly "figure it out." At times the path to understanding is discovered not by solving or defeating dilemmas, but by enduring them as King Lear does, or else by "living the questions" as Hamlet does. Tragic suffering points toward the Christian concept of sin, the consequences of which require the death of some characters and the stubborn endurance of others. Hence, we sometimes find a strong element of Stoicism in Shakespeare's tragedies, a hard-won acceptance of the inevitability of testing as the price of ultimate insight.

It is difficult to know how conversant Shakespeare was with Aristotle's theory of tragedy, but Aristotle's familiar principles in his *Poetics* have been an influential critical tool in understanding these plays; his concepts have received much more critical analysis than can be summarized here. Tragedies focus on the predicaments of noble individuals who suffer because of their acts (or lack of action), which result from a personal "flaw" (*hamartia*), most often linked to pride (*hubris*), and influenced by some divine or superhuman influence (fate, destiny, providence). The complex causality at work in these plays raises profound questions captured in the title of Robert G. Hunter's study *The Mystery of God's Judgements*. The protagonist undergoes a crisis (*catastrophe*), which leads to an insight (*anagnorisis*) and then to death. The audience will be moved to feel pity (a sympathetic or vicarious identification with the tragic hero) and fear (awe, amazement, or horror), leading to its own emotional release (*catharsis*), the gaining of an inner psychic stability and deeper insight.

Aristotle's terms, while obviously not identical with Christian concepts, do present some broad parallels with a Christian reading of the tragedies, though critics debate how closely both approaches can be linked. Roland M. Frye, for example, does not deny "the relevance of theological material to the plays," but he does deny "the consistent analysis of them by theological means" (24, n. 8). In obedience to the will of God, Christ heroically chose to undergo suffering and death, arousing pity and fear among his followers, and his agony in the Garden of Gethsemane (Matthew 26: 36–46) may be seen as a crisis of decision. As Paul states in 1 Corinthians 15: 21, just as man fell through Adam (the first Judaeo-Christian tragic figure), so Christ as the "second Adam" will also die to bring reconciliation with God. But Christ is clearly without any predisposing Aristotelian flaw, a pagan counterpart to the influence of original sin. Hence Roy Battenhouse suggests that the death of a Shakespearean tragic hero is an "ironic or dark analogy" to Christ, while the death of a different, innocent figure, like Cordelia in *King Lear*, "can truly suggest" Christ's death (*Shakespearean Tragedy*, 94). Because *King Lear* has a pre-Christian setting, Cordelia's death while seeking to save her father need not necessarily be seen in Christian terms. Yet when she is moved by the fact that Lear did "hovel" with "swine" (4.7.38), this hint at the Prodigal Son story (Luke 15: 16)—one of many Christian references in the play—overlays, without obscuring, the pagan one. To use an analogy, we may say that to read Shakespeare's tragedies—indeed his whole canon—from a Christian (or indeed any) perspective means reading them as if they were a kind of palimpsest, a manuscript on which several texts have been written but all of whose meanings can still be glimpsed. The expansiveness of meaning Shakespeare achieves is the result of his blending of multiple contexts of meaning, whether they are explicitly depicted or poetically implied.

Titus Andronicus (1593–1594), Shakespeare's first tragedy (if we classify *Richard III* as a history play), has historically been criticized for its unrelieved violence modeled on Seneca's Roman tragedies, but modern directors, such as Julie Taymor in her film version (2000), often see in it a graphic portrayal of war's destructive futility. Titus, returning home with queen Tamora of the Goths and her captured fighters, declines to be elected emperor and defers to Saturninus. But his revenge against Tamora—for his own sons' deaths in battle, Saturninus's evil designs with her, and the rape and mutilation of his daughter Lavinia by Tamora's sadistic sons—prompts him to feed her sons to Tamora at a grisly banquet, a grimly parodic Last Supper. Titus, like some Hotspur in a toga, is devoted to honor, the classic military virtue, but in this play the line between honor and revenge is thin—the word "revenge" occurs twice more here than in any other Shakespearean play. The play's constant pattern of revenge reduces Rome to "a wilderness of Tigers" (3.1.54) in which the pagan gods, called upon to wreak vengeance, remain disturbingly silent. Marcus encourages Lavinia to write her tormentors' names to "display at last / What God will have discovered for revenge" (4.1.74), but he is not sure that divine concern exists: "O heavens, can you hear a good man groan / And not relent, or not compassion him?" (4.1.123–124). Titus and his friends fire arrows into the sky—one each for Jove, Apollo, Mars and Minerva—as he says, "sith [since] there's no justice in earth nor hell, / We will solicit heaven and move the gods / To send down Justice for to wreak our wrongs" (4.3.50–52). But this scene's darkly comic mood makes us suspicious that any justice will be given. Aaron, Tamora's amoral Moorish lover, is contemptuous of religion, and his bitter comment sums up the play's spiritual atmosphere: "Pray to the devils, the gods have given us over" (4.2.48). Sounding like a sneering Protestant, he briefly relents to ask the pious Lucius to pray for his infant son: "I know thou art religious, / And hast a thing within thee called conscience, / With twenty popish tricks and ceremonies . . . " (5.1.74–76). Lucius becomes Rome's new ruler, perhaps hinting at a coming peace strengthened by religious conviction, but the play itself is a gory mayhem unrelieved by any mediating faith in a guiding providence. Whatever gods exist seem indifferent or perversely pleased by suffering, as Marcus laments: "O why should nature build so foul a den, / Unless the gods delight in tragedies?" (4.1.59–60).

Unlike *Titus Andronicus*, in *Romeo and Juliet* (1595–1596) Christianity is decisively present. Despite the play's famous opening announcement of its "star-cross'd lovers" (Prologue, 6) and Romeo's cry that he is "Fortune's fool" (3.1.136), such fatalistic comments are balanced by the Christian context represented by Friar Lawrence. Reminding us of Paolo and Francesca, the lovers condemned in Dante's *Inferno* (Canto V), Romeo and Juliet likewise suffer in part for their headstrong infatuation. The play's imagery depicts Juliet as the almost divine object of Romeo's affection; she is his "bright angel" (2.2.26) who can with a touch "make blessed [his] rude hand" (1.5.51). When they first clasp hands, she describes them as pilgrims (palmers) journeying to each other: "palm to palm is holy palmer's kiss (1.5.100). Romeo's affection—"the religion of mine eye" (1.2.88)—is prompted by her physical beauty, while she calls him "the god of my idolatry" (2.2.114). His powerful adoration of her drives the plot rapidly forward as he fails to heed Friar Lawrence's distinction between "doting" and "loving" (2.3.82). Like Petrarch, Shakespeare uses religious imagery to intensify the language of love, which in medieval theology led to a love of God. Friar Lawrence himself errs in attempting a God-like control over life and death when his drugging of Juliet wrongly convinces Romeo of her death. Romeo's affection turns to "savage-wild" anger (5.3.37), and he kills her suitor Paris in her vault whose "feasting presence full of light" (5.3.86) briefly suggests a religious shrine. Their suicides convince the shamed Friar that "A greater power than we can contradict / Hath thwarted our intents" (5.3.153–154). When the feuding Montagues and Capulets finally make peace, Prince Escalus announces a providential meaning in their deaths: "See what a scourge is laid upon your hate / That Heav'n finds means to kill your joys with love" (5.3.292–293). Capulet admits that the children were "the poor sacrifices of our enmity" (5.3.304). The play conveys the truth of Lancelot Gobbo's comment in *The Merchant of Venice* (echoed in Exodus 20: 5 and elsewhere in the Old Testament) that "the sins of the father are to be laid upon the children" (3.5.1–2). As John F. Andrews observes, the society of the play is "a microcosm of postlapsarian humanity" (416).

In *Julius Caesar* (1599) the conspirator Cassius bitterly remarks that Caesar "is now become a god, and Cassius is / A wretched creature" (1.2.116–117), taking Caesar's divination as another example of the overweening ambition for which he deserves assassination. Though Caesar was historically the first emperor to be glorified as a god, this honor was not out of harmony with polytheistic Roman paganism, which tolerated the worship of many gods besides those it had inherited from the Greeks. The Romans had no central written holy text like the Bible and lacked anything like a consistent "theology" or specific articles of faith. Nor was there a common doctrine of personal salvation, and ideas about the afterlife (if it existed) were vague. But Romans were expected to take part in the rituals and rites of the state religion to ensure that the gods would reward virtue, punish vice, and guide the empire. Portents and omens were thought to indicate this divine will, as Casca says: "the most mighty gods by tokens send / Such dreadful heralds to astonish us" (1.3.55–56). Unlike *King Lear, Hamlet* or *Macbeth*, there is no opposition between clearly contrasting moral values in this play. Though vain and imperfect, Caesar has done much for Rome, while Brutus, though believing he acts for the good of the nation, is still guilty of murder. As John Danby puts it, there is no "Christian core" in the play (149). Although Caesar *was* a divine authority, whereas English monarchs ruled *by* divine authority, his assassination raised for Shakespeare's audience the problem of the misuse of power posed in *Richard II*: is Brutus justified in removing the emperor and for offenses he has not yet committed but "may" in the future? (2.1.27–28). Confronted by this political and moral ambiguity, Brutus is eager that Caesar's death be seen as more of a religious ritual than a criminal massacre: "Let us be sacrificers, not butchers . . . Let's carve him as a dish fit for the gods . . . We shall be called purgers, not murderers" (2.1.166, 173, 180). The play also may suggest Elizabethan religious tensions if the disrobing of Caesar's statues in act 1 reflects Protestant attempts to dismantle the symbols of English Catholic ritual (Kaula 199).

Like *Macbeth*, which opens with a dialogue of three witches, *Hamlet* (1600–1601) inserts the world of spirit into the world of flesh in its opening act, ironically drawing upon medieval Christmas plays in which shepherds await Christ's birth, as Hamlet confronts the ghost of his father, who emerges from purgatorial fires to command his son to avenge his murder by Claudius. Hamlet is thereby compelled into a tragic contradiction: to obey the fourth commandment ("Honor thy father and thy mother") he must violate the sixth ("Thou shalt not kill" [Exodus 20: 1–17]). This contradiction contributes to his much-discussed "hesitation" in completing his mission. Though eager at several points in the play to "sweep to [his] revenge" (1.5.31; 3.2.390–393; 4.4.65–66), he is a frustrated revenger, distraught at having been chosen for this task: "The time is out of joint. O cursed spite, / That ever I was born to set it right!" (1.5.188–189). As he later tells Gertrude, "heaven hath pleas'd it so, / To punish me with this, and this with me, / That I must be their scourge and minister" (3.4.173–175). He berates his mother for her infidelity but does it for her moral betterment and thus attempts to "honor" her: "Confess yourself to heaven: / Repent what's past; avoid what is to come" (3.4.149–150). The progress of his revenge is colored by his religious sensibility; he is overwhelmed by his task but rejects suicide because it is divinely forbidden (1.2.131–132). He devises the "Mousetrap" play to verify his uncle's guilt and confirm the ghost's story for "the devil hath power / T' assume a pleasing shape" (2.2.604–605). He refrains from killing the praying Claudius, assuming (wrongly, because Claudius cannot repent) that his confessed soul would thereby go to heaven. It is only in act 5, after having survived the king's plot against his life during a voyage to England (and "even in that was heaven ordinant" [5.2.48]), that his frantic anxiety is replaced by his faith in a providential plan, which he identifies with an allusion to Matthew 10: 29: "There is special providence in the fall of a sparrow. If it be [now], 'tis not to come; if it be not to come, it will be now; if it be not now, yet it [will] come—the readiness is all" (5.2.219–222). Although Claudius succeeds in having Hamlet killed in a final duel, Laertes, the king, and Gertrude also die as their evil schemes recoil upon them. While perhaps not Shakespeare's most emotionally powerful tragedy, *Hamlet* is the most intellectually complex, and the impact of Christian doctrine upon the hero's behavior is complicated by strong currents of philosophical skepticism.

Like *The Merchant of Venice*, *Othello, the Moor of Venice* (1605) is set in a Catholic city yet is dominated by an outsider, an alien valued for his service to the community but denied social equality because of his cultural difference. Othello's military generalship and baptism as a Christian (2.3.343) are not enough to keep this dark-skinned Moor from being censured by the father of Desdemona, his Caucasian wife.

Nor do they keep Iago, his trusted lieutenant, from tempting and eventually corrupting his mind with thoughts of jealousy by alleging her infidelity. Iago's hatred of Othello is not adequately explained by the fact that Othello promoted Cassio ahead of him. He displays an enmity so deep that Samuel Taylor Coleridge famously called it "motiveless malignity" (Hawkes, 171), and his satanic associations rival those of Richard III. Iago calls attention to his own hypocrisy: "Divinity of hell! / When devils will the blackest sins put on, /They do suggest at first with heavenly shows, / As I do now" (2.3.350–353). By declaring "I am not what I am" (1.1.65), he mocks God's own self-definition in Exodus 3: 14: "I am what I am." The devilish Iago tempts the fall of the Adamic Othello by leading him to the murder of Desdemona. The murder of such innocence connotes the death of a divine light ("Put out the light, and then put out the light" [5.2.7]), and his tremendous anger echoes the raging Herod who ordered the death of the innocents (Matthew 2: 16). Othello's earlier prediction made in the Edenic garden of the castle that the order of creation would suffer a fall into primordial confusion does in fact come true for him: "Perdition catch my soul / But I do love thee! and when I love thee not, / Chaos is come again" (3.3.90–92). Othello's recognition of his error leads to his own suicide, suggesting an affinity with Judas corroborated by a possible reading of the debated passage at 5.2.347. In an irony that blends the play's religious issues with racial and ethnic concerns, Othello's misguided rage against his wife would have aroused for Shakespeare's audience stereotypical ideas about the supposedly ungovernable emotions of Africans, Muslims, and other foreigners (Baker, "Ovid"). The problematical nature of Othello's deepest cultural and religious identity is raised in his final speech, "in which," says Walter Cohen, "the conflict of civilizations reemerges in his identification with the exotic non-European, non-Christian world" (209). Othello's pagan background has prompted close study of the play as a meeting ground of early modern pagan and Christian, Middle Eastern, and European worlds, but Robert N. Watson argues that "the play uses the appeal of romantic love to enhance the appeal of Protestantism, by repeatedly associating Desdemona with [the] pitying Christ, and Othello with her doubtful worshipper" (234–235).

Rather than jealousy, a central theme of *King Lear* (1605) is the suffering caused by Lear's cardinal flaw, pride. It has warped his perception of love, leading him to banish Cordelia, his one loving daughter, and to mistake the greedy flattery of the other two, Regan and Goneril, for genuine affection. After they turn against him, he is driven to a barren heath in a raging storm, a penitential tempest that brings a humbling self-realization of his kinship with commoners as a "poor, bare, forked animal" (3.4.107–108). The storm conveys his disordered emotions, his temporary madness, and the apparent possibility that at the heart of life lies a nothingness, a cosmic indifference to human pain, rather than a providential concern. Lear, by no means innocent, nevertheless feels he suffers more than he deserves: "I am a man more sinned against than sinning" (3.2.59–60). He is accompanied on this dark rite of passage by his Fool, who utters wryly prophetic insights, and Edgar, the loving son of Gloucester, whose disguise as Mad Tom reiterates the theme of psychological fragility as evidence of man's sinfully fallen nature. Gloucester, whose blinding by Regan and her husband parallels the king's sufferings, offers a horribly bleak spiritual vision: "Like flies to wanton boys are we to the gods / They kill us for their sport" (4.1.36–37), a conclusion possibly confirmed by Cordelia's fate. She returns from banishment to rescue her father and forgives him, only to be hanged by the forces of Gloucester's diabolical son Edmund, whom Edgar then kills. Some have seen Cordelia as a Christ-figure owing to her description as one "Who redeems nature from the general curse / Which twain have brought her to" (4.6.206–207)—from the fallen state of humanity caused by Adam and Eve and, in Cordelia's case, Regan and Goneril. Whether Lear's ambiguous final statement at her death is hopeful or despairing has been much debated, as has whether the play is finally Christian or pagan. Peter Milward, for example, finds the image of Lear holding the dead Cordelia to be a version of Michelangelo's Pieta, in which Mary cradles the dead Christ (255). For many this is Shakespeare's greatest tragedy because it finely balances a gripping experience of violent meaninglessness with Cordelia's redemptive love that empties itself totally for Lear, who must suffer greatly before he can learn to accept his own flawed humanity. *King Lear* asks us to consider the existential question of whether the absurdity of an egotistic will-to-power can be met and conquered only by the absurdity of unconditional love.

Macbeth (1606) presents "vaulting ambition" (1.7.27) as the prevailing defect of its protagonist. The brevity of this play (it is the shortest tragedy) reveals the speed with which fragile man can fall victim to diabolical sin. Macbeth's almost instant attraction to the three witches' prophecy of his future kingship suggests that they merely express his own darker purpose, regardless of its required murder of Duncan: "Stars, hide your fires, / Let not light see my black and deep desires" (1.4.50–51). In Duncan's death, Macbeth kills a guest, a king, and a kinsman, the last point linking him to the story of Cain's killing of Abel in Genesis 4. They both quickly learn that "the wages of sin is death" (Romans 6: 23), but it is a living death as they suffer the accusing appearances of Banquo's ghost, "terrible dreams that shake us nightly" producing "torture of the mind" (3.2.18–21), and Lady Macbeth's guilt-ridden sleepwalking scene. Blood and darkness are dominant images here and throughout the play, especially in the porter scene (2.3), which recalls the Harrowing of Hell portions of the medieval mystery plays (Wickham). When the doctor tells Lady Macbeth "you have known what you should not," and the gentleman replies that "heaven knows what she has known" (5.1.46–49), they confirm her fallen state by alluding to the knowledge of good and evil forbidden to Adam and Eve. After news of her death (thought to be suicide) is brought to Macbeth, he reveals his own descent into a spiritual void. Life for him is "a tale told by an idiot, / Full of sound and fury, / Signifying nothing" (5.4.26–28). He has entered Othello's "chaos" (3.3.92); he has become Lear's "forked animal" (3.4.107–108) and Hamlet's "quintessence of dust" (2.2.308). Macbeth's immersion in the void is the result of his own actions, and he is punished by his sins as much as for them. He has less justification for condemning the gods than do Gloucester or Lear because he himself has replaced God by creating his own universe of spiritual negation. This is not so much a play about the loss of religious faith as of its utter absence from the worldview of Macbeth and his wife. His death at the hands of Macduff cleanses the kingdom of "this dead butcher and his fiend-like queen," and Malcolm calls upon the "grace of Grace" (5.9.35–38) to reestablish the nation on a new spiritual footing.

The lovers in Antony and Cleopatra (1606–1607) are not, like the Macbeths, joined in acts of destruction but, rather, in a mutual love that is thwarted by their conflicting cultures and dominating personalities. Their obstacles are not the opposing parents of Romeo and Juliet, but the mutually exclusive values of heroic Roman militarism and self-indulgent Egyptian pleasure. The self-discipline and Stoic endurance that have made Antony a "triple pillar of the earth" (1.1.12) are gradually eroded by the sensual influence of Cleopatra whose "infinite variety" (2.2.235) proves fatally irresistible to him. This play analogously retells the fall of a Roman Adam at the hands of a seductive Egyptian Eve in a lush Edenic setting. Cleopatra is both lover and temptress; for Antony she is "my serpent of old Nile" (1.5.25). Her final suicide through the bite of an asp ("my baby at my breast") also links her with the fatal serpent, and, ironically when Charmian calls her the "eastern star" (5.2.308–309), with the Virgin mother of Bethlehem. The lovers suggest the mythological story of Mars and Venus, but this pagan context implicitly contrasts with the ideal Christian relationship in which love exists not only for itself, but to glorify God. They attempt a love that would possess such supernatural greatness; to contain it, Antony remarks, "Then must thou needs find out new heaven, new earth" (1.1.17), a comment that echoes the biblical "new heaven and new earth" (Isaiah 66: 22, Revelation 21: 1). After Cleopatra's desertion leads to Antony's military defeat by Octavius Caesar, he condemns her, "whose bosom was my crownet, my chief end" (4.12.27), ruefully echoing the first line of Calvin's Genevan Catechism: "What is the chief end of man?" Calvin's answer was "To know God by whom men were created." Antony's is to love the woman for whom he eventually falls on his sword, saying "I will be / A bridegroom in my death" (4.14.99–100). Just before her own suicide Cleopatra refers to him as "Husband" (5.2.287), as if their exclusive devotion to each other will be solemnized only through death, their marriage to be lived out in a heaven of their own imagining, beyond "this [vild] world" (5.2.314).

The title character in Coriolanus (1607–1608) is as devoted to the honor of Rome as Mark Antony was to Cleopatra. Men like Antony are condemned by Volumnia, Coriolanus' strong-willed mother, as those who "voluptuously surfeit out of action" (1.3.25), whereas she prides herself in Coriolanus' strength—also paradoxically his tragic weakness: his pride as a Roman. He despises any, especially commoners, who do not share his high dedication to the state, but his devotion to this earthly empire is seen to be ultimately fruitless. J. L. Simmons has pointed out that, from the Christian perspective of history that the play implies, a thoroughly human institution will contain human flaws that keep it from perfection. "[B]ecause the martial virtue of Rome is in no way directed 'at man's chiefest good' and has no relevance beyond the formalized needs of the Earthly City, it can entail neither an intrinsic nor a metaphysical reward"

(26). Coriolanus thus "was a kind of nothing, titleless, / Till he had forg'd himself a name I' th' fire / Of burning Rome" (5.1.13–15). However, the image of a "burning Rome" ironically suggests the transience of worldly achievements. The single-minded dedication of Coriolanus to the political state leads him to resemble Cleopatra, who recognizes the emptiness of mere earthly accomplishment when she says, "there is nothing left remarkable beneath the visiting moon" (4.15.67–68). In St. Augustine's terms, the "City of Man" cannot hope to equal the ideal virtue of the "City of God."

Timon, in *Timon of Athens* (1607–1608), also becomes "a kind of nothing" after having squandered his money in extravagant generosity and then found himself penniless to pay his creditors. Though there are sparks of idealism in his behavior in the opening acts, his descent into bitter misanthropy in the last two acts is rapid and complete, and he rails endlessly at the world for its devotion to gold. Timon ignores the monetary basis of almost all his relationships; he is a tragic study in obsession just as Ben Jonson's character Volpone is a comic one. In effect worshipping a material god of gold, he loses all respect for his pagan priests and sects—"This yellow slave / Will knit and break religions" (4.3.34–35)—and he confronts the spiritual void with which Shakespeare's tragic figures must contend: "There's nothing level in our cursed natures / But direct villainy" (4.3.19–20). The cave to which he retreats to avoid society resembles Lear's hovel in the storm, his faithful steward Flavius displaying the allegiance of Lear's fool. Flavius reveals to two Senators Timon's tragic pride: "he is set so only to himself / That nothing but himself which looks like man, / Is friendly with him" (5.1.117–119). Timon is isolated in a world of self, cut off from any larger spiritual realities. Unlike Lear, he comes to no moment of insight, no renovating transformation leading to a greater awareness of either humanity or divinity. As Charlton Hinman observes, "One of his chief deficiencies as a tragic hero is certainly his incapacity for spiritual growth" (1139). Timon's bitterness has dissolved his sense of human value; his titanic rages, having no moral conviction to undergird them, are reduced to impotent ranting. His behavior displays the great spiritual flaw that Christianity warns against and which Iago, a similarly twisted soul, suffered from and saw in everyone: "I never found man that knew how to love himself" (*Othello*, 1.3.313–314).

THE ROMANCES

Shakespeare's final four plays, known as romances, have strong tragicomic elements, for they each begin with a conflict or separation within families and end with a reunion, marriage, or reconciliation. But to a much greater extent than his previous comedies, they convey their themes through music; exotic locales; greater use of deities, magicians, and healers; significant lapses of time; and mythic patterns of rebirth. Unlike the tragedies, whose human characters make appeals to the discrete realm of the supernatural, the romances present settings in which the divine and its surprising work seem immediately present and accepted as a matter of course. In their transfiguring of the physical, these plays demand that audiences view the physical world more sacramentally, as both palpable yet somehow holy. To borrow Peter Stitt's observation on Richard Wilbur's poetry, in these plays Shakespeare "no more desires a pure spirituality, divorced from the physical, than he desires a pure materiality, divorced from the spiritual" (15). They require that we more fully suspend our disbelief than with the earlier comedies so as to enter play-worlds that are more fantastic and divine than any others Shakespeare created.

Gower, the chorus in *Pericles, Prince of Tyre* (1607–1608), cautions the audience to "bend your mind" (act 4, line 5) to accommodate the fanciful events of this play, which are punctuated by dumb shows or mimings. After being marked for murder by an incestuous father whose secret he discovers, Pericles escapes but is shipwrecked at Pentapolis, whose princess, Thaisa, he marries. Sailing home he is again shipwrecked, Thaisa dying after having given birth to Marina at sea. Marina is sold to a whoremonger in Tarsus but stoutly retains her virtue. Pericles, believing both wife and daughter dead, is eventually reunited with them, his wife having been revived from apparent death by a healer. Fourteen years elapse before the final reunion, underscoring the gradual but purposive process of providence ("Time's the king of men" [2.3.45]). Pericles's trials teach him a patient faith; he is movingly distraught at his losses but never despairing: "O you gods! / Why do you make us love your goodly gifts, / And snatch them straight away?" (3.1.22–24). He is rewarded at the end with a dream-vision of Diana, goddess of childbirth, and the sound of the mystical music of the spheres, made by the turning heavens and heard only by the blessed. The rebirth of Thaisa blends the pagan myth of spring's return ("see how she 'gins to blow / into life's flower again" [3.2.94–95]) with the Christian image of resurrection from the tomb, and Marina's virtuous rebukes of the brothel's customers draw their amazed respect: "But to have divinity preached there! did you ever dream of such a thing?" (4.5.4–5). These religious suggestions are confirmed at the close, when Gower's final chorus reminds us of the play's morality-like characterization and theme: "Virtue preserv'd from fell destruction's blast, / Led on by heaven, and crown'd with joy at last" (5.3.89–90). Howard Felperin comments that in this play "nature becomes redeemable, for grace, personified in Marina, abounds even to the worst of sinners, just as it had in countless miracle and morality plays before *Pericles*" (162).

Cymbeline (1609–1610), a more episodic tragicomedy, is set, like *King Lear*, in a pre-Christian Britain. King Cymbeline's virtuous daughter Imogene is a Cordelia-figure called upon to suffer for the love she bears Posthumous, whose affection for her is corrupted by the Iago-like Iachimo. But unlike Lear's daughter or Othello's wife, Imogene survives through her disguise as the boy Fidele ("faith") and endures an apparent death. As is typical of the romances, pagan and Christian references imply the presence of a guiding divinity. Ironically, it is the Roman General Caius Lucius who comforts Fidele by alluding to the "fortunate fall" of Adam, which led to Christ's resurrection: "Some falls are means the happier to arise" (4.2.403). Instrumental in her success are two sons of Cymbeline who have been raised in the wild with their exiled kidnapper, Belarius. Like Duke Senior in the Forest of Arden in *As You Like It*, they live close to "divine Nature"

(4.2.170); their lives are marked by moral integrity and religious piety, even to praying "a morning's holy office" (3.3.4). Posthumous repents his distrust of Imogene in a brief speech summarizing the contrition, penance, and satisfaction that were central to the sacrament of pardon and absolution (Hemingway, 146). The play's most stunning theatrical effect, a *deus ex machina* designed to impress courtly audiences, is the descent of Jupiter, who predicts that Posthumous "shall be lord of Lady Imogen, / And happier much by his affliction made" (5.4.107–108). The lovers are reunited, Cymbeline weeps "holy water" on his daughter (5.5.269), and Posthumous forgives Iachimo with words that recall Christ's to the woman taken in adultery (John 8: 11): "Live and deal with others better" (5.5.419–420). Noting that Cymbeline ruled Britain during the lifetime of Jesus, Arthur C. Kirsch comments that "There is certainly a sense of Britain's baptism as a nation at the end of the play in its incorporation into Rome and into the peace that ushered in the birth of Christ" (161).

The Winter's Tale (1610–1611) has the quality of a fable told to pass a winter's evening, and it is perhaps the most lyrical and moving of the romances. The separation that opens the play is not geographical but emotional, as King Leontes is overcome by an irrational jealousy, assuming that his wife Hermione is pregnant by his childhood friend Polixenes. His inexplicably distorted outlook (his "affection" [1.2.138]) afflicts him like an innate sin. He imprisons her and, Herodlike, orders the newborn infant Perdita ("the lost") burned, then ignores a divine oracle proclaiming her innocence. Polixenes denies Leontes' accusation, saying it would make him another Judas, causing his "name / [to] Be yok'd with his that did betray the Best!" (1.2.419). Believing that "pow'rs divine / Behold our human actions" (3.2.28–29), Hermione rejects Leontes' condemnation. When his son dies he suddenly repents, convinced that "the heavens themselves / Do strike at my injustice" (3.2.145–146). Hermione's death is soon announced by Paulina, and Leontes vows to visit their tombs daily as penance for his delusion and impiety. Perdita, having been raised by shepherds, reappears 16 years later, a living testament to the power of "great creating Nature" (4.4.88), and falls in love with the son of Polixenes. Her scenes with the shepherds lend the play a strong pastoral element, with its implied return to an Edenic existence far from the king's madness; a dance of 12 satyrs heralds her coming joyful marriage with Florizel. In the final act, all gather to view Paulina's statue of the dead Hermione, who suddenly revives. This transformation, with clear echoes of the mythological story of Pygmalion, fuses the play's themes of the reproductive cycles of the natural world, the imitative powers of art, the new life granted by belief and forgiveness, and the joys of familial love. To accept this resurrection of Hermione is to believe in the recuperative powers of love; says Paulina, "It is requir'd / You do awake your faith" (5.3.94–95). Such a transformation—like the play itself—seems "monstrous to our human reason" (5.1.41), yet it is "almost a miracle" (4.4.534). Leontes, like King Lear, may not deserve such good fortune, but he receives an act of grace administered by two virtuous women who live to save him, unlike the tragic Cordelia who perished for her father's sake.

The most tightly constructed romance and the last play for which Shakespeare can claim full authorship is the *The Tempest* (1611). As postmodern critics have emphasized, it explores the results of political revolution and the problems of colonization on a remote island, but it also suggests the familiar patterns of personal metamorphosis and redemption that we expect from the final comedies. "Neglecting worldly ends" (1.2.89), Prospero unwittingly contributed to his own political overthrow 12 years before the start of the play by his brother Antonio, who put him and his infant daughter Miranda ("wonderful") to sea. They are blown ashore on an island to later encounter both the usurpers and Caliban (an anagram for "cannibal"), a native of the island and son of the witch Sycorax. Aided by the spirit Ariel, the magically powerful Prospero now has the challenge of governing more wisely than he had in Milan: to guide Miranda's adolescent love for Ferdinand, to administer justice to his usurpers, and to rule Caliban, who had threatened Miranda despite Prospero's efforts to "civilize" him. All of these imperfect characters, including Prospero, make the island, which is a magical place "full of noises, / Sounds and sweet airs, that give delight and hurt not" (3.2.135–136), as well as the site of past and present conflict, a microcosm of the potentials and pitfalls of the fallen world. Prospero eventually places his enemies at his mercy, but, with full knowledge of his own temptation to revenge, he withholds punishment and extends compassion:

> Though with their high wrongs I am strook to th' quick
> Yet, with my nobler reason, 'gainst my fury
> Do I take part. The rarer action is
> In virtue than in vengeance. They being penitent,
> The sole drift of my purpose doth extend
> Not a frown further. Go, release them, Ariel.
> My charms I'll break, their senses I'll restore
> And they shall be themselves. (5.1.25–32)

Prospero leaves the island, where "no man was his own" (5.1.213), and returns to Milan in humility: "what strength I have's mine own, / Which is most faint" (Epilogue, 2–3). The play's patterns of Christian imagery notwithstanding, it is Prospero's combination of strength with forgiveness, his willing relinquishment of power, and his recognition of his own weakness that mark him as a more Christian than Machiavellian ruler.

THE POEMS

In his own day, Shakespeare was as famous for his nondramatic works as for his plays. His most significant poems are *Venus and Adonis* (1593), *The Rape of Lucrece* (1594), *The Phoenix and the Turtle* (1601), and his *Sonnets* (1609). With the exception of *The Phoenix and the Turtle*, religious themes in these works are not as dominant as in many of the plays but are present as minor motifs. *Venus and Adonis* is Shakespeare's retelling of the mythological story of Venus's pursuit of the lovely Adonis. In the version of Ovid's *Metamorphoses* (Ovid was Shakespeare's favorite classical author), Venus succeeds in seducing the boy; in Shakespeare's version, she fails, and Adonis is killed by a boar while hunting. The poem is lushly beautiful, yet its meaning is elusive. Venus unabashedly flaunts her physical desire ("My flesh is soft and plump, my marrow burning" [142]), and at times she justifies her yearning as part of the natural procreative process, a theme prominent in the sonnets: "Seeds spring from seeds, and beauty breedeth beauty: Thou wast begot; to get [beget] it is thy duty" (167–168). But her real motive seems the immediate enjoyment of sexual pleasure rather than a loving relationship more lasting than simple erotic delight. Her sorrow over Adonis's death may imply an ironic Christian censure of a merely physical love. Conversely, the young man's death may be poetic justice for his unnatural resistance to natural desire, a resistance the noblemen in *Love's Labour's Lost* finally had the wisdom to reject. Dympna Callaghan, however, has argued that this epyllion or short epic employs Christian elements for their artistic, rather than religious, meaning. Focusing on the resemblance of the grieving Venus over the dead body of Adonis to Mary holding the dead Christ, she suggests that Shakespeare is employing "a Catholic aesthetic, if you will, with its Christian elements extracted" (42).

Whereas *Venus and Adonis* is erotically comic and undidactic, *The Rape of Lucrece*, drawn from a story in Ovid's *Fasti*, is tragic and moralistic. Lucrece, virtuous wife of Collatinus, is raped by the lustful Sextus Tarquinius (Tarquin) and then, though morally innocent yet shamed at having been violated, commits suicide. Though the early Christians Tertullian and St. Jerome regarded Lucrece as a model of female pagan morality, St. Augustine in his *City of God* "argued that since virtues are properties of the will and not the body, Lucretia was innocent of unchastity. But ironically, her sexual blamelessness rendered her suicide completely inexcusable. Augustine considered her a murderess who had taken her own life out of unchristian pride. By Shakespeare's time, therefore, Lucretia could be held up, variously, as a model of female propriety and as an example of pagan willfulness" (Maus, 515–516). Noting Brutus's comment, "Thy wretched wife mistook the matter so, / To slay herself, that should have slain her foe" (1826–1827), Don Cameron Allen believes that Shakespeare sided with Augustine. Shakespeare "felt that [her story] must be glossed in terms of Christian options. Lucrece should have defended herself to the death, or, having been forced, lived free of blame with a guiltless conscience" (91). Roy Battenhouse goes farther, asserting that Shakespeare "understands Lucrece's staged suicide as paganism's dark substitute for the Christian Passion story" (*Shakespearean Tragedy*, 25).

The Phoenix and the Turtle, first published within a collection of other bird poems, is a brief account of the love between the mythical phoenix, which sprang to life from its own ashes and thus became a resurrection symbol in medieval and Renaissance art, and the turtle dove, traditionally a symbol for faithfulness. Sometimes regarded as Shakespeare's only experiment in the highly allusive metaphysical style made popular by John Donne, this brief poem celebrates the completely loving union ("a mutual flame" 24) of these birds. To express the degree to which they become one creature in love, Shakespeare, according to J. V. Cunningham, employs the language of medieval scholastic philosophy ("essence") and the theology of the trinity to express their spiritual blending. H. Neville Davies finds that "the sequence of stanzas 4–6 corresponds exactly to the ordering of the Elizabethan Burial Service" (527).

Shakespeare's sonnets, composed during the 1590s and published a decade later, are his most notable nondramatic works. In the rather sketchy plot that ties these 154 sonnets together (the final two are not part of the narrative), the speaker addresses the first 126 poems to an attractive male friend, with numbers 1 through 17 encouraging the friend to marry and beget children. The young man is so admirable that he has also drawn the attention of a rival poet. Sonnets 127 through 152 include a "dark lady" (who has been introduced in the earlier section), for whom the speaker feels an overpowering physical desire, which arouses an equally overpowering disgust, and several sonnets also point toward a romance between this lady and the friend. The poems are a notorious mine for biographical speculation about Shakespeare himself, and numerous suggestions have been advanced to identify the true identities of the friend, the rival poet, the lady, and the exact nature of their relationships. It is safer to say that the emotions expressed within them are more valid than any biographical facts they may or may not suggest. The fragmentary narrative is less important than the speaker's meditations on such topics as art, death, love, time, and beauty. As with Shakespeare's works in general, Biblical allusions in the sonnets are not uncommon. Stephen Booth notes that sonnets 137–142 "all have vague and various likenesses to Proverbs 4: 20–27 (Bishops' Version, 1568)" on the avoidance of slander and evil behavior (490). But such allusions may serve ironic rather than obviously doctrinal purposes. Shakespeare, says Thomas P. Roche, Jr., is concerned in these poems with "the inappropriateness of his language to point us to unspoken realities" (428); the speaker "has been playing God throughout the sequence in promising immortality to the young man, a promise he cannot deliver" (429). Richard McCoy contends that, despite the sacrificial and Eucharistic imagery present in numbers 124–126, they (like *The Phoenix and the Turtle*) do not suggest an undying life after death.

Although a poetic immortality is emphasized in the sonnets, at least two of them do record the lived experience of spiritual struggle. Number 146 ("Poor soul, the centre of my sinful earth") presents a traditional medieval contrast between the tormented soul and its sinful, wasting body. It ends with the speaker's exhorting his soul to profit spiritually from the decay of the physical self and prepare for its own release through dying:

> Buy terms divine in selling hours of dross;
> Within be fed, without be rich no more.
> So shalt thou feed on death, that feeds on men,
> And death once dead, there's no more dying then. (11–14)

Number 129 ("Th'expense of spirit in a waste of shame") is an angry denunciation of the sin of lust, which the speaker seems to know only too well and for which he despises himself. His uncontrollable desire is "Past reason hunted, and no sooner had / Past reason hated as a swallowed bait / On purpose laid to make the taker mad" (7–9). Its final couplet could serve as the conclusion to an Elizabethan sermon: "All this the world well knows, yet none knows well / To shun the heaven that leads men to this hell" (13–14).

The strands of religion and spirituality to be found in Shakespeare's plays and poems link them intimately with his era, yet they also lend these works a universality that has made them appealing to centuries of readers. Shakespeare takes these concepts seriously, but he rarely takes them at face value; bishops in the history plays may or may not prove to be pillars of the faith, while unworthy tragic heroes can rise to heights of spiritual maturity. While the exact nature of Shakespeare's own beliefs will continue to be debated, his responsiveness to religious issues remains a central element of his artistry.

REFERENCES

Allen, D. C. "Some Observations on the *Rape of Lucrece*." *Shakespeare Survey* XV (1962): 89–98.

Andrews, John F. "Falling Love: The Tragedy of *Romeo and Juliet*." In *Romeo and Juliet: Critical Essays*. Ed. John F. Andrews. New York: Garland, 1993. 403–422.

Asquith, Clare. *Shadowplay: The Hidden Beliefs and Coded Politics of William Shakespeare*. New York: Public Affairs, 2005.

Auden, W. H. *The Dyer's Hand*. New York: Random House, 1962.

Baker, Christopher. "Ovid, Othello, and the Pontic Scythians." In Paula Harms Payne, ed. *A Search for Meaning: Critical Essays on Early Modern Literature*. New York: Peter Lang, 2004. 61–80.

———. "The Christian Context of Falstaff's 'Finer End.'" *Explorations in Renaissance Culture* 12 (1986): 68–86.

Barton, Anne. "Intro." In *Twelfth Night*. *The Riverside Shakespeare*, 2nd ed. Ed. G. Blakemore Evans, et al. Boston, MA: Houghton Mifflin, 1997. 437–441.

Battenhouse, Roy. "Falstaff as Parodist and Perhaps Holy Fool." *PMLA* 90 (1975): 32–52.

———. "Religion in *King John*: Shakespeare's View." *Connotations* I.2 (1991): 140–149.

———. *Shakespearean Tragedy: Its Art and Its Christian Premises*. Bloomington: Indiana University Press, 1969.

Bevington, David, ed. *The Complete Works of William Shakespeare*. 5th ed. New York: Pearson Longman, 2004.

Bloom, Harold. *The Western Canon*. New York: Harcourt Brace, 1994.

Booth, Stephen, ed. *Shakespeare's Sonnets*. New Haven, CT: Yale University Press, 1977.

Bryant, J. A. *Hippolyta's View: Some Christian Aspects of Shakespeare's Plays*. Lexington: University of Kentucky Press, 1961.

Callaghan, Dympna. "The Book of Changes in a Time of Change: Ovid's *Metamorphoses* in Post-Reformation England and *Venus and Adonis*." *A Companion to Shakespeare's Works. Volume IV: The Poems, Problem Comedies, Late Plays*. Ed. Richard Dutton and Jean E. Howard. Oxford, UK: Blackwell, 2003. 27–45.

Cohen, Walter, ed. *Othello*. *The Norton Shakespeare Based on the Oxford Edition*. New York: Norton, 1997. 2091–2174.

Cornford, F. M. *Origin of Attic Comedy*. Ed. Theodore H. Gaster. Gloucester, MA: Peter Smith, 1968.

Cunningham, J. V. "'Essence' and The Phoenix and Turtle." *ELH* 19.4 (December 1952), 265–276.

Cox, John D. "Was Shakespeare a Christian, and If So, What Kind of Christian Was He?" *Christianity and Literature* 55.4 (Summer 2006): 539–566.

Danby, John F. *Poets on Fortune's Hill: Studies in Sidney, Spenser, Shakespeare, Beaumont and Fletcher.* London, UK: Faber, 1952.

Davies, H. Neville. "The Phoenix and Turtle: Requiem and Rite." *Review of English Studies* XLVI, No. 184 (1995): 525–529.

Dollimore, Jonathan. *Radical Tragedy: Religion, Ideology and Power in the Drama of Shakespeare and his Contemporaries.* Durham, NC: Duke University Press, 2004.

Elton, W. R. *King Lear and the Gods.* San Marino, CA: Huntington Library, 1966.

Evett, David. *Discourses of Service in Shakespeare's England.* New York: Palgrave Macmillan, 2005.

Felperin, Howard. *Shakespearean Romance.* Princeton, NJ: Princeton University Press, 1972.

Fernie, Ewan. *Spiritual Shakespeares.* London, UK: Routledge, 2005.

Fielding, Henry. *Tom Jones.* Ed. Fredson Bowers. Vol. 1. Middletown, CT: Wesleyan University Press, 1975.

Frye, Northrop. *Anatomy of Criticism: Four Essays.* Princeton, NJ: Princeton University Press, 1957.

Frye, Roland M. *Shakespeare and Christian Doctrine.* Princeton, NJ: Princeton University Press, 1963.

Garber, Marjorie. *Shakespeare After All.* New York: Pantheon, 2004.

Greenblatt, Stephen, ed. *Richard III. The Norton Shakespeare Based on the Oxford Edition.* New York: Norton, 1997. 507–600.

———. *Will in the World: How Shakespeare Became Shakespeare.* New York: Norton, 2004.

Groves, Beatrice. *Texts and Traditions: Religion in Shakespeare 1592–1604.* Oxford, UK: Oxford University Press, 2007.

Hamilton, Donna B. "Shakespeare and Religion." In *The Shakespearean International Yearbook 1: Where are we now in Shakespearean studies?* Ed. W. R. Elton and John M. Mucciolo. Aldershot: Ashgate, 1999. 187–202.

Hawkes, Terence, ed. *Coleridge's Writings on Shakespeare.* New York: Capricorn, 1959.

Hemingway, Samuel, ed. *Cymbeline.* New Haven, CT: Yale University Press, 1924.

Hinman, Charlton, ed. *Timon of Athens. The Complete Pelican Shakespeare.* General editor, Alfred Harbage. Baltimore, MD: Pengiun, 1969. 1136–1168.

Holderness, Graham. *Shakespeare: The Histories.* New York: St. Martin's, 2000.

Hooker, Richard. *Of the Laws of Ecclesiastical Polity.* 2 volumes. New York: Dutton, 1907. Rpt. 1965.

Hunt, Maurice. *Shakespeare's Religious Allusivness: Its Play and Tolerance.* Aldershot, UK: Ashgate, 2004.

Hunter, Robert Grams. *Shakespeare and the Comedy of Forgiveness.* New York: Columbia University Press, 1965.

———. *Shakespeare and the Mystery of God's Judgements.* Athens: University of Georgia Press, 1976.

Kaula, David. "'Let us be sacrificers:' Religious Motifs in *Julius Caesar*." *Shakespeare Studies* 14 (1981): 197–214.

Kirsch, Arthur C. *Shakespeare and the Experience of Love.* Cambridge, MA: Cambridge University Press, 1981.

Knapp, Jeffrey. *Church, Nation and Theatre in Renaissance England*. Chicago, IL: University of Chicago Press, 2002.

Joseph, B. L. *Shakespeare's Eden: The Commonwealth of England, 1558–1629*. New York: Barnes and Noble, 1971.

Lewis, C. S. *The Four Loves*. New York: Harcourt, 1991.

Marlowe, Christopher. *The Jew of Malta. Drama of the English Renaissance*. Ed. Russell A. Fraser and Norman Rabkin. 2 vols. New York: Macmillan, 1976. I, 264–294.

Marotti, Arthur. "Shakespeare and Catholicism." In *Theatre and Religion: Lancastrian Shakespeare*. Ed. Richard Dutton, Alison Findlay, and Richard Wilson. Manchester, UK: Manchester University Press, 2003. 218–241.

Marx, Stephen. *Shakespeare and the Bible*. New York: Oxford University Press, 2000.

Maus, Katherine Eisaman, ed. *The Rape of Lucrece. The Norton Shakespeare Based on the Oxford Edition*. New York: Norton, 1997. 635–682.

McCoy, Richard C. "Love's Martyrs: Shakespeare's 'Phoenix and Turtle' and the sacrificial sonnets." In *Religion and Culture in Renaissance England*. Ed. Claire McEachern and Debora Shuger. Cambridge, MA: Cambridge University Press, 1997. 188–208.

Milward, Peter. "The Religious Dimension of *King Lear*." *Shakespeare Studies* (Japan) 8 (1969–1970): 48–73.

Noble, Richmond P. *Shakespeare's Biblical Knowledge and Use of the Book of Common Prayer as Exemplified in the Plays of the First Folio*. London: SPCK and New York: Macmillan, 1935.

Poole, Kristin. *Radical Religion from Shakespeare to Milton*. Cambridge, MA: Cambridge University Press, 2006.

Roche, Thomas P. *Petrarch and the English Sonnet Sequences*. New York: AMS Press, 1989.

Rowse, A. L. *Shakespeare the Man*. Revised ed. New York: St. Martin's, 1988.

Sams, Eric. *The Real Shakespeare: Retrieving the Early Years, 1564–1594*. New Haven, CT: Yale University Press, 1995.

Santyana, George. *Interpretations of Poetry and Religion*. Ed. William G. Hozberger and Herman J. Saatkamp. Cambridge, MA: MIT Press, 1990.

Schoenbaum, Samuel. *William Shakespeare: A Documentary Life*. New York: Oxford University Press, 1975.

Scoufos, Alice-Lyle. "The *Paradiso Terrestre* and the Testing of Love in *As You Like It*." *Shakespeare Studies* 14 (1981): 215–227.

Shapiro, James. *A Year in the Life of William Shakespeare: 1599*. New York: HarperCollins, 2005.

Shaheen, Naseeb. *Biblical References in Shakespeare's Plays*. Newark: University of Delaware Press, 1999.

———. *Biblical References in Shakespeare's Tragedies*. Newark: University of Delaware Press, 1987.

Simmons, J. L. *Shakespeare's Pagan World: The Roman Tragedies*. Charlottesville: University Press of Virginia, 1973.

Spivack, Bernard. *Shakespeare and the Allegory of Evil*. New York: Columbia University Press. 1958.

Stitt, Peter. *The World's Hieroglyphic Beauty: Five American Poets*. Athens: University of Georgia Press, 1985.

Sypher, Wylie. "The Meanings of Comedy." In *Comedy*. Ed. Wylie Sypher. New York: Doubleday, 1956. 193–258.

Tippens, Darryl. "Shakespeare and the Prodigal Son Tradition." *Explorations in Renaissance Culture* 14 (1988): 57–77.

Watson, Robert N. "*Othello* as protestant propaganda." In *Religion and Culture in Renaissance England*. Ed. Claire McEachern and Debora Shuger. Cambridge, MA: Cambridge University Press, 1997. 234–257.

Watterson, William. "*As You Like It* as Christian Pastoral." In *Shakesepare's Christian Dimension*. Ed. Roy Battenhouse. Bloomington: Indiana University Press, 1994. 117–122.

White, R. S., ed. *Hazlitt's Criticism of Shakespeare: A Selection*. Lewiston, NY: The Edwin Mellen Press, 1996.

Wickham, Glynne. "Hell-Castle and its Door-Keeper." *Shakespeare Survey* 19 (1966): 68–74.

Wood, Michael. *Shakespeare*. New York: Basic Books, 2003.

4

RELIGION IN PERFORMANCE

The nineteenth-century essayist and critic Charles Lamb was convinced that Shakespeare's greatest plays (most notably *King Lear*) were incapable of being performed onstage because he felt that their full meaning could never be captured in a theatrical production as fully as it could in the mind of the reader. Although Lamb's view never gained critical favor—or theatrical favor either, as the rich performance histories of the plays attest—it is true that any given production of a play will necessarily be the result of the combined vision of those who have produced, directed, and acted in it and that differing productions will result in different "interpretations." In this sense, every production is thus an adaptation of the play Shakespeare wrote rather than a precise reenactment of an unvarying dramatic event that has been fixed for all time. Directors will shape their productions just as Shakespeare molded and adapted his sources in the creation of his own works. Those performances were influenced as well by the acting style, stage design, and other factors of his own contemporary theatre, as studies such as J. L. Styan's *Perspectives on Shakespeare in Performance* (2000) have documented. As H. R. Coursen notes, "productions do not strive to be 'perfect' or 'definitive'—they freely admit that they are partial and transitory manifestations of an ongoing energy known as script" (43). Orson Welles once quipped that "every single way of playing and staging Shakespeare—as long as the way is effective—is right" (27). The actor Simon Russell Beale echoes this view when he says, speaking of acting from a "cut down" text: "With Shakespeare, quite simply, doing less than the 'full' text is fine if the production that results has its own internal coherence" (Beale 154).

The emphasis given to the religious aspects of a Shakespearean play will also reflect the choices that actors and directors make about the role of those spiritual elements it is thought to express. Many of Shakespeare's plays reveal his use of motifs and character types from medieval morality and mystery plays, so that these plays will contain a religious character that is, so to speak, "embedded" within them. Prince Hal's references to Falstaff in terms of the medieval Vice figure, Richard III's comparison of himself to the vice Iniquity, or Richard II's comparison of his enemies to Judas instantly led Elizabethan audiences to compare these characters to figures whom they resemble in a spiritual way, figures whom audiences themselves may well have recalled from the late medieval plays that persisted in England into the 1560s and 1570s. Alan Dessen, among others, has explored this connection in *Shakespeare and the Late Moral Plays* (1986), finding this influence extending into *Antony and Cleopatra*, *Measure for Measure* and *Troilus and Cressida*. Similarly, Sandra Pyle has argued that the holy fool, a figure from medieval religious drama, contributes to the characterization of Hamlet, Lear's fool, and Feste, among other characters. And Shakesepare's final romances are often marked by language with strongly theological overtones; they present religious themes in ways that need not necessarily look back to the earlier religious drama for a dramatic source, but rely instead on such mythic patterns as the separation and reunion of loved ones, the reformation of harmful characters into virtuous personalities, or the endurance of suffering that leads to a redemptive resolution.

Because of their engagement with the broadest human questions of experience and meaning, Shakespeare's tragedies offer unique opportunities for examining the ways in which religion is treated in performance. This chapter will explore some varieties of religious experience in modern stage and film productions of four tragedies. The films are evidence not only of Shakespeare's continuing influence upon popular culture, but also of the power of this medium to disseminate his dramatic examination of religious issues. Modern audiences are avid consumers of visual media; according to George Barna, "The world of entertainment and mass communications—through television, radio, contemporary music, movies, magazines, art, video games and pop literature—is indisputably the most extensive and influential theological training system in the world" (188). Although "theological training" is too narrow a phrase to describe what Shakespeare was attempting in his work, the theatre of his day was the most popular form of Elizabethan mass media. The complex relationship between Shakespeare's stage and the modern film invites a closer study of religion as it emerges in filmed versions of his plays.

Orson Welles's 1948 film of *Macbeth* presents that play as a collision of sinister pagan belief and medieval Christianity, emphasized through the added character of the Holy Father. Grigori Kozintsev's *King Lear* takes a social approach to that play, placing its religious concerns within the historical context of Lear's kingdom. The world of Peter Brook's cinematic *King Lear* is seemingly devoid of any supernatural dimension, yet its characters appeal to a divinity whose presence can only be found in the midst of absurdity and the language of negative theology; if any god is present in this film, it must be sought within mystery, paradox, and the grotesque, all of which are suggested through Brook's gripping visual style. Far different from Brook's minimalist spiritual experience is Baz Luhrmann's *Romeo + Juliet*, which is flooded with the religious imagery of Hispanic Catholicism combined with the crass commercial values of contemporary urban life. John Caird's National Theatre production of *Hamlet* presented a sympathetic and theologically aware tragic hero whose acute religious sensibility lent pathos to his efforts to fulfill the charge given him by the ghost of his father. Each of these productions represents an individual conception of its play, and each film is a unique attempt to translate the play from a theatrical medium to a cinematic one. Each production also offers a rich field for discussion (beyond the scope of this chapter) of the differences between an *interpretation* of Shakespeare's work and an *adaptation* of it (Friedman).

MACBETH

In 1948 the flamboyant Hollywood actor and director Orson Welles completed his film of *Macbeth*, based upon his earlier version of the play with an all-black cast produced in 1935 and set in Haiti—the so-called "voodoo Macbeth." The shadowy, brooding film was shot in just three weeks at Republic Pictures, a B-movie studio known more for cowboy films and gangster movies, from whose *film noir* techniques Welles's film borrows, along with elements of the horror film (Davies, 88). The film displays an expressionistic cinematic style, with strong use of shadow, frequent high- and low-angle camera shots, and dissolving images, all characteristic of Welles' unique directorial approach, yet insufficient to make this film a critical or popular success in its own day. The film's cinematography invites comparison with Peter Brook's *King Lear,* but the latter film handles its techniques more expertly. Though praised by French critics when it appeared, Welles's film "ought to be judged as an experiment" (Mullin, 138), an inventive conception that never really materialized on the screen, though certain features are now regarded as noteworthy. For example, Welles has been praised for the way in which he links the design of Macbeth's castle to the thane's psyche. Seen in exterior long shots across a misty, shadowed landscape, it is a huge mountaintop structure containing a warren of damp, subterranean rooms. The scenes within these chambers, often shot from a low angle to emphasize the confining ceiling and walls, suggest the oppressive dimensions of Macbeth's psychological state, "cabin'd, cribbed, confin'd, bound in / To saucy doubts and fears" (3.4.23–24). The strong use of shadowing conveys Macbeth's submission to occult forces. Anthony Davies sees this film as a clear influence upon the later Shakespeare films of Akira Kurosawa and Grigori Kozintsev (83–84).

Other features are less successful. Welles required that the actors mimic Scottish accents and then dub their dialogue to the film, which led to a muddied soundtrack. Macbeth's furred helmet in the opening scene suggests that he might be a Mongol warrior rather than a Scottish chieftan, and his oddly-shaped royal crowns lend him a comically alien appearance at odds with his tragic role. Welles said that he viewed the "main point" of his production as

> the struggle between the old and new religions. I saw the witches as representatives of a Druidical pagan religion suppressed by Christianity—itself a new arrival. That's why the long prayer of Saint Michael (not in Shakespeare at all)—that's why the screen is constantly choked with Celtic crosses. These people are holding off not just the forces of darkness but the old religion, which has been forced underground. The witches are the priestesses. Nobody ever paid any attention to that. The whole device of the picture is based on the struggle between two religious systems. (Welles and Bogdanovich, 214–215)

His religious take on the plot is underscored with his opening narration (later cut in the film's final version):

> Our story is laid in Scotland—ancient Scotland, savage, half-lost in the mist that hangs between recorded history and the time of legends. The cross itself is newly arrived here. Plotting against Christian law and order are the agents of Chaos, priests of hell and magic; sorcerers and witches. Their tools are ambitious men. This is the story of such a man, and of his wife. A brave soldier, he hears from witches a prophecy of future greatness and on this cue, murders his way up to a tyrant's throne, only to go down hated and in blood at the end of it all. (qtd. Davies, 87)

While this introductory statement may offer audiences a theme to cling to, it also tends to flatten the play into an allegorical battle of good versus evil in "a Manichean universe" (Coursen, 44), diminishing the complexity of the central tragic character. This spiritual clash is visually symbolized by the contrasting staffs carried by the witches and the Christians. "The film's principal iconic device opposes the spindly forked twigs of the witches—a symbol of their demonism—to the crucifixes of the newly converted Scots" (Pearlman, 251). In Shakespeare's text, while Macbeth is certainly aware of heaven and hell (cf. 2.1.63–64; 3.1.140–141), he chooses to "jump the life to come" (1.7.7), dismissing the moral consequences of his actions. The question of whether he allows himself to be persuaded to commit regicide by the witches' prophecy, or instead believes that they are only confirming those "black and deep desires" (1.4.51) that he has long harbored, is a richly ambiguous problem posed by Shakespeare. Macbeth seems to exist apart from both heaven and hell in a kind of irreligious state that partakes of neither, a spiritual no man's land revealed when he admits that he could not say "Amen" to the grooms' blessing (2.2.26). Macbeth's ambiguous moral stance in the play—knowingly siding with evil, despising himself for it, and yet continuing in it—is one example of the equivocation that marks all of the tragedies (McCoy, 183). Shakespeare refuses to offer us morally neat "either/or" situations, a stance summed up by the porter in act 2, scene 3, who famously refers to "an equivocator, that could swear in both the scales against either scale" (2.3.8–9). This statement likely alludes to an Elizabethan Jesuit tract that advocated the making of carefully qualified statements by captured Catholics to protect their lives. But Welles avoids an equivocating, spiritually complex Macbeth, giving us instead a troubled but recognizable "sinner" who is clearly in the grip of the witches' evil. Not surprisingly, the porter's scene in his film omits any reference to the equivocator. The porter replaces it with Sir Toby Belch's comic complaint about indigestion from *Twelfth Night*: "A plague o' these pickle herring!" (1.5.120–121).

Welles's own religious background seems reflected in this production. "I try to be a Christian," he told an interviewer in 1982, but "I don't pray really, because I don't want to bore God" (Brady, 576). The film's sharply contrasting moral values reflect his personal dislike of spiritual skepticism or religious ambiguity: "I have a great love and respect for religion, great love and respect for atheism.

What I hate is agnosticism, people who do not choose" ("Religious Affiliation," 2). Prominent in the film is a doll of Macbeth made by the witches from mud taken from their cauldron, clearly suggesting that the thane is a pawn of what Lady Macbeth called "metaphysical powers"(1.5.29), his life dominated by sinister forces he cannot control. Macbeth's immersion in evil is made obvious as the witches lift the dripping doll from their bubbling pot and place a tiny crown on its head, later to be violently struck off at the end of the film. The addition of the doll to the film may spring from Welles's own recollections of the ritualistic practices of his paternal grandmother, Mary Head Welles, who in his opinion seems to have been a kind of witch. Welles was convinced that she "had put a curse on his parents" (Brady, 3–4) and practiced sorcery on the top floor of her house in Kenosha, Wisconsin, where he had found dead birds and a bloody altar with a pentagram. He also claimed that she had performed "satanic rites" at his father's death in 1930 (Brady, 14). His memories of his grandmother likely contributed as well to his conception of his all-black production of the play that emphasized native African religion. When Welles staged this production of *Macbeth* at the Lafayette Theatre in Harlem in 1935, he felt that, in Frank Brady's words, "the African nature gods worshiped by voodoo would make a close parallel to some of the ghostly themes found in *Macbeth* . . . He hoped that the voodoo chants, dramatic lighting, strong winds, and lighting and thunder would transform *Macbeth* into a Shakespearean spectacle that would evoke both fear and awe in the hearts of the audience" (82–83).

The demonic religious presence that the doll injects into the film is balanced and finally overcome by the much larger role given to another non-Shakespearean element added by Welles, the figure of the Holy Father. While this character makes clear the clash of spiritual forces Welles finds in the play, it is not a satisfactory addition to the film's artistry. As Anthony Davies points out, "While it is true that Welles introduces the Christian stance both in the spoken prologue and visually, there is not sufficient evidence to show that he really knew how to integrate it" (96). Played by Alan Napier, the Holy Father's Old Testament persona is undercut somewhat by his long, grey braids, but his presence symbolizes the authority of the church that Macbeth has rejected, having conjured the witches to "untie the winds and let them fight / Against the churches" (4.1.52–53). The Holy Father speaks lines taken from the parts of Ross, Lennox, the Old Man, Malcolm, the Messenger, Banquo, and even Macbeth himself, all of his speeches calling attention in some fashion to Macbeth's evil deeds or the carnage that results from them. We first meet him at the opening of the film as Macbeth, Banquo, and he confront the witches; after their brief exchange with Macbeth, the Holy Father drives them off by gesturing at them with his staff topped with a Celtic cross. (The witches carry their own pagan staffs, topped with curious V-shaped sticks.) We next meet him at the execution of the Thane of Cawdor, an event only reported in Shakespeare's play, as he offers a Latin blessing over the rebel just before his beheading. This inserted scene provides a visual foreshadowing of Macbeth's own beheading at the end of the play.

More impressive is the Holy Father's role after Duncan has arrived at Macbeth's castle. Welles emphasizes the contrast between the evil designs of Macbeth and his wife and the saintly presence of the king by having the murderous couple discuss their impending regicide, while the Father simultaneously leads the king's retinue in prayer. As Macbeth considers that the king's "virtues / Will plead like angels, trumpet-tongued against / The deep damnation of his taking-off" (1.7.18–20), the king's men light candles while the Father leads them in the prayer to St. Michael: "St. Michael the archangel, be our safeguard against the wiles and wickedness of the devil. Do thou, O prince of the heavenly host, by thy divine power, thrust into hell Satan and the other evil spirits who roam the world seeking the ruin of souls." Welles here borrows a prayer said to have been composed by Pope Leo XIII during his papacy (1878–1903), after the loss of the Papal States to the Italian army left only the Vatican as a sovereign church territory. Leo ordered the prayer to be said after mass, a practice that continued until 1964. The political context in which the prayer was instituted accords with the film's portrayal of the attempt by the Holy Father (one of the pope's actual ceremonial titles) to protect Duncan's kingdom from usurpation. He next asks the assembled men, "Dost thou renounce Satan? And all his works? And all his pomp?" To each question, they answer in unison, "I do renounce him." Unlike the more recent prayer to St. Michael, these questions and answers are a slightly abbreviated version of part of the church's baptismal service known as the "renunciation of the devil" and were in use as early as the second century. Though they are not part of Shakespeare's play, his audiences would have recognized them for they appear in the rite of public baptism in the 1549 Anglican Book of Common Prayer. The Holy Father is not baptizing Duncan's men, but he is renewing their dedication to oppose the as yet unknown force of evil in the kingdom, which the audience, in the moment of dramatic irony created by Welles's juxtaposition, can easily identify as Macbeth. Welles himself said that his Shakespeare films were "variations" on the plays (qtd. McBride, 109); his addition of this character to the cast clearly crosses the line from interpretation to adaptation, but his consistent thematic purpose is clear.

The Holy Father next comes upon Macbeth in Duncan's chamber immediately after the king's death has been discovered. In a telling closeup, he glares silently at the thane with a penetrating look of suspicion before leaving. When Donalbain asks, "What is amiss?" it is the Father, not Lennox, who replies, "You are, and do not know't." When Malcom inquires who the murderer is, the Father also replies, "Those of his chamber, as it seem'd, had done't" pausing heavily on the middle phrase as a verbal cue back to his previous glance at Macbeth. He appears later, in place of the Messenger, to warn Macduff's wife to flee with her children, and after they have been slaughtered he carries the news to Macduff, speaking the lines originally given to Ross. This scene is especially symbolic, as it is played out beneath a huge Celtic stone cross that dominates the background. As Robert F. Willson, Jr. notes, "this symbol complements the cross atop Holy Father's staff, driving home the point that Scotland under Macbeth is hell, while England is ruled by a Christlike king" (136). The fact that Macduff is given the tragic news by a priest in front of a massive symbol of faith implies that this crime has not been ignored by providence and that a divine justice will finally be meted out to the perpetrator.

The Holy Father's end comes as, with cross in hand, he approaches Macbeth's castle at the head of the English forces led by Macduff and Malcolm. Both of their helmets are topped with crosses, a needless reminder at this point in the film of their spiritual virtue. Atop the battlements and gripping his pronged staff of authority suggesting the witches' V-shaped staffs, Macbeth defies the army with his famous boast that "Our castle's strength will laugh a siege to scorn" (5.5.2–3). He then hurls his staff down, impaling the heart of the Holy Father, an action that "enforces the thematic message that Macbeth has become a Herod, the murderer of innocents and enemy of the Church" (Willson, 137). Having murdered King Duncan, his earthly lord, Macbeth has now murdered the earthly representative of the heavenly lord he has chosen to reject. He and Macduff shortly begin their final duel, but just as Macduff swings the fatal swordstroke, Welles cuts quickly to an image of the witches' doll. We see its crowned head swiftly lopped off and then we quickly jump back to the castle wall where Macbeth's head now rests atop the pikestaff of Macduff, who declares "The time is free"(5.9.21).

Despite the cinematic and religious attention Welles pays to the Holy Father, this character must be judged an oversimplified distraction from the more absorbing moral dilemmas that Shakespeare had originally crafted. Michael Mullin speaks for most modern commentators when he says that "the great discrepancy between what the Holy Father is meant to be and what he looks like—an interfering, greasy prelate—makes Welles' idea ludicrous, a grotesque caricature of the Christian sanctity he is meant to embody" (141). The only moral goodness in the film thus seems contrived and forced. "Despite the Holy Father, the Christian symbols, and the baptismal rites, we never see anything like the world of justice and heroism that Shakespeare embodies in Duncan and his court, later in Malcolm and the English court" (Mullin, 144). Throughout the production, the roles the Holy Father is given by Welles are consistently those of guardian, protector, pastor, and conscience; although the nation has lost its king, Welles seems to be saying, it still retains a spiritual witness as long as the Father remains alive. But the intrusiveness of this character leads Michael Anderegg to conclude that Welles's conception backfired: "That Alan Napier's Holy Father, the object of much ridicule, seems ineffective and even sinister, is precisely the point. Christianity is not offered by the film as a positive alternative to the old religion but rather as an equally oppressive system, itself collaborative with savagery [the execution of Cawdor]" (88–89).

Welles's later movie production of *Othello* (1952) also cast the tragic hero as someone who has forsaken Christianity. "My plan," he said, "was to show much more of the corruption of the Christian Venetian world—this world of what Othello called 'goats and monkeys'" (Welles, 224). Of the play's conclusion he noted, "Othello is so blasted at the end that guilt is really too small an emotion. Anyway, he's not a Christian—that's central to the character. And Shakespeare was very, very aware of who was a Christian and who wasn't . . . " (Welles, 234).

Here again we see Welles's conviction that Shakespeare must have shared his own preference for seeing religious issues in starkly contrasting rather than complex terms. Welles's opinions were controversial, but he was never in doubt about his own views. Not surprisingly, he felt that Shakespeare "would have made a great movie writer" (Welles, 228). Only Welles could have praised Shakespeare by comparing the Bard to himself, but Samuel Crowl has stated that "Welles was the first great postmodern reader of Shakespeare, straddling like a colossus the territory between Twain's King and Duke and Derrida" (52). Welles's productions were not always successful, but they were unmistakably original. In Crowl's opinion "the charge that his manipulation of Shakesepare's text in *Macbeth* and especially in *Othello* and *Chimes at Midnight* was an act of self-aggrandizement is a stale misreading of his achievement" (54).

KING LEAR

King Lear has long provoked discussion about the nature of its religious themes. Its characters' references to "the gods" are not merely passionate outbursts uttered in moments of pain or excitement but convey the presence—at times only tentatively perceived by the characters—of a divinity whose "canons" are far less clear than they are to Hamlet yet with whom these characters retain an intermittent relationship. The bloodily nihilistic world of Macbeth, who "does murther sleep" (2.2.33) is not that of Lear who, echoing Psalm 4: 8, can finally say, "I'll pray, and then I'll sleep" (3.4.27). The setting of the play in pre-Christian Britain renders the precise nature of its deities obscure, yet its characters display moral and spiritual traits familiar to Shakespearean and modern audiences. The play is replete with "fallen" figures who portray a variety of human imperfection: the proud, selfish, and sexually predatory children Regan, Goneril, and Edmund; the smugly ignorant Gloucester; and the tyrannical, petty Lear himself. In contrast are the examples of virtuous humanity, each of whom suffers for the sake of a higher allegiance than self-satisfaction: Lear's loyal servant Kent, Gloucester's faithful son Edgar, and Lear's loving daughter Cordelia. The evil children suffer death resulting from their own "sins" of self-seeking, while the two ignorant fathers live long enough to undergo a conversion, Gloucester recognizing the genuine love of his mistrusted son and Lear willing to kneel for forgiveness before the daughter he finally calls "a soul in bliss" (4.7.45). But the loving characters must endure suffering as the price of showing their love. Edgar undergoes an assumed madness, which comes close to being all too real, and Cordelia ultimately dies as a sacrifice to the chaos that has swept over Lear's kingdom. Kent is so saddened by Lear's death that he chooses suicide.

The impact of this play derives from its ability to blend these religious implications with an insistent emotional reality, confronting us with a succession of inescapable reversals and painful epiphanies. The characters are not merely one-dimensional figures who illustrate a moral point; they are suffering people who must meet what Hamlet called "the thousand natural shocks that flesh is heir to" (3.1.61–62). So overwhelming was the effect of this play on the eighteenth-century critic Samuel Johnson that after his first reading of it, he avoided the play for years until he came to write his famous *Prefaces to Shakespeare* in 1765. Johnson did not avoid the play because he felt that its tragedy was too implausible but, rather, because its shocking enactment of the evil potential of human nature was so profoundly true. Still more provocative was the play's suggestion, certainly contradictory to Johnson's Anglican faith, that a deity might permit such gratuitous agonies as Gloucester's blinding for no apparent purpose.

Johnson favored Nahum Tate's revision of Shakespeare's play, a version that first appeared in 1681. It was to become the only version of the play acted on the English stage for the next century and a half. Tate softened the probing questions of Shakespeare's version, producing a "well-made" play that ends happily and thus greatly diminishes the profound spiritual questioning posed in the original text. In his reworking of Shakespeare's play, which he considered "a Heap of Jewels, unstrung, and unpolish'd" (Tate, 1), Tate eliminates the death of Cordelia and instead has her marry Gloucester's good son Edgar; both of them then proceed to rule Lear's kingdom. Gloucester, though blinded, also remains alive, as does Lear, who invites his loyal courtier Kent (who remains in the kingdom) to "gently pass our short Reserves of Time / In calm Reflections on our Fortunes past" (5.5.148–149). Gone is Lear's anguished lament over Cordelia's death: "Why should a dog, a horse, a rat, have life / And thou no life at all?" (5.3.307–308). The religious implications of Shakespeare's tragic ending are drastically altered by the reassuring survival of these characters, as well as by the obvious spectacle of virtue rewarded instead of being subjected to a shocking fate. As Tate has Edgar tell Cordelia in the play's closing lines:

Thy bright Example shall convince the World
(Whatever Storms of Fortune are decreed)
That Truth and Vertue shall at last succeed. (5.5.158–160)

Tate's revision met the wishes of his contemporaries such as Johnson and Arthur Murphy, who observed of Shakespeare's original ending: "[P]erhaps after all the heart piercing sensations which we have before endured through the whole piece it would be too much to see this actually performed on the stage . . . " (qtd. Bate and Jackson, 83). Tate upheld poetic justice in which goodness is rewarded and evil punished, restoring the audience's confidence in a predictable providence with neat plot solutions instead of disturbing them with unsettling challenges to God's loving governance of the world. Peter Womack has suggested that the questions and inconsistencies in Shakespeare's version were replaced according to Tate's conviction that the story would be more "polish'd" if it possessed an overriding purposefulness (98). However, Tate's imposition of a more rational clarity upon the action obscures any sense of the play's original "transcendence" (101) and the possibility that its events might disclose some unexpected spiritual meaning. Womack notes, for example, that Shakespeare's Cordelia "does not inhabit the probable world" of readily grasped motives that Tate prefers (103). Of six original references to her that stress her symbolic religious importance (especially as one who "redeems nature from the general curse" [4.6.206]), Tate retains only Lear's statement, "Thou art a soul in bliss."

While Tate accomplished a version that satisfied the sentimental and aesthetic demands of eighteenth-century audiences, and likewise a more rationalistic Anglicanism that tended to be suspicious of the mystical, he nevertheless removed an aspect of the play that would later gain importance among Romantic audiences and critics in the mid-nineteenth century, when his version gradually faded from the stage. He omitted the details, for example, that make Gloucester into a character resembling what Womack calls "the stage image of a saint," "both a kind of martyr and a kind of ascetic, moving via a spectacular miracle and an obscurely purgative process to a death which is also a blissful reunion." In Womack's view, Tate ignores the fact that Shakespeare appears to be "reinventing the religious drama which the English Reformation had just brought to an end" and, like Johnson, Tate suppresses "the sacred dimension of early modern theatre" (104). For those familiar with Shakespeare's play, it would be clear that by removing the "distasteful" portions Tate had also removed the thorny religious dilemmas that give Shakespeare's text its driving moral energy. Like a photographic negative that reverses light and dark, Tate's version ironically alerts us to the play's inherent religious themes by replacing their darker passages with a brighter, more reassuring design. His conception of a universe in which poetic justice prevails reflects a confident eighteenth-century optimism about God's dealings with mankind. However, for modern audiences the play's tidy construction, like the fig leaves on a medieval Adam and Eve, only calls attention to what it hides. The play interests us today more for the skill with which Tate has erased the play's original dark spirituality than for the neat resolutions he offers in its place.

Just over three centuries after Tate's version of *King Lear* appeared, the Russian director Grigori Kozintsev brought out his film version in 1967. Unlike the more deeply skeptical movie by Peter Brook that followed four years later, Kozintsev emphasizes the common people of Lear's kingdom at key points throughout his production, as if to remind us that this is a play about the trials of an entire nation, not merely its royal family. Nevertheless, the film contains several details suggesting that, despite the director's Marxist reading of this bleakest of Shakespearean tragedies, the action still retains some Christian implications. As the film opens, a long establishing shot presents a line of bedraggled peasants, some crippled and all ill-clothed, slowly trudging across a barren, rock-strewn landscape towards Lear's enormous mountaintop fortress. As the camera tracks them across the terrain, a boulder carved with a Celtic-style image, possibly of the face of Christ, emerges in the foreground. In contrast to the blatant Christian symbolism of Welles's *Macbeth*, such religious references in Kozintsev's film are brief and muted, but they lend a religious depth to the more obvious historical thrust of the production. Later, after Cordelia has refused to imitate the flattery of her sisters in the opening scene's test of their love, Lear stands high above his peasants on the castle wall to announce publicly his rejection of his "sometime daughter" (1.1.120). The scene then shifts to a windswept beach, presumably in France, where Cordelia and the King of France kneel to be married by a priest.

In front of a crude wooden cross, the priest blesses them in Latin and holds up a rosary for each to kiss. Although Cordelia's later actions are sufficient to reveal her forgiving love for her father, Kozintsev here pointedly links her behavior with Roman Catholic ritual, granting her a more specific religious identity than that of Lear, Albany, or Edgar. Edgar's behavior also invites a religious interpretation. As Lorne Buchman notes, Edgar "decides to assume his disguise after seeing the wandering peasants of the outside world; their wandering and suffering inspire the exiled Edgar to become one with them, to feel what they feel and to seek shelter from the elements in the space of their misery" (56). Whereas Edgar in Brook's film displays a Christlike appearance, Kozintsev's film stresses his Christlike sympathy.

Edgar is discovered in his disguise as Mad Tom by Lear, Kent, and the Fool when they reach the hovel in the storm, the location of Lear's awakening to the suffering of others. Kozintsev's straw hut is filled with peasants huddled together in troubled sleep. Looking directly at them when he speaks of the "poor naked wretches" with their "houseless heads and unfed sides, / [Their] looped and windowed raggedness" (3.4.27–31), Lear's compassion for these lowest members of society momentarily suggests that of Jesus gazing sorrowfully yet lovingly upon Jerusalem (Matthew 23: 37; Luke 13: 34). Buchman contends that "Lear's discovery is not an abstract, philosophical, or theological one" because "Kozintsev takes pains to make the King's learning process as visceral as possible" (56–57). Yet at this point in the film the theological inhabits the visceral. Lear has no need of theoretical propositions about the nature of love; only the felt reality of human need will complete his reformation. What Kozintsev shrewdly offers us is a scene of lived theology, an incarnational instant in which spirit works through flesh. The expression on actor Yuri Yarvet's face at this moment makes this one of the film's transcendent scenes because Lear becomes, and knows what it means to become, a man for others. After the storm has passed, Edgar stops to strip a scarecrow of its rags to provide meager clothing for himself. The gaunt scarecrow continues the sequence of cross imagery, which is taken up again at Gloucester's death. Edgar breaks the staff with which he had killed Oswald and ropes the two pieces together in a cross that he places at the head of his father's grave. He then folds his hands in momentary prayer before heading on, while a mournful choir fills the soundtrack with Dmitry Shostakovitch's requiem-like melody.

Kozintsev's film has been viewed as essentially socialist in outlook because of the recurring presence in it of large groups of impoverished commoners, which infuses the work with a strong awareness of social class. Far removed from the personal struggles of their king, these huddled masses endure poverty and war, making up a silent, collective character in the film. As Kozintsev himself stated, "The process of tracing the spiritual side of Shakespeare's plays cannot be separated from the tracing of the historical process" (qtd. Parker, 82). Yet the occasional small details of religious ritual and symbolism that Kozintsev has added to the plot, while in no way dominating the film, establish a religious presence implying that Lear's tragedy is not played out in a totally materialist world.

Though the two directors respected each other, Kozintsev criticized Peter Brook's 1962 stage version of *King Lear* for its "cold and timeless emptiness" (qtd. Parker, 81) and its failure to give adequate recognition to the historical process. Peter Brook's subsequent filmed version of that production appeared in 1971. It impressed—and shocked—critics with its presentation of an irrational Lear in an irrational universe. Although Brook rejected the widespread belief that his film was strongly influenced by the existentialist interpretation of the play advanced by Polish critic Jan Kott in 1964 (Leggatt, 46), he presents Lear's pre-Christian Britain as analogous to the modern perspective in which traditional religious truths and institutions have been challenged by widely held skepticism or sheer indifference. Brook's self-conscious cinematic techniques, such as shooting the film in black and white; using a hand-held camera to eliminate a reliably steady visual frame; favoring extreme close-ups; and shooting the play in the desolate Jutland peninsula of Denmark, all contribute to its stark, uncompromising portrayal of a barren kingdom ruled by a deluded old man. They also remind us, as Kenneth Rothwell points out, that "Brook was not just making a movie about *King Lear,* but also making a movie about making movies" (249). Brook's interpretation was hotly debated when it appeared, John Simon calling the film "a catastrophe and a scandal," while Frank Kermode dubbed it "the best of all Shakespeare movies" (Rothwell, 250).

The starkness of Brook's film readily invites atheistic, existential interpretations, yet it may also prompt audiences to consider the possible presence of a divinity even within its absurdist world. Shakespeare's tragedies are dramas of questioning, and his greatest tragic protagonists are those willing to ask the most profound, even subversive questions. *Hamlet* famously opens with a question— "Who's there?"—and the substance of his greatest soliloquy is a question: "To be or not to be?" (3.1.55). After he has smothered his wife, Othello plaintively asks, "Where should Othello go?" (5.2.271), and Macbeth, momentarily concerned for his deranged wife, asks the physician, "Canst thou not minister to a mind diseas'd?"(5.3.40). Foundational queries such as these, questions of existence, relationship, and sanity are, it can be argued, fundamentally religious questions, not because they advance a particular theology, but because they have to do with ultimate meanings or larger values that encompass and define the significance of human life. The bleakness of Brook's film version of *King Lear* is not religious in the sense of portraying traditional pieties about the nature of God, far less in offering a theodicy or defense of God's ultimate goodness. But it portrays with graphic power that Lear too is led to pose questions of ultimate meaning concerning himself—"Who is it who can tell me who I am?" (1.4.230)—as well as the moral order of the universe: "Is there any cause in Nature which makes these hard hearts?" (3.6.77–78).

Brook's disconcerting film makes avoiding such questions impossible. It expresses a modern religious sensibility in its willingness to pose such questions in a way that deprives us of the expectation of comfortably predictable answers. These questions can of course be answered without reference to God, although this is not the case in *King Lear,* whose characters call upon divine powers throughout the play; it is filled with what Richard C. McCoy terms "pervasive but painfully ironic god-talk" (189). Just as Lear is stripped of his clothing in the storm, the film's expressionistic style strips us of our reliance upon a more conventionally filmed play by altering or discarding smooth continuity, clear dialogue, or constant visual focus so as to portray on the screen the depth of his struggle. We are also reminded that by asking such questions in the midst of their sufferings, its characters thereby put themselves into some kind of relationship with the possibility of meaning, a meaning to be found within, not in spite of, their predicaments. To adopt, like Job, a posture of quizzical defiance in the face of inexplicable horror is to challenge the notion of ultimate meaninglessness. There is certainly enough in Shakespeare's *King Lear*, and in especially Brook's production of it, to convey the idea of a world that has been abandoned by the very gods upon which the characters call. Yet one aspect of the play's modernity is its honesty in depicting an "unapprehendable" god whose presence is suggested, intimated, or implied, rather than clearly affirmed. The play shares a quality of some modern art that Mircea Eliade has emphasized: The sacred is not absent, but "it has become *unrecognizable*; it is camouflaged in forms, purposes and meanings which are apparently 'profane.' The sacred is not *obvious*, as it was for example in the Middle Ages. One does not recognize it *immediately* and *easily*, because it is no longer expressed in a conventional religious language" (180; emphasis in original).

Some postmodern critics have asserted the inability of language to adequately portray the complexities of experience, a view resembling that of negative theology, the *via negativa* espoused most notably by Nicholas of Cusa (1401?–1464). For Jacques Derrida, for example, the most appropriate language for God is silence (Derrida). The spiritually mature Cordelia similarly recognizes silence as a way of communicating truth when her honestly felt expression of love in the opening scene is expressed in a single word that rejects speech: "Nothing." The "negative way" of mystical theology is far different from medieval scholasticism, which presumed to explain the most abstruse theological truths in terms of Aristotelian logic. Instead, negative theology addresses the limitlessness of God, the essential inexpressibility of divinity, and asserts that the best expression of the divine may be through events that strike us as dangerous, terrifying, or disturbing. To undergo this type of revelation personally is to experience what mystics such as St. John of the Cross (1542–1591) or St. Teresa of Avila (1515–1582) called "the dark night of the soul." Brook depicts the violent stripping away of spiritual misconception to disclose the strangeness, the otherness of the supernatural (Niro). If the film is shocking, that shock can be beneficial if it exposes disturbing spiritual realities that conventional piety might glibly explain away. Kenneth Rothwell understandably resorts to religious terminology to explain the film's achievement. "To a degree the film does represent *King Lear*, but it also allows glimpses into its hidden truths, so that it becomes a Book of Revelation about the play. The last part of the fifth act achieves sublimity in its striving to disclose invisible mysteries in visible images" (250).

Theologian Karl-Josef Kuschel has remarked, "Talk of God is all too easily misused to sidestep the abysses of our own existence, the contradictions of evolution and the absurdities of history" (53). Viewing literature as a form of religious inquiry helps us to recognize that even such unsettling productions of Shakespeare as Brook's may lead to new insights that challenge older assumptions, although the film does not yield up those insights easily. Kuschel's comment on his own belief calls attention to the kinds of questions that Brook's film depicts. "'God'—that is the question of the order of this world and the meaning of this life. It is an open question, sometimes a burning wound. After all, it is precisely the experience of absurdities in one's own life and in the history of this world that provokes the primal question of what this life and this history are all about: who bears ultimate responsibility for their meaning and order?" (55). The world of Brook's Lear is absurd. Yet the root meaning of *absurd* (*surd*, "muted") suggests that this production presents a world in which God is not nonexistent. Instead, God chooses to remain silent or to be known in those very events most marked by human feelings of abandonment, events that will not disclose their religious meaning without first requiring that we interrogate them through tragic suffering, through a conversation that begins with a voice crying "Howl, howl, howl" (5.3.258).

For Jan Kott, Shakespeare's play is a grotesque tragedy that shares the same absurdist vision of the world as the modern plays of Eugene Ionesco or Samuel Beckett. The word "grotesque" itself, derived from the Italian word for the underground chambers found in ancient Roman ruins, *grottesca* (grotto), suggests something ugly, distorted, or misshapen, an object or work of art whose parts are not pleasantly combined but instead appear to clash with each other in an offensive or inharmonious way. G. Wilson Knight argued that "the core of the play is an absurdity, an indignity, and incongruity" (42), which gives rise to a "comedy of the grotesque." For Kott, the nature of tragedy and the element of the grotesque both require that characters find themselves trapped in an "imposed, compulsory and inescapable" situation. "Freedom of choice and decision are part of this compulsory situation, in which both the tragic hero and the grotesque actor must always lose their struggle against the absolute" (132). The absolute is the overriding influence that imposes itself upon the tragic hero, such as "the Gods, Fate, the Christian God, Nature, and History" (133). But the tragic and the grotesque finally lead to different outcomes. "In the final instance tragedy is an appraisal of human fate, a measure of the absolute. The grotesque is a criticism of the absolute in the name of frail human experience. That is why tragedy brings catharsis, while grotesque offers no consolation whatsoever" (132). Thus, at the very close of Brook's film, we are given a grotesque scene as the dying Lear slowly falls backward out of the visual frame as the screen fades to a stark white. The film's "last word" poses a profound question: is this the sterile emptiness of nonbeing or the pure light of an inexplicable divinity?

More recently the grotesque has been examined as a unique path into the realm of theology rather than merely as a symbol of nonmeaning. By disrupting familiar definitions about the "normal," the grotesque may open up glimpses of new ways to understand the boundaries of human meaning or of seeing human experience in relationship to the mysterious nature of the sacred. Roger Hazelton observes that "the grotesque is an 'appropriately odd' disclosure of that mystery, whether forbidding or benign, with which theology is also and necessarily concerned" (75); the grotesque reminds us "that an honest, unsparing awareness of our precariousness before evil, our vulnerability to its fascination and pleasure-ableness, belongs within the scope and reach of faith" (79). By negating our usual ideas of what is holy or sacred with a repulsive image, the grotesque also employs the method of negative theology. Human conceptions of God fall short of truly describing him, language is finally inadequate to capture his essence, and his transcendent distance from humankind may best be suggested not by theological explanations, but through experiences of surprise, disorientation, darkness, or apparent meaninglessness. The Old Testament prophet sums up God's mysteriousness: "For as the heavens are higher than the earth, so are my ways higher than your ways and my thoughts than your thoughts" (Isaiah 55: 9).

Brook's film technique magnifies the grotesque potential of Shakespeare's play, filled as it is with references to "monstrous" children, Gloucester's onstage blinding, and the climactic storm. The grotesque is a style that intentionally breaks neat classifications of what is "normal," bursting their boundaries by purposely introducing contradictory or paradoxical ideas into whatever is considered acceptable or conventional. The familiar becomes distorted and skewed; what is usually respected or worshipped is turned topsy-turvy, as in a carnival where authority figures are mocked and parodied, or as in the festival of Mardi Gras, a period of extreme self-indulgence that purposely yet ironically calls attention to the holy austerity of Lent that follows it. Brook's film is typically seen as the cinematic expression of Kott's nihilistic vision, but if its grotesque features are viewed from the perspective of negative theology, they become a means of glimpsing the hidden presence of the sacred. Rather than an exercise in the futility of living, the play becomes a confrontation with the *mysterium tremendum*, the tremendous mystery of God (Otto).

King Lear is a monarch who, at the start of the play, is convinced that his legacy and the conditions he has set for his daughters' lands will remain fixed, so that, although he will "crawl toward death," (1.1.41) he will still manage those authorities he has given away. Although he has relinquished the throne, he expects that the boundaries of his influence will continue to be respected. Brook implies the king's insistence upon these boundaries by placing his towering throne (reminding us of a Stonehenge monolith) in the very center of his circular throne room, making himself the focus of all who are present. Outside the throne room is a larger space filled with the king's subjects who silently peer into the kingly inner sanctum when the door opens, as if it were some kind of holy temple. Cordelia's refusal to acquiesce to his demands for verbal flattery and his other daughters' refusal to allow him to retain his knights are, to Lear, grotesque restrictions of his power. His evil daughters seek to reduce the boundaries of his authority to their satisfaction. Cordelia, however, will later—through a love that in its own way is just as astounding as her sisters' evil designs—present him with an opposite emotional challenge, which echoes the divine injunction "That ye love one another" (John 13: 34). Both actions are in a way grotesque, the first in its depravity, the second in its amazing grace. Lear has difficulty accepting each; he casts out Cordelia, and Brook has him and his knights demolish the dining room of Goneril's castle. The motif of challenged boundaries or altered expectations is repeated in various forms, and Lear's experiences of the grotesque become the means by which he is led to eventual self-knowledge. The fool who speaks disturbing wisdom, the loyal servant who dares to appear disloyal, the monstrous daughters who seem at first utterly devoted, the beloved daughter who yet says nothing, the trading of a castle for hovel—these grotesque inversions are also echoed in Gloucester's rejection of Edgar, in Edgar's transformation into Mad Tom, and in Gloucester's darkly comic attempted suicide. The great storm itself, rendered onscreen with disjointed sequences, blurred focus, and muddled dialogue, is the freakish denial of nature as an ordered, predictable environment that can be counted on to remain within its boundaries: "The tyranny of the open night's too rough / For nature to endure" (3.4.2–3).

The storm on the heath has perhaps been the most-discussed portion of the film, a self-consciously bizarre depiction of an already horrific upheaval in the natural world. Brook favors extreme, off-center close-ups of Lear and Mad Tom, a rain-streaked lens that distorts their images, low-angle shots of Lear raising his arms to heaven, and rapid reverse shots of the king. Even for admiring critic Vincent Canby, who thought that Brook's Lear looked "like a Michelangelo God somehow fallen to earth," this segment was the one portion of the film that did not succeed: "With the exception of the tempest scenes, which seem to have been shot through a pot of Vaseline and lit with H-bomb flashes, everything works to enhance the meaning of the play" (Canby). Yet if Brook's methods here appear extravagant, they are only as extreme as the struggle within the mind and heart of the king himself. As we hear Lear's voice expressing pity for the "poor naked wretches, whereso'er you are, / That bide the pelting of this pitiless storm" (3.4.28–29), Brook offers us not a huddled mass of peasants as Kozintsev does, but a stark closeup of rats drowned in the relentless flood. According to R. B. Parker, "The implication seems to be less that humanity has reverted to a bestial level than that man is always an animal and nothing more than that, victimized by Nature like all other living things" (80–81). But our revulsion at seeing these dead creatures is at once contradicted by the realization that Lear himself has been led to a compassion not just for the human "wretches" of the world, but for all living things. Shortly after the boundaries of his affection have been so startlingly expanded, we see the boundaries of Lear's egotism just as sharply diminished when he recognizes himself as a "poor, bare, forked animal" (3.4.107–108). Lear's ability to recognize his own creatureliness in fact marks him as both animal and man. His self-knowledge undergoes a drastic change through his confrontation with the storm, which Brook's unsettling cinematic style forces us to share. This is a journey ending with Lear's new ability to give and receive love and to see at last the selfless concern of the daughter he had once rejected but now calls "a soul in bliss" (4.7.45), a phrase that actor Paul Scofield speaks with a mixture of peaceful yet painful recognition.

Cordelia's unwavering devotion takes on a sacramental quality, emphasized by Brook's strong lighting of actress Ana-Lise Gabold's unlined, angelic face. (Robert

Speaight astutely comments that "it is almost incredible that Jan Kott . . . could have devoted forty pages to *King Lear* without mention of Cordelia" [286]). Lear's mythic journey through the dark night of the storm and Cordelia's ability to survive the grotesque designs of her barbarous sisters have revealed to him a glimpse of the sacred, which he, locked within the boundaries of his egotism, could not previously have recognized. He can now say, with great perceptiveness, "Upon such sacrifices, my Cordelia, / The gods themselves throw incense" (5.3.20–21). Shakespeare's choice of the word "sacrifices" alerts us to the way in which these characters' experience of the grotesque has opened for them a window into the sublime. The boundary between the sacred and the profane has been crossed. Lear has suffered the sacrifice of his pride and will shortly experience the loss of his daughter as Cordelia sacrifices her life for him.

Lear and Cordelia have left behind the selfishly calculated stratagems of the opening scene, in which Lear displayed his own misunderstanding of love as merely a commodity to be measured solely by the volume of rhetoric, an emotional economy of profit and loss. Love for him was only a means of affirming his brutal egotism, hence Brook's costuming of Scofield in the opening scene in a mammoth, dehumanizing animal hide, the exact opposite of his later naked state

"He that parts us shall bring a brand from heaven" [5.3.22]. King Lear (Paul Scofield) reunites with Cordelia (Ana-Lise Gabold) in Peter Brook's 1971 film of *King Lear*. Courtesy of Photofest.

in the rainswept hovel. By calling attention to the grotesque elements in the play, Brook's film highlights the ways in which they lead us to appreciate what Lear had to endure to achieve his transformation. He could not be taught to change; he could only be shown. That he loses his daughter is as tragic and shocking to us as it was to Johnson and Tate, but this film confirms the Old Testament truth: "Verily thou art a God that hidest thyself" (Isaiah 45: 15) and suggests that his hiding place may be in just those transforming events that we shun as too abhorrent.

There are virtually no explicit religious symbols in this film, but Edgar as Mad Tom during the storm scene has been termed a Christ-figure; he displays many of the 25 "structural characteristics of the cinematic Christ-figure" identified by Anton Karl Kozlovic. Departing from the frequent jump-cuts in the storm scene, Brook lingers over the grotesque image of the half-naked Tom. Clad only in a loin cloth, and with straw in his hair that mimics a crown of thorns, the open-mouthed and exhausted Tom is seen in an important shot leaning against the wall of the hovel, as the camera pans down his rain-drenched body behind which we can easily imagine a cross. Tom's religious allusiveness is heightened when one of Gloucester's men stones him and when we later see him with Lear in one part of the hovel that protects a small herd of sheep, underscoring the king as one of the lost sheep who must be found. In Lear's moving conversation with the blind Gloucester in act 4 ("I will preach to thee" [4.6.141–142]), they are sitting on a vast beach apparently alone, but the camera moves back to reveal Edgar standing some distance away, observing all as an unseen and loving presence, saying in a voiceover, "I would not take this from report. It is, / And my heart breaks at it" (139–140). The film stresses that Lear's trials bring him to three intimate conversations: with Tom, Kent, and the Fool in the hovel; with Gloucester on the beach; and with Cordelia just before she is led away to death. None of these conversations saves anyone from suffering, but each one of them is a moment of communion, for Lear even a kind of resurrection: "You do me wrong to take me out o' the grave" he tells Cordelia (4.7.45). Brook's film is a gripping rendition of the play's absurd dimension, but it suggests as well a redemptive process that operates under even the most distressing disguises. In his last conversation with her, Lear looks forward to the time when he and Cordelia can "take upon's the mystery of things / As if we were God's spies" (5.3.16–17). Although they will never have the chance to spy in God's behalf upon the mystery of things, they have been privileged to spy upon the mystery of love that is God: "Look there, look there!" (5.3.312).

ROMEO + JULIET

After the popular success of Franco Zefferelli's richly photographed version of *Romeo and Juliet* (1968), young audiences were captivated by the Australian director Baz Luhrmann's film of the play, which appeared in 1995. But critics were divided over whether Luhrmann's setting in a Hispanic community, which suggested both Miami and Los Angeles, was truly effective. The film aroused the ire of traditional Shakespeareans—recalling the controversy over Brook's *King Lear*—not only because of its rapid jump-cutting style (shifting quickly from scene to scene instead of employing a slower narrative pace), but also because of its new setting among feuding Hispanic toughs and its self-conscious allusions to Hollywood westerns, grand opera, and even Tennessee Williams (Lady Capulet is a vamp with a Southern drawl). As if to signal this cheeky adaptation of Shakespeare, Luhrmann replaced the conjunction in the title with "+." Luhrmann's handling of the play's religious dimension is not as theologically nuanced as is Caird's *Hamlet*, as intrusively allegorical as Welles's *Macbeth*, nor as bleak as Brook's *King Lear*. Instead, he offers us a film in which religious images and symbols seem to flood every cultural feature of the screen so that the very idea of spirituality seems somehow cheapened and diminished in the glare of the power politics and glitzy media of Verona Beach. Yet, like the loving couples in John Donne's love poetry, Romeo and Juliet's passionate affection carries its own religiosity as they sanctify and canonize each other with a devotion more genuine than the faith of their fathers.

Andrew Dickson has aptly termed this film's religious style as "in-your-face Catholicism" (314). It also calls attention to the recent scholarly attention given to Shakespeare's own Catholic background. The dominant iconic image in *Romeo + Juliet* is the cross, and the recurring presence of crosses establishes the motif of the lovers as "star-*cross'*d." Luhrmann filmed part of the movie in Veracruz, Mexico, a city whose full name is La Villa Rica de la Vera Cruz ("the rich town of the true cross"), and the "+" in the title may also be linked with the crosses sometimes used to mark obituaries in Spanish newspapers. There is a cross in the very title of the film, a cross on the wedding rings of the tragic couple, a cross atop the back seat of the Montagues' limousine, a cross etched into the windshield of Balthazar's car, small crosses on the rear wall of the elevator in which Romeo and Juliet steal their first kiss, crosses formed by the window panes of the Capulet mansion, and a large, ornate cross tattooed on Friar Laurence's back, to cite only a few. Crosses make their most striking appearance in the final scene within the church where the supposedly dead Juliet lies in state. Romeo approaches her bier walking down a central aisle lined with neon crosses of blue, the traditional color associated with the Virgin Mary. A second visual motif is that of holy statues and the painted faces of saints. Luhrmann opens with an aerial establishing shot of a statue of Christ dominating the city from atop a church (the Catholic church of St. Peter in Mexico City). This opening sequence recalls the famous beginning of Federico Fellini's film *La Dolce Vita* (1960), in which a statue of Christ dangling from a helicopter is flown over the city of Rome. Like Fellini, Luhrmann seems intent on displaying a society for whom religion has been reduced to little more than nostalgic symbols. Unlike Fellini, whose characters lead lives of quiet desperation in "the sweet life," Luhrmann preserves Shakespeare's focus on a pair of young lovers whose vital passion is an earthly experience of the divine that lifts them above the amorality of their surroundings. Throughout the film the statues of Christ and the Virgin Mary reappear in both high- and low-angle shots, suggesting a framing spiritual reality above and beyond the world of the violent city, a reality to which Romeo and Juliet's love offers them access.

The film is so saturated with religious symbolism that these objects at first strike us as little more than stereotypical tokens of Hispanic America, religious "signs" that have been demoted to the garish trappings of pop culture. However, though Romeo and Juliet are immersed in this culture, they are set apart from it in the world of their own romance; they are in Verona Beach but not of it, and these religious symbols point toward their role as "saints of love." As impetuous, even reckless youth, they resemble the other hot-blooded adolescents around them, but as the defiant children of powerful Veronese families, they seek to separate themselves from a culture in which power has replaced piety. In the early scene of the costume ball, Juliet's white angelic wings denote a spiritual dimension to her character that distinguishes her from the other young women, while Romeo's medieval suit of armor marks him as the chivalric knight who will defy all challenges to pursue his paramour. This medieval motif is continued at the movie's conclusion, as the soundtrack plays the "Liebestod" from Wagner's operatic retelling of the doomed love of Tristan and Isolde.

Baz Luhrmann has said that his film is quite consciously Elizabethan in that it employs a variety of styles to reach a varied audience. Shakespeare, he notes, "was an absolutely relentless entertainer. If you look at the plays there would be a joke, a song, violence, tragedy all in one package. There was no such thing as a consistent style." He rejects those who say the film has an "MTV style," pointing out that the film's criteria "came from a direct analysis of the Elizabethan stage" (Adamek). However, as Philippa Sheppard points out, by placing the film's Elizabethan stage motifs in an Hispanic context, he calls up a variety of Latino elements—such as the overbearing Mediterranean father, the historic Black Legend that derides Spanish Catholicism, and Juliet's nurse as the stereotypical Latin American servant—which accomplish a multicultural purpose.

Additionally, Luhrmann's film-world overlays the story with another Latin folk context, the fiesta. By suggesting the Hispanic ethos of both Miami Beach and Los Angeles, "Verona Beach" is a cinematic amalgam of Latino life and its Chicano subculture (West-Durán). The film's color, music, emotional intensity, and unpredictable violence all recreate features of the fiesta, a social phenomenon central to the Mexican identity. The film's rapid cutting, especially in the opening 20 minutes as Montagues and Capulets confront each other; its repeated use of extravagant fireworks and strings of bright, decorative lights; the faded gaiety suggested by the "Sycamore Grove" amusement park on the beach; the customized cars driven by the feuding youths; the everpresent glint of their pistols (given names such as "Sword" and "Rapier"); and the allegorical costuming of Tybalt (wearing devil's horns at the costume ball) and Abra (with a metal plate across his teeth engraved with "Sin")—these and other details combine to create a world of carnival that is both festive and threatening. Two of Tybalt's sidekicks even appear as skeletons at the costume ball, a gesture toward the Mexican festival of the Day of the Dead.

As modern Mexican poet Octavio Paz points out in *The Labyrinth of Solitude*, the celebration of the dead, like those fiestas dedicated to various saints, recognizes the flawed and passionate nature of human life, linking it to a dominant theme of Shakespearean tragedy. These fiestas are windows into Mexican culture which, according to Paz,

> all give [the Mexican] a chance to reveal himself and to converse with God, country, friends, or relations. During these days the silent Mexican whistles, shouts, sings, shoots off fireworks, discharges his pistol into the air. He discharges his soul. . . . This is the night when friends who have not exchanged more than the prescribed courtesies for months get drunk together, trade confidences, weep over the same troubles, discover that they are brothers, and sometimes, to prove it, kill each other. . . . Now and then, it is true, the happiness ends badly, in quarrels, insults, pistol shots, stabbings. But these too are part of the fiesta.(49)

Paz stresses that "The fiesta is by nature sacred, literally or figuratively, and above all it is the advent of the unusual. . . . [T]ime is transformed to a mythical past or a total present; space, the scene of the fiesta, is turned into a gaily decorated world of its own; and the persons taking part cast off all human or social rank and become, for the moment, living images" (50). In ancient Aztec culture, ritual sacrifices to the gods emphasized that life and death were intimately linked, and that all of society thus served a higher destiny. However, with the advent of Christianity, one's fate became an individual matter concerning the afterlife. "To Christians," says Paz, "death is a transition, a somersault between two lives, the temporal and the otherworldly; to the Aztecs it was the profoundest way of participating in the continuous regeneration of the creative forces which were always in danger of being extinguished if they were not provided with blood, the sacred food" (56).

Paz's analysis of the fiesta helps us to appreciate the religious and tragic strands in the fabric of Luhrmann's film. First, the spontaneous, unpredictable nature of fiesta provides a fitting cultural setting for the variety of suprising theatrical effects he borrows from the Elizabethan stage. The fiesta's very theatricality links it to the energetic world of the London stage of Shakespeare's era. While the majority of characters in the film seem oblivious to the religious icons around them, the audience is unavoidably aware of this spiritual presence, most clearly apparent in the two lovers. The religious icons seem to have been crassly degraded by being placed on automobile fenders or garish tropical shirts, but their pervasiveness reveals the underlying spiritual dimension of fiesta. The mixture of sacred and secular, which may seem jarring, is central to this cultural event. Secondly, the fiesta is by nature a religious event that permits an outpouring of uninhibited, blatantly defiant energy in the name of a patron saint or the honored dead. Social conventions are overturned, rules and regulations temporarily suspended, and the whole event recalls the fervent energy of the ancient Greek festivals of Dionysus, the god of procreation and wine, whose festivals gave rise to dramatic tragedy itself. The fiesta reminds us that tragedy had its origin in religious celebration. Nietzsche's theory of tragedy famously linked this type of drama with the release of unbridled powers in the name of the pagan god Dionysus who defies propriety, reveling in the mysterious and the violent. The fiesta is, finally, a celebration with the potential of turning tragic at any moment. Shakespearean tragedy ends in death, but this is typically a sanative, restorative event after which the society of the play may return to a healthier state. The brutal sound of Juliet's final pistol shot shocks us into realizing that these families have unwittingly contributed to their children's deaths. In a dramatic reflection of the propitiatory Aztec rituals cited by Paz, their deaths become an offering that will bring peace to the city.

The religious symbolism in this film is intimately mingled with the mercenary and even sordid details of life in Verona Beach, but a remnant of spiritual presence in these icons, statues, and paintings is never completely obscured by the material culture that sees them as little more than decorative frills. Sacred and profane exist in a dynamic balance, which for Luhrmann resembles the blended relationship of society and religion in Shakespeare's London. As he told an interviewer in 1996: "I wanted to create a place where religion mixed with politics . . . a place with a degree of mysticism. . . . Verona Beach and Shakespeare's Verona are supposed to be worlds where religion is important, where obvious wealth isn't embarrassing, where honor is really a big deal. All those elements exist in the real world, but they don't exist totally in combination—except in Mexico" (Darlington). However, Luhrmann's use of contemporary Hispanic culture to convey the close association between religion and secular culture in Shakespeare's era fails to convey the seriousness with which everyone in Renaissance England was expected

Glowing crosses line the aisle leading to Juliet's bier in Baz Luhrmann's film *Romeo + Juliet* (1995). Courtesy of Photofest.

to take religion, whether Anglican, Catholic, or Puritan. Unlike John Caird's production of *Hamlet*, in which even the morally wrong characters recognize the validity of the divine laws they have broken, Luhrmann's characters—with the exception of Romeo, Juliet, and Friar Laurence—seem unaware of any spiritual dimension in their lives, despite all of their religious tokens. In the opening gas station scene, the lewd behavior of one of the Montague boys, designed to shock the nun and her Catholic schoolgirls, is more typical of the Verona Beach attitude toward religion, far different from Romeo's desire that "He that hath the steerage of my course / Direct my sail" (1.4.112–113). He later loses his course by murdering Tybalt, but actor Leonardo DiCaprio effectively shows the extreme provocation Romeo endures before succumbing to revenge and then guilt. The young lovers also describe their relationship in religious terms. Juliet is Romeo's "bright angel," "a winged messenger of heaven," and "a dear saint" (2.2.26, 28, 55), while Juliet says that he is "the god of my idolatry" (2.2.114). This language might seem to be nothing more than the conventional terms of affection found in Renaissance love poetry if the couple did not then act on their words and have, in the friar's words, "Holy Church incorporate two in one" (2.6.37). Juliet's bedroom is filled with religious kitsch, but we sense that these objects express the most genuine faith in the play. In Shakespeare's text, when Juliet discovers that Romeo has killed Tybalt, she expresses her fears to the nurse (3.2), but Luhrmann significantly has her express these statements while kneeling in prayer to the Virgin. The lovers' devotion sets them apart from their warring families, and they are frequently shot within enclosed spaces that separate them from the secular world: in the Capulet's elevator, in the pool beneath Juliet's balcony, enclosed by the sheets on Juliet's bed, or together in the church where they die.

The placement of religious images often suggests that the church's traditional influence has been compromised by power politics. For example, in the opening shot the large statue of Christ is seen sandwiched between the Montague and Capulet skyscrapers, as if the authority of religion is now dominated by the two wealthy and powerful families. The bizarre juxtaposition of the totem-like image of the Virgin on the pistol grips of some gang members seems to imply their belief that heaven will side with them in the feud. Yet the holy faces that we see of Christ, Mary, and various saints throughout the film compose a ghostly group of silent onlookers to the violence, as if no act committed by these clashing gangs goes unnoticed by the divinity that their culture has debased in its tawdry artwork. Several scenes are shot from a vantage above a statue of Christ, looking down on a traffic circle, as if from a God's-eye view. When the devil-horned Tybalt appears at the costume ball flanked by his two skeleton-clad friends, we glimpse behind them an oil painting of the crucifixion. As Romeo and Friar Laurence leave the church, the camera lingers on a wall painting behind them of the head of Christ sporting Tybalt-like dark sideburns—a Chicano Jesus. Even the outrageously campy dance at the Capulet's ball by Mercutio, portrayed as a black transvestite, is performed on a grand staircase overseen by a colossal painting of the Virgin. These religious juxtapositions are firmly fixed within the palpable world of physical sensation and ethnic values, not apart from it in some spiritually sanitized location free from the contradictions of human experience. This conjunction of the holy and the common would also have been familiar to Shakespeare's audience, who could have seen pagan imps, gargoyles, or naked figures occasionally carved into the sacred corners of their cathedrals, a common medieval practice. Graham Ward accurately captures the provocative religious undercurrent of the film:

> For despite its kitsch attachment to holy accessories and paraphernalia . . . there are moments when the transcendent is taken more seriously, when we view the action from above, from the head of Christ. There are moments of devotional awe and reverence relating both to what the lovers feel for each other and to Christ's own love. These moments run counter to the iconoclasm which sometimes borders on the blasphemous (lending an added *frisson* to the film). The tone of the film's portrayal of Roman Catholicism is ambivalent and irreducibly so. (28–29)

Luhrmann's film displays a society of seductive pleasure, conspicuous consumption, and lethal pride, and the devotion of the two young martyrs to love condemns the faithlessness of their society.

HAMLET

John Caird's noteworthy interpretation of *Hamlet* was first produced in 2000 at the Royal National Theatre in London and was widely hailed as a thoughtful and perceptive rendition of the tragedy. In Michael Dobson's view, this meditative production was "fascinating evidence that at the dawn of the third millennium the religious dimensions of Shakespeare's work are being resurrected in the theatre no less than in criticism" (277). In the opinion of Bernice Kliman, Simon Russell Beale was "an intelligent, sensitive, gentle, and sweet-tempered Hamlet" with "a pleasing wit and a serious intellect" (143). Jonathan Croall's account of the production, *Hamlet Observed* (2001), captured the thoughts and comments of various members of the cast and crew as they sought to bring Caird's conception to the stage, a play of moral struggle informed by the religious culture of its time. Designer Tim Hatley originally conceived the Elsinore of this production as both a prison and a religious place but also a flexible location for the actors. "My original design," he comments, "was a big ruined cathedral, with corridors and tunnels and levels, a banqueting table, lots of icons, and chandeliers inspired by the reference to 'this majestical roof fretted with golden fire.' But this proved too expensive, and not very practical for touring" (Croall, 10). But Hatley did retain costumes that "emphasise the dark, ecclesiastical tone of the production" (Croall, 15). His design suggested to reviewer Suzanne Bixby "a cathedral and the chandeliers swinging on their chains, a priest's censer." John Cameron, music director, decided upon modern adaptations of the music of Orlando di Lassus (c. 1532–1594) "to convey the right spiritual feeling we were looking for" (Croall, 11). As Lizzie Loveridge pointed out in her review, "Every scene gives us church music as if to emphasise that this is a play written by a Catholic, a man who believes in damnation and purgatory and unexpurgated sin." Central to the production was the conviction that "the play was essentially about a group of people who all loved or wanted to love each other, but whose love was destroyed by circumstances" (Croall, 13). In describing her character (Ophelia), actress Cathryn Bradshaw said, "You've got to have someone who understands the importance of spirituality in Ophelia, and she has that kind of imagination" (Croall, 12).

Caird himself saw the play "as both an intensely naturalistic drama and an extraordinary piece of metaphysical poetry and philosophy" (Croall, 14). He consciously chose to cut the political aspects of the play, especially the Fortinbras sections. "The society [of the play] is one that believes in God; Hamlet's thoughts are pre-enlightenment. So the production must be suffused with religious certainty. If you set it after the seventeenth century, an audience loses patience with the religious arguments" (15). Music director John Cameron noted that "[Caird's] decision to lose all the political stuff makes it a much more cerebral production; it gives it a lightness and floatiness, a more spiritual feeling, which I'm trying to match in the original music I'm creating" (27). Caird's religious vision of the play also affected the set design. "How do you physicalise the metaphysical?" he asks. "The production needs a set that allows all the imagery about heaven and earth to be liberated, one that reflects the extraordinary beauty of the form, line and imagery of the play. The solution is to have one that doesn't require conventional scenery" (15). The end result was a collection of suitcases and trunks that were moved about the stage as needed and served a variety of functions. Actor Peter McEnery (Claudius) pointed out that Caird "suggested you could see Claudius not just as the king but also as the chief priest. That's been very helpful to me; it gives him an austerity; it's made it easier to avoid the obvious, moustache-twirling villain" (21). Bence Olveczy noted a "promise of redemption" in the production, saying that "The Christian imagery serves to underscore the hypocrisy and double standard by which the characters go about their business, but it also seems to imply that when all is said and done, there is forgiveness to be had."

Caird's vision of the play gives special emphasis to the ways in which it is not "contemporary," and self-consciously modern interpretations, especially those suggesting a sexual attachment between Hamlet and his mother or Ophelia, he regards as "daft." In his view, there is no evidence that Hamlet's university studies have made him a seventeenth-century skeptic where religion is concerned; "that would be to ignore the religious, ethical, and moral doctrine, which is clearly present in the play" he notes. "My thinking about the play is that you can't really do the play post-Enlightenment. If there's any chance that Hamlet has read Voltaire while at Wittenberg, then he doesn't really have a problem. The whole theological and moral center of the play has fallen away. And I think it's that very fact, that the center of the play is about moral concerns, which is crucial. I think it is the first duty of the director to give the audience some sense of what it would be like to live in a society in which belief in God was axiomatic, in which these moral issues are not theoretical. Whether one was a doer of good or a doer of evil is a vital concern." The play is medieval in that "Hamlet clearly has a belief in the importance of his own relationship to God. Claudius and Hamlet are both concerned about this. Even a man who is guilty of murder [Claudius] is torn apart by what he has done, and a man who was murdered [Hamlet's father] is walking around unhappily." Both Claudius and Gertrude see themselves as sinners and "believe deeply by the end of the play that they are to be judged somewhere other than on earth, and that's central." The play, he concludes, is not narrowly Protestant or Catholic in outlook, but it is profoundly religious. "If you're faithful to its theology, its morality, and its intellect then of course it speaks very loudly to us today, and there is nothing to stop us from saying that it is a completely modern play. But to make it more modern than it is then makes it speak less well to modern audiences" (Caird).

Further insights into this production come from actor Simon Russell Beale's essay on it, which seeks to explain his portrayal of the tragic hero. For Beale, Hamlet's hell, unlike that of Richard III or Iago, was not that of his own inner perversity but, rather, the hellish situation in which he had been placed. Hamlet's nature was in fact the opposite of theirs, and Beale wondered if he was "capable of exploring a character as full of grace as Hamlet" (Beale, 146). The very fact of Hamlet's great love for his father exacerbates the dilemma of this revenge tragedy. "The supernatural element," says Beale, "as with the witches in *Macbeth*, takes away the possibility of choice from the central character; and the fact that here the supernatural element is the father of the hero only makes the emotional landscape more cruel" (149). Significantly, Hamlet never appears startled by the apparition of his father. "The appearance of a ghost does not seem in itself surprising to him. It is the reason for its appearance, the news that it might bring, that is both frightening and exhilarating" (159). (In contrast, Grigori Kozintsev's 1964 film of *Hamlet* treated the ghost far differently, removing the religious context of its appearance and substituting "a prologue that defines the 'strange eruption' in social and political terms" [Buchman, 48]).

Hamlet's confrontation with the destruction of his nuclear family has a devastating impact upon him: "Indeed the play is in some sense a demolition, or at least a questioning, of those certainties, intellectual and spiritual, on which Hamlet has, so far, based his life and thought" (Beale, 149). Beale finds that Hamlet's love for his father is a primal emotion in the prince, and having to hear the ghost tell of his murder is "unbearable." "Unbearable, too, is the fact that Hamlet is forced to watch his father in great pain and hear him admit to past sins. Even for a relatively sophisticated student of theology, this admission must be profoundly distressing . . . " (161). The result of this need to confront a demolished family prompts a theme which "is the most important any man or woman will encounter: that of their own humanity and mortality" (151).

Beale noticeably frames his understanding of the play within religious concepts, and for this reason his comments deserve to be quoted at length. He feels that, in the last act when Hamlet returns from his "short exile," "the playwright's creation of a man somehow at peace and prepared for his death is frankly miraculous" (152). However, this transition is difficult for the actor to portray "especially since his conversion from an active misery to calm resignation happens off stage" (152). Hamlet's "final resignation is also necessarily self-centered, but his trust in some 'special providence' (v.ii.213) . . . is deeply moving and very important" (153). In act 1, Shakespeare identifies Hamlet's university.

Wittenberg was not chosen lightly: Hamlet no doubt studies scholastic—radical or not—theology. So much of the play is, in effect, Hamlet's debate with his god, and the appearance of the ghost overturns or challenges his deeply held convictions (after all, evil, and evil acts, are always a problem theologically). Before meeting the spirit of his father Hamlet can use a conventional church-centered argument against suicide— "Or that the Everlasting had not fixed / His canon 'gainst self-slaughter" (I.ii.131– 132)—which is glossed in a more radical way in 'To be or not to be' (III.i.56–88), where a general fear of an afterlife is a more powerful deterrent than a dread of doing something wrong in the eyes of the church. His famous statement to Horatio—

There are more things in heaven and earth, Horatio, Than are dreamt of in your philosophy (I.i.166–167)

—which is spoken in the excitement of having just talked to the ghost of his father, could come as a surprise to Hamlet, as it does to Horatio, . . . [implying] that previously held convictions are no longer tenable. (157–158)

Hamlet's relationships with women are also deeply influenced by his theological training and beliefs. "It appears," observes Beale, "that Hamlet cannot discard the received wisdom that all women, even Ophelia, are essentially both sinful and the occasion of [opportunity to commit] sin" (158). Hence, he utters a statement that would not have been out of place in a misogynistic medieval religious tract: "Frailty, thy name is woman" (1.2.146). Nevertheless, in his interview with Mary Maher, Beale points out that his own view is "perhaps a twenty-first century perspective. However, given the Hamlet that I do, to a serious divinity student, his outlook would be traditional" (Maher, 232–233). He says that Hamlet's attitude certainly derives as well from his mother's actions: "Since his mother behaved badly, he assumes that is how all women behave" (Maher, 233). Yet in act three, when Hamlet confronts Gertrude, Beale sees an opportunity for the prince to forge a new relationship with the woman who has hurt him so deeply:

The great scene between mother and son became, not so much a discussion about Hamlet's accusation, or, indeed, a violent release of tension (I was keen to avoid any physical abuse), but rather an attempt by both of them to find a *modus vivendi*, to make a new contract based [on] love and respect. This contract involves, too, an observance of Christian procedures—repentance, confession, absolution. I have said earlier that, despite the challenge to his beliefs, Hamlet is ultimately conservative in his response: even in the last act, his fatalism springs from a faith in a benevolent god. (Beale, 171)

Similarly, Beale sees Hamlet's anger toward his uncle Claudius likewise filtered through the prince's religious sensibility. As he told Mary Maher,

I couldn't see doing this play in a godless universe—it has to have a strong Christian Renaissance basis. Even Claudius saying to Laertes's boast to cut Hamlet's throat in the church, "No place, indeed, should murder sanctuarize,"—that is firmly canon law. Equally, Hamlet is not going to kill Claudius in the chapel because he really does believe in purgatory, and he does believe in hell. That is absolutely Catholic, straight down the line. (Maher, 243)

To serve the wishes of his father's ghost, Hamlet must wreak revenge upon the false "father" who has interposed himself into his once-loving family. After his conversation with his mother, he seems imbued with new purposefulness ("Now could I drink hot blood" [3.2.390]). "In this apparently decisive mood, it is not surprising that he comes very near to killing Claudius as the king is praying. What stops Hamlet is, characteristically, a theological argument. This tension between a firm, almost amoral, resolve and a concern over the requirements of his faith is now almost unbearable and brings about, inevitably, the killing of Polonius" (172–173). But simply because Hamlet is aware of the religious implications of his predicament does not mean that he is somehow spiritually superior to those around him; he is as enmeshed in the sinfully fallen world of Elsinore as they are. As Beale reveals, "the fact that, in our production, the dagger used to murder Polonius was the one given to Hamlet by his father's ghost (and therefore a profoundly precious thing) merely intensifies his recognition that not only has he failed, but also that he is, in a fundamental and perhaps irredeemable way, sullied" (Beale, 173). It is worth noting that Beale understands the word "sullied" (from the famous crux in the first soliloquy: "O that this too too solid/sullied flesh would melt" [1.2.129]) to mean "sinful," not merely "besmirched" or "defective." But he and John Caird purposely chose "solid" in that first soliloquy: "We decided on "solid" because it was not overly complicated. Now is the time to be talking about the flesh being solid, to talk about melting away and killing yourself. Now is not the time to be talking about original sin [sullied flesh]. He does that later. That's my decision, my taste" (Maher, 236).

Summing up his written interpretation of *Hamlet*, Beale appears to agree with Charles Lamb's conviction about the sheer unperformability of the great tragedies, but he then notes that, if well-played, any given production can be as valid as another.

> I am acutely aware that almost everything I have written can and should be contradicted, both by other people, of course, but also within my own performance. That's the trouble with writing about *Hamlet*. The play is, quite simply, both too big and too hospitable. . . . [M]ore than any other character I have ever played, the person called Hamlet does not exist. There is only a series of actors' responses to, and reactions, with, the part. It is as if anyone could play him and produce something right and true. (Beale, 177)

Beale's interpretation of the play is one of the most overtly religious versions of it to have been mounted in modern times. As he told Jonathan Croall:

> The play is unquestionably Hamlet's debate with his God, and where it leads him in the final act is probably to a good place. That's what it's been most nights; there's that whole sense that all will be well. Perhaps that's too sentimental, but I think it's a valid reading. I think his line "I am dead, Horatio" is a happy line, because he's meeting his God. I'm playing around with giving it a smile, but it might change every night, depending where I've got to in his journey. I might sometimes feel more resigned, abdicating responsibility and judgement for my own life, or it might be a wonderful moment of happiness and release—or both. (Croall, 68)

Critical opinion of Caird's production was essentially favorable, though some critics lamented the loss of the Fortinbras action. For reviewer Michael Dobson this was "the most religious Hamlet anyone can remember. . . . set either in Purgatory or very near it" (246; 259). In a production that echoed recent scholarly interest in the Roman Catholic background of Shakespeare himself, Caird backlit the stage through a lighted cross-shaped opening through which characters could enter and exit. The modernized music of di Lassus also emphasized that this "Denmark was as much a theocracy as a monarchy," and Claudius, rather than being costumed as clearly a villain, was dressed in a churchly robe. "[H]is first speech led the court in an incense-scented prayer for the dead King Hamlet (as if we were witnessing the closing stages of his state funeral) rather than initating a secular business meeting" (Dobson, 259). A mood of prayer pervaded the production, notes Dobson: "Simon Russell Beale played the whole of 'O that this too, too sullied flesh . . .' kneeling motionless facing the audience as if across an altar rail. . . . it was quite clear that what was on offer was a sacramental Hamlet, its cast priests as much as comedians" (259–260).

Each of the productions examined in this chapter earned varying levels of critical praise, but each reveals how religious issues and questions of theology can inform both stage and screen performances. Orson Welles's Macbeth is shaped by the director's own religious conception of the stark spiritual conflict between a Macbeth, that is completely overwhelmed by demonic forces and an emerging Christianity expressed through the militant righteousness of the Holy Father. Grigori Kozintsev inserts several brief Christian rituals into his film of King Lear, but he is more concerned to show religion as part of larger historical forces affecting not just Lear's household, but the people of his whole realm. A more cosmically oriented Lear is given us by Peter Brook, who pits his protagonist against inscrutable natural and spiritual forces, emphasizing the old king's confrontation less with social and political intrigue than with the awesome presence of a titanic power. For Baz Luhrmann religion is engrained within society, even possibly debased by it into nothing more than an aesthetic style, yet the mixture of violence, passion, and religion in Verona Beach implies the spiritual dimension that is an essential part of the Mexican fiesta. John Caird's Hamlet is, of all these productions, the one most grounded in a theological awareness of his characters, in their response not simply to the presence of the divine, but to specific beliefs concerning sin, guilt, and judgment that characterized Elizabethan Catholicism.

The religious language used in these plays, such as "God," "the gods," "divine powers," and "grace," are not the only vehicles for conveying their religious themes, which are as convincingly expressed through the dramatic play-worlds themselves and through the events faced by their characters. Shakespeare does not preach. The religious meaning of his plays is not taught to his audiences so much as caught by them, through the emotional and intellectual effect of his artistry, through the interplay of character, plot, language, and conflict. We find the spiritual significance of his work not in sermonized statements of belief, but in the substance of the drama itself, at the place where our willing perception meets his dramatically creative questioning. An artistic medium can become a basis for dialogue, as Clive Marsh emphasizes. "Any aspect of human culture—including film—which explores in however slight a fashion such themes as 'the human condition,' the nature of reality, or how people should live is addressing subject-matter of concern to Christian theology, and about which Christian theology has things to say" (27). Precisely because Christians believe that God entered history in physically human form, "God, in Christian perspective, is tangled up with the ordinary, the mundane, the seemingly trivial, in a way which is worthy of close examination" (Marsh and Ortiz, 253). Even the material nature of culture can thus hold a spiritual significance, which "will not be limited to sacred buildings, religious symbols or architecture, or even writings which are religious or theological in character" (Graham, 37). In the words of modern theologian Paul Tillich, "Everything that expresses ultimate reality expresses God whether it intends to do so or not" (220).

REFERENCES

Adamek, Pauline. "*Romeo + Juliet*: Interview with Baz Luhrmann." POP-Film. November 3, 1996. http://members.ozemail.com.au/~catman/pop/film/ci/interviews/baz.html.

Anderegg, Michael. *Orson Welles, Shakespeare, and Popular Culture*. New York: Columbia University Press, 1999.

Barna, George, and Mark Hatch. *Boiling Point: Monitoring Cultural Shifts in the 21st Century*. Ventura, CA: Regal, 2003.

Bate, Jonathan, and Russell Jackson, eds. *Shakespeare: An Illustrated History*. New York: Oxford University Press, 1996.

Beale, Simon Russell. "Hamlet." *Players of Shakespeare 5*. Ed., Robert Smallwood. Cambridge, UK: Cambridge University Press, 2003. 145–177.

Bixby, Suzanne. "Talkin' Broadway: Hamlet." *Boston*. February 26, 2007. http://www.talkinbroadway.com/regional/boston/boston7.html.

Brady, Frank. *Citizen Welles: A Biography of Orson Welles*. New York: Scribner's, 1989.

Buchman, Lorne M. *Still in Movement: Shakespeare on Screen*. New York: Oxford University Press, 1991.

Caird, John. Personal interview. August 19, 2006.

Canby, Vincent. "King Lear." *New York Times*. November 23, 1971. 54.

Coursen, H. R. *Shakespearean Performance as Interpretation*. Newark; University of Delaware Press, 1992.

Croall, Jonathan. *Hamlet Observed: The National Theatre at Work*. London: NT Publications, 2001.

Crowl, Samuel. *Shakespeare Observed: Studies in Performance on Stage and Screen*. Athens: Ohio University Press, 1992.

Darlington, Shasta. "Yo! Romeo!" *Los Angeles Times*. July 21, 1996. www.clairdanes.com/print/latimes072196.html.

Davies, Anthony. *Filming Shakespeare's Plays: The Adaptations of Laurence Olivier, Orson Welles, Peter Brook and Akira Kurosawa*. Cambridge, MA: Cambridge University Press, 1988.

Derrida, Jacques. "How to Avoid Speaking: Denials." In *Languages of the Unsayable: The Play of Negativity in Literature and Literary Theory*. Ed. S. Budick and W. Iser. New York: Columbia University Press, 1989. 3–70.

Dessen, Alan. *Shakespeare and the Late Moral Plays*. Lincoln, NE: University of Nebraska Press, 1986.

Dickson, Andrew. *The Rough Guide to Shakespeare*. London, UK: Rough Guides, 2005.

Dobson, Michael. "Shakespeare Performances in England, 2000." *Shakespeare Survey 54*. Cambridge, UK: Cambridge University Press, 2001. 246–282.

Eliade, Mircea. "The Sacred and the Modern Artist." *Criterion* (Spring 1964): 22–24. Rpt. *Art, Creativity and the Sacred*. Ed. Diane Apostolos-Cappadona. New York: Crossroad, 1992. 179–183.

Friedman, Michael D. "In Defense of Authenticity." *Studies in Philology* 99 (2002): 33–56.

Graham, David John. "The Uses of Film in Theology." In *Explorations in Theology and Film*. Ed. Clive Marsh and Caye Ortiz. Oxford, UK: Blackwell, 1997. 35–44.

Hazelton, Roger. "The Grotesque, Theologically Considered." In *The Grotesque in Art and Literature: Theological Reflections*. Ed. James L. Adams and Wilson Yates. Grand Rapids, MI: Eerdmans, 1997. 75–81.

Kliman, Bernice W. "*Hamlet* Productions Starring Beale, Hawke, and Darling From the Perspective of Performance History." In *A Companion to Shakespeare's Works*. Ed. Richard Dutton and Jean E. Howard. Vol. 1. Malden, MA: Blackwell, 2003. 134–157.

Knight, G. Wilson. "*King Lear* and the Comedy of the Grotesque." In *The Wheel of Fire*. London, UK: Methuen, 1949. 160–176. Rpt. *Twentieth Century Interpretations of King Lear*. Ed. Janet Adelman. Englewood Cliffs, NJ: Prentice-Hall, 1978. 34–49.

Kott, Jan. *Shakespeare Our Contemporary*. Garden City, NY: Doubleday & Company, 1966.

Kozlovic, Anton Karl. "The Structural Characteristics of the Cinematic Christ-figure." *Journal of Religion and Popular Culture* IV (Fall 2004). http://www.usask.ca/relst/jrpc.

Kuschel, Karl-Josef. "Literature and Theology—A Mutual Challenge: Reflections on a Personal Literary Canon." In *Literary Canons and Religious Identity*. Ed. Erik Borgman, Bart Philipsen, and Lea Verstricht. Aldershot, UK: Ashgate, 2004. 51–68.

Leggatt, A. *King Lear*. Manchester, UK: Manchester University Press, 1991.

Loveridge, Lizzie. "Hamlet." *Curtain Up*. September 5, 2000. http://www.curtainup.com/hamletliz.html.

Maher, Mary Z. *Modern Hamlets & Their Soliloquies: An Expanded Edition*. Iowa City: University of Iowa Press, 2003.

Marsh, Clive. "Film and Theologies of Culture." In *Explorations in Theology and Film*. Ed. Clive Marsh and Gaye Ortiz. Oxford, UK: Blackwell, 1997. 21–34.

Marsh, Clive, and Gaye Ortiz. "Theology Beyond the Modern and the Postmodern: A Future Agenda for Theology and Film." In *Explorations in Theology and Film*. Ed. Clive Marsh and Gaye Ortiz. Oxford, UK: Blackwell, 1997. 245–256.

McBride, Joseph. *Orson Welles*. New York: Viking, 1972.

McCoy, Richard C. "Shakespearean Tragedy and Religious Identity." In *A Companion to Shakespeare's Works*. Ed. Richard Dutton and Jean E. Howard. 4 vols. Oxford, UK: Blackwell, 2003. 1:178–198.

Mullin, Michael. "Orson Welles' *Macbeth*: Script and Screen." In *Focus on Orson Welles*. Ed. Ronald Gottesman. Englewood Cliffs, NJ: Prentice Hall, 1976. 136–145.

Niro, August. "King Lear and the Via Negativa." *Shakespeare and Renaissance Association of West Virginia: Selected Papers* 10 (1985): 62–67.

Olveczky, Bence. "Hamlet: The British are Coming!" *The Tech*. 121.9 (April 20, 2001): http://www-tech.mit.edu/V121/N19/Hamlet.19a.html.

Otto, Rudolf. *The Idea of the Holy*. Trans. John W. Harvey. Oxford, UK: Oxford University Press, 1923.

Parker, R.B. "The Use of *Mise-en-Scène* in Three Films of *King Lear*." *Shakespeare Quarterly*, 42(1991), 75–90.

Paz, Octavio. *The Labyrinth of Solitude*. New York: Grove Weidenfeld, 1985.

Pearlman, E. "'Macbeth' on Film: Politics." In *Shakespeare and the Moving Image: The Plays on Film and Television*. Ed. Anthony Davies and Stanley Wells. Cambridge, MA: Cambridge University Press, 1994. 250–261.

Pyle, Sandra. *Mirth and Morality of Shakespeare's Holy Fools*. Lewiston, NY: Edwin Mellin Press, 1998.

"Religious Affiliation of Orson Welles." December 6, 2005. http://www.adherents.com/people/pw/Orson_Welles.html.

Rothwell, Kenneth S. "Classic Film Versions of Shakespeare's Tragedies: A Mirror for the Times." In *A Companion to Shakespeare's Works*. Ed. Richard Dutton and Jean E. Howard. Volume I. Malden, MA: Blackwell, 2003. 241–261.

Sheppard, Philippa. "Latino Elements in Baz Luhrmann's *Romeo + Juliet*." In *Latin American Shakespeares*. Ed. Bernice W. Kliman and Rick J. Santos. Madison, NJ: Fairleigh Dickinson University Press, 2005. 242–262.

Speaight, Robert. *Shakespeare: The Man and his Achievement*. 1977. New ed. New York: Cooper Square Press, 2000.

Styan, J. L. *Perspectives on Shakespeare in Performance*. New York: Peter Lang, 2000.

Tate, Nahum. *The History of King Lear*. Ed. James Black. Lincoln: University of Nebraska Press, 1975.

Tillich, Paul. "Art and Ultimate Reality." Rpt. in *Art, Creativity, and the Sacred*. Ed. Diane Apostolos-Cappadona. New York: Crossroad , 1984, 219–235.

Ward, Graham. *True Religion*. Malden, MA: Blackwell, 2003.

Welles, Orson. *Everybody's Shakespeare*. Woodstock, IL: Todd Press, 1934.

Welles, Orson, and Peter Bogdanovich. *This Is Orson Welles*. New York: HarperCollins, 1992.

West-Durán, Alan. "Crossing Borders: Creative Disorders." In *Latino and Latina Writers*. Ed. Alan West-Durán. 2 vols. New York: Thomson Gale, 2004. I, 21–40.

Willson, Robert F., Jr. *Shakespeare in Hollywood 1929–1956*. Madison, NJ: Fairleigh Dickenson University Press, 2000.

Womack, Peter. "Secularizing *King Lear*: Shakespeare, Tate, and the Sacred." *Shakespeare Survey*, 55 (2002), 96–105.

5

SCHOLARSHIP AND CRITICISM

The various religious allusions and analogues reviewed in the previous two chapters do not reveal for us a consistent Shakespearean theology, but they at least demonstrate what W. Moelwyn Merchant has called "the exploratory pattern in the plays in which Christian attitudes and beliefs play their part" (85). The attention paid by critics to Shakespeare's religious "patterns" has varied with the changes in critical approaches and literary tastes since the dramatist's death. A complete history of critical responses to his employment of religious themes and motifs would require a book in itself, but it is possible to suggest the outlines of that history through a review of representative critics through the centuries who have commented on Shakespeare's use of religious ideas.

The earliest critical comments on Shakespeare, such as those in Francis Meres' *Palladis Tamia: Wit's Treasury* (1598) or Ben Jonson's dedicatory poem in his First Folio (1623), do not make direct reference to religion in his works, but later seventeenth-century writers, in language sometimes verging on the religious, praised his impressive creativity. John Milton's (1608–1674) sonnet "On Shakespeare" refers to his "Delphick lines" (12), comparing his work to the utterances of the Greek oracle at Delphi. Although John Dryden (1631–1700) in his Preface to *Troilus and Cressida* (1679), like most of the eighteenth-century critics who followed him, saw numerous flaws in Shakespeare's diction, style, and plotting, he found the variety and depth of Shakespeare's characters to be signs of genius in the man he called "*that Divine Poet*" (vol 13, p. 246). More emphatically, in his Prologue to *The Tempest*, he declared that "Shakespear's *Pow'r is Sacred as a King's*" (vol. 10, p. 6). Clearly, Shakespeare himself was not thought to be divine, but his "untutored" or "natural" gifts enabled him to create what were regarded as undeniably inspired works.

THE EIGHTEENTH CENTURY

Numerous editions of Shakespeare appeared in the eighteenth century, and their editors occasionally continued Dryden's "divine" praise. In his Preface to *The Works of Shakespear* (1725), Alexander Pope extended Milton's idea of Shakespeare as an oracle: "he is not so much an Imitator, as an Instrument of Nature;

and 'tis not so just [appropriate] to say that he speaks from her, as that she speaks thro' him" (qtd. Smith, 44). In 1740, Lewis Theobald noted that "in the wild extravagant Notes of Shakespeare, you every now and then encounter Strains that recognize the divine Composer" (qtd. Smith, 72). Other critics began to take note of religious implications in the plays, especially as these violated or upheld contemporary expectations for drama. Nicholas Rowe, who cited Dryden's compliments in his own *Account of Shakespeare* (1709), praised Shakespeare's characterization of Henry VI as "showing [the king] . . . wholly resign'd to the severest Dispensations of God's Providence" (qtd. Smith, 16). However, in *On the Genius and Writings of Shakespear* (1712), John Dennis, expecting that all tragedies should exhibit a moral lesson grounded in divine law, found fault with Shakespeare's. "The Good and the Bad then perishing promiscuously [indiscriminately] in the best of *Shakespeare's* Tragedies, there can be either none or very weak Instruction in them: For such promiscuous Events call the Government of Providence into Question, and by Scepticks and Libertines are resolv'd into Chance" (qtd. Smith, 28). He typically considers religion under the larger issue of whether or not the plays adhered to the Aristotelian "rules" of time, place, and action, and the degree to which their language and plots were decorous or logical.

More than most critics of his age, Samuel Johnson (1709–1784) seemed able to rise above this "rule-mongering of lesser neo-classic critics" (Bate, 181) and to appreciate Shakespeare for his own merits rather than judging him too harshly by the critical standards of his day. Johnson, a devout member of the Church of England, had a complex respect for the dramatist (Jain). The two authors shared at least one point of ethical connection, namely a belief in the morally mixed nature of human life. Johnson, observes Jean Hagstrum, "found in human nature a balance of virtues and vices. As he said in one of his earliest works, 'Wherever human nature is to be found, there is a mixture of vice and virtue, a contest of passion and reason . . . '" (69). This statement accords with the comment of the First Lord in *All's Well That Ends Well*, "The web of our life is of a mingled yarn, good and ill together" (4.3.71–72). Johnson's notes on the plays themselves often reveal his own Anglican frame of mind. Rosalind's allusion to Venice in *As You Like It* (4.1.37–38) prompts Johnson to describe this city as one in which "young English gentlemen . . . sometimes lost their religion" (7: 258), while the clown's reference to "the surplice of humility" in *All's Well That Ends Well* (1.3.94–95) is "an allusion, violently enough forced in, to satirise the obstinacy with which the *Puritans* refused the use of the ecclesiastical habits" (7: 381). His defense of Henry IV's planned crusade to the Holy Land has a provocative relevance for modern readers: "If it be part of the religion of the Mahometans, to extirpate by the sword all other religions, it is, by the law of self defence, lawful for men of every other religion, and for Christians among others, to make war upon Mahometans, simply as Mahometans, as men obliged by their own principles to make war upon Christians, and only lying in wait till opportunity shall promise them success" (7: 455).

As authors of two of the best eighteenth-century essays on Shakespeare, Johnson and Pope recognized that despite his flaws, the playwright's unique talents so far outstripped conventional dramatic standards that he was in a category by him-self. As Pope remarked, "To judge therefore of *Shakespear* by *Aristotle's* rules, is like trying a man by the Laws of one Country, who acted under those of another" (Smith, 47). Shakespeare often contradicted neoclassical dramatic conventions not because he could not achieve them, but because his art was conceived in such a radically different way. Thus it was recognized that his seemingly incongruous use of witches and fairies in plays such as *Macbeth, A Midsummer Night's Dream,* and *The Tempest* did not negate the Christian context of his work, but existed together with it as evidence of the popular culture of his time. "The reformation did not immediately arrive at its meridian," commented Johnson in his notes on *Macbeth*, "and tho' day was gradually increasing upon us, the goblins of witchcraft still continued to hover in the twilight" (8: 753). A law passed in 1603, fostered in large part by King James's own treatise on *Daemonologie* (1597), made witch-craft punishable by death, thus validating this widespread superstition. A century and a half later belief in witchcraft had faded, and Johnson confidently attributed its decline to the growing influence of Anglicanism: "The jesuits and sectaries took advantage of this universal error . . . but they were detected and exposed by the clergy of the established church" (8: 755).

A somewhat different defense of Shakespeare's use of pagan or occult deities was made by Elizabeth Montagu in *An Essay on the Writings and Genius of Shake-spear* (1769), which contains a chapter "On the Praeternatural Beings." Montagu notes approvingly that gods, nymphs, and other supernatural deities populate Homer's poetry; "Shakespear saw how useful the popular superstitions had been to the ancient poets: he felt that they were necessary to poetry itself" (135). "Ghosts, fairies, goblins, elves, were as propitious, were as assistant to Shakespear, and gave as much of the sublime, and of the marvelous to his fictions, as nymphs, satyrs, fawns, and even the triple Geryon, to the works of ancient bards" (137). She also notes the influence of native folklore, observing that "The church of Rome adopted many of the Celtic superstitions" (143). Montagu is more inclined than Johnson to view the use of such pagan deities as an asset to Shakespeare's plays, but both critics agree that their presence is part of the native English char-acter of his works. Affirming that Shakespeare was more cultured than his own era, Montagu says, "Shakspear, in the dark shades of Gothic barbarism, had no resources but in the very phantoms that walked in the night of ignorance and superstition. . . . His choice of these subjects was judicious, if we consider the times in which he lived; his management of them so masterly, that he will be admired in all times" (151).

THE NINETEENTH CENTURY

The late eighteenth century saw a critical shift away from the importance of strict neoclassical definitions of dramatic "correctness" towards an emphasis, fostered by literary romanticism, upon Shakespeare's imaginative richness and psychological depth. Foremost among the English Romantic critics was the poet Samuel Taylor Coleridge (1772–1834). Coleridge praises Shakespeare for his inventiveness and the "organic form" of his plays, the wholeness and unity of each work springing from the unique combination of its own elements rather than from some externally imposed standard of excellence. He highlights the religious climate of the sixteenth century as a clear influence upon Shakespeare's work. The Reformation, which "sounded through Europe like a trumpet," fostered the "purer religion" of the poet's culture (94). Unlike eighteenth-century critics who emphasized the "barbarous" tastes of Shakespeare's audience, Coleridge finds their perceptions heightened by the era of religious reform. Shakespeare "lived in an age in which from the religious controversies . . . there was a general energy of thinking, a pleasure in hard thinking and an expectation of it from those who came forward to solicit public praise" (103). Yet Shakespeare himself was no mouthpiece for any particular sect: "he is of no age—nor, I may add, of any religion, party, or profession" (106). Noting the "style of the sermons of the time and the eagerness of the Protestants to distinguish themselves by long and frequent preaching," Coleridge concludes that "no country ever received such a national education as England" (109).

His comments on religion in the plays are infrequent, but he does explain the depth of Romeo's love for Juliet by stressing, like Plato, the divinely created moral tendency of humans to seek out a true love based on more than physical desire. Thus "we become worthy to conceive that infinite in ourselves, without which it is impossible for man to believe in a God. In a word, the grandest and most delightful of all promises has been expressed to us by this practical state—our marriage with the Redeemer of mankind" (135). In notes on Claudius's soliloquy in Hamlet (3.3.36–72), he explains that Claudius cannot gain atonement because of the fundamentally flawed nature of his character: "The divine medium of the Christian doctrine of expiation is this: not what you have done, but what you are, must determine" (152). The ghost of Hamlet's father, being "a superstition connected with the most sacred truths of revealed religion" (158), he considered as totally unrelated to the witches in Macbeth. Coleridge carefully notes that our impression of Desdemona is guided by Othello's perception of her as a spiritually pure being; Othello believes "that she, his angel, had fallen from the heaven of her native innocence . . . and, like him, is almost sanctified in our eyes by her absolute unsuspiciousness and holy entireness of love" (176). And in one of the careful distinctions that Coleridge is fond of making, he sees Iago as "a being next to devil, only *not* quite devil" (171). As for the problematic *Troilus and Cressida*, Coleridge offers the somewhat puzzling observation that Shakespeare's "ruling impulse was to translate the poetic heroes of paganism into the not less rude but more intellectually vigorous, more *featurely* warriors of Christian chivalry" (249).

Shakespeare's characterization received close attention from other noted Romantic critics: Charles Lamb's essay "On the Tragedies of Shakespeare" (1811, asserting that the tragedies are best appreciated only when read, not acted), William Hazlitt's *Characters of Shakespeare's Plays* (1817), and the German critic Augustus Wilhelm Schlegel's *Course of Lectures on Dramatic Art and Literature*, first delivered in 1801–1804 and an influence upon Coleridge. Among these, only Schlegel comments upon religion in the plays and then but briefly. He views the reformation context of *Hamlet* favorably. Hamlet studies at Wittenberg, "and no selection of a place could have been more suitable . . . . it was of particular celebrity in protestant England as Luther had taught and written there shortly before, and the very name must have immediately suggested the idea of freedom in thinking" (356). The frequency of monks in the plays does not result from any religious purpose by Shakespeare but is simply part of his poetic design: "We find in him none of the black and knavish monks, which an enthusiasm for Protestantism, rather than poetical inspiration, has suggested to some of our modern poets. Shakespeare merely gives his monks an inclination to busy themselves in the affairs of others, after renouncing the world for themselves" (388).

In 1841, Thomas Carlyle (1795–1881) broadly addressed Shakespeare's literary strengths in "The Hero as Poet" in his *Lectures on Heroes, Hero-Worship, and the Heroic in History*. Unlike Coleridge, who praised the Reformation's influence on Shakespeare, Carlyle begins by crediting the literary achievements of Elizabethan England, including Shakespeare's, "to the Catholicism of the Middle Ages." Sounding somewhat like contemporary revisionist historians, who find strong evidence for the persistence of English Catholicism even after the rise of Anglicanism, Carlyle notes that "the Christian Faith" created "this Practical Life which Shakespeare was to sing," although "Middle Age Catholicism was abolished, so far as Acts of Parliament could abolish it, before Shakespeare, the noblest product of it, made his appearance" (87). Once again, as with the eighteenth century critics, it is "Nature" which has brought forth in a particular historical age this poet, whom Carlyle acknowledges "the greatest intellect who, in our recorded world, has left record of himself in the way of Literature" (88).

Perhaps in response to Carlyle's hero-worship of Shakespeare, William John Birch (1811–63) published in 1848 *An Inquiry into the Philosophy and Religion of Shakspere*, a shrill and one-sided effort to show that Shakespeare was an atheist or at the very least a philosophical skeptic: "we think we can show that he sympathized with those who had no religion rather than those who had; with infidelity rather than belief" (13). Of Hamlet's "To be or not to be" speech Birch asserts, "That there *may be* an hereafter is the ancient position of the doubter. The Christian knows there is a world to come. . . . But Hamlet passes beyond mere doubt" (24–25). Birch fails to grasp Shakespeare's portrayal of hypocrisy when he notes that the Christians in *The Merchant of Venice* treat Shylock like "a wild beast" and then states, "Surely Christians were never before set, by a Christian, in so execrable a light!" (31). "This voluptuous sinner is the hero of profanity," he says of Falstaff (32), and "There is in King Lear all that grossness of materialism which seeks to degrade man to the level of the beasts" (47). One benefit of reading Birch is to realize how much an ultra-literal reading of Shakespeare can distort his works. Birch clearly believes himself to be a person of impeccable faith, but he strikes one as smugly narrow-minded. Other late Victorians disagreed with his conclusions; Thomas Carter argued for *Shakespeare Puritan and Recusant* (1897), while Richard Simpson and Henry G. Bowden, in *The Religion of Shakspere* (1899), contended that he had been a Catholic.

A far more reasonable attempt to show Shakespeare as irreligious is George Santyana's essay of 1900, "The Absence of Religion in Shakespeare." It is better seen as a reaction against the Romantic and Victorian praise of Shakespeare as a kind of religious seer than as a precursor to twentieth-century views. He sees the poet as more the product of the secular Renaissance than of the religious Reformation. Santayana does not consider Shakespeare's various references to bishops, friars, or rituals as evidence of "true religious feeling," which he finds only in "two or three short passages [from *Richard II* and *Henry V*] and one sonnet [#146]" (161). Believing that the Renaissance lacked a modern religious and philosophical diversity, he asserts that for Shakespeare "in the matter of religion, the choice lay between Christianity and nothing. He chose nothing; he chose to leave his heroes and himself in the presence of life and of death with no other philosophy than that which the profane world can suggest and understand" (162). Shakespeare, living in a society in which "to be religious already began to mean to be Puritanical" (167), failed to produce works that had the unifying vision of Homer or Dante. Santayana's thesis oversimplifies the complexity of the Elizabethan religious scene and Shakespeare's response to it. For most modern readers, Shakespeare's lack of a consistent denominational orientation is evidence of his breadth of vision, but for Santayana it is a drawback. Shakespeare is "without a philosophy and without a religion" (168); lacking a "system" or "unity of conception," our "emotions cannot be steadfast and enlightened" or our imagination "achieve its supreme success" (169). Few if any modern critics have sided completely with Santayana's uncompromising view, but he does call attention to the problem of how a writer with such a seemingly indefinable frame of reference manages to achieve a unified work of art.

THE TWENTIETH CENTURY

The volume of criticism published on Shakespeare in the twentieth century has increased tremendously over what was produced in previous eras. His work has been examined within every major theoretical approach practiced by contemporary readers, whether it be formalist, biographical, historical, psychological, mythological, feminist, deconstructive, sociological (Marxist), new historicist, or some combination of these. Theorists do not speak of a "religious" critical approach to Shakespeare, and discussions of religion in his work typically fall within one or more of these broader literary frameworks. Arthur M. Eastman's *A Short History of Shakeseparean Criticism* (1968) does not list "religion," "Christianity," or "spirituality" in its index, nor does Michael Taylor's *Shakespeare Criticism in the Twentieth Century* (2001), although Taylor does devote a brief section to religion and myth-criticism. "Once taking centre stage," he says, "religious, mythic, and archetypal criticism of Shakespeare now languishes on the sidelines," but he notes that "this critical approach has not yet reached the vanishing point" (214). It may, however, be premature to suggest a "vanishing point" if one consults the World Shakespeare Bibliography Online, which in February,

2007, listed 371 entries for the keyword "religion," more than the number listed for either "psychology" or "Marxism."

Heather Dubrow has divided the history of twentieth-century Shakespeare criticism at 1970, after which the influence of European literary theory made its full impact. Insofar as religion is concerned, it may be more helpful to organize the twentieth-century criticism on his work into three broad and often overlapping categories. What may be called criticism of religion as *doctrine* pays close attention to Christian theological concepts, rituals of worship, forms of prayer, or historic religious texts, whether Catholic or Protestant. This label does not imply that Shakespeare espouses the doctrine of any particular church; instead, this type of analysis looks closely at the parallels, analogues or correspondences between Shakespeare's plays and the content of such works as medieval religious plays, Elizabethan homilies, or biblical passages so as to consider Shakespeare's canon within a carefully defined denominational or intellectual context. Criticism of religion as *spirituality* approaches his works as expressions of a fundamental human engagement with the divine but with less regard to institutional labels or precise theological distinctions. It tends to treat Christianity generically, not in a sectarian or denominational way, and emphasizes broad themes or motifs such as sin, suffering, and redemption. These can be linked as well to discussions of mythic, aesthetic, or anthropological insights into pagan or folkloric beliefs. Finally, criticism of religion as *ideology* reflects the influence of postmodern literary theory by viewing religion as a sociopolitical factor within history. Religious leaders and their policies are seen as exerting a patriarchal and hierarchical influence on racial, ethnic, and cultural groups; religions cannot be regarded as functioning apart from the politics and social conflicts of their believers. Marx's famous definition of religion as "the opium of the people" is one example of an ideological view (a negative one to be sure) of religion. Although book-length discussions are emphasized in what follows, it should be understood that there is a vast body of critical essays on these topics; they can be accessed through the MLA Bibliography or, for items after 1963, in the World Shakespeare Bibliography (both available online). It is significant that, despite the variety of critical approaches that characterize modern Shakespearean scholarship, religion has remained a consistent focus of inquiry and has recently acquired new attention through the greater interest being paid to Shakespeare's Catholic background, as evidenced in Stephen Greenblatt's *Will in the World* and studies by Naseeb Shaheen, Richard Wilson, Richard Dutton, and Dennis Taylor, among others.

Religion as Doctrine

The analysis of Shakespeare's treatment of religion within the historical framework of church doctrine typically links the plays to specific texts such as the Bible, the *Book of Common Prayer*, or theological works, connections which have been documented in several important reference works. Aiming primarily to list parallels and allusions between the plays and these works, rather than critically discussing the meanings of these parallels, are Alfred Hart's *Shakespeare and the Homilies*

(1934) and Richmond P. Noble's study, *Shakespeare's Biblical Knowledge and Use of the Book of Common Prayer, as exemplified in the Plays of the First Folio* (1935). More recently, this approach has been continued by Naseeb Shaheen's *Biblical References in Shakespeare's Plays* (1999) and in R. Chris Hassel's *Shakespeare's Religious Language: A Dictionary* (2005), which assembles an extensive list of words of religious significance in the works.

It should be noted that one danger of a doctrinal approach to the plays is to view them simply as vehicles for theological ideas and to downplay their complex function as dramatic works of art, so that, for example, Iago "is" Satan or Cordelia "is" Christ. This temptation to read the plays as allegories, merely as literary expressions of abstract ideas, has been criticized by many commentators, including Brian Vickers in *Appropriating Shakespeare: Contemporary Critical Quarrels* (1993); indeed, he contends that all of the modern approaches to the plays mentioned in this chapter are subject to being misused or overused. A doctrinal approach can also be allied with attempts to investigate Shakespeare's own religious biography, to closely examine his plays for hints and suggestions that might disclose his personal beliefs. The danger here is of falling into a circular argument: a passage from a play may served as "evidence" suggesting Shakespeare's Catholicism, for example, and this presumed Catholicism might then be used to brand another passage as "evidence," which further confirms his Catholicism as a "fact." This is a pitfall that some have noted in Peter Milward's extensive attempts to show that Shakespeare was not merely writing as the child of Catholic parents, but as a believing Catholic dramatist himself. R. Chris Hassel has summarized these and other critical problems that must be guarded against when studying Shakespeare's literary use of religious ideas ("Love Versus Charity," 17).

Beginning in World War II, critics reacted to the more subjective spiritual approach to religion in the plays that had been taken by A. C. Bradley and G. Wilson Knight (discussed below) and began to look more closely at the theological basis of Shakespeare's plays. In *Shakespeare and the Popular Dramatic Tradition* (1944), S. L. Bethell sought to show that Elizabethan audiences could respond to drama "spontaneously and unconsciously on more than one plane of attention at the same time" (29). Because of this "multi-consciousness" the Duke in *Measure for Measure* and Prospero in *The Tempest,* for example, would be perceived as "symbolic of some aspects of Deity" (106). Since "Every one was familiar with the complex methods of biblical interpretation" (113–114), and the "exotic and sensual" Song of Solomon in the Bible was historically understood as the "marriage of Christ and his Church," he concluded that a play such as "the exotic and sensual *Antony and Cleopatra* might also yield its hidden meaning to an audience simultaneously aware of the two levels of story and significance" (114). Three years later, Bethell applied his concept of "multi-consciousness" to a single play in *The Winter's Tale: A Study*, contending that Shakespeare was either "a Roman Catholic recusant" or "an Anglican inclining more to Hooker than to Calvin" (13) and that he offers "a profoundly Christian interpretation of life" (14). By intentionally choosing an old fable for his basic story, creating an artificial geography for Bohemia, inserting a significant lapse of time in the plot, and making his "dramatic technique crude and apparently incoherent" (47), Shakespeare distances us from the action and reminds us that we are watching a different plane of reality, a work of dramatic art rather than realistic "truth." This alternate plane allows us to see in the play "the Christian scheme of redemption" (76) composed of sin, repentance, and redemption. Bethell does not argue that *The Winter's Tale* is an allegory, but he finds its structure to be founded upon this theological pattern.

Paul N. Siegel also noted the role of theology in his study *Shakespearean Tragedy and the Elizabethan Compromise* (1957). He pointed out that the religious convictions of the Tudor humanists of the early sixteenth century were challenged by a growing skepticism in the early seventeenth century, when Shakespeare was composing his greatest tragedies, and his "villains embody values destructive to the ideal of Christian Humanism" (87). This clash of cultural values is portrayed in tragic characters who are fully rounded individuals yet who display clear religious dimensions. "Concerned though Shakespeare's humanist drama is with the passions and struggles of human individuals rather than with the oppositions of allegorical figures, his characters, following the old patterns of temptation, sin, and retribution and of sin, repentance, and salvation, often are implicitly or explicitly compared with the biblical archetypes of erring humanity, diabolical evil, and divine goodness" (88). While not writing allegories, Siegel says, Shakespeare is able to incorporate biblical figures and patterns in such a way as to deepen the religious meaning of his dramas. Even imperfect characters, for example, might reflect Christ; Desdemona—who lies to Othello about her handkerchief—and the self-indulgent Richard II are both Christ-figures (89–90).

Bernard Spivack likewise avoided arguing that Shakespeare wrote allegories, but in *Shakespeare and the Allegory of Evil* (1958), he demonstrated that Shakespeare had used the allegorical character of the Vice from the medieval morality plays to help shape his most villainous characters. Although the church had fought against the heresy of dualism found among the Manicheans (the belief that the world was the battleground between the forces of good and evil), it did recognize the Devil as a powerful force for sin against which believers had to struggle. The provoking tempter and evil agent in the medieval morality plays who incites humans to sin was the Vice figure. While not Satan himself, this "unique protagonist of evil . . . creates a play to demonstrate a moral text" and "he survives in plays that are not otherwise moralities" (178). Richard III thus brashly compares himself to "the formal Vice, Iniquity" (3.1.82), and Falstaff is a comic variation when Prince Hal refers to him as "that reverent Vice, that grey Iniquity" (2.4.453–454). Spivack also finds the influence of the Vice figure in Aaron in *Titus Andronicus,* Don John in *Much Ado About Nothing,* Edmund in *King Lear,* and, most notably, in Iago in *Othello.* If Coleridge had been aware of Shakespeare's reliance on the Vice figure, Spivack suggests, he would have realized that Iago's behavior was not "motiveless malignity" but the predictable action of a medieval evildoer (27).

It is true that plays are not religious tracts, and that, as Naseeb Shaheen remarks, "Elizabethans did not go to the theatre to be indoctrinated with theology" (155), but these and other similar postwar critics stressed that in Shakespeare's age an awareness of religious doctrine permeated society to a degree that is probably impossible for most twenty-first century readers—even Christians—to appreciate. J. A. Bryant, Jr. emphasized this point in *Hippolyta's View: Some Christian Aspects of Shakespeare's Plays* (1961). In such a religiously-charged context, it was natural for people to make comparisons between religious characters, issues, or situations and similar figures or events in scripture. This use of comparisons, usually to explain what was complex in terms of what was simpler, is known as *analogy*. Analogy is the primary poetic device in the instructive parables of Jesus, as in Matthew 13, where the "kingdom of heaven" is "likened unto a man which sowed good seed in his field" (24), or "leaven, which a woman took and hid in three measures of meal" (33), or "treasure hid in a field" (44), or "a net, that was cast into the sea" (47). Bryant observes: "If the sense of analogy was weakening in [Shakespeare's] day, it is all but lost in ours . . . the analogical use of Scripture, simply because it happens to be well documented in a variety of sources, provides one of our firmest clues to a mode of thinking that was habitual with a great many people" (114). A more specific form of analogy is *typology*, in which the comparison is between events and persons of the Old Testament who are "types" or foreshadowings of figures and actions in the New Testament, most often in the life of Christ himself. Typology is not a doctrine of faith but, rather, a method by which such a doctrine can be expressed and interpreted. "[T]ypology had an opportunity to influence the thinking of practically all Elizabethans, whether literate or illiterate. Almost everybody heard sermons in those days, and almost everybody who heard sermons heard typological interpretations of Scripture" (11). For Bryant, "consciously or unconsciously, Shakespeare was a genuine typologist in his use of Scriptural allusion and analogy" (16). Bryant's own study traces various biblical contexts that illuminate twelve plays. He notes that while viewing *Richard II*, Shakespeare's audience would have recalled that this king had killed his uncle, Thomas of Woodstock. Bolingbroke seizes this fact to brand Thomas as Abel and Richard as Cain; Thomas's blood "like sacrificing Abel's, cries, / Even from the tongueless caverns of the earth" (1.1.104–105). It was common in the New Testament, the Mass, and among early church writings, to equate Abel and Christ and "Cain with the disbelieving Jews who slew him" (28). Later on in the play, Richard identifies himself with Christ and his political enemies with Judas; "the chain of analogies, as Shakespeare conceived it, seems complete: Richard-Christ-antichrist-Cain, all are linked as one" (29). The use of typology leads to an even more complex understanding of Shylock in *The Merchant of Venice*. Bryant draws upon John Foxe's sermon on Romans 11, which notes that "modern Jews, in addition to being descendants of the ones who crucified Jesus, are typological fulfillments of the murderer of Abel, the betrayer of Joseph, the contemner of Moses, the slayer of the Paschal lamb, and the detractors of King David" (49). Typology also links Antony, in *Antony and Cleopatra*, "to the story of Samson, who has often been treated as a type of Christ. Like Samson, Antony has his Delilah to tempt him from his destiny; but, even more important, Antony, like Samson the Nazirite, has a special destiny" (181). A more explicit link occurs when Antony exclaims "O, that I were / Upon the hill of Basan" (3.13126–127), an allusion to Psalm 22: 12, pointing to the contrast between Antony's "common" reputation and his original "image of goodness" (180).

Bryant asserts that there is such a thing as Christian tragedy, a seemingly impossible idea because ultimately through Christ's resurrection death has been defeated. He does not deny the "comedy [of the Resurrection] with its mystery and its revelation," but he emphasizes that a real tragedy first occurs as the result of man's prideful violation of God's will. The suffering in Christian tragedy exists when man realizes the stark contrast between what he could have become and what he has made of himself. "The Christian's fall, however, is far more tragic than Adam's, for as a result of the incarnation of God in Jesus, he can see more clearly the image of the creator in his own flesh and in his own actions" (113). Thus, Antony has lost his former greatness by falling for the enticements of Cleopatra, and Othello, who with his "free and open nature, shows off the divine office . . . is far short of being divine and must, in doing his best, come out a fool" (148).

In 1963 Roland M. Frye published *Shakespeare and Christian Doctrine*, a work that sought to correct the views of such earlier critics as A. C. Bradley and G. Wilson Knight, as well as Bryant. Frye brands most theological analyses of Shakespeare "literally inept and theologically naïve" (6) because they tend to reach unsupportable conclusions. For Frye, Shakespeare is not intent on teaching theology, but refers to it solely for his secular dramatic purposes. Shakespeare "seems to have known Christian doctrine intimately, though not on any professional plane. His references to the commonplace topics of theology are never introduced into the drama for doctrinaire reasons, and the action of the plays is never subservient to the presentation of any systematic theology" (9). Though "his plays do contain more theological allusions than have sometimes been recognized" (9), Frye finds it impossible to track exactly what Shakespeare's personal reading in theology was. Like most of his modern critical predecessors, he rejects an overemphasis upon the use of allegory to explain the plays' religious references, and he dismisses Bryant's reading of Othello as unsupported by evidence (31). The urge to find Christ-figures in the dramas he calls a "mania" (39).

Frye finds no evidence in the works of Luther, Calvin, or Hooker that Elizabethan theologians expected literature to be written or read with a special emphasis upon its possible religious meaning, nor did they expect that any ethical models of moral behavior in literature ought to be drawn only from religious sources. He comments on a variety of topics common to Christian doctrine to which Shakespeare refers and finds that some (e.g., God, Pride, Affliction, the Beastliness of Humanity) are treated in ways that classical thinkers as well as Christians would agree with; they are topics common to humanity. Others are uniquely Christian (e.g., Atonement, Guilt, Sin), and it is these alone that repay Christian analysis, as in the references to two traditional aspects of repentance, mortification and vivification, in *Hamlet* and *The Tempest*. Says Frye, "When [Shakespeare] did not write in such unmistakably Christian terms, we should assume that he did not invite a theological interpretation" (272). Frye's point is that discussion of Christian references in the plays must be made more carefully, be better supported by convincing argument, and should recognize that such references "were enclosed by Shakespeare within clearly secular and this-worldly bounds" (57).

One critic of Frye's approach, Roy Battenhouse, contended, however, that Frye had restricted the scope of theological authority in Shakespeare's England too narrowly. Certainly one should look to Luther, Calvin, and Hooker for insights into Elizabethan theology, but in *Shakespearean Tragedy: Its Art and Its Christian Premises* (1969), Battenhouse argued that attention should also be paid to older theologians from the early church who were still quite influential, such saints as Augustine, Chrysostom, Jerome, Bernard, Ambrose, and Basil. "Hooker in fact," he notes, "represents a position closer to Aquinas than to Calvin" (79). Battenhouse's long and detailed study of tragedy is based on his conviction that the roots of these plays reach back beyond the Renaissance, "that a knowledge of Shakespeare's background in medieval Christian lore—which includes theology, symbolism, and the principle of analogy—can be of particular help toward a better understanding of his tragedies" (46). Battenhouse takes a more open-ended approach than Frye to discovering a play's Christian meaning and does not limit such a meaning to only those statements that accord with Reformation thinkers. "[A] drama can carry clues to interpretation which are beyond the ken of its protagonists. A Christian author when dramatizing pagan times can punctuate his story with a figurative overplot and its diction with an underside of meaning. Thereby he challenges us to grasp the final significance of the action by the light of a Christian *Weltanschauung* [worldview]" (181). Echoing a point made earlier by S. L. Bethell, he feels that even as pagan a play as *Antony and Cleopatra* can reveal a Christian "underside" if we recall "the typological knowledge which all readers of Scripture had, not merely from the book of Exodus but as a continuing symbolism throughout the Old and New Testaments and especially in the book of Revelation" (181).

Battenhouse contends that a clearer understanding of Hamlet's tragic flaw can be gained by "Christianizing" Aristotle's concept of *hamartia* (207). He does this by first referring to Augustine, for whom "inordinate love of self" and "aversion from God" are key sources of sin (220). He then follows Aquinas's thinking in the great work of medieval Catholic theology, the *Summa Theologica*, and points out that in Hamlet this love of self takes the form of "an inordinate apprehension of the imagination," which causes him to see Claudius as a "satyr" and term his mother "bestial" (224). Battenhouse climaxes his discussion by suggesting that a "comprehensive way of viewing the tragedy of Hamlet" (262) is to read it as a tragic parody of the atonement, the reconciliation of man with God achieved through the death of Christ.

> Hamlet as scourge pervertedly imitates Christ's role as suffering servant; his flight from reality pervertedly imitates Christian pilgrimage; his being visited by a ghost is darkly analogous to a baptism or a Pentecost; his longing for "the witching time of night" reverses the Christian hope; his Gnostic wish that his flesh may melt and free him parodies Christian desire for transcendence; his Manichean melodrama of "mighty opposites" counterfeits the Christian concept of a warfare between God and Satan. And, to sum it all up, Hamlet's stealthy strategy for setting the world right is a perverse imitation of the method of Atonement in Christian story. (263)

This interpretation presents an impressive consistency, although it imposes a kind of predictability on the play that threatens to transform it into the very sort of allegory to which Frye and others had objected. Although Battenhouse is in sympathy with the critical method of Bryant, he gives greater emphasis to the importance of Roman Catholic theologians in reaching his conclusions. It should be noted, however, that allegorical interpretations can be revealing, and the benefits of this critical strategy should not ignored; Lionel Basney has said that, unlike the tragedies, the late romances "project other kinds of play-world, in which allegorical and pageant-like representations of salvation are appropriate" (34). One of the better examples of this approach, as applied to a comedy, is Barbara Lewalski's significant 1962 article, "Biblical Allusion and Allegory in *The Merchant of Venice*."

In 1979 R. Chris Hassel investigated the relationships between those Shakespeare plays that had been produced on festival days of the church year and the doctrinal meaning of those festivals. *Renaissance Drama and the English Church Year* pointed out that plays (not merely by Shakespeare) produced at court on such feast days as Epiphany, Candlemas, Shrovetide, Easter, and others, had suggestive parallels with the theological meanings of their respective celebrations. Some, such as *Twelfth Night*, were named for a particular day, while others express a link through theme, character, or plot. The framing story of *The Comedy of Errors*, performed at Gray's Inn on the feast of Holy Innocents (December 28), is that of the separated family of Egeon and Emilia that reiterates the theme of Jeremiah 31: 1–17 as "the Lord's promise to reunite the dispersed and weeping families of Israel" (41). There are clear parallels between *Twelfth Night* and the feast of Epiphany (January 6) as both express the "basic values of the Christmas season, forgivness and humility" (78). This play was also performed on Candlemas (February 2), as was *King Lear*, a surprising choice until, says Hassel, we see the play's use of ideas from the ninth chapter of the book of Wisdom, which was read on that day. In perhaps the most obvious connection, *The Winter's Tale* was performed at Easter, the reappearance of Hermione at the play's end figuring the resurrection of Christ.

Hassel followed this book with a study of the comedies, *Faith and Folly in Shakespeare's Romantic Comedies* (1980), finding that paradoxes from St. Paul and Erasmus concerning "reversals of folly and wisdom" (ix) offer a unifying insight into six different comedies. "There are inconceivable blessings of love and faith for those who can admit with humility the profound folly of their limited knowledge; there is abundant grace and forgiveness for those who can acknowledge with humility the profound folly of their imperfect behavior" (15). This discussion also points to contemporary theological debates. When, in *Love's Labour's Lost* for example, Berowne says "For charity itself fulfills the law, / And who can sever love from charity"? (4.3 361–362), he alludes to the contention over the translation of Romans 13: 10, the Catholics preferring "charity" and the Protestants choosing "love" (30–37). Bottom's visionary speech in *A Midsummer Night's Dream* (4.1.203–219) "alerts us to the possibilities and the impossibilities of our own knowing, the limits of human reason and human behavior evoked by all profound fools of Christian or comic persuasion" (58).

More recently, in a 1994 article on "Hamlet's 'Too, Too Solid Flesh,'" Hassel has argued that Hamlet's delay is the result of a "paralyzing desire for perfect knowledge and perfect doing," an over-reliance upon human capability, which Luther had termed the "wisdom of the flesh" (609). Hassel's Lutheran reading of the play offers an interesting contrast with Stephen Greenblatt's emphasis upon its Catholic context (to be noticed below). Taken together, these interpretations lend support to Maurice Hunt's contention that Shakespeare's allusions to religion are uniquely tolerant of both reformed and Roman viewpoints. "Shakespeare's syncretistic method for incorporating Protestant and Catholic elements into his plays is virtually singular among early modern English playwrights at a time when governmental and social tolerance of Protestantism in the theater was high and criticism of usually stereotyped Catholicism was correspondingly rampant in drama" (ix). Hunt acknowledges that it is difficult for a modern reader to determine whether Shakespeare's balanced view of religion reflected his own personal stance, or his indifference to the details of theological wrangling, or his willingness as a dramatist to use any material at hand to further the dramatic effectiveness of his plays (xiii). Hunt's concept of Shakespeare's religious "tolerance" invites our consideration of a broader doctrinal context for the plays, but one based always in a knowledge of the playwright's contemporary religious environment.

Religion as Spirituality

Criticism of religion as *spirituality* considers religious themes apart from the immediately historical or theological context with which religion as *doctrine* is concerned and minus the focus on political power found in criticism of religion as *ideology*. The work of A. C. Bradley (1851–1935) contains significant comments on the tragedies from this perspective. In his seminal *Shakespearean Tragedy* (1904), Bradley was careful to avoid suggesting that Shakespeare presents an overtly "religious" worldview; religion was not Bradley's primary focus, hence, he is not included among the critics of "doctrine" cited earlier, although those critics often respond to his commentary. Yet he does argue for the presence of a moral order at work in the tragedies that is something more than simply blind fate, and he comments that both Hamlet and Macbeth approach a kind of religious outlook prior to their deaths. "The horror in Macbeth's soul is more than once represented as desperation at the thought that he is eternally 'lost'; the same idea appears in the attempt of Claudius at repentance; and as *Hamlet* nears its close, the 'religious' tone of the tragedy is deepened in two ways" (141). The first way is through Hamlet's chance rescue by pirates, which is designed to be seen as divinely intended. The second is through "that feeling, on Hamlet's part, of his being in the hands of Providence" (142). The religious tone is suggested at the play's opening, when the king's ghost appears from purgatory, and at the end, with "the similar idea of a soul carried by angels to its rest" (142).

In the second half of *King Lear,* Bradley notes "in most of the better characters a preoccupation with the question of the ultimate power, and a passionate need to explain by reference to it what otherwise would drive them to despair." The result of this on the audience's imagination is "in causing it to receive from *King Lear* an impression which is at least as near of kin to the *Divine Comedy* as to *Othello*" (219). He especially takes note of Edgar's "pronounced and conscious religiousness." Of Edgar's statement that "The gods are just, and of our pleasant vices / Make instruments to plague us" (5.3.171–72) Bradley comments, "He interprets everything religiously, and is here speaking from an intense conviction which overrides personal feelings . . . He never thinks of despairing; in the worst circumstances he is sure there is something to be done to make things better. And he is sure of this, not only from temperament, but from faith in 'the clearest gods'" [4.6.73] (244).

Like the Romantic critics with whom he shares a strong interest in character analysis (too great an interest, said critics such as L. C. Knights), Bradley can be movingly perceptive about the ways in which Shakespeare's characters and audience are affected by indefinable realities, as in his comment on the ending of *King Lear.* "Its final and total result is one to which pity and terror, carried perhaps to the extreme limits of art, are so blended with a sense of law and beauty that we feel at last, not depression and much less despair, but a consciousness of greatness in pain, and of solemnity in the mystery we cannot fathom" (223).

One of the most prolific critics of Shakespeare's spiritual dimension was G. Wilson Knight (1897–1984). His most important works appeared before the end of World War II: *Myth and Miracle* (1929), a study of the "mystic symbolism" of Shakespeare; *The Wheel of Fire* (1930), on the major tragedies; *The Imperial Theme* (1931), covering the tragedies and the Roman plays; *The Shakesparean Tempest* (1932), discussing *The Tempest* and musical themes; *The Crown of Life* (1947) on the final plays; and *The Mutual Flame* (1955), focusing on the *Phoenix and the Turtle* and the sonnets. Known for his emphasis upon metaphor and imagery, Knight viewed the plays themselves as metaphors and felt that characters should only be understood within their "spatial" context, the dramatic atmosphere and meaningful surroundings in which they exist on stage. His essays in *The Christian Renaissance* (1962) stress that Shakespeare's plays combine both the spiritual and the material dimensions of experience. Literature and religion thus share a revelatory function by illustrating the fullness of existence. "All religions and all art are purposive towards awaking our sight to the miraculous life which we live, to immediate experience. This exists not in terms of matter or of spirit, but of both; or rather in the matter-spirit continuum which transcends its elements and corresponds to the 'eternal life' of the Gospels" (45). When the worlds of spirit and matter are disconnected the result is tragic; "Our extreme example is *Macbeth*, with its violent disjointing of the spirit-world from nature" (40), evidenced by the ghost of Banquo, the witches, the dagger in the air, and the troublesome dreams. The comedies tend toward a union of spirit and matter, as in *The Tempest*. "Prospero controls both Ariel and Caliban: here the excessively spiritual and the excessively earthly are shown under human control.

The spirit-nature harmony is always our ideal, though it need not preclude the possibility of divine beings, conceived as self-sufficient personalities in contrast to ghosts which are only hideous abstractions from the human" (43). Similarly, Theseus in A Midsummer Night's Dream "stands over the action as a man in whom discords are resolved. He shares with Bottom and Oberon the dominance of the drama, refusing to believe in the frenzied imaginations of lunatic, lover, or poet (V.i.2–22). His poetry is incarnated in life. He is almost a Christ-figure possessing the Christ-harmony" (44).

Like Shakespeare's plays, the New Testament itself is for Knight an art form and "has many correspondences with ancient myth" (49); it is "a divine poetry in that it blends the poetic world with the world's history" (53). The poet of this creative work is Jesus himself. "Jesus is a person corresponding to the art-form of the poet. He is in himself the incarnation the poet accomplishes in art. He creates in his imagination his own poetry and then acts it, making himself the protagonist in his own drama. Shakespeare's tragic heroes may sometimes be regarded as figures of Christ-like endurance and martyrdom" though without his moral perfection. (52). While Knight's approach to criticism is quite personal and subjective, he does raise for us the value of the reader's "intuition" as a critical tool, and asks us to "consider again our impressions" (51) as guides into the plays. Hugh Grady has called for new attention to the importance of Knight as a modernist critic of Shakespeare. Chris Baldick praises Knight for having offered a way of understanding the problem play Measure for Measure "as a consistent Christian allegory or parable of justice and forgiveness, with the Duke cast as God" and for his overarching view of the tragedies—a view praised by T. S. Eliot—which "are made to follow a redemptive Christian scheme in which Macbeth is hell, King Lear purgatory, and Antony and Cleopatra heaven, while Timon plays the role of Christ" (94–95).

Fifteen years younger than Knight, Northrop Frye (1912–1991) developed a theory of criticism grounded in the mythic language of poetry, spelled out in his Anatomy of Criticism: Four Essays (1957) and later applied in such works as Fables of Identity (1963), A Natural Perspective: The Development of Shakespearean Comedy and Romance (1965), Fools of Time: Studies in Shakespearean Tragedy (1967), Spiritus Mundi (1976), The Myth of Deliverance: Reflections on Shakespeare's Problem Comedies (1983) and two studies of the Bible, The Great Code (1983) and Words with Power (1992). Among many other sources, Frye draws upon the work of earlier anthropological studies of literature, including Sir James Frazer's Golden Bough (1890), which examined such motifs as the dying and resurrected god, and upon the archetypal psychology of Carl Jung (1875–1961). In Heather Dubrow's words, "Frye's interest lies not in the close scrutiny of particular texts but rather in the comprehensive discovery and classification of recurrent generic, mythic, and Christian patterns" (37). Religious themes in Shakespeare are thus one of several patterns of underlying meaning that compose the works. The words "wonder" and "grace" echo throughout The Winter's Tale with several levels of meaning, two of them being "the power of God (the Classical gods in this play) that makes the redemption of humanity possible and, second, the quality that distinguishes civilized life, of the kind 'natural' to man, from the untutored or boorish" (Northrop

Frye on Shakespeare, 167). The recurring, mythic patterns of Shakespeare's comedies reiterate the redemptive pattern of Christianity itself. "The framework of the Christian myth is the comic framework of the Bible, where man loses a peaceable kingdom, staggers through the long nightmare of tyranny and injustice which is human history, and eventually regains his original vision. Within this myth is the corresponding comedy of the Christian life" (*A Natural Perspective*, 133).

> When we find Falstaff invited to the final feast in *The Merry Wives*, Caliban reprieved, attempts made to mollify Malvolio, and Angelo and Parolles allowed to live down their disgrace, we are seeing a fundamental principle of comedy at work. The tendency of the comic society to include rather than exclude is the reason for the traditional importance of the parasite, who has no business to be at the final festival but is nevertheless there. The word "grace" with all its Renaissance overtones from the graceful courtier of Castiglione [author of the 1528 conduct book *The Courtier*] to the gracious God of Christianity, is a most important thematic word in Shakespeare. (*Anatomy*, 165–166)

In the comedies and romances, references to the providence of God are less explicit than in the histories, but we do find "characters or powers who act as though they were agents of providence. In three of the romances a deity—Diana in *Pericles*, Jupiter in *Cymbeline*, and a hidden off-stage Apollo in *The Winter's Tale*—brings about or is involved in the redemptive conclusion. Where it is accomplished by a human being, as it is in *The Tempest* and *Measure for Measure*, that character has about him something of the mysterious aura of divinity, symbolized by magic or sanctity" (*A Natural Perspective*, 125). Frye is careful to note that the processes of nature may resemble some Christian principles without being identical to them. In *Fables of Identity*, his discussion of "Recognition in the *Winter's Tale*" points out that Hermione pointedly refers to "grace" several times during the play. "But such grace is not Christian or theological grace, which is superior to the order of nature, but a secular analogy of Christian grace which is identical with nature" (111). The only romance in which he finds explicit links to Christianity is *Cymbeline*. "Cymbeline was king of Britain at the birth of Christ, and in such scenes as the Jailer's speculations about death and his wistful 'I would we were all of one mind, and that mind good,' there are hints that some far-reaching change in the human situation is taking place off-stage" (112). In his notebooks, Frye noted that there was "no evidence" that Shakespeare had himself reached a meditative "higher consciousness" of the divine, but his work "certainly manifests that world," and Frye wondered if by reading Shakespeare it is not possible for one to reach "a genuine Logos vision" (qtd. Denham, 186).

Frye's emphasis on mythology is linked with anthropology in the work of René Girard (born 1923). Girard draws upon several disciplines in exploring the relationships among religion, violence, mimesis, literature, and the Bible in such works as *Violence and the Sacred* (1977), *The Scapegoat* (1986), *Things Hidden Since the Foundation of the World* (1987), and *I See Satan Fall Like Lightning* (2001). His interest in the relationship between religion and violence and in the concept of human mimesis (the imitation by people of each others' actions or desires) appears in *Theatre of Envy* (1991), a study of how Shakespeare depicts imitative acts and concepts and their resulting influence on dramatic meaning. Girard notes that in *Julius Caesar,* while mere butchery seems to imitate a sacrificial death, the two are quite different, which is why Brutus wishes Caesar's death to seem a religious act. Sacrifice is "a *good* violence that seems and therefore is mysteriously different from the *bad* violence of the crisis" (214); Shakespeare's "understanding of sacrificial religion is the highest peak of his mimetic vision" (216). In *The Merchant of Venice,* there is likewise a mimetic parallel between "the explicit venality of Shylock and the implicit venality of the other Venetians" (244) that influences the play's theme; "the Christians will easily destroy Shylock, but they will go on living in a world that is sad without knowing why, a world in which even the difference between revenge and charity has been abolished" (247). For Leontes in *The Winter's Tale,* the stone statue of Hermione imitates the "stone" or obstacle preventing his understanding of the truth about her and also suggests the stone that sealed the tomb of Jesus. When her statue comes to life, she is released, and he is freed from delusion; these "stones" are rolled away in a kind of resurrection (340–341). Girard's work is a challenging combination of psychology, mythology, religion, and symbolic meaning, informed as well by his own Roman Catholicism.

Ewan Fernie's recent anthology of essays, *Spiritual Shakespeares* (2005), combines an interest in varying definitions of "spirituality" with the application of postmodern critical concepts. Fernie's conception of spirituality is one that purposely defies neat definition, as he announces: "It is necessary to think in terms not so much of spiritual truth as truths" (7). Spirituality is not quite the same as ideology, nor is it a synonym for religion. "Spirituality is an experience of truth, and of living in accordance with truth, but it is concerned with the truth not of this world but of a world that has not yet and perhaps never will come to be. Spirituality is a mode of opposition to what is" (9). This conception is linked closely with the ideas of the French theorist Jacques Derrida, for whom God is the indefinable Other for which we experience a yearning (14). Two chapters from this volume will suggest its critical path. Richard Kearny's essay approaches *Hamlet* as "a play about a crisis of narrative memory" involving "holy and unholy ghosts" (155), which he examines from psychoanalytic, existential, deconstructive, and theological vantages. He concludes that play is a "metamorphosis of melancholy into a miracle of mourning" and "deep spiritual enlightenment" (184). John J. Joughin examines Bottom's famous visionary speech from *A Midsummer Night's Dream* and Leontes' experience of the sacred reappearance of his wife in *The Winter's Tale* as moments of the apparently illogical and inexpressible reality of faith, of "the untranslatable *mysterium tremendum* [tremendous mystery]" (140). Drawing upon Derrida and the existential philosopher Kierkegaard, Joughin argues that within such dramas "A faith in the absurd, beyond knowledge in any conventional sense, entails a touching without touching, a sharing without sharing, remaining responsive to the irreducible otherness of the other, in an encounter with alterity, a 'dis-figuring' that refuses categorisation and which forgoes philosophical knowing . . . " (150).

Religion as Ideology

To better understand contemporary theoretical approaches to Shakespeare and religion, it is first necessary to briefly review some key assumptions of these complex critical strategies. Since about 1970, criticism of Shakespeare has been fundamentally affected by the broad impact of continental literary theorists such as Jacques Derrida, Michel Foucault, and Jacques Lacan, who have questioned the methods of earlier critical approaches, including, among the deconstructionists led by Derrida, the reliability of language itself to accurately communicate truth. The so-called postmodern approaches view Shakespeare's era as "early modern" rather than post-medieval, revealing the presence of "proto-capitalism," "subjectivity," and "patriarchal suppression" (Dubrow, 39). "New historicism" and its more politically radical British version "cultural materialism" view Shakespeare's plays, says David Bevington, as "shot through with the multiple and contradictory discourses of its time." Such critics are "apt to be skeptical of the accepted canon of literary texts and drawn to a markedly politicized reading of Renaissance plays" with "a deep ambivalence toward political authority" (cvii). The influence of feminism has also played a part within postmodern criticism, as has increasing attention to previously marginalized ethnic, racial, or sexual groups and newer interpretations of older thinkers such as Freud (who viewed religion as a childlike desire for a father) and Marx (who saw religion as an oppressive social force for controlling the masses).

Postmodern theorists see religion—like any other human institution—as embedded within, rather than above or beyond, its historical and social setting; they view with suspicion any historic claims it makes for special authority. They also question the validity of what Jean-François Lyotard termed "metanarratives," the all-compassing myths that have been used to understand human existence. They contend that religious thinking, while still expressing a human interaction with the divine, must make its case without assuming a special superiority just as do political thinking or psychological thinking or any other discourse that attempts to comment on experience. Religion is therefore an "ideology" or a worldview employed as a means of defining experience but always subject to challenge and review. As Hugh Grady notes, "ideologies came into existence in part to replace the older mythic and symbolic belief-systems of religion" (9). An openness to debate and a refusal to take unchallengeable positions must now be a feature of postmodern theology. In the words of Rowan Williams, "religious and theological integrity is possible as and when discourse about God *declines the attempt to take God's point of view* (i.e., a 'total perspective')" (6). Lionel Basney has noted that postmodern (or what he terms "skeptical") criticism shares with "Christian criticism" a concern for "moral criticism" though each approach defines morality differently (22).

The allusive, "de-centered" quality of postmodern criticism, its effort to encompass diverse kinds of literary analysis, and its awareness that it, like literature itself, is a socially constructed activity (not "divinely inspired" or the result of "individual genius") are key features of new historicism. One of its foremost proponents is Stephen Greenblatt, whose influence has been discussed by John Brannigan. Greenblatt's book *Shakespearean Negotiations* sets out the place of the dramatist within the sociopolitical net of forces that he sees operating within Elizabethan culture. Greenblatt's goal is "to know how cultural objects, expressions and practices"—which include Shakespeare's plays—"acquire compelling force" (5). Rather than being the product of a single creative imagination, these plays are "cultural objects" because their creation cannot be separated from the sum total of all of the cultural influences that affect their composition; works of literature are "the products of extended borrowings, collective exchanges, and mutual enchantments" (7). Greenblatt's chapter on "Invisible Bullets: Renaissance Authority and its Subversion, *Henry IV* and *Henry V*" examines those history plays from the perspective of Thomas Harriot's 1588 account of Sir Walter Raleigh's settlement in Virginia, which reveals "the coercive power of religious belief, and the source of this power is the impression made by advanced technology upon a 'backward' people [the Native Americans]" (440). Prince Hal's crafty "redeeming" of himself from a life of waywardness also employs the language of religion to control the subversive social elements represented by Falstaff and his cronies and to insure his own rise to power.

In *Hamlet in Purgatory* (2001), Greenblatt offers an analysis of the religious and nonreligious impact of the concept of purgatory in Shakespeare's era, drawing upon artistic, theological, and literary sources. Noting that Protestants had redefined purgatory as a poetic fable, he observes that "They charted the ways in which certain elemental human fears, longings, and fantasies were being shaped and exploited by an intellectual elite who carefully packaged fraudulent, profit-making innovations as if they were ancient traditions" (45). Hamlet, "a young man from Wittenberg, with a distinctly Protestant temperament, is haunted by a distinctly Catholic ghost" (240), who strongly suggests Shakespeare's own Catholic father (249). In Greenblatt's view, John Foxe's disparaging contemporary view of purgatory contributed to the climate in which *Hamlet* was received "by participating in a violent ideological struggle that turned negotiations with the dead from an institutional process governed by the church to a poetic process governed by guilt, projection, and imagination" (252). Greenblatt and Catherine Gallagher have also suggested that Hamlet's famous comment about worms eating the body of Polonius (4.3.20–22) alludes to "a grotesquely materialist reimagining of the Eucharist" (Gallagher and Greenblatt 153); within the play's imagery of disease and death, it is linked to "the deep anxiety about the yoking of the divine spirit to corrupting and corruptible matter that haunted Eucharistic controversies for centuries" (Gallagher and Greenblatt 160).

Alan Sinfield, a prominent English cultural materialist, argues that the contending ideologies in Shakespeare's England made for a much less cohesive society than the more traditional critical view presented. That view, says Michael Bristol, held that Shakespeare is "the poet of tradition, of religious orthodoxy, and of a politically conservative view of the individual contained within the hierarchy of master and servant" (145). Sinfield instead argues, for example, that Hamlet's allusion to the "special providence in the fall of the sparrow" in act 5, scene 2, rather than pointing to a reassuring sense of purpose in the prince, reveals a conflict within Hamlet between his desire to practice the single-minded Stoic endurance of tragic heroes in Senecan tragedies and his willingness to accept a Calvinist understanding of God's providence. Hamlet's audience "may come to feel that this Christianity cannot separate itself satisfactorily from a Stoic paganism that claims no divine revelation and no divine beneficence . . . such a tyrannical deity need inspire no more than passive acquiescence" (230).

Jonathan Dollimore's important materialist analyses of Shakespeare presented in *Radical Tragedy* (2nd ed. 1993) are based upon the power of ideology to mold individual and social behavior. Ideology refers most directly to "a system of illusory beliefs which serve to perpetuate a particular social formation or power structure; typically this power structure is itself represented by that ideology as *eternally or naturally given*—i.e. as inevitable, immutable" (9). Dollimore emphasizes Calvin's statement in his *Institutes* (I.3.2) that "in order to hold Men's minds in greater subjection, clever men have devised many things in religion by which to inspire the common folk with reverence and strike them with terror" (11). The problem for the Christian is to distinguish true religion from false ideology; in Calvin's case, the false would have been Catholicism, with its emphasis upon papal authority and its deemphasis upon individual scriptural interpretation. The Renaissance theatre thus becomes a means of displaying the struggles between competing ideologies, including skeptical philosophies such as those of Machiavelli and Montaigne. In Dollimore's view, religion is not insulated from paradox or internal divisions by claiming to be "divine." "Christianity, like any ideology, is characterized by contradictions, points at which it falters, and the dogma(tic) is specially and crucially reinforced by faith; in effect, the contradiction is dissolved in and by the paradox of faith. The Elizabethan period was one in which that shift from contradiction to faithful resolution, became, for many, too difficult" (20). Shakespeare's plays, therefore, do not depict a harmonious cosmos ruled by a reliably providential god, as Ulysses's speech on order in *Troilus and Cressida* or the king's singing of Psalm 115 after the Battle of Agincourt in *Henry V* would seem to suggest. These utterances are part of an ideology of hope, an ideal that is contradicted at many points in each play.

Dollimore asserts that, "*Lear* is only one of several texts which confirm that the concept of natural law was nowhere near as stable and coherent as advocates of organic providence would have us believe" (91). Furthermore, *King Lear* is a play "above all, about power, property, and inheritance . . . we see the cherished norms of human kind-ness [*sic*] shown to have no 'natural' sanction at all" (197). Whereas Bradley could read Edgar's statement that "the gods are just" and find in it an assertion of faith, Dollimore, commenting on the same passage, contends that Edgar "is making his society supernaturally intelligible at the cost of rendering the concept of divine justice so punitive and 'poetic' as to be, humanly speaking, almost unintelligible" (203). If, Dollimore seems to be saying, the brutal suffering and death in this play is somehow evidence of a loving God, then who could—or would want to—believe in such a God? In short, "Of one thing we can be fairly certain: in the Renaissance, God was in trouble; 'he' was being subjected to skeptical interrogation, not least in the theatre" (xxix).

The personal and social impact of religion has also been a concern of feminist critics, especially because Christianity has historically been a hierarchical and patriarchal institution. Contemporary feminist theologians have stressed biblical references to inclusiveness and the ways in which scripture reveals a decisive female agency. Old Testament figures such as Esther and Deborah display vital leadership qualities; the virgin Mary not only gives birth to the savior, but "is also the author of the Magnificat [Luke 1: 46–55], the first theological reflection in the New Testament of what the coming of the kingdom means" (Maggay); and the news of the resurrection was given first to three women, Mary Magdalene, Mary the mother of James, and Salome (Mark 16: 1–8). The Bible also contains female images of God, reminders that God is neither male nor female, but beyond gender (Houts). Feminist approaches to Renaissance literature and religion have gained added momentum with studies of such figures as Aemilia Lanyer (1569–1643), Rachel Speght (born 1597?), Lady Mary Wroth (1587?–1651/53), Dorothy Leigh (died c. 1616), and Lucy Hutchinson (1620–1681).

Apart from such poets however, a feminist approach to the Bible was largely unknown in Shakespeare's era, a time in which Christian ideology was exclusively masculine, institutionally as well as theologically. Eve, the traditional commentators asserted, was the second human to be created, not the first, and she was created out of Adam's substance, two factors that appeared to give primary authority to the male. Furthermore, she was the first to fall into sin, and Satan's ability to trick her only confirmed her innate moral weakness when compared to Adam. Kathleen McLuskie observes that "the misogyny of King Lear, both the play and its hero, is constructed out of an ascetic tradition which presents women as the source of the primal sin of lust, combining with concerns about the threat to the family posed by female insubordination" (qtd. Dolliimore, xxxiv).

In her 1975 study Shakespeare and the Nature of Women, Juliet Dusinberre argued that the arrival of Puritanism in England was a liberating event for women because the Puritans, wishing to downplay the Catholic church's stress on celibacy, championed marriage as an equally spiritual choice of life. This "led ultimately to the Puritan assertion of spiritual equality between men and women with its significant implications for the relation of man and wife" (3). It also resulted in demands for "reform of inhumane marriage customs in a middle-class context and refusing to tolerate the double standard for adultery" (5). The erosion of Catholic rituals, especially devotion to the virgin Mary, also began to diminish the traditional idolization of women, to which the portrayal of idealized women in medieval courtly love poems had contributed. The Anglican "Homily against Peril of Idolatry" also warned against elevating anything other than God, including one's romantic beloved, to a divine plane. The feisty energy of many Shakespearean female characters reflects this newfound freedom linked to religious change (though outspoken medieval women such as Margery Kemp and Chaucer's Wife of Bath were not unknown). They do not hesitate to disrupt men's illusions, like the ladies' destruction of the Muscovite masque in Love's

Labour's Lost (162), or to instruct them in more realistic attitudes, like Rosaline's guidance of Orlando in *As You Like It* (167).

However, in 1983 Lisa Jardine challenged this positive view by contending that the Protestant emphasis upon biblical authority also meant that the scriptures were employed to enforce female submissiveness and confine women to the mastery of domestic skills, such as are summarized in Proverbs 31: 10–29. The new "freedom in thinking" for which Schlegel had praised the Reformation existed in her view primarily for men, not women. Jardine points to the situation of Adriana in *The Comedy of Errors* as a realistic example of the "double bind" in which Elizabethan women found themselves. Adriana is victimized by being married to one of the identical Antipholus twins, who unfairly scorns her when she mistakenly locks him out of the house. Jardine points out that while a "liberalized" marriage "laid strong emphasis on dialogue between partners," it "continued . . . to treat articulateness in women as unseemly and unreliable" and did so with Biblical endorsement (46). In *The Taming of the Shrew* "it is by no means the case that Kate is obliged in Christian humility to serve her breadwinner husband: he is a fortune-hunting rascal, supported by *her* fine dowry" (60). Likewise, in *The Merchant of Venice*, Portia relinquishes to Bassanio the vast wealth that has made her such a desirable catch for him ("This house, these servants, and this same myself, / Are yours—my lord's" [3.2.170–171]), yet this submissiveness is called into question when she "pleads as an accomplished advocate later in the play" (61). For Jardine, the tension between assertiveness and acquiescence in Shakespeare's women is the result of a contradictory effect of the Reformation: "Protestantism may have encouraged women, and then in practice withdrawn much of that encouragement" (51).

M. Lindsay Kaplan finds that Shylock and Portia are in somewhat similar situations as regards the male and Christian ruling authority of Vienna. Each is regarded as an "other," a person of lesser influence, Shylock for his Jewishness and Portia for her womanhood. Traditional statements from St. John Chrysostom and St. Augustine advocated that Jews be subservient to Christians (and eventually converted) and that women be subservient to their husbands. "[B]oth Shylock and Portia attempt to protect their independence from forces which would work to nullify it" (345). "However, as a white, aristocratic Christian, Portia also participates in the dominant culture of the play which is intolerant of difference" (349). Kaplan points out that Portia relinquishes her self and her goods to Bassanio in marriage only as long as he retains her ring; when he gives that away, she is technically released from her bond just as Shylock is legally separated from his. "Unlike Shylock who is forced to convert to Christianity, and Jessica who willingly chooses it and a conventional marriage, Portia only appears to 'convert' (III.ii.167) to a subordinate wife while protecting herself by making use of the law" (356).

Isabella, in *Measure for Measure*, has also attracted scholarly attention for her confrontation with issues of sexuality, religion, and political authority. Barbara Baines has argued that Isabella's chastity is not essentially a religious quality, but a social one. Because "the play presents a society in which the health of the nation and the authority of the ruler are jeopardized by sexual license" (284), her chastity, although "a theologically prescribed virtue" (284), is a form of social power, and "the laws mandating chastity constitute a prohibition placed on the individual for the greater good of society as a whole" (285). Viewing the religious value of chastity in new historicist terms, Baines states that Isabella's "choice of her chastity over her brother's life" is best explained by "the social and psychological, rather than the religious, construct in which she and the other characters function" (284). Isabella herself fails to see how much her belief in chastity is shaped by nonreligious forces; her preference for convent life is an attempt to retain some freedom "in a world where sexuality means submission to men and degradation in that submission" (287). Angelo's attraction to her is driven not only by his sexual desire, but by his envy of the power her chastity represents. The play ends, according to Baines, with Isabella's marriage to the Duke, who "takes this prospective bride of Christ as his own in the ultimate act of appropriation that asserts his power as indeed 'like pow'r divine' (V.i.369)" (298).

Laura Lunger Knoppers addresses the topic of shame in the play and sees it from a "materialist feminist" point of view, contending that Isabella suffers public humiliation for her behavior, much as the clergy publicly punished prostitutes by making them wear a white sheet in public and kneel in church, separated from the congregation, until their penance was done. Knoppers points out that in the later civil punishment for prostitution, this religious process of "confession, forgiveness, and reintegration is no longer prominent," being replaced by public shaming as the primary "deterrent" (455). Isabella must endure a similar "punitive process of juridical shaming and ends as silent spectacle" (460). Like Baines, Knoppers recognizes that Angelo reacts to Isabella's power as he is threatened by her chastity; she must be made to appear submissive. "As she kneels for Angelo in her final speech in the play, Isabella significantly and strikingly places herself in the position she has been resisting all along—as the sexualized object of the male gaze" (468). Despite her marriage to the Duke, Isabella is nevertheless shamed in a way similar to the whores punished by church authorities.

Unlike Baines and Knoppers, Jessica Slights and Michael Morgan Holmes pay much more attention in their analysis to the importance of convent life to Isabella, stressing "the long-standing belief held by numerous English Protestant women that the dissolution of the convents [during the Reformation] had stripped them of an important alternative to married life" (267). These critics stress historical evidence that for them contradicts the view "that few if any in Shakespeare's audiences would have imagined a cloistered vocation to be a fulfilling life" (269). Many women "continued to turn to Catholicism and to convent life in order to assert their independence and to express politically unorthodox views" (268). Isabella's motivation for entering the convent is thus not only religious, but also political in that she wishes to "resist coercive authority in [her] daily [life]" (272). Previous critics have too easily agreed with "a paternalist ideology that ignores early modern nuns' many positive evaluations of convent life" (285). Isabella's oft-mentioned silence in the play is a sign of her reluctance to give up the practices of her order. Unlike the previous critics, Slights and Holmes point out that "there is little textual evidence that Isabella happily betroths herself to Vincentio" (287). Her silence at the end of the play denotes "a firm determination to return to a life of religious devotion" (288).

Just as there is no single best path into Shakespeare's work, there is likewise no one critical approach to the topic of religion in his plays and poems that will render a complete and final picture of the ways in which spiritual belief informs his artistry. Newer critical approaches to Shakespeare have been faulted by some as suffering from "presentism," a tendency to read his work more from the vantage of modern religious or philosophical perspectives than from the position that his own contemporaries may have held. This debate returns us to the antithesis famously phrased by Ben Jonson: is Shakespeare of "an age" or "for all time"? By stressing the latter idea, Jonson sought to predict Shakespeare's enduring prominence in the annals of English literature. Four hundred years later, modern readers can recognize not only his greatness among his Renaisance peers, but also his ability to speak to each succeeding age. He was of an age *and* for all time. As succeeding generations read his works through differing critical lenses, Shakespeare will continue to reveal new perspectives on the religion of his era. The variety of strategies used to appreciate his work will be matched by the variety within his works themselves.

REFERENCES

Baines, Barbara J. "Assaying the Power of Chastity in *Measure for Measure*." *Studies in English Literature, 1500–1900* 30.2 (Spring 1990): 283–301.

Baldick, Chris. *Criticism and Literary Theory 1890 to the Present*. London, UK: Longman, 1996.

Basney, Lionel. "Is a Christian Perspective on Shakespeare Productive and/or Necessary?" In *Shakespeare and the Christian Tradition*. Ed. E. Beatrice Batson. Lewiston, NY: The Edwin Mellen Press, 1994. 19–35.

Bate, Walter Jackson. *The Achievement of Samuel Johnson*. New York: Oxford University Press, 1955.

Battenhouse, Roy W. *Shakespearean Tragedy: Its Art and Its Christian Premises*. Bloomington: Indiana University Press, 1969.

Bethell, Samuel Leslie. *Shakespeare and the Popular Dramatic Tradition*. Durham, NC: Duke University Press, 1944.

———. *The Winter's Tale: A Study*. London and New York: Staples Press, 1947.

Bevington, David, ed. *The Complete Works of Shakespeare*. 5th ed. New York: Pearson Longman, 2004.

Birch, William John. *An Inquiry into the Philosophy and Religion of Shakespeare*. New York: Haskell House Publishers, 1972.

Bradley, A. C. *Shakespearean Tragedy: Lecture on* Hamlet, Othello, King Lear, *and* MacBeth. New York: Meridian Books, 1955.

Brannigan, John. *New Historicism and Cultural Materialism*. New York: St. Martin's Press, 1998.

Bristol, Michael. *Shakespeare's America, America's Shakespeare*. London, UK: Routledge, 1990.

Bryant, J. A. *Hippolyta's View: Some Christian Aspects of Shakespeare's Plays*. Lexington: University of Kentucky Press, 1961.

Carlyle, Thomas. *On Heroes, Hero-Worship, and the Heroic in History*. Michael K. Goldberg, notes and introduction. Berkley: University of California Press, 1993.

Coleridge, Samuel Taylor. *Coleridge's Writings on Shakespeare*. Ed. Terence Hawkes. New York: Putnam Capricorn, 1959.

Denham, Robert D. *Northrop Frye: Religious Visionary and Architect of the Spiritual World*. Charlottesville: University of Virginia Press, 2004.

Dollimore, Jonathan. *Radical Tragedy: Religion, Ideology and Power in the Drama of Shakesepare and his Contemporaries*. 2nd ed. Durham, NC: Duke University Press, 1993.

Dubrow, Heather. "Twentieth Century Shakespeare Criticism." In *The Riverside Shakespeare*. 2nd ed. Ed. G. Blakemore Evans. Boston, MA: Houghton Mifflin, 1997. 27–54.

Dusinberre, Juliet. *Shakespeare and the Nature of Women*. New York: Barnes and Noble, 1975.

Dryden, John. *The Works of John Dryden*. Vol. X. Ed. E. N. Hooker and H. T. Swedenberg, Jr. 20 vols. Berkeley: University of California Press, 1956.

Eastman, Arthur M. *A Short History of Shakespearean Criticism*. New York: Norton, 1968.

Fernie, Ewan, ed. *Spiritual Shakespeares*. London: Routledge, 2005.

Frazer, James George, Sir. *The Golden Bough: a study in comparative religion*. 15 vols. New York: Palgrave Macmillian, 2005.

Frye, Northrop. *Anatomy of Criticism: Four essays*. Princeton, NJ: Princeton University Press, 1957

———. *Fables of Indentity: studies in poetic mythology*. New York: Harcourt, Brace, & World, 1963

———. *Fools of Time: studies in Shakespearean tragedy*. Toronto: University of Toronto Press, 1967.

———. *The Great Code: the Bible and literature*. New York: Harcourt Brace Jovanovich, 1982

———. *The Myth of Deliverance: Reflections on Shakespeare's Problem Comedies*. Toronto: University of Toronto Press 1965.

———. *A Natural Perspective; the development of Shakespearean comedy and romance*. New York: Columbia University Press, 1965.

———. *Northrop Frye on Shakespeare*. New Haven, CT: Yale University Press, 1986.

———. *Spiritus Mundi: essays on literature, myth, and society*. Bloomington, IN: Indiana University Press, 1976.

———. *Words with power: being a second study of "the Bible and literature."* San Diego, CA: Harcourt Brace Jovanovich, 1990.

Frye, Roland M. *Shakespeare and Christian Doctrine*. Princeton, NJ: Princeton University Press, 1963.

Gallagher, Catherine, and Stephen Greenblatt. *Practicing New Historicism*. Chicago, IL: University of Chicago Press, 2000.

Girard, René. *I See Satan Fall like Lightning*. Trans. James G. Williams. Maryknoll, NY: Orbis Books, 2001

———. *The Scapegoat*. Baltimore: Johns Hopkins University Press, 1986.

———. *A Theatre of Envy*. New York: Oxford University Press, 1991.

———. *Things Hidden since the foundation of the world*. Trans. Stephen Bann (I&II) and Michael Meteer (III). Stanford, CA: Stanford University Press, 1987.

————. *Violence and the Sacred*. Trans. Patrick Gregory. Baltimore: Johns Hopkins University Press, 1977.

Grady, Hugh. *The Modernist Shakespeare*. Oxford, UK: Oxford University Press, 1991.

Greenblatt, Stephen. *Hamlet in Purgatory*. Princeton, NJ: Princeton Univesity Press, 2001.

————. *Shaksperean Negotiations: The Circulation of Social Energy in Renaissance England*. Berkeley: University of California Press, 1988.

Hagstrum, Jean H. *Samuel Johnson's Literary Criticism*. Chicago, IL: University of Chicago Press, 1952.

Hart, Alfred. Shakespeare and the Homilies. 1934. Rpt. New York: Octagon Books, 1970.

Hassel, R. Chris, Jr. *Faith and Folly in Shakespeare's Romantic Comedies*. Athens: University of Georgia Press, 1980.

————. "Hamlet's 'Too, Too Solid Flesh.'" *Sixteenth Century Journal* 25.3 (Autumn 1994): 609–622.

————. "Love Versus Charity in *Love's Labour's Lost*." *Shakespeare Studies* 10 (1977): 17–41.

————. *Renaissance Drama and the English Church Year*. Lincoln: University of Nebraska Press, 1979.

————. *Shakespeare's Religious Language: A Dictionary*. London: Thoemmes Continuum, 2005.

Houts, Margo G. "Images of God as Female." In *The IVP Women's Bible Commentary*. Ed. Catherine Clark Kroeger and Mary J. Evans. Downers Grove: InterVarsity Press, 2002. 356–358.

Hunt, Maurice. *Shakespeare's Religious Allusiveness: Its Play and Tolerance*. Aldershot, UK: Ashgate, 2004.

Jain, Nalini. "Johnson's Shakespeare: A Moral and Religious Quest." In *Re-Viewing Samuel Johnson*. Ed. Nalini Jain. Bombay, India: Popular Prakashan, 1991. 82–101.

Jardine, Lisa. *Still Harping on Daughters: Women and Drama in the Age of Shakespeare*. Sussex, UK: Harvester Press, 1983. Rpt. with new preface, New York: Columbia University Press, 1989.

Joughin, John J. "Bottom's Secret . . ." In *Spiritual Shakespeares*. Ed. Ewan Fernie. London: Routledge, 2005. 130–156.

Kaplan, M. Lindsay. "Others and Lovers in *The Merchant of Venice*." In *A Feminist Companion to Shakespeare*. Ed. Dympna Callaghan. Oxford, UK: Blackwell, 2000. 341–357.

Kearney, Richard. "Spectres of *Hamlet*." In *Spiritual Shakespeares*. Ed. Ewan Fernie. London and New York. Routledge, 2005. 157–185.

Knight, G. Wilson. *The Christian Renaissance*. New York: Norton, 1962.

————. *The Crown of Life*. London: Oxford University Press, 1947.

————. *The Imperial Theme*. London: H. Milford, Oxford University Press, 1931.

————. *The Mutual Flame*. New York: Macmillan, 1955.

————. *Myth and Miracle: an essay on the mystic symbolism of Shakespeare*. London: E. J. Burrow, 1929.

————. *The Shakespearean Tempest*. London: H. Milford, Oxford University Press, 1931.

————. *The Wheel of Fire*. London: Oxford University Press, 1930.

Knoppers, Laura Lunger. "(En)gendering Shame: *Measure for Measure* and the Spectacles of Power." *English Literary Renaissance* 23 (1993): 450–471.

Lewalski, Barbara. "Biblical Allusion and Allegory in *The Merchant of Venice*." *Shakespeare Quarterly* 13(1962), 327–343.

Maggay, Melba Padilla. "The Power & Potential of Women." In *The IVP Women's Bible Commentary*. Ed. Catherine Clark Kroeger and Mary J. Evans. Downer's Grove: InterVarsity Press, 2002. 268–270.

Merchant, W. Moelwyn. "Shakespeare's Theology." A *Review of English Literature* 5.2 (1964): 72–88.

Montagu, Elizabeth. *An Essay on the Writings and Genius of Shakespear, Compared with the Greek and French Dramatic Poets*. New York: Augustus M. Kelley, 1970.

Noble, Richmond P. *Shakespeare's Biblical Knowledge and Use of the Book of Common Prayer*. London, UK: Society for Promoting Christian knowledge and New York: Macmillian, 1935.

Santyana, George. *Interpretations of Poetry and Religion*. Ed. William G. Hozberger and Herman J. Saatkamp. Cambridge, MA: MIT Press 1990.

Schlegel, Augustus William. *Course of Lectures on Dramatic Art and Literature*. Trans. John Black. London, UK: Henry G. Bohn, 1846. Rpt. New York: AMS Press, 1965.

Sinfield, Alan. *Faultlines: Cultural Materialism and the Politics of Dissident Reading*. Berkeley: University of California Press, 1992.

Shaheen, Naseeb. *Biblical References in Shakespeare's Plays*. Newark: University of Delaware Press, 1999.

Siegel, Paul N. *Shakespearean Tragedy and the Elizabethan Compromise*. New York: New York University Press, 1957.

Slights, Jessica, and Michael Morgan Holmes. "Isabella's Order: Religious Acts and Personal Desires in Measure for Measure." *Studies in Philology* XCV.3: (Summer 1998): 263–292.

Smith, D. Nichol, ed. *Eighteenth Century Essays on Shakespeare*. Oxford, UK: Clarendon Press, 1963.

Spivack, Bernard. *Shakespeare and the Allegory of Evil: The History of a Metaphor in Relation to his Major Villains*. New York: Columbia University Press, 1958.

Taylor, Michael. *Shakespeare Criticism in the Twentieth Century*. Oxford, UK: Oxford University Press, 2001.

Vickers, Brian. *Appropriating Shakespeare: Contemporary critical quarrels*. New Haven; London: Yale University Press, 1994, c. 1993.

Williams, Rowan. *On Christian Theology*. Oxford, UK: Blackwell, 2000.

PRIMARY DOCUMENTS

The intellectual core of the Renaissance was humanism, a close and sustained interest in the written works of the Greeks and Romans by European scholars. The study of classical texts by these humanists demanded an intimate knowledge of their languages and works and of the transmission of their writings through history. One immediate result of humanism was thus an increased attention paid to the written (and, later, printed) page, whether ancient or early modern. Shakespeare's works were produced during the great flowering of printed books and pamphlets which marked the European Renaissance. This broad print culture was fed by innumerable authors of brief tracts as well as longer works in literature, religion, history, political theory, and numerous other fields. These writers were also greatly enabled in their efforts by the increasing availability of printing houses through which to publish their works, so that—at least by the time of the folio publication of Ben Jonson's works in 1616—literary authorship gradually became a recognized profession in its own right and not merely the accomplishment of an educated elite uninterested in publication, as had been the case about a century earlier. This mutual relationship between author and printer was further aided by a gradually rising literacy rate, creating a growing market of readers who awaited the rising tide of publications. Religious issues were key themes or supporting ideas within many of these works, which meant that the various spiritual denominations of the day were not the only sources of information about belief and its role in society. Secular authors did not hesitate to appeal to religion in their discussions of other topics, as Sidney does in his *Defense of Poesie* (see Primary Documents 27–28). Popular poets did not refrain from issuing their own compositions or translations for devotional purposes (see Primary Document 29). As Michael Drayton says "To the curteous Reader" in the preface to his *Heavenly Harmony of Spirituall Songes*, "I doubt not, but thou wilt take as great delight in these, as in any Poetical fiction." In the cultural context of Shakespeare's age, religious issues were omnipresent and available for him to draw upon and adapt to his own dramatic purposes. Poetic examples of such works may be found in Primary Documents 31–49.

The following selections illustrate this religious emphasis in—with one medieval exception—a variety of sixteenth century works written before Shakespeare's death in 1616. They are arranged chronologically and then by the author's name or title of the work. Spelling, phrasing and punctuation have in most cases been modernized, with two exceptions for the sake of literary style. Edmund Spenser's intentionally archaic spellings and diction have been largely retained, especially for the sake of his poetic rhythm and rhyme. Secondly, the five examples of English translations of the Bible (out of many more that appeared during the sixteenth century) retain their original phrasing and spelling (such as the double "v" for "w" in the Rheims-Douai version) to illustrate the variations made by different translators and to suggest the path that led ultimately to the profoundly influential King James Version. Reading these texts in their original spelling also suggests something of the visual experience of the printed page that early modern readers had.

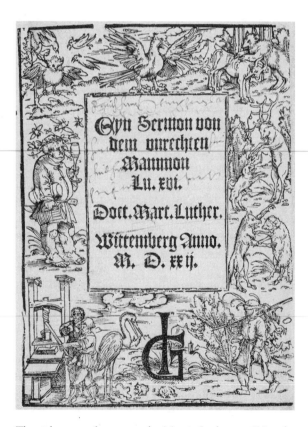

The title page of a sermon by Martin Luther on "Unrighteous Mammon" (Luke 16: 11) printed in 1522. Note the printing press in the lower left. By permission of the Folger Shakespeare Library.

PROSE

1383

John Wyclif (c. 1330–1384). A preacher and religious reformer, Wyclif's opposition to church abuses during the fourteenth century called attention to issues that the major Protestant reformers later attacked in their proposals for church improvement. Wyclif's followers were known as Lollards ("mumblers"), one of whom was Sir John Oldcastle, executed in 1417. Shakespeare originally named Falstaff after this person, as if to poke fun at the extreme Puritan reformers of his own day. But after being reprimanded by Lord Cobham, a descendant of Oldcastle, Shakespeare removed Oldcastle's name from *Henry IV, Part I* and bluntly stated in the epilogue to *Henry IV, Part II* that "Oldcastle died [a] martyr and this [Falstaff] is not the man" (Epilogue 32). This selection, from a Wycliffite tract called *The Great Sentence of Curse Expounded* (1383), vigorously condemns the practice of simony, a favorite target of reformers. Compare Wyclif's praise of honest priests with Chaucer's description of the simple parson in the Prologue to *The Canterbury Tales*. (*Select English Works of John Wyclif*. Ed. Thomas Arnold. 3 volumes. Oxford, UK: 1871. III, 287–289.)

DOCUMENT 1: FROM *THE GREAT SENTENCE OF CURSE EXPOUN)DED*

Ah! Lord, how much is our king and our realm helped by masses and prayers of simonists and heretics, full of pride, covetousness, and envy? They hate the poor priests so much, who teach Christ's life and the gospel to maintain the holy life of the Christian people and the king's royalty, that they curse them and imprison them without answer who are ruled by all goodness and truth according to holy writ. Namely, our prelates live in open extortion and Lucifer's pride, and sell men permission to lie in the sin of lechery and adultery for annual rent, and live in the pomp of worldly array and gluttony and drunkenness, and waste poor men's lifeblood in great feasts and fat horses, and eat up and drink up poor men's lives and build great palaces out of Christian men's blood and then are clothed in them and sleep in them. Where do they please God in offering this sacrament of unity and peace, while their hands are full of the hot blood of Christ's children and heirs of heaven? . . . [C]ertainly these wayward heretics stir God rather to vengeance than to mercy, as Saint Gregory proves, and their blessing turns to cursing and their prayer into sin. And Saint Paul says that they befoul God's son as much as they can, and therefore, as to themselves, they offer befouled bread, as Saint Gregory and Saint Jerome witness, with the common law of holy church. Certainly the Jews allowed Christ to be laid in a clean stone tomb after his death, but these vicious priests, full of pride, covetousness and heresy, put his body into their souls that are a thousand times more foul than any stinking privy on earth. And since their foul soul is in the devil's possession they take Christ's body into the fiend's power as much as they can. Nevertheless, as the saying of the mass while living an unclean life, and without devotion and unworthily receiving this blessed sacrament, frequently and close at hand, most displeases God, so the saying of the mass with the cleanness of a holy life and burning devotion, frequently and close at hand, pleases God almighty and profits Christian souls in purgatory and men living on earth to withstand temptations of sin and increase peace and charity. Therefore, you clean priests, think how much you are beholden to God, that gave you power to sacrifice his own precious body and blood of bread and wine, a power he granted neither to his own mother nor to the angels of heaven. Therefore with all your desire and reverence and devotion do your official duties and perform the sacraments.

1532

Sir Thomas More (1478–1535). Sir Thomas More rose rapidly in the court of Henry VIII, becoming Lord Chancellor in 1529. However, after the king declared himself head of the English church, More resigned this post in 1532. A witty and famous humanist author, he defended Roman Catholicism and engaged in spirited controversies against Lutherans and English Protestants, notably William Tyndale. His *History of King Richard III* (1557) was eventually included in Holinshed's *Chronicles* (1577), thereby offering Shakespeare a source for many of the more notorious details of Richard's reign, which appear in the play *Richard III*. He refused to accept the Act of Supremacy and was beheaded in 1535. In 1935 More was canonized a Roman Catholic saint. (*The Wit and Wisdom of Blessed Thomas More.* Ed. Rev. T. E. Bridgett. London, UK: Burns and Oates, 1892. 111–112, 114.)

DOCUMENT 2: FROM *THE CONFUTATION OF TINDALE*

Of all the heretics that ever sprang in Christ's Church, the very worst and the most beastly be these Lutherans, as their opinions and their lewd living shows. And let us never doubt but all that be of that sect, if any seem good, as very few do, yet will they in conclusion decline to the like lewd living as their master and their fellows do, if they might once (as by God's grace they never shall) frame the people to their own frantic fantasy. Which dissolute living they be driven to dissemble, because their audience is not yet brought to the point to hear, which they surely trust to bring about, and to frame this realm after the fashion of Switzerland or Saxony, or some other parts of Germany, where their sect hath already fordone [destroyed] the faith, pulled down the churches, polluted the temples, put out and despoiled [robbed] all good religious folk, joined friars and nuns together in lechery, despited [shown contempt for] all saints, blasphemed our Blessed Lady, cast down Christ's Cross, thrown out the Blessed Sacrament, refused all good laws, abhorred all good governance, rebelled against all rulers, fallen to fight among themselves, and so many thousand slain, that the land lieth in many places desert and desolate. And finally, that most abominable is of all, of all their own ungracious deeds they lay the fault on God, taking away the liberty of man's will, ascribing all our deeds to destiny, with all reward or punishment pursuing upon all our doings; whereby they take away all diligence and good endeavour to virtue, all withstanding and striving against vice, all care of heaven, all fear of hell, all cause of prayer, all desire of devotion, all exhortation to good, all dehortation from [persuasion against] evil, all praise of well-doing, all rebuke of sin, all the laws of the world, all reason among men, set all wretchedness abroach [astir], no man at liberty, and yet every man do what he will, calling it not his will, but his destiny, laying their sin to God's ordinance and their punishment to God's cruelty, and, finally, turning the nature of man into worse than a beast, and the goodness of God into worse than a devil. And all this good fruit would a few mischievous persons, some for desire of a large liberty to an unbridled lewdness, and some of a high devilish pride cloaked under pretext of good zeal and simpleness, undoubtedly bring into this realm, if the prince and prelates and the good faithful people did not in the beginning meet with their malice. . . .

Now where the wretch (Tindale) rails by name upon that holy doctor, St. Thomas [Aquinas, the greatest medieval Scholastic theologian], a man of that [such] learning that the great excellent wits and the most cunning men that the Church of Christ has had since his days, have esteemed and called the very flower of theology; and a man of the true perfect faith and Christian living thereto, that God has Himself testified His Holiness by many a great miracle, and made him honoured here in His Church in earth, as he has exalted him to great glory in heaven;—this glorious saint of God does this devilish, drunken soul abominably blaspheme, and calls him liar and falsifier of Scripture, and makes him no better than "draff" [dregs]. But this drowsy drudge has drunken so deep in the devil's dregs, that, but if he wake and repent himself the sooner, he may hap, ere aught [before too] long, to fall into the mashing-vat, as the hogs of hell shall feed upon and fill their bellies thereof.

1534

Act of Supremacy. This act formally established the English monarch as supreme head of the Church of England, something the king had personally done three years earlier. It had been preceded in Henry VIII's reign by other acts that forbade papal dispensations within England and payments of money to the pope; these acts also established the succession of the crown by voiding the king's marriage to Catherine of Aragon, declaring that all children of Anne Boleyn and the king be considered legitimate heirs, including Elizabeth (should there be no male children). The Supremacy Act formalized Henry's ability to exercise direct administrative influence over the church, including the dissolution of the monasteries (Acts of 1536 and 1539 and others) and the behavior of clergy (such as in the Royal Injunctions of 1536 and 1538). (*Documents Illustrative of English Church History*. Ed. Henry Gee and William John Hardy. London, UK: Macmillan, 1896. 243–244.)

DOCUMENT 3: THE ACT OF SUPREMACY

Albeit the king's majesty justly and rightfully is and ought to be the supreme head of the Church of England, and so is recognized by the clergy of this realm in their Convocations, yet nevertheless for corroboration and confirmation thereof, and for increase of virtue in Christ's religion within this realm of England, and to repress and extirp [eradicate] all errors, heresies, and other enormities and abuses heretofore used in the same; be it enacted by authority of this present Parliament, that the king our sovereign lord, his heirs and successors, kings of this realm, shall be taken, accepted, and reputed to the only supreme head in earth of the Church of England, called *Anglicana Ecclesia*; and shall have and enjoy, annexed and united to the imperial crown of this realm, as well the title and style thereof, as all honours, dignities, pre-eminences, jurisdictions, privileges, authorities, immunities, profits, and commodities to the said dignity of supreme head of the same Church belonging and appertaining; and that our said sovereign lord, his heirs and successors, kings of this realm, shall have full power and authority from time to time to visit, repress, redress, reform, order, correct, restrain, and amend all such errors, heresies, abuses, offences, contempts, and enormities, whatsoever they be, which by any manner spiritual authority or jurisdiction ought or may lawfully be reformed, repressed, ordered, redressed, corrected, restrained, or amended, most to the pleasure of Almighty God, the increase of virtue in Christ's religion and for the conservation of the peace, unity, and tranquility of this realm; any usage, custom, foreign law, foreign authority, prescription, or any other thing or things to the contrary hereof notwithstanding.

William Tyndale (c. 1494–1536). Tyndale's skillful English translation of the New Testament, based upon the original Greek, became the foundation for the later and better-known King James Version of 1611. Meeting with opposition in England, Tyndale journeyed to Germany, where he met Martin Luther and finally published his translation in 1525 at Cologne and Worms. The Protestant theology of Tyndale's translation is evident in his substitution of "congregation" for "church" and "elder" for "priest," changes criticized by Sir Thomas More. He also published translations of the first five books of the Old Testament and the Book of Jonah and engaged in a lengthy theological controversy with More. He was arrested in 1535 in Antwerp, Belgium and executed for heresy the following year. (*The English Hexapla*. London, UK: Samuel Bagster, 1841. n.p.)

DOCUMENT 4: FROM TYNDALE'S NEW TESTAMENT

1 Corinthians 13: 1–13

Though I spake with the tounges of men and angels, and yet had no love, I were even as soundinge brass: or as a tynklynge Cymball. And though I coulde prophesy, and understode all secretes, and all knowledge: yee, yf I had all faith so that I coulde move mountains oute of ther places, and yet had no love, I were nothynge. And though I bestowed all my gooddes to fede the poore, and though I gave my body even that I burned, and yet had no love, it profeteth me nothinge.

Love suffreth longe, and is corteous. Love envieth not. Love doth not frowardly, swelleth not[,] dealeth not dishonestly, seketh not her awne, is not provoked to anger, thynketh not evyll, reioyseth not in iniquite: but reioyseth in the trueth, suffreth all thynge, beleveth all thynges, hopeth all thynges, endureth in all thynges. Though that prophesyinge fayle, other tonges shall cease, or knowledge vanysshe awaye, yet love falleth never awaye.

For oure knowledge is vnparfect, and oure prophesyinge is vnperfet. But when that which is parfect is come, then that which is vnparfet shall be done awaye. When I was a chylde, I spake as a chylde, I vnderstode as a childe, I ymagened as a chylde. But assone as I was a man, I put awaye childesshnes. Now we se in a glasse even in a darke speakynge: but then shall we se face to face. Now I knowe vnparfectly: but then shall I knowe even as I am knowen. Now abideth faith, hope and love, even these thre: but the chefe of these is love.

1539

The Great Bible. Thomas Cranmer had planned an authorized Bible as early as 1537; chief among the scholars who prepared a new translation was Miles Coverdale (1488–1569), who had published his own English version of the entire Bible in 1535. The so-called Great Bible appeared in 1539; a second edition (of an eventual seven), known as "Cranmer's Bible" because of the long preface he authored, was published in 1540. The version of the Psalms contained in Cranmer's *Book of Common Prayer* is Coverdale's translation from the Great Bible. (*The English Hexapla*. London, UK: Samuel Bagster, 1841. n.p.)

Document 5: From the Great Bible, 1539

1 Corinthians 13: 1–13

Though I spake with the tonges of men and of angels, and haue no loue, I am euen as sounding brasse: or as a tynklinge cymbal. And though I coulde prophesy, and vnderstode all secretes, and all knowledge: yee yf I haue all faith, so that I can moue mountains oute of their places, and yet haue no loue, I am nothinge. And though I bestowe all my goodes to fede the poore, and though I geue my body euen that I burned, and yet haue no loue, it profyteth me nothynge.

Loue suffreth longe, and is curteous. Loue enuyeth not. Loue doth not forwardly, swelleth not, dealeth not dishonestly[,] seketh not her awne, is not prouoked to anger, thinketh no euyll, reioyseth not in iniquitie: but reioyseth in the trueth, suffreth all thynges, beleueth all thynges, hopeth all thinges, endureth all thynges. Though that prophesyinges fayle, other tonges cease, or knowledge vanysshe awaye, yet loue falleth neuer awaye.

For oure knowledge is vnperfect, and oure prophesyinge is vnperfect. But when that which is perfect, is come, then that which vnperfect, shall be done awaye. When I was a chylde, I spake as a chylde, I vnderstode as a chyulde, I ymagined as a childe. But assone as I was a man, I put awaye chyldeshnes.

Now we se in a glasse, euen in a darcke speaking: but then shall we se face to face. Now I knowe vnperfectly: but then shall I know euen as I am knowen. Now abydeth faith, hope, and loue, euen these thre: but the chefe of these is loue.

1547

Thomas Cranmer (1489–1556). Cranmer, Archbishop of Canterbury under Henry VIII and Edward VI, was burned at the stake as a heretic under Mary Tudor. The key clerical figure in the development of the Anglican church, he was the most significant compiler of the *Book of Common Prayer* (1549), oversaw publication of the English Great Bible of 1539, and composed a preface for its second edition in 1540, which advocates biblical translation in the common (or "vulgar") language spoken by most people. He also drafted the 39 articles of doctrine for the English church, among other significant works. In about 1547 he composed a Latin *Confutation of Unwritten Verities,* which was later translated and published during Mary's reign, and then republished in 1582. Its Preface may be the work of the translator, but it was certainly prepared from Cranmer's own materials and is therefore included among his works. The vivid language of the Preface to the *Confutation* conveys the intensity of the religious debate during the mid-sixteenth century; the 1540 preface to the Bible illustrates the Protestant emphasis upon widespread Bible reading in their own language by people in all walks of life. Cranmer appears in Shakespeare's *Henry VIII,* where, in act 5, he and the king dominate the Roman Catholic interests of Bishop Gardiner and the Lord Chancellor. (*Miscellaneous Writings and Letters of Thomas Cranmer.* Ed. John Edmund Cox. Parker Society. Cambridge, MA: University Press, 1856. 9–10; 119–121.)

DOCUMENT 6: FROM THE PREFACE TO *THE CONFUTATION* OF *UNWRITTEN VERITIES* [TRUTHS]

What christian heart, dearly beloved countrymen and brethren in our Savior Christ, can abstain from deep sobs and sorrowful sighings? What natural and kind-hearted man can forbear weeping; so often as he calls to remembrance the Lord's vineyard within the realm of England (which he himself had of late so strongly hedged, walled, and fenced round about by the princes of most famous memory, king Henry the eighth and Edward the sixth, and planted therein the pure vine of his own blessed word by godly preachers, his gardeners,) to be so suddenly broken down, destroyed, wasted, and rooted up by the roots, by the wild boar of the wood and the beasts of the field, that is, by the Romish [Roman Catholic] bishop [the pope, the bishop of Rome] and his bloody ministers; and now in the same vineyard to see planted, take root, and prosper, brambles, briars, and hemlocks; that is, gross ignorance, naughty doctrine, false worship of God, and such other kinds of most stinking, vile, and filthy weeds? O what a sweet and pleasant grape of godly doctrine was then gathered in England to the great comfort and rejoicing of all them that lovingly tasted thereof! Then was God's word (for that is the sweet and pleasant grape "that maketh glad the heart of man") with great freedom preached, earnestly embraced, and with greedy hearts in all places received.

. . . Then was there the common prayer rightly used, and the sacraments (baptism, I mean, and the holy communion) in such a tongue and language set forth that all people might understand them. Then were they plainly ministered, without any juggling or sorcery, according to Christ's institution and the rule of his holy word: which word at that time had the prize and bare [carried] the bell away throughout the whole land.

. . . This bloody boar, besides all mischiefs that he hath done to the vineyard, yet ceases he not, with fagot, fire, and all other cruel torments to constrain and compel men to worship images, the work of men's hands, to kneel to them, to reverence them, to bow to them, and with all manner of obeisance to honor them, clean contrary to God's commandment. . . . But yet these shameless wretches be not abashed to say, that images are necessary, because they be layman's books, teaching them, instructing them, and leading them to the true worship of God. Oh great blasphemy! Oh sacrilege! Oh spiteful robbery! What is blasphemy, what is sacrilege, what is robbery, if this be none? God giveth his word written to be every man's book, and his pure, everlasting, and undefiled commandments as sufficient instructions for all men to the true worship of him. But these earthly wroters [rooters, boars] (the pope, I mean, and his prelates) as though they were wiser than God, will teach men to worship him with images, although the same be utterly forbidden by God throughout the whole course of his holy scriptures.

DOCUMENT 7: FROM THE PREFACE TO THE BIBLE (1540)

For it is not much above one hundred years ago, since scripture hath not been accustomed to be read in the vulgar [common, vernacular] tongues within this realm; and many hundred years before that it was translated and read in the Saxons' tongue, which at that time was our mother's tongue: whereof there remaineth yet divers copies found lately in old abbeys, of such antique manners of writing and speaking, that few men now been able to read and understand them. And when this language waxed [grew] old and out of common usage, because folk should not lack the fruit of reading, it was again translated in the newer language. Whereof yet many copies remain and be daily found. [Cranmer then quotes extensively from a sermon by St. Chrysostom.]

Hitherto, all that I have said, I have taken and gathered out of the foresaid sermon of this holy doctor, St. John Chrysostom. . . . In the scriptures be the fat pastures of the soul; therein is no venomous meat, no unwholesome thing; they be the very dainty and pure feeding. He that is ignorant, shall find there what he should learn. He that is a perverse sinner, shall there find his damnation to make him to tremble for fear. . . . Herein may princes learn how to govern their subjects; subjects obedience, love and dread to their princes: husbands, how they should behave them unto their wives; how to educate their children and servants: and contrary the wives, children, and servants may know their duty to their husbands, parents and masters. Here may all manner of persons, men, women, young, old, learned, unlearned, rich, poor, priests, laymen, lords, ladies, officers, tenants, and mean men, virgins, wives, widows, lawyers, merchants, artificers, husbandmen, and all manner of persons, of what estate or condition soever they be, may in this book learn all things what they ought to believe, what they ought to do, and what they should not do, as well concerning Almighty God, as also concerning themselves and all other. Briefly, to the reading of the scripture none can be enemy, but that either be so sick that they love not to hear of any medicine, or else that [they] be so ignorant that they know not scripture to be the most healthful medicine.

1549

Book of Common Prayer. The Book of Common Prayer contains the rites of worship for the Church of England. It was compiled primarily by Thomas Cranmer (see headnote to **1547**) largely from the more complicated Sarum rite used at Salisbury Cathedral and in most of England. It was revised in 1552 and again in 1559. Together with the King James Version of the Bible, its literary style had a broad and lasting impact upon the development of English prose. The Prayer Book's preface ("Concerning the Service of the Church") emphasizes Cranmer's goal of a liturgy more simplified than the Roman Catholics' yet with a fixed and dignified order of worship similar to that which the early church ("the old Fathers") was thought to have had. Especially noteworthy are the book's collects, brief prayers for specific purposes or days of the church year; they combine a brevity of statement with a nobility of tone and memorable, rhythmic phrasing. (*The Book of Common Prayer.* Ed. Archibald John Stephens. 2 vols. London, UK: Ecclesiastical History Society, 1849. Volume I: 115–120, 393, 432, 579–580.)

DOCUMENT 8: FROM "CONCERNING THE SERVICE OF THE CHURCH"

There never was anything by the wit of man so well devised, or so sure established, which, in continuance of time, hath not been corrupted, as, among other things, it may plainly appear by the Common Prayers in the Church, commonly called Divine Service. The first original and ground whereof if a man would search out by the ancient Fathers, he shall find, that the same was not ordained, but of a good purpose, and for a great advancement of godliness. For they so ordered the matter, that all the whole Bible (or the greatest part thereof) should be read over once every year; intending thereby, that the clergy, and especially such as were ministers in the congregation, should (by often reading, and meditation in God's word) be stirred up to godliness themselves, and be more able to exhort others by wholesome doctrine, and to confute them that were adversaries to the truth; and further, that the people (by daily hearing of holy Scripture read in the church) might continually profit more and more in the knowledge of God, and be more inflamed with the love of his true religion.

But these many years passed, this godly and decent order of the ancient fathers hath been so altered, broken, and neglected, by planting in uncertain stories and legends, with multitude of responds [responses], verses, vain repetitions, commemorations, and synodals [gifts to bishops], that commonly when any book of the Bible was begun, after three or four chapters were read out the rest were unread. And in this sort the Book of Isaiah was begun in Advent [the four weeks prior to Christmas], and the Book of Genesis in Septuagesima [the third Sunday before Lent], but they were only begun and never read through. After like sort [in the same way] were other books of Holy Scripture used. And moreover, whereas St. Paul would have such language spoken to the people in the church as they might understand and have profit by hearing the same, the service in this Church of England these many years hath been read in Latin to the people, which they understand not, so that they have heard with their ears only, and their heart, spirit, and mind have not been edified thereby. And furthermore, notwithstanding that the ancient Fathers have divided the Psalms into seven portions, whereof every one was called a nocturn, now of late time a few of them have been daily said, and the rest utterly omitted. Moreover, the number and hardness of the rules called the Pie [lists of books], and the manifold changings of the service was the cause, that to turn the book only was so hard and intricate a matter, that many times there was more business to find out what should be read than to read it when it was found out.

These inconveniences therefore considered, here is set forth such an order, whereby the same shall be redressed. And for a readiness in this matter, here is drawn out a calendar for that purpose, which is plain and easy to be understood, wherein (so much as may be) the reading of holy Scripture is so set forth that all things shall be done in order without one piece from another. For this cause be cut off anthems, responds, invitatories, and such like things as did break the continual course of the reading of the Scripture.

Yet because there is no remedy but that of necessity, there must be some rules. Therefore, certain rules are here set forth, which, as they are few in number, so they are plain and easy to be understood. So that here you have an order for prayer and for the reading of the holy Scripture much agreeable to the mind and purpose of the old Fathers, and a great deal more profitable and commodious than that which of late was used. It is more profitable, because here are left out many things, whereof some are untrue, some uncertain, some vain and superstitious, and nothing is ordained to be read, but the very pure word of God, the holy Scriptures, or that which is agreeable to the same, and that in such a language and order, as is most easy and plain for the understanding of both the readers and the hearers.

DOCUMENT 9: THE GENERAL CONFESSION

Almighty and most merciful Father, we have erred and strayed from thy ways like lost sheep. We have followed too much the devices and desires of our own hearts. We have offended against thy holy laws. We have left undone those things which we ought to have done and we have done those things which we ought not to have done, and there is no health in us. But thou, O Lord, have mercy upon us, miserable offenders. Spare thou them, O God, which confess their faults. Restore them that are penitent according to thy promises declared unto mankind in Christ Jesu our Lord. And grant, O most merciful father, for his sake, that we may hereafter lead a godly, righteous, and sober life, to the glory of thy holy name. Amen.

Document 10: The Second Collect, for Peace, from Morning Prayer

O God, who art the author of peace and lover of concord, in knowledge of whom standeth our eternal life, whose service is perfect freedom, defend us thy humble servants in all assaults of our enemies, that we surely trusting in thy defense, may not fear the power of any adversaries, through the might of Jesus Christ our Lord. Amen.

Document 11: A Prayer in the Time of War and Tumults

O Almighty God, king of all kings, and governor of all things, whose power no creature is able to resist, to whom it belongeth justly to punish sinners, and to be merciful to them that truly repent; save and deliver us we humbly beseech thee, from the hands of our enemies; abate their pride, assuage their malice, and confound their devices, that we, being armed with thy defense, may be preserved evermore from all perils to glorify thee, who art the only giver of all victory, through the merits of thy only Son Jesus Christ our Lord. Amen.

1553

Mary I (1516–1558; reigned 1553–1558). Mary Tudor, Queen Mary I, the staunchly Catholic daughter of Catherine of Aragon and Henry VIII, ascended the throne after the death of King Edward VI (reigned 1547–1553), the son of Henry VIII and Jane Seymour. Mary's *First Proclamation about Religion* declared her intention to return England to Catholicism and dismantle the Church of England. Her request for a peaceable transition to the old church expresses the common desire of Tudor monarchs for social stability in times of transition, as seen also in *An Homily Against Disobedience* (Document 17). Her commands against "evil-disposed" books, plays, and poetry also reveal her concern about the power of literature to influence popular religious feeling; "interludes" were brief, often comic, dramatic pieces performed between the acts of longer plays. Her persecutions of non-Catholics earned her the name "Bloody Mary." (*Documents Illustrative of English Church History*. Ed, Henry Gee and William John Hardy. London, UK: Macmillan, 1896. 373–375.)

Document 12: From the *First Proclamation about Religion*

First, her majesty being presently by the only goodness of God settled in her just possession of the imperial crown of this realm . . . cannot now hide that religion, which God and the world know she has ever professed from her infancy hitherto; which as her majesty is minded to observe and maintain for herself by God's grace during her time, so doth her highness much desire, and would be glad, the same were of all her subjects quietly and charitably embraced.

And yet she doth signify unto all her majesty's loving subjects, that of her most gracious disposition and clemency, her highness minds not to compel any her said subject thereunto, unto such time as further order, by common assent, may be taken therein; forbidding nevertheless all her subjects of all degrees, at their perils, to move seditions or stir unquietness in her people, by interrupting the laws of this realm after [according to] their brains and fancies but quietly to continue for the time till (as before is said) further order may be taken; and therefore wills and straitly [strictly] charges and commands all her said good loving subjects to live together in quiet sort and Christian charity, leaving those new-found devilish terms of papist or heretic and such like, and travail to live in the fear of God . . . and in so doing they shall best please God and live without dangers of the laws, and maintain the tranquility of the realm, whereof her highness shall be most glad, so if any man shall rashly presume to make any assemblies of people, or at any public assemblies or otherwise shall go about to stir the people to disorder or disquiet, she minds, according to her duty, to see the same most severely reformed and punished, according to her highness's laws.

And furthermore, forasmuch as it is well known that seditions and false rumours have been nourished and maintained in this realm by the subtlety and malice of some evil-disposed persons, which take upon them, without sufficient authority, to preach and interpret the word of God after their own brain in churches and other places, both public and private, and also by playing of interludes, and printing of false fond [foolish] books and ballads, rhymes, and other lewd [unlearned] treatises in the English tongue, concerning doctrine in matters now in question and controversy touching the high points and mysteries of Christian religion, which books, ballads, rhymes, and treatises are chiefly by the printers and stationers set out to sale to her grace's subjects, of an evil zeal for lucre [profit], and covetous of vile gain; her highness therefore straitly charges and commands all and every of her said subjects, of whatsoever state, condition, or degree they be, that none of them presume from henceforth to preach, or by way of reading in churches or other public or private places, except in the schools of the University, to interpret or teach any Scriptures or any manner points of doctrine concerning religion; neither also to print any book, matter, ballad, rhyme, interlude, process, or treatise, nor to play any interlude, except they have her grace's special licence in writing for the same, upon pain to incur her highness's indignation and displeasure.

1556

An Account of the Death of Thomas Cranmer—Cranmer was one of many martyrs who died for the Protestant cause under the reign of Mary I; their lives took on a religious significance comparable to the Roman Catholic martyrs and saints. The eyewitness account given here in a letter by a Roman Catholic onlooker was later collected by church historian John Strype in 1694; it differs somewhat from the account contained in Foxe's "Book of Martyrs." Cranmer's death by burning is noteworthy for his having thrust first into the fire his right hand, with which he had signed a recantation of his views during his trial. (Harleian Mss. 422. Plut. Lxv. E. fol. 48–52. Rpt. John Strype, *Memorials of Archbishop Cranmer* (1694). 3 vols. Oxford: Ecclesiastical History Society, 1854. III: 247, 252, 253, 254.)

Document 13: From John Strype, *Memorials of Archbishop Cranmer*

[The execution occurred near St. Mary's Church, Oxford, and was preceded by a sermon by Dr. Cole.] "When he had ended his sermon, he desired all the people to pray for him: Mr. Cranmer kneeling down with them, and praying for himself. I think there was never such a number so earnestly praying together. For they, that hated him before, now loved him for his conversion, and hope of continuance. They that loved him before could not suddenly hate him, having hope of his confession again of his fall. So love and hope increased devotion of [on] every side.

"I shall not need, for the time of sermon, to describe his behavior, his sorrowful countenance, his heavy cheer, his face bedewed with tears; sometime lifting his eyes to heaven in hope, sometime casting them down to the earth for shame; to be brief, an image of sorrow; the dolor [sadness] of his heart bursting out at his eyes in plenty of tears: retaining ever a quiet and grave behavior. . . .

[Cranmer then spoke to the onlookers and rejected his earlier recantation.] . . . "And now I come to the great thing that troubles my conscience more than any other thing that ever I said or did in my life: and that is, the setting abroad of writings contrary to the truth. Which here now I renounce and refuse, as things written with my hand, contrary to the truth which I thought in my heart, and written for fear of death, and to save my life, if it might be: and that is, all such bills [official documents], which I have written or signed with my own hand since my degradation: wherein I have written many things untrue. And forasmuch as my hand offended in writing contrary to my heart, therefore my hand shall first be punished [therefore]: for if I may come to the fire, it shall be first burned. And as for the pope, I refuse him, as Christ's enemy and antichrist, with all his false doctrine. . . .

"Coming to the stake with a cheerful countenance and willing mind he put off his garments with haste, and stood upright in his shirt; and a bachelor of divinity, named Elye, of Brazen-nose college [in Oxford University], labored to convert him to his former recantation, with two Spanish friars. . . . Unto [Elye] he answered, that, as concerning his recantation, he repented it right sore [very strongly], because he knew it was against the truth; with other words more. Whereby the lord Williams cried, Make short, make short. . . .

"Fire being now put to him, he stretched out his right hand, and thrust it into the flame, and held it there a good space, before the fire came to any other part of his body; where his hand was seen of [by] every man sensibly [visibly] burning, crying with a loud voice, *This hand hath offended*. As soon as the fire got up, he was very soon dead, never stirring or crying all the while."

1559

Foxe's Book of Martyrs. John Foxe (1516–1587) is the greatest English martyrologist. He had begun work on his famous history of the martyrs of Protestanism in England before Mary Tudor became queen, whose accession forced him to escape to Strasbourg, Germany, a center of the Reformation. A Latin version of the work (1559) was finished before he returned to England, and it was followed by an expanded English translation entitled *The Acts and Monuments of These Latter and Perilous Days* (1563), popularly known as "Foxe's Book of Martyrs." The courage of Nicholas Ridley (who had ordained Foxe a deacon) and Bishop Hugh Latimer during their martyrdom, and Foxe's graphic details of the scene, make this one of the most oft-cited passages in the volume. (Ingram Cobbin, ed. *Foxe's Book of Martyrs*. London, UK: Knight, 1856.)

DOCUMENT 14: FROM JOHN FOXE, *ACTS AND MONUMENTS*

Then, being in his shirt, [Ridley] stood upon the foresaid stone, and held up his hand and said, "O heavenly Father, I give unto thee most hearty thanks, for that thou has called me to be a professor of thee, even unto death. I beseech thee, Lord God, take mercy upon this realm of England, and deliver the same from all her enemies." Then the smith took a chain of iron, and brought the same about both their middles: and as he was knocking in a staple, Dr. Ridley took the chain in his hand, and shaked the same, for it did gird in his belly, and looking aside to the smith said, "Good fellow, knock it in hard, for the flesh will have its course." Then the smith's brother did bring him a bag of gunpowder, and would have tied the same about his neck. Dr. Ridley asked what it was; and being told it was gunpowder, he said, "I will take it to be sent of God. And have you any for my brother?" meaning Latimer. "Yea, sir, that I have," said the man. "Then give it unto him betime [quickly]," said Ridley, lest ye come too late." So the man carried of the same gunpowder unto master Latimer. . . .

Then they brought a lighted fagot, and laid the same down at Ridley's feet; upon which Latimer said, "Be of good comfort, master Ridley, and play the man. We shall this day light such a candle, by God's grace, in England, as I trust shall never be put out." And so the fire being given unto them, when Dr. Ridley saw the fire flaming up towards him, he cried with a wonderful loud voice, "In manus tuas, Domine, commendo spiritum meum: Domine recipe spiritum meum." [Into your hands, O Lord, I commend my spirit: Lord receive my spirit.] And after repeated this latter part often in English, "Lord, Lord receive my spirit!" Master Latimer cried as vehemently, on the other side, "O Father of heaven, receive my soul!" who received the flame as if he were embracing it. After that he had stroked his face with his hands, and as it were bathed them a little in the fire, he soon died (as it appeareth) with very little pain or none. And thus much concerning the end of this old and blessed servant of God, Master Latimer, for whose laborious travails, fruitful life, and constant death, the whole realm hath cause to give great thanks to Almighty God.

But Dr. Ridley, by reason of the evil making of the fire unto him, because the fagots were laid about the gorse [shrubs], and overhigh built, the fire burned first beneath, being kept down by the wood; which when he felt he desired them, for Christ's sake, to let the fire come unto him. Which when his brother-in-law heard, but not well understood, intending to rid him out of his pain, (for the which cause he gave attendance), as one in such sorrow not well advised what he did, heaped fagots upon him, so that he clean covered him, which made the fire more vehement beneath, that it burned all his nether parts before it once touched the upper; and that made him leap up and down under the fagots, and often desire them to let the fire come unto him, saying, "I cannot burn." Which indeed appeared well; for, after his legs were consumed by reason of his struggling through the pain, (whereof he had no release, but only his contentation [contentment] in God), he showed that side towards us clean, shirt and all untouched with flame. Yet in all this torment he forgot not to call upon God, still having in his mouth, "Lord have mercy upon me," intermingling his cry, "Let the fire come unto me, I cannot burn!" In which pangs he laboured till one of the standers by with his bill [spear with a hook-shaped blade] pulled the fagots off above; and where he saw the fire flame up, he wrested himself unto that side. And when the flame touched the gunpowder, he was seen to stir no more, but burned on the other side, falling down at master Latimer's feet. In beholding of which horrible sight hundreds were moved to tears, and signs of sorrow there were on every side.

1560

The Geneva Bible. Many of the Protestant exiles who fled England during the reign of the Catholic Queen Mary settled in Geneva, the European center of Calvinism. A small group of translators there led by William Whittingham (c. 1524–1579) translated the Bible, relying heavily on Tyndale's earlier version. The New Testament portion of Whittingham's translation was published in 1557; the complete version appeared in 1560. This clearly printed and reasonably priced version also had explanatory notes in the margins, some of them quite obviously Protestant in tone. Words or phrases not literally present in the original manuscripts were printed in italics. This translation was extremely popular and was still in print even after the King James Version of 1611. The Geneva version was the translation Shakespeare knew.

DOCUMENT 15: FROM THE GENEVA BIBLE

1 Corinthians 13: 1–13

Thogh I spake with the tonges of men and Angels, and haue not loue, I am euen as sounding brasse, or as a tinkling cymbal. And thogh I could prophecie, and vnderstand all secretes, and all knowledge: yea, yf I had all faith, so that I could moue mountains out of their places, and yet had not loue, I were nothing. And thogh I bestowe all my goodes *to fede the poore,* and thogh I gyue my body that I be burned, and yet haue not loue, it profiteth me nothing.

Loue suffreth long, is courteous: loue enuieth not: loue doth not boast it selfe, swelleth not, Disdaineth nothing as vnbeseeming, seketh not her owne things, is not prouoked to anger, thinketh not euil, Reioyseth not in iniquitie, but reioyseth in the trueth. Suffreth all thinges, beleueth all thinges, hopeth all thinges, endureth all thinges.

Loue doth neuer fall away, thogh that both propheciinges shalbe abolished, and tongues shal cease, and learning shal vanishe away. For we learne in part, and we prophecie in part. But when that which is perfect, is come, then that which is in part, shalbe done away.

When I was a chylde, I spake as a childe, I vnderstode as a chylde, I thoght as a childe, but assone as I was a man, I put away chyldesh things. For now we se in a glasse, and in a darcke speaking: but then *shal we se* face to face. Now I knowe in part: but then shal I know euen as I am knowen. Now abydeth fayth, hope, and loue, euen these thre: but the chiefest of these is loue.

1559

The Act of Uniformity. Elizabeth I was crowned queen on January 13, 1559. The Act of Uniformity was passed that same year and repealed the laws of Mary I, which had sought to reestablish Catholicism as the national religion. (*Documents Illustrative of English Church History*. Ed. Henry Gee and William John Hardy. London, UK: Macmillan, 1896. 458–459.)

DOCUMENT 16: FROM THE ACT OF UNIFORMITY

Where at the death of our late sovereign lord King Edward VI there remained one uniform order of common service and prayer, and of the administration of sacraments, rites, and ceremonies in the Church of England, which was set forth in one book, intituled: The Book of Common Prayer, and Administration of Sacraments, and other rites and ceremonies in the Church of England; authorized by Act of Parliament holden in the fifth and sixth years of our said late sovereign lord King Edward VI, intituled: And for the uniformity of common prayer, and administration of the sacraments; the which was repealed and taken away by Act of Parliament in the first year of the reign of our late sovereign lady Queen Mary, to the great decay of the due honor of God, and discomfort to the professors of the truth of Christ's religion:

Be it therefore enacted by the authority of this present Parliament, that the said statute of repeal, and everything therein contained, only concerning the said book, and the service, administration of sacraments, rites, and ceremonies contained or appointed in or by the said book, shall be void and of none effect, from and after the feast of the Nativity of St. John Baptist [June 24] next coming; and that the said book, with the order of service, and of the administration of sacraments, rites, and ceremonies, with the alterations and additions therein added and appointed by this statute, shall stand and be, from and after the said feast of the Nativity of St. John the Baptist, in full force and effect, according to the tenor and effect of this statute; anything in the aforesaid statute of repeal to the contrary notwithstanding.

1563

An Homily Against Disobedience and Wilful Rebellion. In 1547 Thomas Cranmer issued a collection of 12 homilies, or sermons, to be read in all Anglican churches to disseminate the theology of the new faith of England. Queen Mary withdrew the homilies during her attempt to return the country to Catholicism, but in 1563 a second set of 21 more homilies appeared after Elizabeth I had repealed Mary's injunctions. These sermons, heard regularly by parishioners throughout England, helped shape the religious thinking of the nation and echoes of them can be found in Shakespeare, as Alfred Hart and others have pointed out. *The Homily Against Disobedience* appeared in the second volume and clearly defines obedience to earthly rulers as a religious virtue, even if the "the prince be undiscreet and evil indeed." This attitude of submission can be found in John of Gaunt's attitude toward the failures of the king in *Richard II:* "I may never lift / An angry arm against [God's] minister" (1.2.40–41). (*The Two Books of Homilies Appointed to be Read in Churches.* Oxford, UK: University Press, 1859. 555–557.)

DOCUMENT 17: FROM *AN HOMILY AGAINST DISOBEDIENCE AND WILFUL REBELLION*

What shall subjects do then? Shall they obey valiant, stout, wise, and good princes, and contemn, disobey, and rebel against children being their princes, or against undiscreet and evil governors? God forbid. For first what a perilous thing were it to commit unto the subjects the judgment, which prince is wise and godly and his government good, and which is otherwise; as though the foot must judge of the head; and enterprise very heinous, and must needs breed rebellion. For who else be they that are most inclined to rebellion, but such haughty spirits? From whom springeth such foul ruin of realms? Is not rebellion the greatest of all mischiefs? And who are most ready to the greatest mischiefs, but the worst men? Rebels therefore, the worst of all subjects, are most ready to rebellion, as being the worst of all vices and furthest from the duty of a good subject; as, on the contrary part, the best subjects are most firm and constant in obedience, as in the special and peculiar virtue of good subjects. What an unworthy matter were it then to make the naughtiest subjects, and most inclined to rebellion and all evil, judges over their princes, over their government, and over their counsellors, to determine which of them be good or tolerable, and which be evil and so intolerable that they must needs be removed by rebels; being ever ready, as the naughtiest subjects, soonest to rebel against the best princes, specially if they be young in age, women in sex, or gentle and courteous in government; as trusting by their wicked boldness easily to overthrow their weakness and gentleness, or at the least so to fear the minds of such princes, that they may have impunity of their mischievous doings. But, whereas indeed a rebel is worse than the worst prince, and rebellion worse than the worst government of the worst prince, that hitherto hath been, both are rebels unmeet ministers, and rebellion an unfit and unwholesome medicine, to reform any small lacks in a prince, or to cure any little griefs in government; such lewd [ignorant] remedies being far worse than any other maladies and disorders that can be in the body of a commonwealth. . . .

But what if the prince be undiscreet and evil indeed, and it also evident to all men's eyes that he is so? I ask again, what if it be long of [caused by] the wickedness of the subjects that the prince is undiscreet or evil? Shall the subjects both by their wickedness provoke God for their deserved punishment to give them an undiscreet or evil prince, and also rebel against him, and withal against

God, who for the punishment of their sins did give them such a prince? Will you hear the Scriptures concerning this point? *God, say the holy Scriptures, maketh a wicked man to reign for the sins of the people*. Again, *God giveth a prince in his anger*, meaning an evil one, *and taketh away a prince in his displeasure*, meaning specially when he taketh away a good prince for the sins of the people, as in our memory he took away our good Josias, King Edward, in his young and good years for our wickedness. And contrarily the scriptures do teach, that God giveth wisdom unto princes, and maketh a wise and good king to reign over that people whom he loveth, and who loveth him. Again, If the people obey God, both they and their king shall prosper and be safe, else both shall perish, saith God by the mouth of Samuel. Here you see that God placeth as well evil princes as good, and for what cause he doth both. If we therefore will have a good prince either to be given us or to continue, now we have such a one, let us by our obedience to God and to our prince move God thereunto. If we will have an evil prince (when god shall send such a one) taken away, and a good in his place, let us take away our wickedness, which provoketh God to place such an one over us, and God will either displace him or of an evil prince make him a good prince, so that we first will change our evil into good. . . . Wherefore let us turn from our sins unto the Lord with all our hearts, and he will turn the heart of the prince unto our quiet and wealth. Else for subjects to deserve through their sins to have an evil prince, and then to rebel against him, were double and treble evil, by provoking God more to plague them. Nay let us either deserve to have a good prince, or let us patiently suffer and obey such as we deserve.

1579

Stephen Gosson (1554–1624). Gosson wrote some poetry and three plays (now lost) early in his career, but he is best known for two works published in 1579: *The School of Abuse* and *A Short Apologie [Defense] of the School of Abuse*. These vigorous satires condemned the contemporary London theatres not so much for their plays themselves as for serving as a nucleus of immoral and licentious behavior. They thus expressed and fed the Puritan view of the public stage as a contributor to the general moral decline of society. Gosson dedicated *The School of Abuse* to Sir Philip Sidney, who replied with his famous *Defense of Poesie* in 1595. (*The School of Abuse*. Ed. Edward Arber. Westminster: A. Constable, 1895. 42–43, 44, 70–72.)

DOCUMENT 18: FROM *THE SCHOOL OF ABUSE*

Thus have I set down the abuses of poets, pipers, and players which bring us to pleasure, sloth, sleep, sin, and without repentance to death and the Devil, which I have not confirmed by authority of the Scriptures, because they are not able to stand up in the sight of God. And since they dare not abide the field, where the word of God doth bid them battle, but run to antiquities (though nothing be more ancient than holy Scriptures) I have given them a volley of profane writers to begin the skirmish and done my endeavor to beat them from their holds with their own weapons. The patient that will be cured, of his own accord, must seek the means; if every man desire to save one, and draw his own feet from the theaters, it shall prevail as much against these abuses, as Homer's Moly against witchcraft, or Pliny's Peristerion against the biting of dogs.

God hath armed every creature against his enemy: the lion with paws; the bull with horns; the boar with tusks; the vulture with talons; harts, hinds, hares and such like with swiftness of feet, because they are fearful, every one of them putting his gift in practice. But man, which is lord of the whole earth, for whose service herbs, trees, roots, plants, fish, fowl and beasts of the field were first made, is far worse than the brute beasts. For they, endued but with sense, do *Appetere salutaria, et declinare noxia,* seek that which helps them, and forsake that which hurts them.

Man is enriched with reason and knowledge: with knowledge, to serve his maker and govern himself; with reason to distinguish good and ill, and choose the best, neither referring the one to the glory of God, nor using the other to his own profit. Fire and air mount upwards, earth and water sink down, and every insensible body else [in addition] never rests, until it bring itself to his [its] own home. But we which have both sense, reason, wit, and understanding, are ever overlashing [exaggerating], passing our bounds, going beyond our limits, never keeping ourselves within compass, nor once looking after the place from whence we came, and whither we must in spite of our hearts....

Let us but shut up our ears to poets, pipers, and players, pull our feet back from resort to theaters, and turn away our eyes from beholding of vanity, the greatest storm of abuse will be overblown, and a fair path trodden to amendment of life. Were not we so foolish to taste every drug, and buy every trifle, players would shut in their shops, and carry their trash to some other country.

DOCUMENT 19: FROM *AN APOLOGY OF THE SCHOOL OF ABUSE*

If players take a little more counsel of their pillow, they shall find themselves to be the worst and the dangerousest people in the world. A thief is a shrewd member in a commonwealth: he empties our bags by force, these ransack our purses by permission; he spoils us secretly, these rifle us openly; he gets the upper hand by blows, these by merry jests; he sucks our blood, these our manners; he wounds our body, these our soul. O God, O men, O heaven, O earth, O times, O manners, O miserable days! He suffers for his offense; these strut without punishment under our noses, and like unto a consuming fire are nourished still with our decay. . . . [I]f Diogenes were alive now to see the abuses that grow by plays, I believe he would wish rather to be a Londoner's hound than his apprentice, because he rateth [scolds] his dog for wallowing in carrion, but rebukes not his servant for resorting to plays that are rank poison. So corrupt is our judgment in these matters that we account him a murderer whom we see delight in shedding of blood, and make him a jester that woundeth our conscience. We call that a slaughterhouse where brute beasts are killed, and hold that a pastime, which is the very butchery of Christian souls. We perceive not that trouble and toil draw us to life, ease and idleness bring destruction; that sorrow and anguish are virtuous books, pleasure and sport the devil's baits; that honest recreation quickens the spirits, and plays are the venomous arrows to the mind; that hunters deceive most, when seeming to walk for their delight they craftily fetch the deer about; that players counterfeiting a show to make us merry, shoot their nets to work our misery; that when Comedy comes upon the stage, Cupid sets up a springe [snare] for woodcocks, which are entangled before they descry [see] the line, and caught before they mistrust the snare.

1582

The Rheims-Douai Bible. Just as Protestant exiles under Mary Tudor produced an English translation of the Bible in Switzerland, so Roman Catholics who fled to France to avoid prosecution under Elizabeth I produced an English version to counteract the Protestant tone of the Geneva text. Based largely on a new translation of the Latin Vulgate version (the approved text of the Catholic Counter-Reformation), their New Testament appeared in 1582 at the English College of Rheims; an Old Testament translation followed in 1609–1610, published at Douai. (*The English Hexapla.* London, UK: Samuel Bagster, 1841. n.p.)

DOCUMENT 20: FROM THE RHEIMS-DOUAI BIBLE

1 Corinthians 13: 1–3

If I speake vvith the tonges of men and of Angels, and haue not charitie: I am become as sounding brasse, or a tinkling cymbal. And if I should haue prophecie, and knevv al mysteries, and al knovvledge, and if I should haue al faith so that I could remoue mountains, and haue not charitie, I am nothing. And if I should distribute al my goods to be meate for the poore, and if I should deliuer my body so that I burne, and haue not charitie, it doth profit me nothing.

Charitie is patient, is benigne: Charitie enuieth not, dealeth not peruersly: is not puffed vp, is not ambitious, seeketh not her ovvne, is not prouoked to anger, thinketh not euil: reioyceth not vpon iniquitie, but reioyceth vviwth the truth: suffereth al things, beleeueth al things, hopeth al things, beareth al things.

Charitie neuer falleth avvay: vvhether prophecies shal be made voide, or tonges shal cease, or knovvledge shal be destroyed. For in part vve know, and in part vve prophecie. But vvhen that shal come that is perfect, that shal be made voide that is in part. Vven I vvas a little one, I spake as a little one, I vnderstood as a little one. But vvhen I vvas made a man, I did avvay the things that belonged to a litle one. Vve see novv by a glasse in a darke sort: but then face to face. Novv I knovvin part: but then I shal knovv as also I am knovven. And novv there remaine, faith, hope, charitie, these three[,] but the greater of these is charitie.

1583

Philip Stubbes (c. 1555–c. 1610). Details about Stubbes' life are scanty. His fame rests on *The Anatomy of Abuses* (1583), a sprawling condemnation of every defect and shortcoming he could find in late sixteenth-century England, from cheating shopkeepers and "beastly ruffians who wear long hair" to "rascally lawyers" and corrupt clergymen. Though not theologically an extreme Puritan (he defends the usefulness of bishops in the English church), the vigor of his prose attacks against social ills links him to the Puritan religious reformers of his day, as in his condemnation of Roman Catholics ("Papists"). (*The Anatomy of Abuses in England. Part II: The Display of Corruptions Requiring Reformation.* Ed. Frederick J. Furnivall. The New Shakespere Society. London, UK: N. Trübner, 1882. 5–6.)

DOCUMENT 21: FROM *THE ANATOMY OF ABUSES,* PART II

It is an old saying and true: *Ex incertis, & ambiguis rebus optimum tenere sapientis est:* Of things uncertain, a Christian man ought to judge and hope the best. They hope well that all are their friends and well-willers, but it is thought (and I fear me too true) that they are so far from being their friends . . . that they have vowed and sworn their destruction, if they could as easily achieve it as they secretly intend it. Which thing to be true, some of their late practices have (yet to their own confusion, God's name be praised) proved true. For how many times hath that man of sin, that son of the devil, that Italian Antichrist of Rome, interdicted, excommunicated, suspended, and accursed with book, bell, and candle, both the prince, the nobility, the commons, and whole Realm? How often hath he sent forth his roaring bulls [papal pronouncements] against her Majesty, excommunicating (as I have said) her Grace, and discharging her Highness' liege people and natural subjects from their allegiance to her Grace? How often hath he with his adherents conspired and intended the death and overthrow of her Majesty and Nobility, by conjuration [spells], necromancy [magic], exorcisms, art, magic, witchcraft, and all kind of devilry besides, wherein the most part of them are skilfuller than in divinity? And when these devices would not take place, nor effect as they wished, then attempted they by other ways and means to overthrow the estate, the prince, nobles, people and country, sometimes by secret irruption [outbreak], sometime by open invasion and rebellion, sometime by open treason, sometime by secret conspiracy, and sometimes by one means, sometimes by another. And now of late attempted they the overthrow and subversion of her Majesty, people, country, and all by sending into the realm a sort of cutthroats, false traitors, and bloodthirsty Papists, who under the pretence of religious men (in whom for the most part there is as much religion as is in a dog) should not only lurk in corners like howlets [screech owls] that abhor the light, creep into noble men's bosoms, thereby to withdraw her Majesty's subjects from their allegiance, but also to move them to rebellion, and to take sword in hand against prince, country, yea, and against God himself (if it were possible) and to dispense with them that shall thus mischievously behave themselves. And forsooth [truly] these goodly fellows, the devil's agents, that must work these feats, are called (in the devil's name) by the name of Jesuits, seminary priests, and catholics, usurping to themselves a name never heard of till of late days, being indeed a name very blasphemously derived from the name of Jesus, and improperly alluded and attributed to themselves.

But what will it prevail them to be like unto Jesus in name only or how can they, nay, how dare they, arrogate that name unto themselves, whereas their doctrine, religion, life and whole profession, together with their corrupt lives and conversations are directly contrary to the doctrine, religion, life and profession of Christ Jesus? There is nothing in the world more contradictory one to another, than all their proceedings in general are to Christ Jesus and his laws, and yet will they, under the pretense of a bare and naked name, promise to themselves such excellencie, such integrity and perfection, as GOD cannot require more, yea such as doth merit *Ex opere operato* ["from the work itself"] eternal felicity in the heavens. And thus they deceive themselves, and delude the world also with their trash: but of them enough.

1587

Phillipe Du Plessis-Mornay (1549–1623). Du Plessis-Mornay was a French Huguenot leader and controversialist who fled to England for a year after the St. Bartholomew's Day Massacre in 1572. His *A Work Concerning the Trueness of the Christian Religion* was translated into English by Sir Philip Sidney and Arthur Golding and published in 1587. Part of his argument for Christianity asserts the traditional point that reason and faith are not contrary human activities, but that faith can move beyond the capabilities of reason. Though Hamlet certainly respects reason, he seems to echo du Plessis-Mornay's view of truth as extending beyond the limits of reason when he says, "There are more things in heaven and earth, Horatio / Than are dreamt of in your philosophy" (1.5.166–67). (*The Prose Works of Sir Philip Sidney*. Ed. Albert Feuillerat. 4 vols. Cambridge, 1912. Rpt. 1963. III, 194–195.)

Document 22: From *A Work Concerning the Trueness of the Christian Religion*

For what a great way does the truth of things extend further than man's reason? But we say that man's reason is able to lead us to that point; namely that we ought to believe even beyond reason, I mean the things whereto all the capacity of man cannot attain. And likewise, that when things are revealed to us, which reason could never have entered into nor once imagined, no not even when it was at the soundest, the same reason (which never could have found them out) makes us to allow of them. The reason I say (whereto those mysteries were invisible before) makes them credible to us, surely even after the same manner that our eye makes us to see that in the visible things, which we ought to believe of the invisible, without which the visible could have no being, that is to wit, the invisible God, by the visible Son, and also to see many things when the Sun is up, which were hidden before in darkness. Not that the eyesight was of less force, or the thing itself less visible before but because the Son is now up, which lightens the air with his brightness, which is the means by which the eye sees and by which the thing is seen. As for example, we believe that there is one God, the Father, the Son, and the holy Ghost. This is the article which they [adversaries of Christianity] oppose against us, and therefore do I take [up] the very same [point]. This article cannot in any wise fall within the compass of understanding, much less be comprehended by man's reason. But yet reason does lead us to this point, that there is a God: that he has created man to live for ever, that whereas man has stepped out of the way, to follow his own sway, he reforms him again by his word. That this word (as I have already said heretofore) is the old and new Testament, which contains things that cannot proceed from creatures. Here Reason stays, and holds itself contented. For seeing that God speaks, it is becoming for man to hold his peace, and seeing that he vouchsafes to teach us, it becomes us to believe. Now we read this doctrine in God's aforesaid books, oftentimes repeated. Lo, how Reason teaches us that which she herself neither knew nor believed, namely by leading us to the teacher, whom we ought to hear and believe, and to the book wherein he vouchsafes to open himself to us, in giving us infallible marks and tokens, whereby to discern what comes from God, and what does not come from him.

1589

The Martin Marprelate Tracts. The Marprelate Tracts, a series of seven anonymous pamphlets issued between 1588 and 1589, vigorously satirized the ability and authority of Anglican bishops and the entire structure of the Church of England. Their blunt, vigorous, evangelical Protestant style makes them the best example of Elizabethan prose satire. Of the three men involved in the tracts' production, one escaped to Scotland, one was hanged, and Job Throckmorton, likely the actual author, eventually escaped punishment. The aim of "Marprelate," the fictional author, is to mar the Anglican prelates (ruling bishops), while "Martin" may be a backward glance at Martin Luther. The fourth pamphlet's title, "Hay any Work for Cooper," was the street-cry of a London cooper or barrel-maker, but here the allusion is to Bishop Thomas Cooper of Winchester. (*The Marprelate Tracts 1588, 1589.* Ed. William Pierce. London, UK: James Clarke, 1911. 238–240, 243, 250.)

DOCUMENT 23: FROM "HAY ANY WORK FOR COOPER"

I am not disposed to jest in this serious matter. I am called Martin Marprelate. There be many that greatly dislike my doings. I may have my wants [deficiencies] I know; for I am a man. But my course [purpose] I know to be ordinary and lawful. I saw the cause of Christ's government, and of the Bishops' antichristian dealing to be hidden. The most part of men could not be gotten to read anything written in the defence of the one, and against the other. I bethought me, therefore, of a way whereby men might be drawn to do both; perceiving the humours [moods] of men in these times (especially of those that are in any place) to be given to mirth. I took that course. I might lawfully do it. Aye, for jesting is lawful by circumstances, even in the greatest matters. The circumstances of time, place, and persons urged me thereunto. I never profaned the Word in any jest. Other mirth I used as a covert, wherein I would bring the truth into light. The Lord being the author both of mirth and gravity, is it not lawful in itself, for the truth to use either of these ways, when the circumstances do make it lawful?

My purpose was, and is, to do good. I know I have done no harm, howsoever some may judge Martin to mar all. They are very weak ones that so think. In that which I have written, I know undoubtedly that I have done the Lord, and the State of this Kingdom, great service. Because I have in some sort discovered the greatest enemies thereof. And, by so much the most pestilent enemies, because they wound God's religion, and corrupt the State with atheism and looseness, and so call for God's vengeance upon us all, even under the colour of religion. I affirm them to be the greatest enemies that now our State hath; for if it were not for them, the truth should have more free passage herein, than now it hath. All states [portions of society] thereby would be amended. And so, we should not be subject unto God's displeasure, as now we are by reason of them. . . .

Now, you wretches (archbishops and lord bishops, I mean), you Mar-State, Mar-Law, Mar-Prince, Mar-Magistrate, Mar-Commonwealth, Mar-Church, and Mar-Religion! Are you able for your lives to answer any part of the former syl-logism [logical argument], whereby you are concluded to be the greatest enemies to her Majesty and the State? You dare not attempt it, I know. . . .

. . . And shall I, being a Christian English subject, abide to hear a wicked crew of ungodly bishops, with their hang-ons and parasites, affirm that our Queen and our State must needs be subject to the greatest danger that may be; viz. [videlicet: namely] the wrath of God for deforming his Church, and that God's Church must needs be maimed and deformed among us; because otherwise, a few civilians shall not be able to live? Shall I hear and see these things professed and published, and in the love I owe unto God's religion and her Majesty say nothing? I cannot; I will not; I may not be silent at this speech; come what will of it. The love of a Chris-tian Church, Prince and State shall work more in me than the love of a heathen empire and state should do.

1593

An Act against Recusants. This act was passed to ensure conformity to the wor-ship of the Church of England. Recusancy was any disobedience to established governmental authority, but it was applied more specifically to Roman Catholics who refused to take part in the rites of the Anglican church. Recusancy had been a crime since the 1559 Act of Uniformity. The 1593 act viewed Roman Catholics as both a religious and political threat and is one of several acts passed under Elizabeth I to control groups regarded as enemies of the Anglican settlement; an act against Jesuits and seminarians had been passed in 1585 and one against Pu-ritans in 1593. John Shakespeare, the dramatist's father, was charged with recu-sancy in 1592, a fact which has been used to support claims of the playwright's own Catholicism. (*Documents Illustrative of English Church History*. Ed. Henry Gee and William John Hardy. London, UK: Macmillan, 1896. 499–501, 505.)

DOCUMENT 24: FROM AN ACT AGAINST RECUSANTS

For the better discovering and avoiding of all such traitorous and most dan-gerous conspiracies and attempts as are daily devised and practiced against our most gracious sovereign lady the queen's majesty and the happy estate of this commonweal, by sundry wicked and seditious persons, who, terming themselves Catholics, and being indeed spies and intelligencers, not only for her majesty's foreign enemies, but also for rebellious and traitorous subjects born within her highness's realms and dominions, and hiding their most detestable and devilish purposes under a false pretext of religion and conscience, do secretly wander and shift from place to place within this realm, to corrupt and seduce her majesty's subjects, and to stir them to sedition and rebellion:

Be it ordained and enacted . . . that every person above the age of sixteen years, born within any of the queen's majesty's realms and dominions, or made denizen [inhabitant], being a popish recusant, and before the end of this session of Parliament, convicted for not repairing [returning] to some church, chapel, or usual place of common prayer, to hear divine service there, but forbearing the same, . . . shall . . . repair to their place of dwelling where they usually heretofore made their common abode, and shall not, any time after, pass or remove above five miles from thence. . . . [E]very person and persons that shall offend against the tenor and intent of this Act in anything before mentioned, shall lose and forfeit all his and their goods and chattels, and shall also forfeit to the queen's majesty all the lands, tenements, and hereditaments [inheritable property], and all the rents and annuities of every person so offending, during the life of the same offender.

. . . And be it further enacted and ordained by the authority aforesaid, that if any person which shall be suspected to be a Jesuit, seminary or massing priest [one saying the Catholic mass], being examined by any person having lawful authority . . . shall refuse to answer directly and truly whether he be a Jesuit, or a seminary or massing priest, as is aforesaid, every such person so refusing to answer shall for his disobedience and contempt in that behalf, be committed to prison . . . and . . . shall remain and continue in prison without bail or mainprize [a writ of release], until he shall make direct and true answer to the said questions whereupon he shall be so examined.

Richard Hooker (1554–1600). If Thomas Cranmer's *Book of Common Prayer* is the essential pattern for the liturgy of Anglicanism, Hooker's *Laws of Ecclesiastical Polity* is its earliest and most formative theological treatise. Its first four books appeared in 1594; a total of seven were eventually published in 1662. The work does more than just present a description of polity or church government. Its first book presents a discussion of the nature of law itself, rooted in God's divine plan and visible in the physical design and operation of the universe. Whereas Tudor politicians viewed obedience to authority as a political necessity for social order, Hooker viewed it as a theological response to God's purposes. The second book presents an Anglican defense of the role of individual reason in the interpretation of holy scripture, objecting both to Roman Catholicism's ranking of church pronouncements as equal to the Bible and to the Puritan assumption that the Bible directly answers any and every human question or problem. Hooker's style is a model of latinate English prose. (*The Laws of Ecclesiastical Polity*, Books I–IV. Intro. Henry Morley. London, UK: George Routledge, 1888. 64–68; 165–166.)

DOCUMENT 25: FROM *THE LAWS OF ECCLESIASTICAL POLITY,* BOOK I

Now that law which, as it is laid up in the bosom of God, they call eternal, receiveth, according unto the different kind of things which are subject unto it, different and sundry kinds of names. That part of it which ordereth natural agents we call usually Nature's law; that which angels do clearly behold, and without any swerving observe, is a law celestial and heavenly. The law of reason, that which binds creatures reasonable in this world, and with which by reason they may most plainly perceive themselves bound; that which bindeth them, and is not known but by special revelation from God, Divine law; human law, that which out of the law either of reason or of God, men probably gathering to be expedient, they make it a law. . . . This world's first creation, and the preservation since of things created, what is it but only so far forth a manifestation by execution what the eternal law of God is concerning things natural? . . . He made a law for the rain, He gave His decree unto the sea that the waters should not pass His commandment. Now if nature should intermit [interrupt] her course, and leave altogether, though it were but for a while, the observation of her own laws; if those principal and mother elements of the world whereof all things in this lower world are made should lose the qualities which now they have; if the frame of that heavenly arch erected over our heads should loosen and dissolve itself; if celestial spheres should forget their wonted motions and by irregular volubility [twisting] turn themselves any way as it might happen; if the prince of the lights of heaven, which now as a giant doth run his unwearied course, should as it were, through a languishing faintness, begin to stand and to rest himself; if the moon should wander from her beaten [accustomed] way, the times and seasons of the year blend themselves by disordered and confused mixture, the winds breathe out their last gasp, the clouds yield no rain, the earth be defeated of heavenly influence, the fruits of the earth pine away as children at the withered breasts of their mother, no longer able to yield them relief—what would become of man himself whom these things now do all serve? See we not plainly that obedience of creatures unto the law of nature is the stay of the whole world? . . . That law the performance whereof we behold in things natural, is as it were an authentical or an original draft written in the bosom of God himself; whose spirit being to execute the same, useth every particular nature, every mere natural agent, only as an instrument created at the beginning, and ever since the beginning used to work His own will and pleasure withal. Nature, therefore, is nothing else but God's instrument . . .

DOCUMENT 26: FROM *THE LAWS OF ECCLESIASTICAL POLITY,* BOOK II

. . . let them with whom we have hitherto disputed consider well how it can stand with reason to make the bare mandate of sacred Scripture the only rule of all good and evil in the actions of mortal men. . . . Whatsoever to make up the doctrine of man's salvation is added as in supply of the Scripture's insufficiency, we reject it. Scripture, purposing this, hath perfectly and fully done it. Again, the scope and purpose of God in delivering the Holy Scripture, such as do take more largely than behoveth [more broadly than is necessary], they on the contrary side, racking and stretching it further than by Him was meant, are drawn into sundry as great inconveniences. These, pretending the Scripture's perfection, infer thereupon that in Scripture all things lawful to be done must needs be contained. . . . So that if hereupon we conclude that because the Scripture is perfect therefore all things lawful to be done are comprehended in the Scripture, we may even as well conclude so of every sentence as of the whole sum and body thereof, unless we first of all prove that it was the drift, scope and purpose of Almighty God in Holy Scripture to comprise all things which many may practice. But admit this and mark, I beseech you, what would follow. God, in delivering Scripture to His Church, should clean have abrogated amongst them the law of Nature, which is an infallible knowledge imprinted in the minds of all the children of men, whereby both general principles for directing of human actions are comprehended and conclusions derived from them, upon which conclusions groweth in particularity the choice of good and evil in the daily affairs of this life. Not that the Scripture itself doth cause any such thing, for it tendeth to the clean contrary, and the fruit thereof is resolute assurance and certainty in that it teacheth; but the necessities of this life urging men to do that which the light of Nature, common discretion and judgment of itself directeth them unto.

1595

Sir Philip Sidney (1554–1586). Sidney was a renowned poet, courtier, statesman, and author. His *Defence of Poesie* (1595) ("poesie" included all forms of creative writing) justified literature against the criticism of Puritans who felt that it posed too great a temptation to sin and against the Platonic idea that it presented a false image of truth. Sidney's elaborate essay, a major work of English Renaissance literary criticism, drew upon classical and Christian authorities to make its argument that literature was as valuable a branch of learning as either history or philosophy. (*The Prose Works of Sir Philip Sidney*. Ed. Albert Feuillerat. 4 vols. Cambridge: Cambridge University Press, 1912. III, 6–7, 15–16.)

DOCUMENT 27: FROM *THE DEFENCE OF POESIE*

Among the Romans a Poet was called Vates, which is as much as a diviner, foreseer, or Prophet . . . And may I not presume a little farther, to show the reasonableness of this word Vates, and say that the holy Davids Psalms are a divine Poem? If I do, I shall not do it without the testimony of great learned men, both ancient and modern. But even the name of Psalms will speak for me, which being interpreted, is nothing but Songs. Then that it is fully written in meter as all learned Hebritians [scholars of Hebrew] agree, although the rules are not yet fully found. Lastly and principally, his handling his prophecy, which is merely [purely] Poetical. For what else is the awaking his musical Instruments, the often and free changing of persons, his notable Prosopopeias [personifications], when he makes you as it were see God coming in his majesty, his telling of the beasts' joyfulness, and hills leaping, but a heavenly poetry, in which almost he shows himself a passionate lover of that unspeakable and everlasting beauty, to be seen by the eyes of the mind, only cleared by faith? But truly now having named him, I fear I seem to profane that holy name, applying it to Poetry, which is among us thrown down to so ridiculous an estimation. But they that with quiet judgements will look a little deeper into it, shall find the end and working of it such, as being rightly applied, deserves not to be scourged out of the Church of God. . . . For the question is, whether the fained [artistically created] Image of Poetry, or the regular instruction of Philosophy, has the more force in teaching? . . . Certainly even our Savior Christ could as well have given the moral commonplaces of uncharitableness and humbleness, as the divine narration of Dives and Lazarus, or of disobedience and mercy, as that heavenly discourse of the lost child and the gracious Father, but that his thorough, searching wisdom knew the estate of Dives burning in hell, and of Lazarus in Abraham's bosom, would more constantly as it were, inhabit both the memory and judgement. Truly for myself (it seems to me) I see before my eyes the lost child's disdainful prodigality turned to envy a swine's dinner: which by the learned Divines are thought not Historical acts, but instructing Parables. For conclusion, I say the Philosopher teaches, but he teaches obscurely, so as only the learned can understand him, that is to say, he teaches them that are already taught. But the Poet is the food for the tenderest stomachs; the Poet is indeed the truly popular Philosopher.

1606

Lancelot Andrewes (1555–1626). Andrewes was one of the most accomplished preachers of the English church in an age that valued skillful preaching. Beginning in 1606 and continuing almost annually for the next 12 years, he preached a series of sermons before the king, which celebrated England's escape (praised as an act of divine providence) from the Gunpowder Plot of November 5, 1605. On that day, 36 barrels of gunpowder were found beneath Parliament, evidence of a Roman Catholic plot against the crown. Among the conspirators were Guy Fawkes (after whom this day, still commemorated in England, is named) and Henry Garnett, a Jesuit priest whose equivocal answers to his interrogators is assumed to be the source of the porter's remarks about "the equivocator" in *Macbeth* (2.3.11). (Lancelot Andrewes, *Ninety-six sermons*. 5 vols. Oxford, UK: J. H. Parker, 1841–1843. Vol. IV, 203–204, 211–212, 221–222.)

DOCUMENT 28: FROM SERMON I OF THE GUNPOWDER TREASON PREACHED BEFORE THE KING'S MAJESTY AT WHITEHALL, ON THE FIFTH OF NOVEMBER A.D. MDCVI

Psalm cxviii.23, 24

This is the Lord's doing, and it is marvelous in our eyes.
This is the day which the Lord hath made; let us rejoice and be glad in it.

To entitle this time to this text, or to show it pertinent to the present occasion, will ask no long process. This day of ours, this fifth of November, a day of God's making; that which was done upon it was "the Lord's doing." Christ's own application, which is the best, may well be applied here: "This day is this Scripture fulfilled in our ears." For if ever there were a deed done, or a day made, by God in our days, this day, and the deed of this day, was it. If ever he gave cause of marveling, as in the first, of rejoicing, as in the second verse, to any land, to us this day he gave both. If ever saved, prospered, blessed any, this day he saved, prospered, and, as we say, fairly blessed us.

The day, we all know, was meant to be the day of all our deaths; and we, and many were appointed, as sheep to the slaughter, nay worse than so. There was a thing doing on it, if it had been done, we all had been undone. And the very same day, we all know, the day wherein that appointment was disappointed by God and we all saved, that we might "not die but live, and declare the praise of the Lord," the Lord of whose doing that marvelous deed was, of whose making this joyful day is that we celebrate....

We have therefore well done and upon good warrant, to tread in the same steps, and by law to provide that this day should not die, nor the memorial thereof perish, from ourselves or from our seed; but be consecrated to a perpetual memory, by a yearly acknowledgment to be made of it throughout all generations. In accomplishment of which order, we are all now here in the presence of God, on this day that he first, by his act of doing, hath made: and we secondly, by our act of decreeing have made before him, his holy Angels and men, to confess this his goodness, and ourselves eternally bound to him for it. And being to confess it, with what words of scripture can we better or fitter do it than those we have read out of this psalm? . . .

But this, that this so abominable and desolatory a plot stood "in the holy place," this is the pitch [most extreme point] of all. For there it stood, and thence it came abroad. Undertaken with a holy oath, bound with the holy sacrament—that must needs be in "a holy place," warranted for a holy act tending to the advancement of a holy religion, and by holy persons called by a most holy name, the name of Jesus. That these holy religious persons, even the chief of all religious persons, the Jesuits, gave not only absolution but resolution, that all this was well done; that it was by them justified as lawful, sanctified as meritorious, and should have been glorified—but it wants [lacks] glorifying, because the event failed, that is the grief; if it had not, glorified—long ere this, and canonized as a very good and holy act, and we had had orations out of the conclave [a private meeting of Catholic clergy] in commendation of it. Now I think we shall hear no more it. These good fathers they were David's "bees" here, came hither to bring us honey, right honey they; not to sting any body; or, as in the twenty-second verse, they as "builders" came into the land only for edification, not to pull down or to destroy any thing. We see their practice, they begun with rejecting this stone, as one that favoured heretics at least, and therefore excommunicate, and therefore deposed, and therefore exposed to any that could handle a spade well to make a mine to blow him up—him, and all his estates with him to attend him: the corner stone being gone, the walls must needs follow. But then this shrining it—such an abomination—setting it "in the holy place," so ugly and odious, making such a treason as this, a religious, missal, sacramental treason, hallowing it with orison [prayer], oath, and eucharist, this passeth all the rest. . . .

. . . All these were undone and blown over, all the undermining disappointed, all this murder and cruelty and desolation defeated. The mine is discovered, the snare is broken, and we are delivered. All these, the king, queen, prince, nobles, bishops, judges, both houses [of Parliament], alive all; not so much as "the smell of fire" on any their garments. . . .

To end then. "This day, which the Lord hath" thus "made" so marvelously, so marvelously and mercifully, let us rejoice in the maker, for the making of it, by his doing on it that deed that is so "marvelous in our eyes," in all eyes; returning to the beginning of the psalm, and saying with the prophet, "O give thanks to the Lord, for he is gracious," &c. "Let Israel, let the house of Aaron, yea let all that fear the Lord, confess that his mercy endureth for ever."

"Who only doeth great wonders." "Who remembered us when we were in danger." "And hath delivered us from our enemies," "with a mighty hand and stretched-out arm." And, so for them, has turned their device upon their own head. And has made this day, to us, a day of joy and gladness. To this God of Gods, the Lord of heaven, "glorious in holiness, fearful in power, doing wonders," be &c.

1606

Thomas Dekker (c. 1572–1632). Dekker was a prolific pamphleteer and dramatist whose works offer graphic glimpses of London life around the turn of the seventeenth century. The plague had struck London in 1603, and Dekker's pamphlet, excerpted here, three years later responded to this calamity as a secular sermon with a call to repentance and purity of life. It documents the common belief that great national events, whether successes like the defeat of the Spanish Armada in 1588 or disasters like the plague, were acts of divine mercy or punishment as well as human or natural occurrences. The pamphlet's complete title is *The Seven Deadly Sins of London drawn in seven several coaches, through the seven several gates of the City; bringing the plague with them. (The Seven Deadly Sins of London.* Ed. Edward Arber. English Scholar's Library, No. 7. London, UK: Edward Arber, 1879. 7–10.)

DOCUMENT 29: FROM *THE SEVEN DEADLY SINS OF LONDON*

O London, thou art great in glory, and envied for thy greatness. Thy towers, thy temples, and thy pinnacles stand upon thy head like borders of fine gold, thy waters like fringes of silver hang at the hems of thy garments. Thou art the goodliest of thy neighbors, but the proudest; the wealthiest, but the most wanton. Thou hast all things in thee to make thee fairest, and all things in thee to make thee foulest; for thou art attired like a bride, drawing all that look upon thee to be in love with thee, but there is much harlot in thine eyes. Thou sitst in thy gates heated with Wines, and in thy Chambers with lust. What miseries have of late overtaken thee? Yet (like a fool that laughs when he is putting on fetters [chains]) thou hast been merry in height of thy misfortunes. . . .

Here I could make thee weep thyself away into waters, by calling back those sad and dismal hours wherein thou consumed almost to nothing with shrieks and lamentations, in that wonderful [astounding] year when these miserable calamities entered in at thy gates, slaying 30,000 and more as thou heldst them in thine arms, but they are fresh in thy memory . . . How quickly notwithstanding didst thou forget that beating? The wrath of him that smote thee was no sooner (in mere pity of thy stripes [wounds]) appeased, but hourly (again) thou wert in the company of evildoers, even before thou couldst find leisure to ask him for forgiveness.

Ever since that time hath he winked at [overlooked] thy errors, and suffered thee (though now thou art grown old, and lookest very ancient) to go on still in the follies of thy youth. He hath tenfold restored thy lost sons and daughters, and such sweet, lively, fresh colors hath he put upon thy cheeks that kings have come to behold thee, and Princes to delight their eyes with thy beauty. None of all these favors (for all this) can draw thee from thy wickedness. Graces have poured down out of heaven upon thee, and thou art rich in all things, saving in [except for] goodness. So that now once again hath he gone about (and but gone about) to call thee to the dreadful bar of his judgement. . . . O thou beautifullest daughter of two united monarchies [England and Scotland]! From thy womb received I my being, from thy breasts my nourishment; yet give me leave to tell thee, that thou hast seven devils within thee, and till they be clean cast out, the arrows of pestilence will fall upon thee by day, and the hand of the invader strike thee by night. The sun will shine, but not be a comfort to thee, and the moon looks pale with anger when she gives thee light. Thy lovers will disdain to court thee; thy temples will no more send out divine oracles. Justice will take her flight, and dwell elsewhere, and that desolation, which now for three years together hath hovered round about thee, will at last enter and turn thy gardens of pleasure into churchyards [graveyards], thy fields that served thee for walks, into Golgotha, and thy high-built houses into heaps of dead men's skulls. . . . Lift up therefore thy head (thou mother of so many people) and awaken out of thy dead dangers slumbers, and with a full and fearless eye behold those seven monsters, that with extended jaws gape to swallow up thy memory. For I will into so large a field single every one of them, that thou and all the world shall see their ugliness, for by seeing them, thou mayst avoid them, and by avoiding them, be the happiest and most renowned of cities.

1611

The King James Bible. In 1604 King James I, displeased with existing English translations of the Bible, expressed a desire for a new rendition that would become the authorized version for use throughout the nation. For almost three years, a committee of more than 50 scholars led by Lancelot Andrewes consulted previous translations before finally arriving at what became known as the Authorized or King James Version (the king was not one of the revisers). Relying heavily on the Bishop's Bible (1568), they also consulted Tyndale's version, as well as the Geneva, Rheims-Douai, and Greek and Hebrew editions, among others. The result was a version of great beauty and expressiveness that eclipsed all other translations in popularity, becoming a formative influence not only upon English religious faith, but upon the English language itself. (*The English Hexapla.* London, UK: Samuel Bagster, 1841. n.p.)

DOCUMENT 30: FROM THE KING JAMES BIBLE

1 Corinthians 13: 1–13

Though I speake with the tongues of men and of Angels, and haue not charity, I am become as sounding brasse or a tinkling cymbal. And though I haue the gift of prophesie, and vnderstand all mysteries and all knowledge: and though I haue all faith, so that I could remooue mountains, and haue no charitie, I am nothing. And though I bestowe all my goods to feede the poore, and though I giue my body to bee burned, and haue not charitie, it profiteth me nothing. Charitie suffereth long, and is kinde: charitie enuieth not: charitie vaunteth not it selfe, is not puffed vp, Doeth not behaue it selfe vnseemly, seeketh not her owne, is not easily prouoked, thinketh no euill, Reioyceth not in iniquitie, but reioyceth in the trueth: Beareth all things, beleeueth all things, hopeth all things, endureth all things.

Charitie neuer faileth: but whether there be prophesies *they* shall faile; whether there bee tongues, *they* shall cease; whether there bee knowledge, *it* shall vanish away. For we know in part, and we prophesie in part. But when that which is perfect is come, then that which is in part, shalbe done away. When I was a childe, I spake as a childe, I vnderstood as a childe, I thought as a childe: but when I became a man, I put away childish things. For now we see through a glasse, darkely: but then face to face: now I know in part, but then shall I know euen as also I am knowen. And now abideth faith, hope, charitie, these three, but the greatest of these is charitie.

POETRY

1562

John Hopkins (c. 1520/1521–1570). Versifying the psalms (setting these biblical prayers into poetic form especially for singing) was a popular activity among Elizabethan poets and laymen. Beginning with an edition of metrical psalms published the same year as the first Book of Common Prayer (1549), Hopkins, along with Thomas Sternhold (d. 1549), contributed significantly to this vogue of singable biblical verse. *The Whole Book of Psalms* (1562) was largely the work of Sternhold and Hopkins, and their versions were the standard musical psalm lyrics heard in Anglican churches through the seventeenth century. Though not distinguished poetry, their ballad measure was easily sung and memorized. (John Holland. *The Psalmists of Britain.* 2 vols. London, UK: R. Groombridge, 1843. I, 112–113.)

DOCUMENT 31: FROM *THE WHOLE BOOK OF PSALMS*

Psalm LXXXIV, 1–5

David exiled his country; desires ardently to return to God's tabernacle, and assembly of the saints to praise God. Then he praises the courage of the people, that pass the wilderness to assemble themselves in Sion.

1. How pleasant is thy dwelling place,
     O Lord of hosts to me?
   The tabernacles of thy grace,
     how pleasant Lord they be?
2. My soul doth long full sore to go,
     into thy courts abroad;
   My heart doth *lust, my flesh also,   *desire*
     In thee the living God.
3. The sparrows find a room to rest,
     and save themselves from wrong:
   And *eke the swallow hath a nest,   *also*
     wherein to keep her young.
4. These birds full *nigh thine altar may   *near*
     have place to sit and sing:
   O Lord of hosts thou art I say,
     my God and eke my king.
5. O they be blessed that may dwell,
     within thy house always:
   For they all times thy facts do tell,
     and ever give thee praise.

1595

Robert Southwell (1561–1595). Southwell, the best Roman Catholic clerical poet of the Elizabethan period, was a Jesuit priest who worked as a missionary in the south of England and ministered to Roman Catholic recusants. He was eventually arrested, tortured, and hanged. A collection of his poems, *St. Peter's Complaint,* first appeared in 1595 with several expanded later editions. "The Burning Babe" is regarded as his finest poem; contemporary poet and playwright Ben Jonson remarked that he would have been content to destroy many of his own poems if he could have written it. Southwell composed several deeply felt poems on the Virgin Mary, and his "Holy Hymn" asserts the Roman Catholic doctrine of transubstantiation, that the bread and wine of communion spiritually become the body and blood of Christ "in each kind wholly." (*The Poetical Works of the Rev. Robert Southwell.* Ed. William B. Turnbull. London, UK: John Russell Smith, 1856. 98–99, 123–124, 125–128.)

DOCUMENT 32: "THE BURNING BABE"

As I in *hoary winter's night stood shivering in the snow,   *white*
Surprised I was with sudden heat which made my heart to glow;
And lifting up a fearful eye to view what fire was near,

A pretty babe all burning bright did in the air appear,
Who scorchèd with exceeding heat such floods of tears did shed,
As though His floods should quench His flames with what His tears were fed;
Alas! quoth He, but newly born in fiery heats I fry,
Yet none approach to warm their hearts or feel my fire but I!
My faultless breast the furnace is, the fuel wounding thorns;
Love is the fire and sighs the smoke, the ashes shame and scorns;
The fuel Justice layeth on, and Mercy blows the coals;
The metal in this furnace wrought are men's defiled souls;
For which, as now on fire I am, to work them to their good,
So will I melt into a bath, to wash them in my blood:
With this He vanish'd out of sight, and swiftly shrunk away,
And straight I callèd unto mind that it was Christmas-day.

DOCUMENT 33: "THE VIRGIN MARY TO CHRIST ON THE CROSS"

What mist hath dimm'd that glorious face?
   What seas of grief my sun doth toss?
The golden rays of heavenly grace
   Lie now eclipsèd on the cross.
Jesus, my love, my Son, my God,
   Behold Thy mother wash'd in tears:
Thy bloody wounds be made a rod
   To chasten these my later years.
You cruel Jews, come work your ire
   Upon this worthless flesh of mine,
And kindle no eternal fire
   By wounding Him who is divine.
Thou messenger that didst impart
   His first descent into my womb,
Come help me now to cleave my heart,
   That there I may my Son entomb.
You angels, all that present were
   To show His birth with harmony,
Why are you not now ready here,
   To make a mourning symphony?
The cause I know you wail alone,
   And shed your tears in secrecy,
Lest I should moved be to moan,
   By force of heavy company.
But wail, my soul, thy comfort dies,
   My woful womb, lament thy fruit;
My heart give tears unto mine eyes,
   Let sorrow string my heavy lute.

DOCUMENT 34: "A HOLY HYMN"

Praise, O Sion! praise thy Saviour,
Praise thy captain and thy pastor,

With hymns and solemn harmony.
What power affords perform in deed;
His worths all praises far exceed,
   No praise can reach His dignity.
A special theme of praise is read,
A living and life-giving bread,
   Is on this day exhibited;
Which in the supper of our Lord,
To twelve disciples at His board
   None doubts was delivered.
Let our praise be loud and free,
Full of joy and decent glee,
   With minds' and voices' melody;
For now solemnize we that day,
Which doth with joy to us display
   The prince of this mystery.
At this board of our new ruler,
Of new law, new *paschal order   *Easter*
   The ancient rite abolisheth;
Old decrees be new annulled,
Shadows are in truths fulfilled
   Day former darkness finisheth.
That at supper Christ performed,
To be done He *straitly charged   *strictly*
   For His eternal memory.
Guided by His sacred orders,
Bread and wine upon our altars
   To saving host we sanctify.
Christians are by faith assured
That to flesh the bread is changed,
   The wine to blood most precious:
That no wit nor sense conceiveth,
Firm and grounded faith believeth,
   In strange effects not curious.
Under two kinds in appearance,
Two in show but one in substance,
   Lie things beyond comparison;
Flesh is meat, blood drink most heavenly,
Yet is Christ in each kind wholly,
   Most free from all division.
None that eateth Him doth chew Him,
None that takes Him doth divide Him,
   Received He whole persevereth.
Be there one or thousands hosted,
One as much as all receivèd,
   He by no eating perisheth.
Both the good and bad receive Him,
But effects are diverse in them,
   True life or due destruction.
Life to the good, death to the wicked,

Mark how both alike received
   With far unlike conclusion.
When the priest the host divideth,
Know that in each part abideth
   All that the whole host covered.
Form of bread, no Christ is broken,
Not of Christ, but of His token,
   Is state or stature altered.
Angels' bread made pilgrim's feeding,
Truly bread for children's eating,
   To dogs not to be offered.
Signed by Isaac on the altar,
By the lamb and paschal supper,
   And in the manna figured.
Jesu, food and feeder of us,
Here with mercy feed and friend us,
   Then grant in heaven felicity!
Lord of all, whom here Thou feedest,
Fellows, heirs, guests with Thy dearest,
   Make us in heavenly company! Amen.

Edmund Spenser (1552–1559). Spenser's greatest work, *The Faerie Queene,* is an allegorical epic honoring Queen Elizabeth and portraying Christian virtues from a Protestant perspective. Spenser published only the first six books of the epic (1596). His "Hymn to Heavenly Beauty" is one of his "Four Hymns" (1596) that praise human and divine love and beauty. Influenced by Platonic philosophy, it carries praise of the beloved to its most ethereal, praising physical beauty as an earthly expression of the highest beauty, God's. Extolling Christ's beauty as an expression of his divinity, Spenser reiterates the divinely ordained structure of the universe to which Richard Hooker alludes and Ulysses' famous speech in *Troilus and Cressida* refers. His sonnet sequence, the *Amoretti,* published in 1595, praises an ideal mistress in spiritual terms combined with the language of Petrarchan poetry, much as Shakespeare combined them in *Romeo and Juliet,* probably composed at about the same time. Book II of *The Faerie Queene* recounts the adventures of Guyon, the knight of Temperance. The "Bower of Bliss" episode depicts allegorically the Christian soul confronted with sensual temptations. This garden, unlike the Garden of Eden, is a place of uncontrolled indulgence, unchecked by any spiritual restraint. Spenser's lush style evokes the sensations of physical pleasure, but Guyon, along with his guide the Palmer, resists these blandishments and ensnares the enchantress Acrasia ("uncontrolled desire"), destroys her Bower, and frees those who have succumbed to its allure. Book II is also a humanist praising of the classical virtue of moderation and self-control. (*Poetical Works,* ed. J. C. Smith and E. De Selincourt. Oxford, 1912. 136–139, 566, 572–573, 596–599.)

DOCUMENT 35: *AMORETTI, SONNET XXII*

This holy season, fit to fast and pray,
Men to devotion ought to be inclined:
Therefore, I likewise, on so holy day,

For my sweet saint some service fit will find.
Her temple fair is built within my mind,
In which her glorious image placed is,
On which my thoughts do day and night attend,
Like sacred priests that never think amiss!
There I to her, as th' author of my bliss,
Will build an altar to appease her *ire;   **anger**
And on the same my heart will sacrifice,
Burning in flames of pure and chaste desire:
    The which vouchsafe, O goddess, to accept,
    Amongst thy dearest relics to be kept.

DOCUMENT 36: *AMORETTI, SONNET LXI*

The glorious image of the Maker's beauty,
My sovereign saint, the idol of my thought,
Dare not henceforth, above the bounds of duty,
T'accuse of pride, or rashly blame for *aught. **anything**
For being, as she is, divinely wrought,
And of the brood of angels heavenly born;
And with the crew of blessed Saints upbrought,
Each of which did her with their gifts adorn;
The bud of joy, the blossom of the morn,
The beam of light, whom mortal eyes admire;
What reason is it then but she should scorn
Base things, that to her love too bold aspire?
    Such heavenly forms ought rather worshipped be,
    Than dare be lov'd by men of mean degree.

DOCUMENT 37: *AMORETTI, SONNET LXVIII*

Most glorious Lord of life! That, on this day,
Did'st make thy triumph over death and sin;
And, having *harrow'd hell, did'st bring away   **tormented**
Captivity thence captive, us to win:
This joyous day, dear Lord, with joy begin;
And grant that we, for whom thou diddest die,
Being with thy dear blood clean wash'd from sin,
May live for ever in felicity!
And that thy love we weighing worthily,
May likewise love thee for the same again;
And for thy sake, that all like *dear did'st buy,   **at equal cost**
With love many one another entertain!
    So let us love, dear love, like as we ought:
    Love is the lesson which the Lord us taught.

DOCUMENT 38: AN HYMN OF HEAVENLY BEAUTY

*Rapt with the rage of mine own ravished thought,   **enraptured**
    Through contemplation of those goodly sights,

And glorious images in heaven wrought,
Whose wondrous beauty breathing sweet delights,
Do kindle love in high *conceited sprites: *imagined*
I *faine to tell the things that I behold,   *desire*
But feel my wits to fail, and my tongue to fold.
*Vouchsafe then, O thou most almighty Sprite,   *grant*
From whom all gifts of wit and knowledge flow,
To shed into my breast some sparkling light
Of thine eternall Truth, that I may show
Some little beams to moral eyes below,
Of that immortal beauty, there with thee,
Which in my weak *distraughted mind I see.   *anxious*
That with the glory of so goodly sight,
The hearts of men, which fondly here admire
Fair seeming shows, and feed on vain delight,
Transported with celestiall desire
Of those fair forms, may lift themselves up higher,
And learn to love with zealous humble duty
Th'eternal fountain of that heavenly beauty.
Beginning then below, with th'easy view
Of this base world, subject to fleshly eye,
From thence to mount aloft by order due,
To contemplation of th'immortal sky,
Of the *soare falcon so I learn to fly,   *soaring*
That flags awhile her fluttering wings beneath,
Till she herself for stronger flight can breathe.
Then look who *list, thy gazefull eyes to feed   *wishes*
With sight of that is fair, look on the frame
Of this wide universe, and therein read
The endless kinds of creatures, which by name
Thou canst no count, much less their nature aim:
All which are made with wondrous wise respect,
And all with admirable beauty decked.
First th' Earth, on adamantine pillars founded,
Amid the Sea engirt with *brazen bands;   *made of brass*
Then th' Air still flitting, but yet firmly bounded
On every side, with piles of flaming *brands,   *torches*
Never consumed nor quencht with mortal hands;
And last, that mighty shining crystal wall,
Wherewith he hath encompassed this All.
By view whereof, it plainly may appear,
That still as every thing doth upward tend,
And further is from earth, so still more clear
And fair it grows, till to his perfect end
Of purest beauty, it at last ascend:
Air more than water, fire much more than air,
And heaven than fire appears more pure and fair.
Look thou no further, but affixe thine eye
On that bright shiny round still moving Mass,

The house of blessed Gods, which men call Sky,
All sowed with *glistering stars more thick than grass,   *glittering*
Whereof each other doth in brightness pass,
But those two most, which ruling night and day,
As King and Queen, the heavens Empire sway.
And tell me then what thou hast ever seen,
   That to their beauty may compared be,
   Or can the sight that is most sharp and keen,
   Endure their Captain's flaming head to see?
   How much less those, much higher in degree,
   And so much fairer, and much more than these,
   As these fairer than the land and seas?
For far above these heavens which here we see,
   Be others far exceeding these in light,
   Not bounded, not corrupt, as these same be,
   But infinite in largeness and in height,
   Unmoving, uncorrupt, and spotless bright,
   That need no Sun t'illuminate their spheres,
   But their own native light far passing theirs.
And as these heavens still by degrees arise,
   Until they come to their first Movers bound,
   That in his mighty compass doth comprise,
   And carry all the rest with him around,
   So those likewise do by degrees *redound,   *accumulate*
   And rise more fair, till they at last arrive
   To the most fair, whereto they all do strive.
Fair is the heaven, where happy souls have place,
   In full enjoyment of felicity,
   Whence they do still behold the glorious face
   Of the divine eternal Majesty;
   More faire is that, where those *Ideas* on high
   Enranged be, which *Plato* so admired,
   And pure *Intelligences* from God inspired.
Yet fairer is that heaven, in which do reign
   The sovereign *Powers* and mighty *Potentates*,
   Which in their high protections do contain
   All mortal princes, and imperial states;
   And fairer yet, whereas the royal seats
   And heavenly *Dominations* are set,
   From whom all earthly governance is *fet.   *fetched*
Yet far more fair be those bright *Cherubins,   *lower angels*
   Which all with golden wings are *overdight,   *covered over*
   And those eternal burning *Seraphins,   *higher angels*
   Which from their faces dart out fiery light;
   Yet fairer than they both, and much more bright
   Be th' Angels and Archangels, which attend
   On God's own person, without rest or end.
These thus in fair each other far excelling,
   As to the Highest they approach more near,
   Yet is that Highest far beyond all telling,

Fairer than all the rest which there appear,
    Though all their beauties joined together were:
    How then can mortal tongue hope to express,
    The image of such endless perfectness?
Cease then my tongue, and lend unto my mind
    *Leave to bethink how great that beauty is   **freedom**
    Whose utmost parts so beautiful I find:
    How much more those essential parts of his,
    His truth, his love, his wisdom, and his bliss,
    His grace, his *doom, his mercy, and his might,   **judgment**
    By which he lends us of himself a sight.
Those unto all he daily doth display,
    And shew himself in th'image of his grace,
    As in a looking glass, through which he may
    Be seen, of all his creatures vile and base
    That are unable else to see his face,
    His glorious face which glistereth else so bright,
    That th' Angels selves can not endure the sight.
But we frail *wights, whose sight cannot sustain   **humans**
    The Sun's bright beams, when he on us doth shine
    But that their points rebutted back again
    Are dulled, how can we see with feeble *eyen,   **eyes**
    The glory of that Majesty divine,
    In sight of whom both Sun and Moon are dark,
    Compared to his least resplendent spark?
The means therefore which unto us is leant,
    Him to behold, is on his works to look,
    Which he hath made in beauty excellent,
    And in the same, as in a brazen book,
    To read enregistered in every nook
    His goodness, which his beauty doth declare.
    For all that's good, is beautiful and fair.
Thence gathering plumes of perfect speculation,
    To *imp the wings of thy high flying mind,   **repair**
    Mount up aloft through heavenly contemplation,
    From this dark world, whose damps the soul do blind,
    And like the native brood of Eagles *kind,   **species**
    On that bright Sun of glories fix thine eyes,
    Clear'd from gross mists of frail infirmities.
Humbled with fear and awful reverence,
    Before the footstool of his Majesty,
    Throw thyself down with trembling innocence,
    Nor dare look up with corruptible eye
    On the dred face of that great Deity,
    For feare, lest if he chance to look on thee,
    Though turn to naught, and quite confounded be.
But lowly fall before his mercy seat,
    Close covered with the Lamb's integrity,
    From the just wrath of his avengeful threat,
    That sits upon the righteous throne on high:

His throne is built upon Eternity,
   More firm and durable than steel or brass,
   Or the hard diamond, which them doth pass.
His scepter is the rod of Righteousness,
   With which he bruiseth all his foes to dust,
   And the great Dragon strongly doth repress,
   Under the rigor of his judgment just;
   His seat is Truth, to which the faithful trust;
   From whence proceed her beams so pure and bright,
   That all about him sheddeth glorious light.
Light far exceeding that bright blazing spark,
   Which darted from *Titan*'s flaming head,
   That with his beams enlumineth the dark
   And dampish air, whereby al things are red:
   Whose nature yet so much is marveled
   Of mortal wits, that it doth much amaze
   The greatest wizards, that thereon do gaze.
But that immortal light which there doth shine,
   Is many thousand times more bright, more clear,
   More excellent, more glorious, more divine,
   Through which to God all mortal actions here,
   And even the thoughts of men, do plain appear
   For from th' eternal Truth it doth proceed,
   Through heavenly virtue, which her beams do breed.
With the great glory of that wondrous light,
   His throne is all encompassed around,
   And his in his own brightness from the sight
   Of all that look thereon with eyes unsound:
   And underneath his feet are to be found
   Thunder, and lightning, and tempestuous fire,
   The instruments of his avenging ire.
There in his bosom *Sapience* doth sit,   **wisdom**
   The sovereign, darling of the *Deity*,
   Clad like a Queen in royal robes, most fit
   For so great power and peerless majesty.
   And all with gems and jewels gorgeously
   Adorned, that brighter than the stars appear,
   And make her brightness seem more clear.
And on her head a crown of purest gold
   Is set, in sign of highest sovereignty,
   And in her hand a scepter she doth hold,
   With which she rules the house of God on high,
   And manages the ever-moving sky,
   And in the same these lower creatures all,
   Subjected to her power imperial.
Both heaven and earth obey unto her will,
   And all the creatures which they both containe:
   For of her fullness which the world doth fill,
   They all partake, and do in state remaine,

As their great Maker did at first ordain,
Through observation of her high behest,
By which they first were made, and still increased.
The fairness of her face no tongue can tell,
  For she the daughters of all women's race,
  And Angels *eke, in beauty doth excel,   *also*
  Sparkled on her from God's own glorious face,
  And more increased by her own goodly grace,
  That it doth far exceed all human thought,
  *Ne can on earth compared be to aught.   **Nor**
Ne could that Painter (had he lived yet)
  Which pictured *Venus* with so curious quill,
  That all posterity admired it,
  Have portrayed this for all his mastering skill:
  Ne she herself, had she remained still,
  And were as fair, as fabling wits do *feign,   *imagine*
  Could once come near this beauty sovereign.
But had those wits the wonders of their days
  That sweet *Teian* Poet which did spend   ***the poet Anacreon***
  His plenteous vein in setting forth her praise,
  Seen but a glimpse of this, which I pretend,
  How wondrously would he her face commend,
  Above that Idol of his feigning thought,
  That all the world should with his rhymes be fraught?
How then dare I, the novice of his Art,
  Presume to picture so divine a wight,
  Or hope t'express her least perfection's part,
  Whose beauty fills the heavens with her light,
  And darks the earth with shadow of her sight?
  Ah gentle Muse thou art too weak and faint,
  The portrait of so heavenly hue to paint.
Let Angels which her goodly face behold
  And see at will, her soverign praises sing,
  And those most sacred mysteries unfold,
  Of that fair love of mighty heaven's king.
  Enough is me t'admire so heavenly thing,
  And being thus with her huge love possessed,
  In th'only wonder of her selfe to rest.
But who so may, thrice happy man him hold,
  Of all on earth, whom God so much doth grace,
  And lets his own Beloved to behold:
  For in the view of her celestial face,
  All joy, all bliss, all happiness have place,
  Ne aught on earth can want unto the wight,
  Who of herself can win the wishful sight.
For she out of her secret treasury,
  Plenty of riches forth on him will pour,
  Even heavenly riches, which there hidden lie
  Within the closet of her chastest bowre,

Th'eternal portion of her precious dower,
Which mighty God hath given to her free,
And to all those which thereof worthy be.
None thereof worthy be, but those whom she
Vouchsafeth to her presence to receive,
And letteth them her lovely face to see,
Whereof such wondrous pleasures they conceive,
And sweet contentment, that it doth bereave
Their soul of sense, though infinite delight,
And them transport from flesh into the sprite.
In which they see such admirable things,
As carries them into an ecstasy,
And hear such heavenly notes, and carolings,
Of God's high praise, that fills the brazen sky,
And feel such joy and pleasure inwardly,
That maketh them all worldy cares forget,
And only think on that before them set.
Ne from thenceforth doth any fleshly sense,
Or idle thought of earthly things remaine:
But all that *erst seemed sweet, seems now offense   *formerly*
And all that pleased erst, now seems to pain.
Their joy, their comfort, their desire, their gain,
Is fixed on all that which now they see,
All other sights but fained shadows be.
And that faire lamp, with useth to enflame
~~The hearts of men with self-consuming fire,~~
Thenceforth seems foul, and full of sinful blame;
And all that pompe, to which proud minds aspire
By name of honor, and so much desire
Seems to them baseness, and all riches dross,
And all mirth sadness, and all *lucre loss.   *profit*
So full their eyes are of that glorious sight,
And senses fraught with such satietie,
That in naught else on earth can delight,
But in th'aspect of that felicity,
Which they have written in their inward eye;
On which they feed, and in their fastened mind
All happy joy and full contentment find.
Ah then my hungry soul, which long has fed
On idle fancies of thy foolish thought,
And with false beauty's flattering bait misled,
Hast after vain deceitful shadows sought,
Which all are fled, and now have left thee naught
But late repentance through thy follies *prief;   *proof*
Ah cease to gaze on matter of thy grief.
And look at last up to that sovereign light,
From whose pure beams all perfect beauty springs,
That kindles love in every godly sprite,
Even the love of God, which loathing brings

Of this vile world, and these gay seeming things;
With whose sweet pleasures being so possessed,
Thy straying thought henceforth for ever rest.

Document 39: From *The Faerie Queene,* Book II, Canto XII

58

There the most dainty Paradise on ground,
    Itself doth offer to his sober eye,
    In which all pleasures plenteously abound,
    And none does others happiness envy:
    The painted flowers, the trees upshooting high,
    The dales for shade, the hills for breathing space,
    The trembling groves, the Crystal running by;
    And that, which all faire works doth most aggrace,
The art, which all that wrought, appeared in no place.

59

One would have thought, (so cunningly, the rude,
    And scorned parts were mingled with the fine,)
    That nature had for wantonness ensued
    Art, and that Art at nature did repine;
    So striving each th' other to undermine,
    Each did the others work more beautify;
    So differing both in wills, agreed in fine:
    So all agreed through sweet diversity,
This Garden to adorn with all variety.

60

And in the midst of all, a fountain stood,
    Of richest substance, that on earth might bee,
    So pure and shiny, that the silver flood
    Through every channel running one might see;
    Most goodly it with curious imagery
    Was over-wrought, and shapes of naked boys,
    Of which some seemed with lively jollity,
    To fly about, playing their wanton toys,
Whilst others did themselves *embay in liquid joys.   **shelter**

61

And over all, of purest gold was spread,
    A trail of ivy in his native hue:
    For the rich metal was so colored,
    That wight, who did not well *avised it view,   **advised**
    Would surely deem it to be ivy true:
    Low his lascivious arms adown did creep,

That themselves dipping in the silver dew,
Their fleecy flowers they tenderly did steep,
Which drops of Crystal seemed for wantonness to weep.

63

And all the margent round about was set,
   With shady Laurell trees, thence to defend
   The sunny beams, which on the billows *bet,   **beat**
   And those which therein bathed, *mote offend.   **might**
   As Guyon happened by the same to *wend,   **turn**
   Two naked Damsels he therein espied,
   Which therein bathing, seemed to contend,
   And wrestle wantonly, nor cared to hide,
Their dainty parts from view of any, which them eyed.

64

Sometimes the one would lift the other quite
   Above the waters, and then down again
   Her plunge, as overmastered by might,
   Where both awhile would covered remain,
   And each the other from to rise restrain;
   The whiles their snowy limbs, as through a veil,
   So through the crystal waves appeared plain:
   Then suddenly both would themselves *unhele   **uncover**
And the amorous sweet spoils to greedy eyes reveal.

66

The wanton maidens him espying, stood
   Gazing a while at his unwonted *guise   **appearance**
   Then the one herself low ducked in the flood,
   Abashed, that her a stranger did *avise: **advise**
   But the other rather higher did arise,
   And her two lilly paps aloft displayed,
   And all, that might his melting heart entice
   To her delights, she unto him *bewrayed: **revealed**
The rest hid underneath, him more desirous made.

67

With that, the other likewise up arose,
   And with her fair locks, which formerly were bound
   Up in one knot, she low adown did loose:
   Which flowing long and thick, her clothed around,
   And the ivory in golden mantle gowned:
   So that faire spectacle from him was *reft   **removed**
   Yet that, which reft it, no less fair was found:
   So hid in lockes and waves from looker's theft
Nought but her lovely face she for his looking left.

68

*Withall she laughed, and she blushed withal   *in addition*
   That blushing to her laughter gave more grace,
   And laughter to her blushing, as did fall:
   Now when they spied the knight to slack his pace,
   Them to behold, and in his sparkling face
   The secret signs of kindled lust appear,
   Their wanton merriments they did increase,
   And to him beckoned, to approach more near,
And showed him many sights, that courage cold could rear.

69

On which when gazing him the *Palmer saw,   *pilgrim*
   He much rebuked those wandering eyes of his,
   And counseled well, him forward thence did draw.
   Now are they come nigh to the Bower of bliss
   Of her fond favorites so named amiss:
   When thus the Palmer: "Now Sir, well avise;
   For here the end of all our travel is:
   Here *wones Acrasia, whom we must surprise   *lives*
Else she will slip away, and all our drift despise."

72

There, whence that Music seemed heard to be,
   Was the fair witch herself now solacing,
   With a new lover, whom through sorcery
   And witchcraft, she from far did thither bring:
   There she had him now laid aslumbering,
   In secret shade, after long wanton joys:
   Whilst round about them pleasantly did sing
   Many fair Ladies, and lascivious boys,
That ever mixed their song with light licentious toys.

73

And all that while, right over him she hung,
   With her false eyes fast fixed in his sight,
   As seeking medicine, whence she was stung,
   Or greedily *depasturing delight   *devouring*
   And oft inclining down with kisses light,
   For fear of waking him, his lips bedewed,
   And through his humid eyes did suck his *spright   *spirit*
   Quite molten into lust and pleasure lewd;
Wherewith she sighed soft, as if his case she *rued.   *regretted*

77

Upon a bed of Roses she was laid,
   As faint through heat, or *dight to pleasant sin,   *prepared*

And was arrayed, or rather disarrayed,
  All in a veil of silk and silver thin,
  That hid no *whit her alablaster skin   *part*
  But rather showed more white, if more might be:
  More subtle web Arachne cannot spin,
  Nor the fine nets, which oft we woven see
Of scorched dew, do not in the air more lightly flee.

79

The young man sleeping by her, seemed to be
  Some goodly swain of honorable place,
  That *certes it great pity was to see   *certainly*
  Him his nobility so foul deface;
  A sweet regard, and amiable grace,
  Mixed with manly sternness did appear,
  Yet sleeping, in his well proportioned face,
  And on his tender lips the downy hair
Did now but freshly spring, and silken blossoms bear.

80

His warlike arms, the idle instruments
  Of sleeping praise, were hung upon a tree,
  And his brave shield, full of old monuments,
  Was foully *rased, that none the signs might see;   *erased*
  *Ne for them, *ne for honor cared he   **Neither . . . nor**
  Ne ought, that did to his advancement tend,
  But in lewd loves, and wasteful luxury,
  His days, his goods, his body did he spend:
O horrible enchantment, that him so did *blend.

81

The noble Elf, and careful Palmer drew
  So nigh them, minding nought but lustful game,
  That sudden forth they on them rushed, and threw
  A *subtle net, which only for the same   *delicate*
  The skillful Palmer *formally did frame.   *intricately*
  So held them under *fast, the whiles the rest   *firmly*
  Fled all away for fear of fouler shame.
  The fair Enchantress, so unawares oppressed,
Tried all her arts, and all her sleights, thence out to wrest.

82

And eke her lover strove: but all in vain;
  For that same net so cunningly was wound,
  That neither guile nor force might it *distrain. **hinder**
  They took them both, and both them strongly bound

In captive bands, which there they ready found:
But her in chains of adamant he tied;
For nothing else might keep her safe and sound:
But Verdant (so he *hight) he soon untied,   *was called*
And counsel sage instead thereof to him applied.

83

But all those pleasant bowers and Palace *brave,   *showy*
Guyon broke down with rigor pitiless;
Ne ought their goodly workmanship might save
Them from the tempest of his wrathfulness,
But that their bliss he turned to balefulness:
Their groves he felled, their gardens did deface,
Their arbors spoil, their *Cabinets suppress   *summer homes*
Their banquet houses burn, their buildings raze,
And of the fairest late, now made the foulest place.

84

They led her away, and eke that knight
They with them led, both sorrowful and sad:
The way they came, the same returned they right,
Till they arrived, where they lately had
Charmed those wild beasts, that raged with fury mad.
Which now awaking, fierce at them gan fly,
As in their mistress' rescue, whom they *lad;   *led*
But them the Palmer soon did pacify.
Then Guyon asked, what meant those beasts which there did lie.

85

Said he, "These seeming beasts are men indeed,
Whom this Enchantress hath transformed thus,
*Whilom her lovers, which her lusts did feed,   *formerly*
Now turned into figures hideous,
According to their minds like monstrous."
"Sad end," (quoth he) of life intemperate,
And mournful *meed of joys delicious   *reward*
But Palmer, if it mote thee so *aggrate,   *please*
Let them returned be unto their former state.

86

Straight way he with his virtuous staff them struck,
And straight of beasts they comely men became,
Yet being men they did unmanly look,
And stared ghastly, some for inward shame,
And some for wrath, to see their captive Dame:
But one above the rest in special,

That had an hog been late, hight Grill by name,
   Repined greatly, and did him miscall,
That had from hoggish form him brought to natural.

87

Said Guyon, "See the mind of beastly man,
   That hath so soon forgot the excellence
   Of his creation, when he life began,
   That now he chooseth, with vile difference,
   To be a beast and lack intelligence."
   To whom the Palmer thus, "The dunghill kind
   Delights in filth and foul incontinence:
   Let Grill be Grill and have his hoggish mind,
But let us hence depart, whilst weather serves and wind."

1609

John Donne (1572–1631). Donne's claim as the foremost religious poet of the Church of England is challenged only by the verse of George Herbert, his close friend. Donne is the best practitioner of the metaphysical poetic style, employing a colloquial tone, intricate and startling metaphors (metaphysical conceits), and wide-ranging allusions. The order of his 19 "Holy Sonnets" is uncertain; most are thought to have been composed around 1609, six years before his ordination to the priesthood in 1615. He later became Dean of St. Paul's Cathedral and a highly renowned preacher. "A Hymn to God the Father" dates from late 1623. The first edition of his poems appeared posthumously in 1633. (*Poems of John Donne.* Ed. E. K. Chambers. The Muses' Library. 2 vols. London, UK: George Routledge, 1896. I, 158–165, 213.)

DOCUMENT 40: FROM THE "HOLY SONNETS"

What if this present were the world's last night?
Mark in my heart, O soul, where thou dost dwell,
The picture of Christ crucified, and tell
Whether His countenance can thee affright.
Tears in his eyes quench the amazing light;
Blood fills his frowns, which from his pierced head fell;
And can that tongue adjudge thee unto hell
Which prayed forgiveness for His foes' fierce spite?
No, no; but as in my idolatry
I said to all my profane mistresses,
Beauty of pity, foulness only is,
A sign of rigor; so I say to thee,
To wicked spirits are horrid shapes assigned;
This beauteous form assumes a *piteous mind.   ***compassionate***

DOCUMENT 41: FROM THE "HOLY SONNETS"

O, my black soul, now thou art summoned
By sickness, Death's herald and champion;

Thou'rt like a pilgrim, which abroad hath done
Treason, and durst not turn to whence he's fled;
Or like a thief, which till death's doom be read,
Wisheth himself delivered from prison,
But damned and haled to execution,
Wisheth that still he might be imprisoned.
Yet grace, if thou repent, thou canst not lack;
But who shall give thee that grace to begin?
O, make thyself with holy mourning black,
And red with blushing, as thou art with sin;
Or wash thee in Christ's blood, which hath this might,
That being red, it dyes red souls to white.

DOCUMENT 42: FROM THE "HOLY SONNETS"

At the round earth's imagined corners blow
Your trumpets, angels; and arise, arise
From death, you numberless infinities
Of souls, and to your scattered bodies go;
All whom the flood did, and fire shall overthrow,
All whom war, death, age, agues, tyrannies,
Despair, law, chance, hath slain; and you whose eyes
Shall behold God, and never taste death's woe.
But let them sleep, Lord, and me mourn a space;
For, if above all these my sins abound,
'Tis late to ask abundance of thy grace,
When we are there. Here, on this lowly ground,
Teach me how to repent, for that's as good
As if Thou hadst sealed my pardon with thy blood.

DOCUMENT 43: FROM THE "HOLY SONNETS"

Death, be not proud, though some have called thee
Mighty and dreadful, for thou art not so;
For those, whom thou think'st thou dost overthrow
Die not, poor Death, nor yet canst thou kill me.
From rest and sleep, which but thy pictures be,
Much pleasure, then from thee much more must flow,
And soonest our best men with thee do go,
Rest of their bones, and souls' delivery.
Thou'rt slave to Fate, chance, kings, and desperate men,
And doth with poison, war, and sickness dwell,
And poppy, or charms can make us sleep as well,
And better than thy stroke; why swell'st thou then?
Our short sleep past, we wake eternally,
And Death shall be no more; Death, thou shalt die.

DOCUMENT 44: FROM THE "HOLY SONNETS"

Batter my heart, three-personed God; for you
As yet but knock; breathe, shine, and seek to mend;

That I may rise, and stand, o'erthrow me, and bend
Your force, to break, blow, burn, and make me new.
I, like an usurped town, to another due,
Labour to admit you, but O, to no end.
Reason, your viceroy in me, me should defend,
But is captived, and proves weak or untrue.
Yet dearly I love you, and would be loved fain,
But am betrothed unto your enemy;
Divorce me, untie, or break that knot again,
Take me to you, imprison me, for I,
Except you enthrall me, never shall be free,
Nor ever chaste, except you ravish me.

DOCUMENT 45: "A HYMN TO GOD THE FATHER"

I.

Wilt thou forgive that sin where I begun,
    Which was my sin, though it were done before?
Wilt thou forgive that sin, through which I run,
    And do run still, though still I do deplore?
        When thou has done, thou hast not done,
            For I have more.

II.

Wilt thou forgive that sin which I have won
    Others to sin, and made my sin their door?
Wilt thou forgive that sin which I did shun
    A year or two, but wallowed in a score?
        When thou hast done, thou has not done,
            For I have more.

III.

I have a sin of fear, that when I have spun
    My last thread, I shall perish on the shore;
But swear by Thyself, that at my death Thy Son
    Shall shine as he shines now, and heretofore;
        And, having done that, Thou has done—
            I fear no more.

1610

Michael Drayton (1563–1631). Drayton is best known for his epic about British geography, *Poly-olbion* (completed in 1622) and for "England's Heroical Epistles" (1597). In 1610 he issued a small collection of poetic biblical translations designed to be read as a popular form of religious devotion. The fourth chapter of the *Song of Songs* employs the "blazon" or praise of the beloved's body, a frequent feature of

Renaissance love sonnets and one that Shakespeare parodies in sonnet 130 ("My mistress eyes are nothing like the sun"). Drayton here uses "poulter's measure," alternating lines of iambic hexameter and iambic heptameter. (*A Heavenly Harmonie of Spirituall Songes, and holy Himnes, of godly Men, Patriarkes, and Prophets*. London, UK: Thomas Owen [reissued probably by W. White], 1610. Facsimile rpt., 1891.)

DOCUMENT 46: FROM *SONG OF SONGS*, CHAPTER IV

Behold, thou art all fair my Love, my heart's delight,
Thine eyes so lovely like the Dove's, appear to me in sight,
Thy hair surpassing fair and seemly to the eye,
Like to a goodly heard of Goats, on Gilead mountain high.
Thy teeth like new washed sheep, returning from the flood,
Whereas not one is barren found, but beareth ewes so good.
Thy lips like scarlet thread, thy talk doth breed delight,
Thy temples like pomgranet fair doth show to me in sight.
Thy neck like David's Tower, which for defense doth stand,
Wherein the shields and targets be, of men of mightie hand.
Thy breasts like twinned Roes, in prime and youthful age,
Which feed among the lilies sweet, their hunger to assuage.
Until the day do spring, and might be banished hence:
I will ascend into the mount of Myrrh and Frankincense.
Thou art all fair my love, most seemly *eke to see,   ***also***
From head to foot, from top to toe, there is no spot in thee.
Come down from Lebanon, from Lebanon above,
And from Amana's mountain high, come to thine own true love.
From Shener's stately top, from Hermon hill so high,
From Lion's dens and from the cliffs, where lurking Leopards lie,
My Spouse and sister dear, thy love hath wounded me,
Thy lovely eye and seemly neck, hath made me yield to thee.
Thy love far better is, than any wine to me,
Thy odors sweet doth far surpass, the smell where spices be.
Thy lips like honey comb, under thy tongue doth lie
The honey sweet: thy garments smell, like Lebanon on high.
My spouse a garden is, fast under lock and key,
Or like a Fountain closely kept, where sealed is the way.
Like to a pleasant plot I may thee well compare,
Where Camphor, Spikenard, dainty fruits, with sweet Pomgranets are.
Even Spikenard, Saffron, Calamus, and Cinnamon do grow,
With Incense, Myrrhe and Aloes, with many spices *moe.   ***more***
Oh fountain passing pure, oh Well of life most dear,
Of spring of lofty Lebanon, of water crystal clear.
The North and Southern winds upon my garden blow,
That the sweet spice that is therein, on every side may flow.
Unto this garden place, my Love for his repast
Shall walk, and of the fruits therein, shall take a pleasant taste.

1611

Emilia Lanyer (1569–1645). Lanyer's primary work was *Salve Deus Rex Judaeo-rum* ("Hail, God, King of the Jews"). This poem on Christ's passion emphasizes the sympathy shown to Jesus by the women around him, who are portrayed as more devout than his male followers. Lanyer's religious poetry typically adopts a distinctively feminine point of view. (*Select Poetry Chiefly Sacred of the Reign of King James I.* Ed. Edward Farr. Cambridge, UK: J. & J. J. Deighton and John W. Parker, 1847. 229–230.)

DOCUMENT 47: "THE TEARS OF THE DAUGHTERS OF JERUSALEM." FROM *SALVE DEUS REX JUDAEORUM*

Thrice happy women! That obtain'd such grace
From Him whose worth the world could not contain,
Immediately to turn about his face,
As not remembering his great grief and pain,
To comfort you, whose tears poured forth apace
On Flora's banks, like showers of April's rain:
　　Your cries enforced mercy, grace, and love,
　　From Him whom greatest princes would not move.
To speak one word, nor once to lift his eyes,
Unto proud Pilate—no, nor Herod, king,
By all the questions that they would devise,
Could make him answer to no manner of thing:
Yet these poor women, by their piteous cries,
Did move their Lord, their lover, and their king,
　　To take compassion, turn about and speak
　　To them whose hearts were ready now to break.
Most blessed daughters of Jerusalem,
Who found such favor in your Savior's sight,
To turn his face when you did pity him;
Your tearfull eyes beheld his eyes more bright;
Your faith and love unto such grace did clime
To have reflection from this heav'nly light:
　　Your eagles' eyes did gaze against this sun,
　　Your hearts did think, he dead, the world were done.
When spiteful men with torments did oppress
Th' afflicted body of this innocent dove,
Poor women, seeing how much they did transgress,
By tears, by sighs, by cries entreat,—nay, prove
What may be done among the thickest press;
They labor still these tyrants' hearts to move,
　　In pity and compassion to forbear
　　Their whipping, spurning, tearing of his hair.
But all in vain—their malice hath no end;
Their hearts more hard than flint, or marble stone:
Now, to his grief, his greatness they attend,
Where he, God knows, had rather be alone;

They are his guard, yet seek all means to offend:
Well may he grieve, well may he sigh and groan;
   Under the burden of a heavy cross
   He faintly goes to make their gain his loss.

William Warner (1558–1609). Warner is best known for his long poetic history, *Albion's England*. Its first edition (1592) carried the history of the nation through the reign of Elizabeth; the second edition (1612) continued the story through the rule of James I. In the portion reprinted here, Warner employs the popular but tedious 14-syllable line to summarize such key points of Anglicanism as the monarch as head of the church and the use of only two valid sacraments, while rejecting belief in the intercession of the saints and use of the Latin Bible. He uses "Catholic" to refer to the "universal" church, in contrast to the "Roman Catholic" or "Papist" church. (*Select Poetry Chiefly Sacred of the Reign of King James the First.* Ed. Edward Farr. Cambridge, UK: J. & J. J. Deighton and John W. Parker, 1847. 295–299.)

DOCUMENT 48: FROM ALBION'S ENGLAND. "HOW OUR RELIGION IS AUTHENTIC. OF THE CHIEF POINTS WHEREIN WE DISSENT FROM THE PAPISTS." CHAPTER 52 OF THE NINTH BOOK.

Upon the only scriptures doth our church foundation lay,
Let patriarchs, prophets, gospel and the apostles for us say:
For soul and body we affirm, and all-sufficient they;
Yet ye add *canons, part corrupt, some books ye quite deny.   *church laws*
We by the Hebrew and the Greek (their primer *penores*) expound
Each scripture by the eldest clerks whom doubtful texts be found,
Not by the Latin only, as ye would that all were bound:
So far forth yet the Fathers and the councils we approve,
As do their expositions tend to sincere faith and love.
Else fully scriptures in themselves explain themselves, say we,
If searched with the humble spirit by which they written be:
Through which is oft from literal speech a spiritual sense set free,
Upon which sense the Catholic Church did, does, and must agree.
Nor does our church admit, at least allow, of those in her
That teach not faith sincerely, win to heaven, from hell deter.
That with new *glozes tant the text, or such as be unread   *glosses taint*
In that sweet promise of the seed should bruise the serpent's head—
The Alpha and Omega of all scriptures, and whereby
Of grace, through faith in Christ, our soles revive, and sin does die:
Our Church affects, how so effects, such pure theologies
And guides, and to our natural prince grants sole supremacy.
God's covenant with the patriarchs, and extending to the seed,
Us gentiles to coequall, is a primate in our creed;
And Christ we know the end of it; in circumcision's place
Is baptism; and entirely we the tables two embrace,
Which God himself in *Synia wrote, and gave to Moses then,   *Sinai*
To publish to the people, two commandements in ten:
Scriptures' idea, crouched in our love to God and men.

The Apostles', Athanasian, *Nice, and Bizain creeds we hold   **Nicaean,**
Authentic by the Holy Spirit in sacred writ enrolled.   **Byzantine**

1613

John Donne (See also **1609**). This poem expresses Donne's typical use of paradox in his religious verse. The speaker, traveling westwards away from Jerusalem
on Good Friday, feels guilty for turning his back on Christ's death and seemingly
neglecting those devotions on the crucifixion which his "soul's form" desires. Yet
by presenting his back to Christ and his tormentors, he is symbolically better able
to be scourged for his own sins and thus to vicariously share in Christ's suffering.
(*Poems of John Donne*. Ed. E. K. Chambers. The Muses' Library. 2 Vols. London,
UK: Routledge, 1896. I, 172–73.)

DOCUMENT 49: "GOOD FRIDAY, 1613, RIDING WESTWARD"

Let man's soul be a sphere, and then, in this,
The intelligence that moves, devotion is;
And as the other spheres, by being grown
Subject to foreign motion, lose their own,
And being by others hurried every day,
Scarce in a year their natural form obey;
Pleasure or business, so, our souls admit
For their first mover, and are whirled by it.
Hence is't that I am carried towards the west
This day, when my soul's form leads towar ds the East.
There I should see a Sun by rising set,
And by that setting endless day beget.
But that Christ on His cross did rise and fall,
Sin had eternally benighted all.
Yet dare I almost be glad, I do not see
That spectacle of too much weight for me.
Who sees God's face, that is self-life, must die;
What a death were it then to see God die!
It made His own lieutenant, Nature, shrink,
It made His footstool crack, and the sun wink.
Could I behold those hands which span the poles
And tune all spheres at once, pierced with those holes?
Could I behold that endless height, which is
Zenith to us and our *antipodes,   **opposite point on the globe**
Humbled below us? or that blood which is
The seat of all our souls, if not of His,
Made dust of dust? or that flesh which was worn
By God, for His apparel, ragg'd and torn?
If on these things I durst no look, durst I
On His distressed Mother cast mine eye,
Who was God's partner here, and furnish'd thus
Half of that sacrifice which ransomed us?
Though these things as I ride be from mine eye,

They're present yet unto my memory,
For that looks towards them; and Thou look'st towards me,
O Savior, as Thou hang'st upon the tree:
I turn my back to Thee but to receive
Corrections till Thy mercies bid Thee leave.
O think me worth Thine anger, punish me,
Burn off my rust, and my deformity;
Restore Thine image, so much, by Thy grace
That Thou may'st know me, and I'll turn my face.

GLOSSARY

This glossary lists a selection of the key literary, theatrical, religious, and Biblical topics that appear in the text. Cross-referenced words appear in **bold.**

Allegory—Literary work in which the characters, actions, or setting stand for specific concepts or values to which that work refers, such as *Everyman,* a medieval **morality play.**

Anabaptist—("Re-baptizer"). Sixteenth-century German denomination requiring an adult decision for baptism; those baptized as infants had to be rebaptized. Modern descendants are the Amish, Mennonites, and Quakers.

Anagnorisis—The "recognition" or "insight" gained by a tragic protagonist that produces a significant change.

Anglicanism—Protestant denomination founded in England, resulting from the **Henrician Reformation** and established by the **Elizabethan Settlement,** which generally retains many worship features, especially in its **liturgy,** of **Roman Catholicism** but denies obedience to the **Pope** and adheres to more Protestant theology. The Church of England and the Protestant Episcopal Church in the United States are branches of Anglicanism.

Annulment—Distinct from divorce, a declaration that a marriage is not valid in the view of the Roman Catholic church; that a marriage had never formally existed.

Apocrypha—(Greek, "hidden things"). Books (*e.g.*, Tobit, Ecclesiasticus) not in the Hebrew Bible and omitted from the Protestant Bible but included in the Roman Catholic Bible.

Authorized Version of the Bible—See **King James Version.**

Ave Maria—The "Hail Mary," a prayer of **Roman Catholicism** based upon Luke 1: 28 and repeated in the saying of the rosary.

Baptism—A **sacrament** in which a person is formally inducted into the Christian faith, usually by immersion or sprinkling with water, based upon Christ's baptism (*cf.* Mark 1: 9–11).

Beatitudes—See **Sermon on the Mount.**

Bible—The sacred text of Judaism (**Old Testament**) and Christianity (**Old and New Testaments**).

Book of Common Prayer—Book of service and basic summary of doctrine (The Thirty-nine Articles) of **Anglicanism,** published in 1549. Includes collects, the Psalms, and a calendar of biblical readings for the church year.

Calvinism—Protestant religious belief established by John Calvin (1509–1564), emphasizing God's sovereignty (absolute authority over all of creation), man's innate depravity (total sinfulness and loss of free will resulting from the **Fall of Adam and Eve**), the **Bible** as final authority in matters of faith, **predestination** of man (God's authority to decide who shall be saved and damned), adherence to two sacraments (**Baptism** and **Communion**), and **justification by faith** (man becomes acceptable or made righteous to God only through faith and **grace**, not works of devotion).

Catastrophe—The final stage of a tragedy, including the death of the tragic hero.

Catechism—A written summary of important church doctrine, presented in question-and-answer format.

Catharsis—The complex psychological and emotional release experienced by the audience of tragedy.

Catholic Reformation—Self-improvement within Renaissance **Roman Catholicism** in response to internal demands for renewal and external pressures from the Protestant Reformation. Also called the Counter-Reformation.

Celibacy—The traditional rejection of marriage by Roman Catholic clergy as means of improving their dedication to ministry in imitation of the life of Christ.

Collect—(Pronounced "COL-lect"). A short prayer, including an invocation to God, presentation of a petition, and a final statement of divine praise.

Comedy—A drama that resolves plot conflicts without death and typically arouses humor.

Communion—That portion of a Christian worship service in which bread and wine (or grape juice) are shared by minister and congregation in remembrance of Christ's last supper. See also **Transubstantiation, Consubstantiation, Eucharist.**

Confession—Acknowledgement of one's sins as preparation for absolution or forgiveness of sins.

Consubstantiation—Luther's understanding of the nature of communion, in contrast to **transubstantiation;** the sacramental bread and wine are not transformed into the substance of Christ's body and blood but remain with them, unchanged.

Counter-Reformation—See **Catholic Reformation**.

Creed—(Latin, "credo," "I believe"). Statement of Christian belief. Some historically significant creeds are the Apostles' Creed, the Nicene Creed, and the creed of St. Athanasius.

Cultural Materialism—See **New Historicism.**

Denomination—A branch of Christianity, such as **Roman Catholicism** or **Lutheranism.** Christianity itself is a religion, not a denomination.

Deus ex machina—(Latin, "god from the machine"). A plot twist that quickly (almost in a godlike way) resolves dramatic conflicts, often through use of coincidence or surprise. In ancient Greek drama, gods appeared by being lowered from above with a mechanical device.

Divine Providence—Belief that God lovingly cares for creation, guiding the course of human events to fulfill his will eventually.

Divine Right—Concept that the authority of monarchs to rule ultimately derives from God.

Docetism—(Greek, *dokein*, "to seem"). Heresy of the second and third centuries A.D., derived from **Gnosticism,** opposed by Irenaeus and Tertullian, claiming that Jesus Christ only seemed to be human.

Dogma—Belief or teaching of the church (primarily Roman Catholic) grounded in scripture and sanctioned by a specific church authority, such as the pope or a church council. See **orthodoxy.**

Donatism—Schismatic movement of the fourth century A.D. contending that the moral state of the minister determined the effectiveness of the **sacraments.** Condemned by the Council of Carthage in 404.

Double Predestination—See **Predestination.**

Eden—Paradise. Home of Adam and Eve before the **Fall of Adam and Eve.** A place of ideal beauty,happiness, and spiritual goodness.

Elect—In **Calvinism,** those chosen by God's **predestination** to receive **salvation.**

Elizabethan Settlement—Elizabeth I's attempt to resolve tensions between English Catholics and Protestants by establishing a *via media* ("middle way") combining aspects of both faiths in a national denomination. Legally established by two acts of Parliament in 1559: the Act of Uniformity (requiring church attendance and use of the **Book of Common Prayer**) and the Act of Supremacy (declaring the queen "Supreme Governor" of the Anglican church).

Epiphany—(Greek, "manifestation"). Christian feast day (January 6) celebrating the visit of the Three Wise Men to the infant Jesus. In literature, a moment of insight or sudden awareness.

Epistles—Letters of Paul to the early Christian churches of Asia Minor (Corinth, Galatia, Philippi, etc.) explaining doctrine and exhorting unity and faith. They are printed after the **Gospels** in the **New Testament.**

Epyllion—A narrative poem with epic elements; a "brief epic."

Erastianism—After Thomas Erastus (1524–1583); theory that the monarch or secular authority in a state rules over all religious authorities.

Eucharist—(Greek, "thanksgiving"). In **Roman Catholicism,** the **Orthodox Church,** and some branches of **Protestantism,** the sacramental reenactment with bread and wine of Christ's sacrificial offering of his body and blood for mankind (hence for Catholics the "sacrifice of the Mass"). See also **Communion, Mass.**

Excommunication—An official act of the church formally excluding someone from membership.

Ex opere operato—"From the work performed" or "By the work itself." The Roman Catholic doctrine that the sacrament of **communion (Eucharist)** is valid because of the true presence of Christ in the bread and wine rather than because of the worshipper's belief in his presence or the priest's moral condition as he administers the sacraments.

Fall of Adam and Eve—In Genesis 2, the ejection of Adam and Eve from Eden as sinners, after they had disobeyed God's command not to eat from the Tree of the Knowledge of Good and Evil. Once fallen (lapsed), they existed in a **postlapsarian** ("after the fall") world.

Feminism—Broad cultural and intellectual movement of the twentieth century emphasizing a fuller acknowledgement of the nature and role of women in society.

Garden of Gethsemane—Garden in which Jesus prayed agonizingly to God the night before his crucifixion, and where he was betrayed by Judas and seized by the Romans (Matthew 26: 36–46).

Gnosticism—(Greek, *gnosis*, "knowledge"). Religious belief beginning in the first century A.D. and opposed by church fathers (e.g., Irenaeus). Drew upon a variety of religious and mythical beliefs. Denied the physical humanity of Jesus, advocated the superiority of spirit over matter, and stressed individually revealed sacred knowledge as necessary to salvation. See also **Docetism** and **Marcionism.**

Gospels—(Greek, "good news"). The **New Testament** books of Matthew, Mark, Luke, and John recounting the life and ministry of Jesus Christ.

Gothic—Predominant style of medieval Roman Catholic cathedral architecture, employing high, narrow naves; cruciform floor plan; pointed arches; stained glass windows; and flying buttresses.

Grace—Divine favor granted by God to believers, enabling their salvation. Calvin believed that God's grace could not be resisted, being part of his predestined plan for the **elect.**

Great Chain of Being—Hierarchical conception of the structure of the cosmos, with God as the supreme being and descending levels of creation below him.

Hamartia—In Aristotle's definition of tragedy, the key act, error, or weakness of the protagonist that vitally contributes to his or her "fall" into tragic suffering. Sometimes defined as "flaw."

Henrician reformation—The actions instigated by Henry VIII that politically and ecclesiastically separated him from **Roman Catholicism,** formally drawing England into Protestantism with the creation of the Church of England.

Heresy—Theological belief held by a baptized Christian but contrary to church **dogma** or **orthodoxy.**

History plays—Shakespearean plays focusing on events from English history. See also **tetralogy.**

Homily—A sermon.

Hubris—(Greek, "pride"). The most common flaw of tragic heroes in drama, leading to their downfall; also the worst of the seven deadly sins in Christianity.

Huguenots—French Protestants. Their freedom to worship was established by the Edict of Nantes (1598) but withdrawn in 1685.

Humanism—Intellectual movement during the Renaissance that emphasized the capabilities and potential of human nature, based upon the study of ancient Greek and Roman texts. It was rooted in the classical respect for the individual and the Christian recognition of man's place in God's creation, thus was more properly a Christian humanism rather than a secular humanism.

Humours—According to ancient and Renaissance psychology, four substances in the body (blood, phlegm, yellow bile, and black bile) whose balance is necessary for a well-adjusted personality and avoidance of a "bad humour."

Ideology—Term deriving from Marxism for any belief system used to exert power over a class or group.

Indulgence—Remission of the punishment for sin in exchange for the saying of prayers or the performance of charitable works. The buying, rather than the earning, of indulgences became an abuse in the medieval and Renaissance church and one of Luther's targets of reform. See also **Ninety-Five Theses.**

Innate Depravity—See **Calvinism.**

Inquisition—Process for discovering and punishing heretics in the Roman Catholic church, beginning in the thirteenth century. The Spanish Inquisition, begun in 1479 to disclose converted Jews and Muslims suspected of practicing their former faith, was not officially ended until 1834.

Jesuits—Members of the Society of Jesus, a Roman Catholic religious order, a result of the **Catholic Reformation,** established by St. Ignatius Loyola in 1540. Well educated and highly motivated, its members became teachers and missionaries.

Justification by faith—Justification is God's rendering a believer righteous and spiritually acceptable. Reformation Protestants held that the believer made this possible by faith alone (*sola fides*), in contrast with Roman Catholics who emphasized justification by works, the completion of devotional acts and prayers. See also **Calvinism.**

King James Version—Published in 1611, the most influential English Biblical translation of the Renaissance and probably of all time. James did not formally order or take part in the translation, completed by a committee of 54 scholars, but it was completed during his reign. Also known as the Authorized Version.

Liturgy—(Greek, "work of the people"). The public, corporate worship of the church according to set rituals and prescribed prayers, especially in reference to the **Eucharist.**

Lollards—English, late medieval reform-minded followers of John Wycliffe (c. 1330–1384). Not strictly part of the later **Protestant Reformation,** Lollards advocated many similar convictions, such as increased emphasis upon scripture and reform of church abuses. The name was originally pejorative, meaning "mumblers."

Lord of Misrule—An irreverent, jolly overseer appointed to "rule" festivities as a mock-king at court or in country houses during times of holiday. Shakespeare's Falstaff has traits of the Lord of Misrule.

Lord's Prayer—Christ's summary of how to pray, recited in Luke 11: 2–4 (also in Matthew 6: 9–13). Also called the "Our Father."

Lutheranism—Protestant religious belief established by Martin Luther (1483–1546), emphasizing **justification by faith,** the **sacraments** of **Baptism** and **Eucharist,** and a more Roman Catholic set of rituals than the **Reformed** (Calvinist) churches. Important to historic Lutheranism is the assertion of *sola gratia, sol fides, sola scriptura* ("grace alone, faith alone, scripture alone") as a devotional method, and replacement of the doctrine of **transubstantiation** with **consubstantiation.**

Machiavel—Dramatic character in English Renaissance drama who foments rebellion or discord, defying established authority. Richard III (*Richard III*), Iago (*Othello*), Aaron (*Titus Andronicus*), and Edmund (*King Lear*) are machiavels. Named after Niccolo Machiavelli (1469–1527), author of *The Prince*.

Magisterium—The instructional authority of the Roman Catholic church and the hierarchy of church officials who teach church **dogma.**

Manichaeism—Third century A.D. dualistic heresy originating from the Persian thinker Mani. Held that man is caught in a struggle between good (spirit) and evil (matter). Influenced by **Gnosticism.**

Marcionism—Heresy of Marcion (c. 85–c. 160), who revised and shortened the New Testament; argued (somewhat like **Docetism**) that Jesus could not have had a physical body because matter was evil, and that the **Old Testament** God differed from that of the **New Testament.**

Marxism—Political and social theory established by Karl Marx (1818–1883). Advocates a materialistic, atheistic society that develops through class struggle as workers overthrow middle-class owners of economic production and replace capitalism with communism, the truly egalitarian society.

Mass—The liturgy of the Roman Catholic church, more specifically the **Eucharist.**

Metaphysical poetry—Style of English poetry popular in the early seventeenth century, characterized by a colloquial tone; uneven, spontaneous rhythms; varied stanza forms; and surprising, intellectually challenging metaphors and similes, known as "metaphysical conceits." Shakespeare's "Phoenix and the Turtle" appears to reflect a metaphysical style.

Microcosm—(Latin, "little world"). Based upon the Renaissance belief in the symbolic correspondences between the individual and the cosmos, any feature of human society that resembles or suggests a similar, larger structure in the universe. The kingdom of England is an earthly microcosm of God's universal kingdom; the individual human being is an even smaller microcosm. Cf. King Lear's "little world of man" (3.1.10).

Monasticism—Form of Roman Catholic clerical life in which men (monks) and women (nuns) vow to observe a disciplined life of prayer and meditation more strict than that followed by priests and nuns who minister directly to the laity.

Montanism—Montanus (second century A.D.) and two women, Prisca and Maximilla, claimed themselves as prophets of the Holy Spirit, announcing the imminent end of the world and the need for disciplined living in preparation. They denied the absolution of sins, defied the authority of the church, and were excommunicated.

Morality play—Medieval drama whose dramatic purpose is the teaching of a moral or religious truth and whose characters are allegorical figures (e.g., Death, Beauty, Fellowship in *Everyman*).

Myth—Any story or narrative, written or oral and usually quite old, that explains natural or human events in supernatural terms, thus placing them in a larger, divine context. Myths can express significant and similar meanings across cultures; for example, both Satan and Prometheus convey the idea of defiance of the divine.

New Covenant—A covenant is an agreement between parties. The Old Covenant was God's promise to guide the chosen people of Israel if they obeyed his commands as spelled out in the **Old Testament.** The New Covenant of the **New Testament** enhances and verifies this agreement through the sacrifice of Christ, motivating the believer to follow his example.

New Historicism—Critical method that views literature as a cultural "object" and the result of social factors beyond the author's personal composition.

New Testament—Books of the Bible that include the four Christian **gospels** (Matthew, Mark, Luke, and John) as well as the **epistles** (letters) of St. Paul to the early churches.

Old Covenant—See **New Covenant.**

Old Testament—Books of the Bible that recount the pre-Christian story of God's relationship with the ancient Hebrews. The first five books (Genesis, Exodus, Leviticus, Numbers, Deuteronomy) are also called the Pentateuch or Torah.

Orthodox Church—Those churches in the eastern portion of the Roman empire that, after the Great Schism (1054), recognized the authority of the patriarch of Constantinople rather than the pope.

Orthodoxy—(Greek, "right belief"). Correct doctrine believed by the faithful; the opposite of **heresy.** See also **dogma.**

Paganism—Any religious belief not connected with the worship of the God of Abraham; the religion of someone not a Christian, Jew, or Muslim. The term was often used pejoratively in the Renaissance, yet the pagan cultures of Greece and Rome were respected for their accomplishments, despite their **polytheism.**

Papal Bull—(Latin, *bulla,* "official seal"). An official pronouncement by the pope.

Parable—A short instructive story told by Jesus in the **gospels** to illustrate a moral or religious point.

Pax Romana—(Latin, "the Roman peace"). The long period of peace within the Roman empire during which Christ was born, from 27 B.C. until 180 A.D. (from the rise of Caesar Augustus until the end of Marcus Aurelius's reign).

Pelagianism—Belief advanced by Pelagius (c. 350–c. 425 A.D.) that each individual through free will could overcome **original sin,** thereby aiding his own salvation; attacked by St. Augustine and condemned as a heresy in 418 on grounds that it denied the necessity of **grace.**

Penance—Performance of prayer or works done to express **repentance,** after the confession of sins.

Petrarchan poetry—Verse in the style of Petrarch (1304–1374); typically love poetry directed toward an idealized beloved who is morally purer (at times eliciting religious language of praise) than the speaker of the poem, whose unrequited love for her arouses his intense emotions of passion and longing.

Polytheism—Belief in more than one god.

Pope—(Latin, *papa,* "father"). Supreme cleric of the Roman Catholic church.

Postlapsarian—See **Fall of Adam and Eve.**

Postmodernism—In literary criticism, the collection of critical strategies that generally rejects older methods that stressed the primacy of the individual author, the reliable validity of language, and close attention to issues of form, structure, and meaning unaffected by social or cultural factors. In their place postmodernism emphasizes the unpredictability, social context, psychological complexity, and political power of literature. Generally challenges the assumptions of **rationalism.**

Prayer Book—See **Book of Common Prayer.**

Predestination—Belief that God elects those to be saved. Augustine, opposing **Pelagianism,** asserted that human free will (corrupted by the **Fall of Adam and Eve**) played no part in one's salvation. This view was extended by **Calvinism** in double predestination, which stated that God determines both those to be saved and those to be damned.

Presbyterianism—(Greek *presbyter,* "elder"). A **reformed church** governed by councils of elected elders known as a presbytery; under the leadership of John Knox (1513–1572) it became the state church of Scotland.

Problem comedies—Shakespearean **comedies** (*All's Well That Ends Well, Measure for Measure,* and *Troilus and Cressida;* some scholars include *The Merchant of Venice*) possessing a dominant mood of seriousness or even satirical cynicism, raising difficult moral or religious issues, and with plots that diminish the relative importance of romantic love.

Prodigal Son—One of the **parables** of Jesus (Luke 15: 11–32); a young man wastes his wealth in "riotous living," then returns humbly to his father, who welcomes him, just as God will welcome sinners. Alluded to in Shakespeare's *The Merchant of Venice, Henry IV Part II,* and *The Winter's Tale,* among others.

Primogniture—Principle of succession in a monarchy in which the throne passes to the eldest son first.

Protestant Reformation—Historical stage in the development of Christianity in which the authority and theology of **Roman Catholicism** was challenged during the sixteenth century by creation of the Protestant churches of **Lutheranism** and **Calvinism.** They protested such abuses as the corruption of the clergy, rule of the papacy, and sale of indulgences and church offices, resulting in such reforms as the marriage of ministers, reinterpretation of the **Eucharist, salvation** by faith, and vernacular translations of the Bible.

Purgatory—A state after death in which the soul is purged of imperfections before proceeding to salvation; not, like Hell, a place of final punishment. Alluded to by the ghost of Hamlet's father (1.5.10–13).

Puritanism—An extreme form of English Calvinism. Puritans sought to "purify" **Anglicanism** by ridding it of apparent remnants of **Roman Catholicism,** especially in rituals of worship and clerical dress; often regarded as self-righteously pious, hence satirized by some writers. Some, following Robert Browne (c. 1550–1630)—alluded to in *Twelfth Night* (3.2.31)—broke with the Church of England entirely and were known as Separatists; a group of these, the Pilgrims, settled in Plymouth, Massachusetts in 1620.

Rationalism—Belief in the final authority of human reason as the guide to understanding experience; logic, the scientific method, and observable data are the basis for reaching valid conclusions. Emerged in the eighteenth century, the so-called "age of reason."

Real Presence—Theological understanding of the **Eucharist** within **Anglicanism,** which rejects **transubstantiation** and asserts the "real" or "spiritual" presence of Christ in the sacrament, without specifying precisely the exact nature of this presence.

Recusant—One (typically Roman Catholic or Separatist **Puritan)** who refused, in Elizabethan England, to acknowledge the authority the Church of England and avoided its worship services.

Reformed Church—A Protestant church that follows the doctrines of **Calvinism** as opposed to **Lutheranism.**

Renaissance—European cultural movement affecting all branches of the liberal arts beginning in Italy and lasting from about 1300 to 1700; emphasized **humanism** and, in the sixteenth century, coincided with the **Protestant** and **Catholic Reformations** in a complex historical relationship. Historian Jakob Burkhardt (1818–1897) believed it a unique cultural flowering, whereas some later historians such as Johann Huizinga (1872–1945) found in it the "waning" of medievalism. The term "Renaissance" has been replaced by many scholars with "Early Modern" to denote its foreshadowing of contemporary issues.

Repentance—Sorrow for sin, especially as expressed through **penance.**

Resurrection—The rising of Jesus Christ from the dead after his crucifixion.

Roman Catholicism—The Christian denomination that existed in Europe prior to the **Protestant Reformation,** characterized by a hierarchical clerical structure (**magisterium**), governing authority of the **pope,** adherence to seven **sacraments** and the **Mass,** a theology of **scholasticism,** and an historic tradition of **monasticism.**

Romances—The final **comedies** of Shakespeare, distinguished from the **problem comedies** and earlier romantic comedies by greater use of music and masque-like elements, presence of supernatural beings, thematic patterns of separation and reuniting of families, and more prominent mythic and Christian elements.

Rood Screen—(Old English *rood,* "cross"). A broad, open screen of wood or stone in front of the altar, often topped by a cross or crucifix. Most were destroyed as remnants of **Roman Catholicism** during the **Protestant Reformation** in England.

Sacrament—Any of seven rites within the church through which God's grace is made available. Augustine called sacraments the "visible form of invisible grace." **Baptism** and the **Eucharist** are the sacraments referred to in the **gospels; Roman Catholicism** observes these plus confirmation, penance, extreme unction (anointing the dying, "last rites"), ordination, and matrimony.

Salvation—Ultimate forgiveness of sin and restoration of humanity to its right relationship with God, achieved through faith in Jesus Christ.

Scholasticism—Dominant medieval school of philosophy, using a rigorously logical, systematic method for analyzing the truth of scripture, often with reference to ancient authors (such as Aristotle) for support. Scholastic philosophers, such as Aquinas, were known as the "schoolmen" (Latin, *schola,* "school").

Sermon on the Mount—Christ's sermon delivered in Matthew chapters 5–7, summarizing his moral teaching. It includes the nine **Beatitudes,** statements of praise for specific virtues (e.g., "Blessed are the pure in heart, for they shall see God"), and the **Lord's Prayer.**

Skepticism—Generally, a refusal to come to final statements about truth, based upon a belief in the limitations or unverifiability of knowledge. Skeptical thinkers who influenced the later Renaissance were Machiavelli, who doubted the claims of divine monarchic authority and asserted that fear often was the essential political tool rather than divine authority; and Montaigne, whose essays reveal a subjectively perceived world of relative, changing values rather than absolute truths.

Simony—Any attempt to buy or sell spiritual offices; after Simon Magus, who attempted to buy the Holy Spirit (Acts 8: 18–24).

Sovereignty of God—See **Calvinism.**

Stoicism—Ancient philosophy put forth primarily by Zeno (335–263 B.C.); taught that life should be lived "according to nature," or the divine model of behavior exhibited in the natural world, which included a self-disciplined indifference to pain and pleasure.

Synoptic Gospels—See **Gospels.**

Tetralogy—Group of four plays. Eight of Shakespeare's ten history plays form two tetralogies. The first tetralogy comprises the three parts of *Henry VI* plus *Richard III;* the second comprises *Richard II,* the two parts of *Henry IV,* and *Henry V.* The other two histories are *King John* and *Henry VIII.*

Thirty-nine Articles—See **Book of Common Prayer.**

Torah—See **Old Testament.**

Tragedy—A drama that, for Aristotle, contained a noble protagonist who, through a personal flaw or characteristic (hamartia), undergoes a tragic downfall (catastrophe) to endure suffering and death, arousing a catharsis of pity and fear in the audience.

Tragicomedy—A drama whose plot may potentially lead to a tragic ending but which ends happily, without a death, as a comedy.

Transubstantiation—Understanding of communion within **Roman Catholicism;** the sacramental bread and wine are themselves transformed into the "substance" of Christ's body and blood. See **Consubstantiation.**

Tudor Myth—View of English history in which the rise of the Tudor dynasty was crucial to the peace and prosperity of the nation during the sixteenth century.

Typology—System of correspondence between the **Old** and **New Testaments** in which events or persons in the Old ("types") prefigure or foreshadow parallel events in the New ("antitypes").

Via media—See **Elizabethan Settlement.**

Vice figure—Dramatic character from medieval drama, influential on Shakespearean villains, who incited social mischief or discord.

Zwinglianism—Branch of Protestantism in Reformation Switzerland led by Ulrich Zwingli (1484–1531), based in Zurich. Against Lutheran **consubstantiation**, Zwingli held that the belief of the communicant determines Christ's sacramental presence in the **Eucharist;** against the **Anabaptists** he argued for infant baptism.

BIBLIOGRAPHY

CULTURAL AND RELIGIOUS BACKGROUND

Print Sources

Arthur, Ross G. "Literary Jews and the Breakdown of the Medieval Testamental Pattern." In *Jewish Presences in English Literature*. Ed. Derek Cohen and Deborah Heller. Montreal, Canada: McGill-Queen's University Press, 1990. 113–127.

Aston, Margaret. *Faith and Fire: Popular and Unpopular Religion 1350–1600*. London, UK: Hambledon Press, 1993.

———. *Lollards and Reformers: Images and Literacy in Late Medieval Religion*. London, UK: Hambledon Press, 1984.

Bicknell, E. J. *A Theological Introduction to the Thirty-Nine Articles of the Church of England*. London, UK: Longmans, Green, 1947.

Carlson, Eric Josef, ed. *Religion and the English People 1500–1640*. Sixteenth Century Essays and Studies. Volume 45. Kirksville, MO: Thomas Jefferson University Press at Truman State University, 1998.

Clark, Stuart. *Thinking with Demons: The Idea of Witchcraft in Early Modern Europe*. Oxford, UK: Clarendon Press, 1997.

Coffey, John. *Persecution and Toleration in Protestant England, 1558–1689*. Harlow, UK: Longman, 2000.

Collinson, Patrick. "The Era of Elizabeth and James VI: Literature and the Church." In *The Cambridge History of Early Modern English Literature*. Ed. David Lowenstein and Janel Mueller. Cambridge, MA: Cambridge University Press, 2002. 374–398.

———. *The Birthpangs of Protestant England: Religious and Cultural Change in the Sixteenth and Seventeenth Centuries*. Basingstoke, UK: Macmillan and New York: St. Martin's, 1988.

———. *Godly People: Essays on English Protestantism and Puritanism*. London, UK: Hambledon, 1983.

———. *The Religion of Protestants: The Church in English Society 1559–1625*. Oxford, UK: Clarendon, 1982.

———. *Archbishop Grindal, 1519–1583: The Struggle for a Reformed Church*. Berkeley: University of California Press, 1979.

Crawford, Patricia. *Women and Religion in England, 1500–1720*. London, UK: Routledge, 1993.

Cressy, David. *Birth, Marriage and Death: Ritual, Religion, and the Life-Cycle in Tudor and Stuart England*. Oxford, UK: Oxford University Press, 1997.

Crystal, David, and Ben Crystal. *The Shakespeare Miscellany*. Woodstock, NY: Overbrook Press, 2005.

Davies, Horton. *Worship and Theology in England from Cranmer to Baxter and Fox, 1534–1690*. Grand Rapids, MI: Eerdmans, 1996.

Elton, G. R. *Reform and Reformation: England 1509–1558*. Cambridge, MA: Harvard University Press, 1977.

Fletcher, Anthony, and Peter Roberts, eds. *Religion, Culture, and Society in Early Modern Britain*. Cambridge, MA: Cambridge University Press,1994.

Green, Ian. *The Christian's ABC: Catechism and Catechizing in English c. 1530–1740*. Oxford, UK: Oxford University Press, 1996.

———. *Print and Protestantism in Early Modern England*. Oxford, UK: Oxford University Press, 2000.

Gregory, Brad. *Salvation at Stake: Christian Martyrdom in Early Modern Europe*. Cambridge, MA: Harvard University Press, 1999.

Haigh, Christopher. *English Reformations: Religion, Politics, and Society under the Tudors*. Oxford. UK: Oxford University Press, 1993.

———, ed. *The English Reformation Revisited*. Cambridge, MA: Cambridge University Press, 1987.

Hudson, Elizabeth K. "English Protestants and the *Imitatio Christi*, 1580–1620." *Sixteenth Century Journal* 19 (1988): 541–558.

Kendall, R. T. *Calvin and English Calvinism to 1649*. Oxford, UK: Oxford University Press, 1979.

King, John N. *Voices of the English Reformation: A Sourcebook*. Philadelphia: University of Pennsylvania Press, 2004.

Kirby, W. J. Torrance. *Richard Hooker, Reformer and Platonist*. Aldershot, UK: Ashgate, 2005.

Knott, John R. *The Sword and the Spirit: Puritan Responses to the Bible*. Chicago, IL: University of Chicago Press, 1980.

Luebke, David Martin, ed. *The Counter-Reformation: The Essential Readings*. Oxford, UK: Blackwell, 1999.

MacCulloch, Diarmaid. *The Later Reformation in England: 1547–1603*. 2nd ed. New York: Palgrave Macmillan, 2001.

MacCulloch, Diarmaid, Mary Laven, and Eamon Duffy. "Recent Trends in the Study of Christianity in Sixteenth Century Europe." *Renaissance Quarterly* 59 (Fall 2006): 697–731.

Maltby, Judith. *Prayer Book and People in Elizabethan and Early Stuart England*. Cambridge, MA: Cambridge University Press, 1998.

Marshall, Peter. *Religious Identities in Henry VIII's England*. Aldershot, UK: Ashgate, 2006.

Matar, Nabil. *Islam in Britain, 1558–1685*. Cambridge, MA: Cambridge University Press, 1998.

McEachern, Claire, and Debora Shuger, eds. *Religion and Culture in Renaissance England*. Cambridge, MA: Cambridge University Press, 1997.

Milward, Peter. *Religious Controversies of the Elizabethan Age: A Survey of Printed Sources*. Lincoln: University of Nebraska Press, 1977.

Morgan, John. *Godly Learning: Puritan Attitudes towards Reason, Learning and Education, 1560–1640*. Cambridge, MA: Cambridge University Press, 1986.

Mueller, Janel. "The Tudor Era from the Reformation to Elizabeth I: Literature and the Church." *The Cambridge History of Early Modern English Literature*. Ed. David Lowenstein and Janel Mueller. Cambridge, MA: Cambridge University Press, 2002. 257–312.

Nuttall, Geoffrey. *The Holy Spirit in Puritan Faith and Experience*. 3rd ed. Chicago, IL: University of Chicago Press, 1992.

Olsen, V. Norskov. *John Foxe and the Elizabethan Church*. Berkeley: University of California Press, 1973.

Questier, Michael. *Conversion, Politics and Religion in England, 1580–1625*. Cambridge, MA: Cambridge University Press, 1996.

Rex, Richard. *The Theology of John Fisher*. Cambridge, MA: Cambridge University Press,1991.

Patterson, Bruce. *Music and Poetry of the English Renaissance*. London, UK: Methuen, 1948.

Scarisbrick, J. J. *The Reformation and the English People*. Oxford, UK: Blackwell, 1984.

Shuger, Debora. *Renaissance Habits of Thought in the English: Religion, Politics, and the Dominant Culture*. Berkeley: University of California Press, 1990.

———. *The Renaissance Bible: Scholarship, Sacrifice, and Subjectivity*. Berkeley: University of California Press, 1994.

———. "The Earlier Stuart Era: Literature and the Church." In *The Cambridge History of Early Modern English Literature*. Ed. David Lowenstein and Janel Mueller. Cambridge: Cambridge University Press, 2002. 512–543.

Sinfield Alan. *Literature in Protestant England, 1560–1660*. New York: Barnes and Noble, 1983.

Electronic Sources

Anglican Church History Resources. anglicansonline.org/resources/history.html.

British Broadcasting Corporation. *Church and Reformation*. www.bbc.co.uk/history/state/church_reformation/index.html.

Calvinism Resources Database. www.calvin.edu/library/database/card/.

Catholic Encyclopedia. www.newadvent.org/cathen/index.html.

Center for Reformation and Renaissance Studies. University of Toronto. www.crrs.ca.

Christian Classics Ethereal Library. http://www.ccel.org/.

Early Modern Resources. www.earlymodernweb.org.uk/emr/.

The Garden, the Ark, the Tower, the Temple: Biblical Metaphors of Knowledge in Early Modern Europe. www.mhs.ox.ac.uk/gatt.

Hooker, Thomas. *World Cultures to 1500: Discovery and Reformation*. Washington State University. www.wsu.edu/~dee/REFORM/REFORM.HTM.

Internet Archive of Texts and Documents. Protestant Reformation and Catholic Reformation. http://history.hanover.edu/texts.html.

Martin Luther: The Reluctant Revolutionary. www.pbs.org/empires/martinluther/.

Project Wittenberg. Concordia Theological Seminary. www.iclnet.org/pub/resources/text/wittenberg/wittenberg-home.html.

Redefining the Sacred in Early Modern England. The Folger Shakespeare Library. Washington, D.C. www.folger.edu/html/folger_institute/sacred/index.html.

Reformation and Counter-Reformation.www2.sunysuffolk.edu/westn/reformation.html.

The Reformation Guide. Michigan State University.www.educ.msu.edu/homepages/laurence/reformation/index.htm.

Reformation Ink. http://homepage.mac.com/shanerosenthal/reformationink/index.html.

Religious Reformation and Conflict: Bibliography. Idaho State University. www.isu.edu/
~owenjack/rrc/bib.html.

Research Guide for Christianity. Yale Divinity School. www.library.yale.edu/div/xtiangde.
htm.

Top Religion Sites. Wabash College. http://www.wabashcenter.wabash.edu/Internet/
topsites.htm.

Tudor History. www.tudorhistory.org.

LITERATURE AND RELIGION IN RENAISSANCE ENGLAND

Print Sources

Barnet, Sylvan. "Some Limitations of a Christian Approach to Shakespeare." *ELH* 22
(1955): 81–92.

Battenhouse, Roy, ed. *Shakespeare's Christian Dimension: An Anthology of Commentary.*
Bloomington: Indiana University Press, 1994.

———. "Shakespeare's Christianity: The Future for Scholarship." *The Upstart Crow* 14
(1994): 4–10.

Bernthal, Craig. *The Trial of Man: Christianity and Judgment in the World of Shakespeare.*
Wilmington, DE: ISI Books, 2003.

Betteridge, Tom. *Literature and Politics in the English Reformation.* Manchester, UK: Manchester University Press, 2004.

Burnham, Douglas, and Enrico Giaccherini. *The Poetics of Transubstantiation: from Theology to Metaphor.* Aldershot, UK: Ashgate, 2005.

Burton, Jonathan. *Traffic and Turning: Islam and English Drama, 1579–1624.* Newark: University of Delaware Press, 2005.

Bryant, James C. *Tudor Drama and Religious Controversy.* Macon, GA: Mercer University
Press, 1984.

Cox, John D. "Shakespeare's Religious and Moral Thinking: Skepticism or Suspicion?"
Religion and Literature 36.1 (2004): 39–66.

Crockett, Bryan. *Stage and Sermon in Renaissance England.* Philadelphia: University of
Pennsylvania Press, 1995.

Diehl, Huston. *Staging Reform, Reforming the Stage: Protestantism and Popular Theater in
Early Modern England.* Ithaca, NY: Cornell University Press, 1997.

Dimmock, Matthew. *New Turkes: Dramatizing Islam and the Ottomans in Early Modern England.* Aldershot, UK: Ashgate, 2005.

Dutton, Richard, Alison Findlay, and Richard Wilson, eds. *Theatre and Religion: Lancastrian
Shakespeare.* Manchester, UK: Manchester University Press, 2003.

Hamilton, Donna B. *Shakespeare and the Politics of Protestant England.* Lexington: University Press of Kentucky, 1992.

Hamilton, Donna B., and Richard Strier, eds. *Religion, Literature, and Politics in Post-
Reformation England, 1540–1688.* Cambridge, MA: Cambridge University Press,
1996.

Hammond, Gerald. *The Making of the English Bible.* Manchester, UK: Manchester University Press, 1982.

Hannay, Margaret, ed. *Silent but for the Word: Tudor Women as Patrons, Translators, and
Writers of Religious Works.* Kent, OH: Kent State University Press, 1985.

Harris, Max. *Theater and Incarnation.* New York: St. Martin's Press, 1990.

Hassel, R. Chris. "Shakespeare's Comic Epilogues: Invitations to Festive Communion."
Shakespeare-Jahrbuch 106 (1970): 160–169.

Howse, E. M. *Spiritual Values in Shakespeare*. Toronto, Canada: Abingdon Press, 1965.

Hughes, Ted. *Shakespeare and the Goddess of Complete Being*. London, UK: Faber, 1992.

Jones, Richard Foster. *The Triumph of the English Language: A Survey of Opinions concerning the Vernacular from the Introduction of Printing to the Restoration*. Palo Alto, CA: Stanford University Press, 1953.

Kendall, Ritchie D. *The Drama of Dissent: The Radical Poetics of Nonconformity, 1380–1590*. Chapel Hill: University of North Carolina Press, 1986.

King, John N. *English Reformation Literature: The Tudor Origins of the Protestant Tradition*. Princeton, NJ: Princeton University Press, 1982.

———. *Tudor Royal Iconography: Literature and Art in an Age of Religious Crisis*. Princeton, NJ: Princeton University Press, 1982.

Lake, Peter. *The Antichrist's Lewd Hat: Protestants, Papists, and Players in Post- Reformation England*. New Haven, CT: Yale University Press, 2002.

Lewis, Cynthia. *Particular Saints: Shakespeare's Four Antonios, Their Contexts, and Their Plays*. Newark: University of Delaware Press, 1997.

Mahon, John W. " 'For now we sit to chat as well as eat': Conviviality and Conflict in Shakespeare's Meals." *"Fanned and Winnowed Opinions": Shakespearean Essays Presented to Harold Jenkins*. Ed. John W. Mahon and Thomas A. Pendleton. London, UK: Methuen, 1987.

Manley, Lawrence. *Literature and Culture in Early Modern London*. Cambridge, MA: Cambridge University Press, 1995.

Marshall, Sherrin, ed. *Women in Reformation and Counter-Reformation Europe: Public and Private Worlds*. Bloomington: University of Indiana Press, 1989.

McCullough, Peter. *Sermons at Court: Politics and Religion in Elizabethan and Jacobean Preaching*. Cambridge, MA: Cambridge University Press, 1998.

Milward, Peter. "Wise Fools in Shakespeare." *Christianity and Literature* 33.2 (1984): 21–27.

Pendergast, John S. *Religion, Allegory, and Literacy in Early Modern England, 1560–1640: The Control of the Word*. Aldershot, UK: Ashgate, 2006.

Pinciss, Gerald M. *Forbidden Matter: Religion in the Drama of Shakespeare and His Contemporaries*. Newark: University of Delaware Press, 2000.

Ranald, Margaret Loftus. *Shakespeare and His Social Context: Essays in Osmotic Knowledge and Literary Interpretation*. New York: AMS Press, 1987.

Rose, Mary Beth, ed. *Renaissance Drama as Cultural History*. Evanston, IL: Northwestern University Press, 1990.

Salter, David. "Shakespeare and Catholicism: The Franciscan Connection." *Cahiers élisabéthains* 66 (2004): 9–22.

Shapiro, James. *Shakespeare and the Jews*. New York: Columbia University Press, 1996.

Shell, Alison. *Catholicism, Controversy and the English Literary Imagination, 1558–1660*. Cambridge, MA: Cambridge University Press, 1999.

Sims, James H. *Dramatic Uses of Biblical Allusions in Marlowe and Shakespeare*. Humanities Monographs No. 24. Gainesville: University of Florida Press, 1967.

———. "Shakespeare and the Christian Reader: A Consideration of Shakespeare's Faith and Moral Vision as Communicated Through the Text of His Plays." *A Search for Meaning: Critical Essays on Early Modern Literature*. Ed. Paula Harms Payne. New York: Peter Lang, 2004. 39–60.

Skulsky, Harold. *Spirits Finely Touched: The Testing of Value and Integrity in Four Shakespearean Plays*. Athens: University of Georgia Press, 1976.

Stachniewski, John. *The Persecutory Imagination: English Puritanism and the Literature of Religious Despair*. Oxford, UK: Oxford University Press, 1991.

Strier, Richard. "Shakespeare and the Skeptics." *Religion and Literature* 32.2 (2000): 171–196.

Strong, Roy. *The Cult of Elizabeth: Elizabethan Portraiture and Pageantry.* London, UK: Thames and Hudson, 1977.

Targoff, Ramie. *Common Prayer: The Language of Public Devotion in Early Modern England.* Chicago, IL: University of Chicago Press, 2001.

Taylor, Dennis, ed. *Religion and the Arts* 5 (2001). Special issue: Shakespeare and Catholicism.

Todd, Margot, ed. *Reformation to Revolution: Politics and Religion in Early Modern England.* London, UK: Routledge, 1995.

Trevor-Roper, Hugh R. *Archbishop Laud, 1573–1645.* 2nd ed. London: Macmillan, 1962.

Walsham, Alexandra. *Church Papists: Catholicism, Conformity and Confessional Polemic in Early Modern England.* 2nd Rev. ed. Woodbridge, UK: Boydell and Brewer, 2000.

Watson, Curtis Brown. *Shakespeare and the Renaissance Concept of Honor.* Princeton, NJ: Princeton University Press, 1960.

White, Helen. *Tudor Books of Private Devotion.* Madison: University of Wisconsin ress, 1951.

White, Paul Whitfield. "Theatre and Religious Culture." *A New History of Early English Drama,* ed. John D. Cox and David Scott Kastan. New York: Columbia University Press, 1997. 133–152.

Electronic Sources

Complete Works of William Shakespeare Online. Massachusetts Institute of Technology. http://www-tech.mit.edu/Shakespeare/works.html.

English Literature and Religion. William S. Peterson. University of Maryland, College Park. http://www.english.umd.edu/englfac/WPeterson/ELR/elr.htm.

Internet Shakespeare Editions. University of Victoria. http://ise.uvic.ca/index.html.

Mr. William Shakespeare and the Internet. Palomar College. http://shakespeare.palomar.edu.

Shakespeare and Religion. Boston College. http://www.bc.edu/publications/relarts/supplements/Shakespeare/.

Touchstone: Resource for Shakespeare Studies. The British Library. http://www.touchstone.bham.ac.uk/.

Shakespeare's Staging: Shakespeare's Performance. University of California, Berkeley. http://shakespearestaging.berkeley.edu/index.php?option=com_content&task=view&id=28&Itemid=201.

SHAKESPEARE'S PLAYS AND POEMS

The Histories

Battenhouse, Roy. "Religion in *King John:* Shakespeare's View." *Connotations* 1 (1991): 140–149.

Bishop, Tom. "The Burning hand: Poetry and Reformation I in Shakespeare's *Richard II.*" *Religion and Literature* 32.2 (Summer 2000): 29–47.

Bryant, J. A., Jr. "Prince Hal and the Ephesians." *Sewanee Review* 67 (1959): 204–219.

Candido, Joseph. "King Richard's 'I'." *Religion and the Arts* 5.4 (2001): 464–484. [On *Richard II*].

Cubeta, Paul M. "Falstaff and the Art of Dying." *Studies in English Literature: 1500–1900* 27 (1987): 197–211.

Goodland, Katharine. "'Obsequious Laments': Mourning and Communal Memory in Shakespeare's *Richard III.*" *Shakespeare and the Culture of Christianity in Early Modern England.* Ed. Dennis Taylor and David N. Beauregard. New York: Fordham University Press, 2003. 44–79.

Hamilton, Gary D. "Mocking Oldcastle: Notes Towards Exploring a Possible Catholic Presence in Shakespeare's Henriad." *Shakespeare and the Culture of Christianity in Early Modern England.* Ed. Dennis Taylor and David N. Beauregard. New York: Fordham University Press, 2003. 141–158.

Huffman, Clifford Chalmers. "'Unvalued Jewels': The Religious Perspective in *Richard III.*" *Bucknell Review* 26.2 (1982): 58–73.

Hunt, Maurice. "The Hybrid Reformations of Shakespeare's Second Henriad." *Comparative Drama* 32.1 (Spring 1998): 176–206.

Kelly, Henry Ansgar. *Divine Providence in the England of Shakespeare's Histories.* Cambridge, MA: Harvard University Press, 1970.

Klause, John. "New Sources for Shakespeare's *King John:* The Writings of Robert Southwell." *Studies in Philology* 98 (2001): 401–427.

Marx, Stephen. "Holy War in *Henry V.*" *Shakespeare Survey* 48 (1996): 85–97.

Martin, Randall. "Catilines and Machiavels: reading Catholic resistance in *3 Henry VI.*" *Theatre and Religion: Lancastrian Shakespeare.* Ed. Richard Dutton, Alison Findlay, and Richard Wilson. Manchester, UK: Manchester University Press, 2003. 105–115.

Mayer, Jean-Christophe. "Revisiting the Reformation: Shakespeare and Fletcher's King *Henry VIII.*" *Renaissance and Reformation* 5.2 (2003): 188–203.

———. "Shakespeare's Religious Background Revisited: *Richard II* in a New Context." *Shakespeare and the Culture of Christianity in Early Modern England.* Ed. Dennis Taylor and David N. Beauregard. New York: Fordham University Press, 2003. 103–120.

McAlindon, Thomas. "Pilgrims of Grace: Henry IV Historicized." *Shakespeare Survey* 48 (1996): 69–84.

Monta, Susannah Brietz. "'Thou Fall'st a Blessed Martyr': Shakespeare's *Henry VIII* and the Polemics of Conscience." *English Literary Renaissance* 30.2 (Spring 2000): 262–283.

Narkin, Anthony P. "Day-Residue and Christian Reference in Clarence's Dream." *Texas Studies in Literature and Language* 9 (1967): 147–150.

Palmer, David J. "Casting off the Old Man: History and St. Paul in *Henry V.*" *Critical Quarterly* 12 (1970): 267–283.

Ranald, Margaret Loftus. "The Degradation of Richard II: An Inquiry into the Ritual Background." *English Literary Renaissance* 7 (1977): 170–196.

Richmond, Hugh M. "*Richard III* and the Reformation." *Journal of English and Germanic Philology* 83 (1984): 509–521.

Rosendale, Timothy. "Sacral and Sacramental Kingship in the Lancastrian Tetralogy." *Shakespeare and the Culture of Christianity in Early Modern England.* Ed. Dennis Taylor and David N. Beauregard. New York: Fordham University Press, 2003. 121–140.

Slights, Camille Wells. "Politics of Conscience in *All Is True* (or *Henry VIII*)." *Shakespeare Survey* 43 (1991): 59–68.

Spencer, Janet M. "Violence and the Sacred: Holy Fragments, Shakespeare and the Postmodern." *Christianity and Literature* 50 (2000–2001): 613–629.

Taylor, Gary. "Forms of Opposition: Shakespeare and Middleton." *English Literary Renaissance* 24.2 (Spring 1994): 283–314. [On *Henry IV*].

Tricomi, Albert H. "Joan La Pucelle and the Inverted Saints Play in *1 Henry VI.*" *Renaissance and Reformation* 25.2 (2001): 5–31.

Wilders, John. *The Lost Garden: A View of Shakespeare's English and Roman History Plays.* Totowa: Rowman and Littlefield, 1978.

The Comedies

Andreas, James R. "Remythologizing The Knight's Tale: *A Midsummer Night's Dream* and *The Two Noble Kinsmen.*" *Shakespeare Yearbook* 2 (1991): 49–67.

Austen, Glyn. "Ephesus Restored: Sacramentalism and Redemption in *The Comedy of Errors.*" *Literature and Theology* 1 (1987): 54–69.

Beauregard, David N. "'Inspired Merit': Shakespeare's Theology of Grace in *All's Well That Ends Well.*" *Renascence* 51.4 (1999): 219–239.

Bennett, Robert B. "The Law Enforces Itself: Richard Hooker and the Law against Fornication in *Measure for Measure.*" *Shakespeare and Renaissance Association of West Virginia: Selected Papers* 16 (1993): 43–51.

Brown, Carolyn E. "Erotic Religious Flagellation and Shakespeare's *Measure for Measure.*" *English Literary Renaissance* 16 (1986): 139–165.

Buccola, Regina M. "Shakespeare's Fairy Dance with Religio-Political Controversy in *The Merry Wives of Windsor.*" *Shakespeare and the Culture of Christianity in Early Modern England.* Ed. Dennis Taylor and David N. Beauregard. New York: Fordham University Press, 2003. 159–179.

Cantor, Paul A. "Religion and the Limits of Community in *The Merchant of Venice.*" *Soundings* 70 (Spring–Summer 1987): 239–258.

De Alvarez, Leo Paul S. "Biblical Allusions in *The Comedy of Errors.*" *Law and Philosophy: The Practice of Theory: Essays in Honor of George Anastaplo.* 2 vols. Athens: Ohio University Press, 1992. 981–988.

Dean, Paul. "'Comfortable Doctrine': *Twelfth Night* and the Trinity." *Review of English Studies* 52 (2001): 500–515.

———. "The Harrowing of Malvolio: The Theological Background of *Twelfth Night*, Act 4, Scene 2." *Connotations* 7 (1997 / 98): 203–214.

Dessen, Alan C. "The Elizabethan Stage Jew and Christian Example: Gerontus, Barabbas, and Shylock." *Modern Language Quarterly* 35 (1974): 231–245.

DeVillier, Mary Anne G. "*Much Ado About Nothing*: The Moral and Religious Approach to Shakespeare Criticism." *West Georgia College Review* 2.1 (1969): 26–31.

Dobbins, Austin C., and Roy Battenhouse. "Jessica's Morals: A Theological View." *Shakespeare Studies* 9 (1976): 107–120.

Dutton, Richard. "*The Comedy of Errors* and *The Calumny of Apelles*: An Exercise in Source Study." *Religion and the Arts* 7 (2003): 11–30.

Enos, Carol. "Catholic Exiles in Flanders and *As You Like It*; or, What If You Don't Like It At All?" *Theatre and religion: Lancastrian Shakespeare.* Ed. Richard Dutton, Alison Findlay, and Richard Wilson. Manchester, UK: Manchester University Press, 2003. 130–142.

Ephraim, Michelle. "Jephthah's Kin: The Sacrificing Father in *The Merchant of Venice.*" *Journal for Early Modern Cultural Studies* 5.2 (2005): 71–93.

Ferber, Michael. "The Ideology of *The Merchant of Venice.*" *English Literary Renaissance* 20 (1990): 431–464.

Forrest, James F. "Malvolio and Puritan 'Singularity.'" *English Language Notes* 11 (1973): 259–264.

Gill, Roma. "Masques and Shadows." *Drama and Religion.* Ed. James Redmond. Themes in Drama Number 5. Cambridge, MA: Cambridge University Press, 1983. [On *The Winter's Tale.*]

Godshalk, William L. "*All's Well That Ends Well* and the Morality Play." *Shakespeare Quarterly* 25 (1974): 61–70.

Hassel, R. Chris. "Love Versus Charity in *Love's Labour's Lost.*" *Shakespeare Studies* 10 (1977): 17–41.

Hennings, Thomas P. "The Anglican Doctrine of the Affectionate Marriage in *The Comedy of Errors.*" *Modern Language Quarterly* 47 (1986): 91–107.

Hopkins, Lisa. "*The Comedy of Errors* and the Date of Easter." *Ben Jonson Journal* 7 (2000): 55–64.

Hunt, Maurice. "All's Well That Ends Well and the Triumph of the Word." *Texas Studies in Literature and Language* 30 (1988): 388–411.

———. "On the Catholicism of *The Two Gentlemen of Verona.*" *CCTE Studies* 67 (2002): 43–52.

———. "The Religion of *Twelfth Night.*" *CLA Journal* 37 (1993–94): 189–203.

———. "Shakespeare's *Troilus and Cressida* and Christian Epistemology." *Christianity and Literature* 42 (1993): 243–260.

Klause, John. "Catholic and Protestant, Jesuit and Jew: Historical Religion in *The Merchant of Venice.*" *Religion and the Arts* 7 (2003): 65–102.

Laird, David. "'If we offend, it is with our goodwill': Staging Dissent in *A Midsummer Night's Dream.*" *Connotations* 12 (2002–2003): 33–51.

Liston, William T. "Paradoxical Chastity in *A Midsummer Night's Dream.*" *Dayton Review* 21. 2 (1991): 153–160.

Martin, Randall. "Rediscovering Artemis in *The Comedy of Errors.*" *Shakespeare and the Mediterranean: The Selected Proceedings of the International Shakespeare World Association World Congress, Valencia 2001.* Ed. Thomas Clayton, et al. Newark: University of Delaware Press, 2004. 363–379.

Mikesell, Margaret Leal. "Love wrought these miracles': Marriage and Genre in *The Taming of the Shrew.*" *Renaissance Drama* new series 20 (1989): 141–167.

Milward, Peter. "Religion in Arden." *Shakespeare Survey* 54 (2001): 115–121.

Palmer, D. J. "Comedy and the Protestant Spirit in *All's Well That Ends Well.*" *Bulletin of the John Rylands Public Library* 71 (1989): 95–107.

Pinciss, Gerald. *Forbidden Matter: Religion in the Drama of Shakespeare and His Contemporaries.* Newark: University of Delaware Press, 2000. [Chapter 3 on *Measure for Measure.*]

Priest, Dale. "Katherine's Conversion in *The Taming of the Shrew:* A Theological Heuristic." *Renascence* 47(1994), 31–40.

Rist, Thomas. "Topical Comedy: On the Unity of *Love's Labour's Lost.*" *Ben Jonson Journal* 7 (2000): 65–87.

Sexton, Joyce H. "'Rooted love': Metaphors for Baptism in *All's Well That Ends Well.*" *Christianity and Literature* 43 (1994–1995): 261–287.

Sichi, Edward, Jr. "Religious Imagery in *The Two Gentlemen of Verona:* Or, Why Does Proteus Get the Girl?" *Shakespeare and Renaissance Association of West Virginia: Selected Papers* 6 (1981): 42–49.

Shaheen, Naseeb. "A Young Scholar from Rheims." *English Language Notes* 30.3 (1993): 7–13. [On *The Taming of the Shrew*].

Stockard, Emily E. "'Transposed to form and dignity': Christian Folly and the Subversion of Hierarchy in *A Midsummer Night's Dream*." *Religion and Literature* 29.3 (1997): 1–20.

Wilson, Richard. "'Every third thought': Shakespeare's Milan." *Shakespeare and the Mediterranean: The Selected Proceedings of the International Shakespeare AssociationWorld Congress, Valencia, 2001*. Ed. Thomas Clayton, et. al. Newark:University of Delaware Press, 2004. 416–424. [On *Two Gentlemen of Verona*].

Yang, Sharon R. "*The Comedy of Errors*: Variation on a Festive Theme." *Upstart Crow* 14 (1994): 11–27.

The Tragedies

Cantor, Paul A. "'A soldier and afeard': Macbeth and the Gospelling of Scotland." *Interpretation: A Journal of Political Philosophy* 24 (1997): 287–318.

Cavell, Stanley. "'Who does the wolf love?' Reading *Coriolanus*." *Representations* 1.3 (1983): 1–20.

Coursen, H. R., Jr. *Christian Ritual and the World of Shakespeare's Tragedies*. Lewisburg, PA: Bucknell University Press, 1976.

Bell, Millicent. *Shakespeare's Tragic Skepticism*. New Haven, CT: Yale University Press, 2002.

Bethell, S. L. "Shakespeare's Imagery: The Diabolical Imagery of *Othello*." *Shakespeare Survey* 5 (1952): 62–80.

Crawford, John W. "The Religious Question in *Julius Caesar*." *Southern Quarterly* 15 (1977): 297–302.

Erne, Lukas. "'Popish tricks' and 'a ruinous monastery': *Titus Andronicus* and the Question of Shakespeare's Catholicism." *The Limits of Textuality*. Ed. Lukas Erne and Guillemette Bolens. Swiss Papers in English Language and Literature 13. Tübingen, Germany: Narr, 2000. 135–155.

Fichter, Andrew. "Antony and Cleopatra: 'The Time of Universal Peace'." *Shakespeare Survey* 33 (1980): 99–111.

Fisch, Harold. *The Biblical Presence in Shakespeare, Milton, and Blake*. Oxford, UK: Oxford University Press, 1999

Guilfoyle, Cherrell. "The Redemption of *King Lear*." *Comparative Drama* 23 (1989–1990): 50–69.

Hughes, John. "The Politics of Forgiveness: A Theological Exploration of *King Lear*." *Modern Theology* 17 (2001): 261–287.

Hunt, Barbara Joan. *The Paradox of Christian Tragedy*. Troy, NY: Whitston Publishing Company, 1985.

Holderness, Graham. "Vanishing Point: Looking for *Hamlet*." *Shakespeare* (British Shakespeare Association) 1.1–2 (2005): 154–173.

Keefer, Michael H. "Accomodation and Synecdoche: Calvin's God in *King Lear*." *Shakespeare Studies* 20 (1988): 147–168.

King, Laura S. "Blessed When They Were Riggish: Shakespeare's Cleopatra and Christian Penitent Prostitutes." *Journal of Medieval and Renaissance Studies* 22 (1992): 429–449.

Klause, John. "Politics, Heresy, and Martyrdom in Shakespeare's Sonnet 124 and *Titus Andronicus*." *Shakespeare's Sonnets: Critical Essays*. Ed. James Schiffer. New York: Garland, 1999. 219–240.

Knight, W. Nicholas. "*Julius Caesar*: A Case of Pre- and Post-Christian Story." *Christianity and Literature* 28.4 (1979): 27–35.

Lawrence, Sean. "'Gods that we adore': The Divine in *King Lear*." *Renascence* 56.3 (2004): 143–159.

Levitsky, Ruth M. "'the elements were so mix'd'. . . . " *PMLA* 88 (1973): 240–245. [On *Julius Caesar*.]

McPherson, James A. "Three Great Ones of the City and One Perfect Soul: Well Met at Cyprus." *Othello: New Essays by Black Writers*. Ed. Mythili Kaul. Washington, DC: Howard University Press, 1997. 45–76.

Morris, Ivor. *Shakespeare's God: The Role of Religion in the Tragedies*. London: George Allen & Unwin, 1972.

Moschovakis, Nicholas. "'Irreligious Piety' and Christian History: Persecution as Pagan Anachronism in *Titus Andronicus*." *Shakesepeare Quarterly* 53 (2002): 460–486.

Myrick, Kenneth O. "The Theme of Damnation in Shakespearean Tragedy." *Studies in Philology* 38 (1941): 221–245.

O'Riordan, Rachel. "Religion, Language and Performance in *Hamlet*." *Studies in Theatre and Performance* 24.2 (2004): 22–93.

Parker, Barbara L. "The Whore of Babylon and Shakespeare's *Julius Caesar*." *Studies in English Literature 1500–1900* 35 (1995): 251–269.

Riebling, Barbara. "Virtue's Sacrifice: A Machiavellian Reading of *Macbeth*." *Studies in English Literature 1500–1900* 31(1991): 273–286.

Ronan, Clifford J. "Keeping Faith: Water Imagery and Religious Diversity in *Othello*." *Othello: New Critical Essays*. Ed. Philip C. Kolin. New York: Routledge, 2002. 271–291.

Roston, Murray. "Hamlet and Suicide." *Hamlet Studies* 25 (2003): 16–40.

Rubenstein, Frankie. "Speculating on Mysteries: Religion and Politics in *King Lear*." *Renaissance Studies* 16 (2002): 234–262.

Spinrad, Phoebe S. "The Fall of the Sparrow and the Map of Hamlet's Mind." *Modern Philology* 102 (2004–2005): 453–477.

Synder, Susan. "Theology as Tragedy in *Macbeth*." *Christianity and Literature* 43 (1994–1995): 289–300.

Traci, Philip. "Religious Controversy in *Romeo and Juliet*: The Play and Its Historical Context." *Michigan Academician* 8 (1975–1976): 319–325.

Ulrich, Simon. *Pity and Terror: Christianity and Tragedy*. New York: St. Martin's Press, 1989.

Vitkus, Daniel. "Turning Turk in Othello: The Conversion And Damnation of the Moor." *Shakespeare Quarterly* 48 (1997): 145–176.

Walker, Lewis. "Fortune and Friendship in *Timon of Athens*." *Texas Studies in Literature and Language* 18 (1977): 577–600.

Waters, D. Douglas. *Christian Settings in Shakespeare's Tragedies*. Rutherford, NJ: Fairleigh Dickinson University Press, 1994.

The Romances

Beattie, Paul H. "*The Winter's Tale*: Shakespeare's Answer to Easter." *Religious Humanism* 23.1 (1989): 24–31; 23.2 (1989).

Beauregard, David N. "New Light on Shakespeare's Catholicism: Prospero's Epilogue in *The Tempest*." *Renascence* 49 (1997): 159–174.

Cox, John D. "Recovering Something Christian about *The Tempest*." *Christianity and Literature* 50 (2000–2001): 31–51.

Grant, R. A.D. "Providence, Authority, and the Moral Life in *The Tempest.*" *Shakespeare Studies* 16 (1983): 235–263.

Hall, Grace R. W. *The Tempest as Mystery Play.* Jefferson, NC: McFarland, 1999.

Hanna, Sara. "Christian Vision and Iconography in Pericles." *Upstart Crow* 11 (1991): 92–116.

Hunt, Maurice. "Dismemberment, Corporal Reconstitution, and the Body Politic." *Studies in Philology* 99 (2002): 404–431.

———. "Shakespeare's *Pericles* and the Acts of the Apostles." *Christianity and Literature* 49 (1999–2000): 295–309.

———. "Visionary Christianity in Shakesepare's Late Romances." *CLA Journal* 47 (2003–2004): 212–230.

Jensen, Phebe. "Singing Psalms to Horn-Pipes: Festivity, Iconoclasm, and Catholicismin *The Winter's Tale.*" *Shakespeare Quarterly* 55 (2004): 279–306.

Jones-Davies, Margaret. "*Cymbeline* and the Sleep of Faith." *Theatre and religion: Lancastrian Shakespeare.* Ed. Richard Dutton, Alison Findlay, and Richard Wilson. Manchester, UK: Manchester University Press, 2003.

Lim, Walter S. H. "Knowledge and Belief in *The Winter's Tale.*" *Studies in English Literature 1500–1900* 41 (2001): 317–334.

Marshall, Cynthia. *Last Things and Last Plays: Shakeseparean Eschatology.* Carbondale: Southern Illinois University Press, 1991.

Tiffany, Grace. "Calvinist Grace in Shakesepeare's Romances: Upending Tragedy." *Christianity and Literature* 49 (1999–2000): 421–425.

Young, R. V. "'Fresh piece of excellent witchcraft': Contemporary Theory and Shakespeare's Romances." *Shakespeare's Last Plays: Essays in Literature and Politics.* Ed. Stephen W. Smith and Travis Curtright. Lanham, MD: Lexington Books, 2002. 217–238.

The Poems

Asquith, Clare. "A Phoenix for Palm Sunday: Was Shakespeare's Poem a Requiem for Catholic Martyrs?" *Times Literary Supplement,* April 23 2001, 14–15.

Callaghan, Dympna. "Comedy and Epyllion in Post-Reformation England." *Shakespeare Survey* 56 (2003): 27–38.

Devereaux, James A. "Shakespeare's Sonnets of Participation." *Shakespeare Newsletter* 26 (1976): 40.

Haskin, Dayton, S. J. "Pardon as a Weapon against Time in Shakespeare's Sonnets." *Xavier University Studies* 11.3 (1972): 27–37.

Hendricks, Margo. "'A word, sweet Lucrece': Confession, Feminism, and *The Rape of Lucrece.*" In *A Feminist Companion to Shakespeare.* Ed. Dympna Callaghan. Oxford: Blackwell, 2000. 103–120.

Klause, John. "The Phoenix and the Turtle in Its Time." In *In the Company of Shakespeare: Essays in Honor of G. Blakemore Evans.* Ed. Thomas Moisan and Douglas Bruster. Madison, NJ: Fairleigh Dickinson University Press, 2002. 206–230.

———. "Politics, Heresy and Martyrdom in Shakespeare's Sonnet 124 and *Titus Andronicus.*" In *Shakespeare's Sonnets: Critical Essays.* Ed. James Schiffer. New York and London: Garland, 1999. 219–240.

Richmond, Hugh M. "The Dark Lady as Reformation Mistress." *Kenyon Review* 8.2 (1986): 91–105.

Ricks, Christopher. "Shakespeare and the Anagram." *Proceedings of the British Academy* 121 (2003): 111–146.

Skretkowicz, Victor. "Philhellenic Shakespeare and the Sidneys." *Sidney Journal* 17.1 (1999): 78–104.

Wilson, Robert. "A Bloody Question: The Politics of Venus and Adonis." *Religion and the Arts* 5.3 (2001): 297–316.

INDEX

About the Author

CHRISTOPHER BAKER is Professor of English at Armstrong Atlantic State University. He edited *Absolutism and the Scientific Revolution, 1600–1720: A Biographical Dictionary* (Greenwood, 2002), and his articles have appeared in such journals as *Comparative Drama*, *Explorations in Renaissance Culture*, and the *Journal of Modern Literature*.